BOTTLES

IDENTIFICATION AND PRICE GUIDE

SECOND EDITION

BOTTLES

IDENTIFICATION AND PRICE GUIDE
SECOND EDITION

MICHAEL POLAK

The CONFIDENT
COLLECTOR™

AVON BOOKS ◆ NEW YORK

AVON BOOKS
A division of
The Hearst Corporation
1350 Avenue of the Americas
New York, New York 10019

Copyright © 1997 by Michael Polak
Cover photographs by Dale Mooney and Jeff Wichmann
The Confident Collector and its logo are trademarked properties of Avon Books.
Published by arrangement with the author
Visit our website at **http://AvonBooks.com**
Library of Congress Catalog Card Number: 96-95440
ISBN: 0-380-72814-1

First Avon Books Trade Printing, Second Edition: August 1997

AVON TRADEMARK REG. U.S. PAT. OFF. AND IN OTHER COUNTRIES, MARCA REGISTRADA, HECHO EN U.S.A.

Printed in the U.S.A.

OPM   10 9 8 7 6 5 4 3 2 1

This book is dedicated to all of the antique bottle collectors of the World. Because of you, the hobby of bottle collecting just keeps getting better.

Acknowledgments

When it came to writing the second edition of this book, I found I still needed a little help from my friends. I had plenty of that sort of help from those with real expertise, and I'd like to say *thank you* to those special people.

Fred Holabird—Once again, thanks for your fine contribution to this book, the special chapter on Bottles of Nevada, and for your great friendship.

Jacque Pace Polak—A special thank you to my wife for her continued patience and invaluable moral support.

Jeff Wichmann (Pacific Glass Auctions)—Thank you for providing great photographic assortments, pricing inputs, and additional insights on the history of the bottles.

David Spaid—Thank you for providing a complete understanding of the miniature bottle–collecting field and some great photographs.

Bob Jones—Thank you for the history lesson in Rexall Drug Store bottles and some great photographs.

John "Digger" Odell—Thanks to one of the premier bottle diggers in the country, for his help and input on outhouse and privy digging.

Mark Churchill—Thank you for your help and information on the techniques of outhouse and privy digging.

John Tutton—Thank you sharing your thorough understanding of milk bottles and for the great photographs.

Rick Sweeney—Thank you for the photographs and additional thanks to the Painted Soda Bottle Collectors Association for promoting soda bottle collecting.

Photo Credits

The H. J. Heinz Company
Fred Holabird
Bob Jones
Dale Mooney
Jennifer M. Polak
David Spaid
Jeff Wichmann
John Tutton
Rick Sweeney

Contents

Foreword

I want to take a moment and say *thank you* to my readers for their support. They helped make the first edition of this book a huge success. Since that first edition was published, I have received positive feedback and valuable input from bottle collectors, clubs, and dealers across the United States, Europe, and the Asia-Pacific.

I've been an antique bottle collector/junkie for over twenty years and have enjoyed writing this second edition of the book. Once again, I did it with the help of my fellow bottle collectors.

In order to write a second edition that would be as informative, as good a reference and pricing guide, and as enjoyable to read as the first edition, I have tried to provide the beginner and veteran collector with an even broader cross-section of information and material. In an attempt to create the best reference guide available, this second edition includes updated pricing, an expanded section on bottle digging, a revised and expanded bottle club and dealer section, a new chapter on miniature bottle collecting, and more than 100 new photographs.

My goal is to continue to bring a positive influence to the hobby of bottle collecting for beginners and experts alike. As I said in the first edition, I want others to experience the excitement of antique bottle collecting, especially the thrill of making that special find.

Have fun with the hobby of bottle collecting, and good digging!

1

Introduction

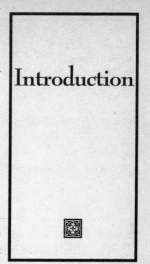

Welcome to the world of antique bottle collecting. Over the years, while selling at antique shows, flea markets, or just talking with friends, I find that these are the most frequently asked questions: What makes a bottle old? What makes a bottle interesting? What makes a bottle valuable? Invariably someone asks about how to get started in antique bottle collecting. In writing this second edition, I have included essentials such as the history and origin of bottles, how the beginning collector gets started, a detailed section on basic bottle facts, bottle sources, and handling suggestions. Because of the heavy response from collectors who purchased the first edition, I have expanded the chapter, Digging for Bottles, specifically in the area of outhouse or privy digging. Also included are separate pricing and information sections updated with the latest information for both old bottles (pre-1900) and new bottles (post-1900). The new bottles section includes a new chapter on miniature bottle collecting. For reference and research purposes, the sections on trademarks, bottle clubs and dealers, bibliography, and a glossary of most used terms have been thoroughly updated. To help collectors make the most of their experience, the bottle clubs and dealers chapters have undergone extensive and detailed updating and expansion.

Over the past few years bottle collecting has become an incredibly popular activity. As a result, bottle clubs continue to form throughout the United States, with more and more people spending their free time digging through old dumps, foraging through ghost towns, digging out old outhouses (that's right), exploring abandoned mine shafts, and searching out their favorite swap meet, flea market, or garage sale. For many collectors and dealers, bottle collecting is a big business, as evidenced by the prices in this book. It is worth noting that many bottles of recent make and origin have become greatly sought after owing to their limited availability.

Most collectors look beyond the type and value of a bottle into the origin and history. In fact, I find that researching the history of bottles has at times proved to be more interesting than finding the bottles themselves. I love both pursuits because of their close ties to the rich history of the settling of the United States and the early methods of merchandising. I hope this book will make you feel the same way.

How to
Use
This
Book

This book is designed to assist collectors—
from the complete novice to the seasoned veteran. The Contents clearly indicates those
chapters, such as The Beginning Collector, that
veterans may want to skip over. However, other introductory chapters,
including those on history, facts, sources, handling of bottles, Fred Holabird's chapter on Nevada bottles, and the new chapter on miniature
bottles, should even contribute something to the expert's store of knowledge about bottles and collecting.

The pricing information is divided into two main sections. The first
begins on page 63 and covers older collectibles, those manufactured
almost exclusively before 1900, broken down into categories based on
physical type and the bottle's original contents. Where applicable, trade
names are listed alphabetically within these sections. In some categories,
such as flasks, trade names were not embossed on the bottles, so pieces
are listed by embossing or other identification that does appear on the
bottles themselves. Descriptive terms used to identify these pieces are
explained in the introductory sections and are also listed in the Glossary.
The second pricing section, which begins on page 281, is a guide to
pieces produced after the turn of the century and are broken down by
manufacturer alone.

Since it is difficult to list prices for every available bottle, I've produced
a cross-section of collectibles in various price ranges. The dollar amount
attached to any listing indicates the value of that particular piece. Similar
but not identical bottles could be more or less valuable than those specifically mentioned. This listing will provide a good starting point for
pricing pieces in your collection or those you are considering as additions.

What's Happening in the World of Bottle Collecting?

◼

Since the first edition of this book, there have been numerous noteworthy events in the bottle collecting community, great bottle discoveries, and an overall increased awareness of the hobby. One of the most exciting events was the Listerine bottle hunt that took place in 1994.

The contest was held by the Warner-Lambert Company to commemorate the change from the barbell-shaped glass bottle to plastic after 115 years. Approximately 6,500 entries (including one from this collector) were submitted for consideration. The feature that distinguished the winning bottle, which was dated between 1895 and 1906, was its unique two-part unembossed rear label. This label was in excellent condition and contained historically characteristic information and product claims not displayed by other finalist bottles. The winner, Michael Peden of Willsboro, New York, received $1,000 as the top prize. The bottle itself was donated to the Smithsonian Museum of American History.

Speaking of museums, The National Bottle Museum in Ballston Spa, New York, had a great 1995 with visitors numbering in the thousands. New exhibits introduced in 1996 featured Saratoga-type mineral water bottles and calabash bottles. These new exhibits were made possible by the assistance of the Hudson Valley Antique Bottle Club. The Corning Museum of Glass, which offers the world's most comprehensive collection and library of glass artifacts and materials, began a major expansion in 1996 to be completed by the year 2000. The Wheaton Glass Museum at Wheaton, New Jersey, plans on publishing a booklet on figural bottles that would accompany a new exhibit.

The Coca-Cola Bottling Company is once again hard at work. In May 1995, Coke introduced a new bottle-shaped aluminum can and in May 1996 released a curvy aluminum can resembling the sharply defined features of the Coke bottle. Also, Coca-Cola issued a limited commemorative edition of bottles for the 1996 Olympics.

And finally, bottle collecting has discovered the supernetwork of communication, the Internet. Simply put, the Internet is the foundation of the fabled information superhighway. The world is now ours. There are numerous bottle collecting Web sites throughout the United States, Canada, and Europe that provide information about clubs, individuals, and numerous antique publications. The following represents a few of these Internet addresses, beginning with my own.

Michael F. Polak—Author: Bottles Identification and Price Guide
    bottle king@msn.com
Pacific Glass Auctions
    http://www.pacglass.com
The Federation of Historical Bottle Collectors
    http://www.av.qnet.com/glassman/
The Miniature Bottle Collector
    http://mediapulse.com/mbc/
The Canadian Online Bottle Network
    http://www.netaccess.on.ca/mhall/
The Internet Collectibles Resource Guide
    http://www.tias.com/dealers.html

As you can see, interest in bottle collecting continues to grow, and with it the resources available to collectors increase.

You never know what you'll find when digging for bottles. Recently, a husband and wife team set out with some friends to dig for bottles and do some metal detecting. While her husband and friends were digging for treasures, the wife decided to do a little searching on her own with the metal detector. She got a strong signal and suspected it might be an old tin can. Instead, it turned out to be three gold coins. After about 20 minutes, she had located a total of eight $20 Double-Eagle gold coins dating from 1866 to 1882. They were valued at $9,000. Here's another one: Joan and Larry Arico, owners of the Julian Drug Store and Soda Fountain in Julian, California, were pulling up floorboards to earthquake-proof their 109-year-old building. Well, they unearthed some very rare Western whiskey bottles, coins, and a rusty tin can full of gold nuggets. Julian, a turn-of-the-century gold mining community, is located in the mountains near San Diego. Ready to go digging?

Bottles: History and Origin

Glass bottles are not as new as some people might think. In fact, the glass bottle has been around for about 3,000 years. In the late first century B.C., the Romans began to make glass bottles that the local doctors and pharmacists used to dispense pills, healing powders, and potions. These were small cylindrical bottles, 3 to 4 inches in length and very narrow. As we will read later, the majority of early bottles produced after Roman times were sealed with a cork or glass stopper, whereas the Romans used a small stone rolled in tar to seal vials. Also, the finished bottles contained many impurities such as sand particles and bubbles caused by the crude glass-producing process. Because of the thickness of the glass and the crude finish, Roman glass was very resilient compared to the glass of later times, which accounts for the survival and good preservation of some Roman bottles that have been dated as 2,500 years old. The Romans also get credit for originating what we think of today as the basic store bottle and early merchandising techniques.

The first effort to manufacture glass in America is thought to have taken place at the Jamestown settlement in Virginia around 1608. It is interesting to note that the majority of glass produced at the Jamestown settlement was in fact earmarked for shipment back to England (owing to England's lack of resources) and not for the new settlements. As it turned out, the Jamestown glasshouse enterprise ended up being a failure almost before it got started. The poor quality of glass produced simply couldn't support England's needs.

The first successful American glasshouse was started in 1739 in New Jersey by Caspar Wistar, a button manufacturer who immigrated to the United States from Germany. The next major glasshouse operation was started by Henry Stiegel in the Manheim, Pennsylvania, area between 1763 and 1774. He later established several more. The Pitkin glassworks was started in East Hartford, Connecticut, around 1783 and was the first American glasshouse to provide figural flasks. It also became the most successful glasshouse of its time, until it closed around 1830 because of the high cost of wood for fuel. In order to understand early glasshouse history, both the successes and far more numerous failures, we need to understand the problems of availability of raw materials and the concerns of constructing the glasshouse itself.

The glass factory of the nineteenth century was usually built near abundant sources of sand and wood or coal, and in close proximity to numerous roads and waterways for transportation of the raw materials to the glasshouse and the finished products to major eastern markets such as Boston, New York, and Philadelphia. Finding a suitable location was usually not a problem, but once production was under way resources would quickly diminish.

The glasshouse building itself was usually a large wooden structure, which housed a primitive furnace that was shaped like a beehive about 9 feet in diameter. A major financial drain on the glass companies, and the major reason so many of the businesses went broke, was the large pot that fit inside the furnace to hold the molten glass. The melting pot, which cost about $100 and took eight months to build, was made by hand from a long coil of clay and was the only substance known that would not melt when the glass was heated to 2,700°. Although the material could withstand the temperatures, the life span of each pot was only about eight weeks; the high temperatures over a long period of time caused the clay itself to turn into glass. The cost of regularly replacing these melting pots proved the downfall of many an early glass factory.

Throughout the nineteenth century, glasshouses continued to come and go because of changes in demand and technological improvements. Between 1840 and 1890, there was an enormous demand for glass containers to satisfy the whiskey and beer businesses and the medicine and food-packing industries. Owing largely to this steady demand, glass manufacturing in the United States finally expanded enough to become a stable industry. This demand was caused in large part by the settling of the western United States and the great gold and silver strikes between 1850 and 1900. Unlike other industries of the time that saw major changes in manufacturing processes, the technique for producing glass bottles remained the same. This process gave each bottle special character, producing unique shapes, imperfections, irregularities, and various colors until 1900.

At the turn of the century, Michael J. Owens invented the first fully automated bottle-making machine. Although many fine bottles were manufactured between 1900 and 1930, Owens's invention ended an era of unique bottle design that no machine process could ever duplicate. In order for a bottle collector, especially a new bottle collector, to better understand the history and origin of antique bottles, it is important to take a look at the chronological history of bottle manufacturing.

Free-Blown Bottles: First Century B.C. to 1860 (see Figure 1)
During the first century B.C., the blowpipe, which was nothing more than a long hollow metal rod, was invented. The tip was dipped into molten glass, and by blowing into the other end, a glassblower formed the desired bottle, bowl, or other container.

Pontil Marks: 1618 to 1866
Once the bottle was blown, it was removed from the rod through the use of a three-foot metal pontil rod, which was dipped into the tank of molten glass and applied to the bottom of the bottle. The neck of the bottle was then touched with a wet rod or stick, which separated it from the blowpipe.

The finishing process could include a variety of applied and tooled rings and collars. In the final step, an iron was inserted into the neck of the bottle, or held by tongs, while the pontil was separated from the bottle. If the bottle was to be molded for body form, the gather was inserted in a mold and further expanded to take on the shape of the interior of the mold, usually cylindrical, square, or polygonal.

Snap, Cases, Snap-Cases: 1860 to 1903 (see Figure 2)
Between 1850 and 1860, the first major invention for bottle making since the invention of the blowpipe appeared, an instrument known as the snap, which replaced the pontil. The basic snap-case was a 5-foot metal rod that had claws to grasp the bottle. A snap locked the claw into place in order to hold the bottle more securely while the neck was being finished. It should be noted that each snap-case was tailor-made to fit bottles of a certain size and shape. These bottles have no pontil scars or marks, which left the bases of the bottles free from lettering or design. There may, however, be some minor grip marks on the side as a result of the claw device.

Free-Blown Bottle-Making Process
Figure 1

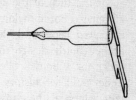

1. The blowpipe was inserted into the pot of red-hot metal and twisted to gather the requisite amount onto the end of the pipe.

5. The body and neck were then formed by the bottom of the bottle being flattened with a wooden paddle called a Battledore (named after a glassblower who designed the paddle concept).

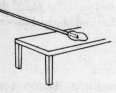

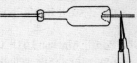

2. The blowpipe was then rolled slowly on a metal table to allow the red-hot metal to cool slightly on the outside and to sag.

6. One of the irons (pontil) was attached to the center bottom of the bottle for easy handling during the finishing of the bottle neck and lip. At this time, a kick-up could be formed in the bottom of the bottle by pushing inward when attaching the iron.

3. The blower than blew into the pipe to form an internal central bubble.

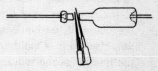

7. The bottle was whetted, or cracked off the blowpipe, by touching the hot glass at the end of the pipe with a tool dipped in cold water.

4. The gathered amount of metal was further expanded and sometimes turned in a wooden block that had been dipped in cold water to prevent charring by the hot metal, or possibly rolled again on the metal table.

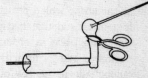

8. With the bottle held on a pontil, the blower reheated the neck to polish the lip and further smoothed it by tooling.

Snap, Cases, Snap-Cases: 1860–1903
Figure 2

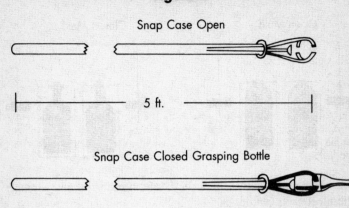

Snap Case Open

5 ft.

Snap Case Closed Grasping Bottle

The snap-case instrument was used for small-mouth bottle production until the automatic bottle machine came into existence in 1903.

Molds: First Century B.C. to 1900

The use of molds in bottle making, which really took hold in the early 1800s, actually dates back to the first century with the Romans. As detailed earlier, in the free-blown process the glassblower shaped the bottle, or vessel, by blowing and turning it in the air. When using a mold, the glassblower would begin in the same way, then take a deep breath while lowering the red-hot shaped mass into the hollow mold. The blower would continue blowing air into the tube until the glass compressed itself against the sides of the mold to acquire the finished shape.

Molds were usually made in two or more sections in order to enable the mold to come apart. The hardened bottle could then be easily removed. Since it was impossible to have the molds fit precisely, the seams show on the surface of the finished article, giving a clue about the manufacturing methods used in the production of the bottle. The molds were categorized as "open," where only the body of the bottle was forced, with the neck and lip being added afterward, and "closed," in which the neck and lip were part of the original mold (Figure 3). Later two specific types of molds came into use: the three-piece mold, in use from 1809 to 1880, which consisted of two main types; and the turn mold or paste mold, in use from 1880 to 1900.

Molds: First Century B.C.-1900
Figure 3

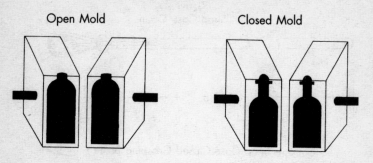

Open Mold   Closed Mold

The three-piece mold helped the bottle industry become stronger in the nineteenth century.

Three-Piece Molds (see Figure 4)

Three-piece dip mold—the bottom section of the bottle mold was one piece, and the top, from the shoulder up, was two separate pieces. The mold seams appeared circling the bottle at the shoulder and on each side of the neck.

Full-height molds—the entire bottle was formed in the mold and the two seams run vertically to below the lip on both sides of the bottle.

Turn Mold or Paste Mold

Wooden molds used in the manufacture of bottles were kept wet to prevent them from igniting, but as the hot glass came into contact with the mold, the walls of the mold became charred. By turning the mold, however, manufacturers discovered that they could erase seams and mold marks, give a high finish to the completed bottle, and prevent charring. After metal molds replaced wooden ones, manufacturers used a paste inside the mold that allowed the bottle to slide easily during the turning process, which explains the origins of the terms "turn mold" and "paste mold."

Mason Food Jars: 1858

In 1858, John Mason invented the wide-mouth jar that became famous as a preserved food container. His new screw-top neck was formed in the same mold as the body. The jar was then broken away from the

Three-Piece Mold
Figure 4

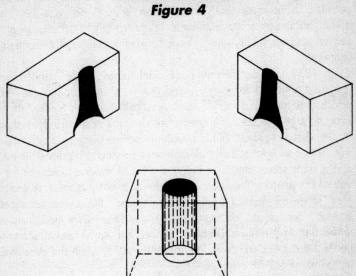

blowpipe and sent to the annealing oven to temper the glass, making it more resistant to breakage. After this, the jagged edges of the rims were ground down. In fact, earlier jars can be distinguished from later ones by looking for rough and sharp edges produced by this grinding process.

Press-and-Blow Process: 1892

In 1892, a semiautomatic process called "press and blow" was invented. This process could only be used in the production of wide-mouth containers formed by pressing molten glass into the mold to form the mouth and lip first. Then a metal plunger was inserted through the mouth and applied air pressure formed the body of the bottle. This process was utilized for the production of early fruit jars and milk bottles.

The Automatic Bottle-Making Machine: 1903

Michael J. Owens is recognized as the inventor of the first automatic bottle-making machine. Owens first introduced his invention in 1899, but the machine was not perfected until 1903. In the beginning, the

Owens machine made only heavy bottles since the demand for them was the greatest. In 1909, improvements to the machine made it possible to produce small prescription bottles. Between 1909 and 1917, numerous other automatic bottle-making machines were invented and soon all bottles were formed automatically throughout the world.

In 1917, another invention of mechanized bottle manufacturing provided a way of forming a measured amount of molten glass from which a bottle could be blown. It was called a "gob feeder." In this process, a gob of glass is drawn from the tank and cut off by shears.

One last note about bottle making concerns the process of producing screw-top bottles. Early glassblowers produced bottles with inside and outside screw caps long before the bottle-making machines mechanized the process. Because early methods of production were so complex, screw-top bottles produced before the 1800s were considered specialty bottles and expensive to replace. Today they are considered to be rare and quite collectible. In fact, the conventional screw-top bottle did not become common until after 1924, when the glass industry standardized the threads.

The Beginning Collector

Now that you have learned something about the history and origin of bottle making, it's time to provide information about how to approach the hobby of bottle collecting, as well as suggestions on books and reference guides, start-up costs, old versus new bottles, and some information on bottle clubs.

So, what approach should you take toward getting started, and what might influence that approach? The first thing to understand about antique bottle collecting is that there aren't any rules. Everyone's finances, spare time, available storage space, and preferences are different and will influence his or her approach. As a collector, you will need to think about whether to specialize and focus on a specific type of bottle or group of bottles, or whether you're more of a general or "maverick" collector who acquires everything that becomes available. The majority of bottle collectors I have talked with over the years, me included, took the "maverick" approach as new collectors. We grabbed everything in sight, ending up with bottles of every type, shape, and color. Now, after twenty years of collecting, my recommendation to newcomers is to specialize. Of course, taking the more general approach in the early years has given me a wider spectrum of knowledge about bottles and glass in general. But specializing has distinct advantages over the "maverick" approach:

- It reduces the field of collection, which helps organize study and research.
- The specialist becomes an authority on bottles in a particular field.
- Trading becomes easier with other specialists who may have duplicate and unwanted bottles.

- By becoming more of an authority within a specialty, the collector can negotiate a better deal by spotting those bottles that are underpriced.

I need to mention, however, that specialized collectors will always be tempted by bottles that don't quite fit into their collections. So they cheat a little and give in to that maverick urge. This occasional cheating sometimes results in a smaller side collection, or, in extreme cases, turns the collector away from a specialty and back to being a maverick. But that's all right. Remember, there are no set rules, with the exception of having a lot of fun.

Now, what does it cost to start a collection and how do you know the value of a bottle? Aside from digging excursions, which have travel and daily expenses, starting a collection can be accomplished by spending just a few dollars or maybe just a few cents per bottle. Digging, which we will discuss in detail later, is in this writer's opinion the ultimate way of adding to your collection.

Knowing what and where the best deals are obviously takes some time and experience. But the beginner can do well with just a few pointers.

Over the years, I've developed a quick-look method of buying bottles by grouping candidates into one of three categories:

- **Low end or common bottles:** Bottles reflect noticeable wear and the label is usually missing or not very visible. In most cases the label is completely gone and there is never embossing. The bottle is dirty (which can usually be fixed), with some scrapes, and free of chips. These bottles are usually clear and colorless.
- **Average grade/common bottles:** Bottles reflect some wear and a label may be visible but is usually faded. They are generally clear in color and free of scrapes or chips. Some of these may have minimal embossing.
- **High end and unique bottles:** These bottles can be empty or sometimes partially or completely full, with the original stopper and label or embossing. The color is clear and the bottle has no chips or scrapes and very little or no wear. If it has been stored in a box it is very likely in good condition. Also the box must be in good condition.

We will discuss price ranges just briefly here since values will be covered in detail in the two price sections. Usually, low-end bottles can be found for 50¢ to $1, average-grade bottles will range from $3 to $10, and basic high-end bottles will range from $10 to $25. Anything over $25 should be looked at closely by someone who has been collecting for a while.

As a rule, I try not to spend more than $1 per bottle for the low end and $3 for the average grade. It's easier to stick to this guideline when you've done your homework, but sometimes you just get lucky. During the 1992 Reno, Nevada, Bottle and Antique Show (one of the best, by the way), I stopped at a table where the seller had "Grab Bags," shopping bags full of bottles for $2 a bag. Well, I couldn't pass up this bargain. Later, when I had time to examine my treasures, I discovered a total of nine bottles, some purple, all earlier than 1900, in great shape, with embossing, for a total cost of 22¢ per bottle. Now what could be better than that! In the high-end category, deals are usually made after some good old horse trading and bartering. But, hey, that's part of the fun. Always let the seller know that you are a new collector with a limited budget. It really helps. I have never run across a bottle seller who wouldn't work with a new collector to try to give the best deal for a limited budget.

A collector should also be aware of old bottles versus new bottles and what distinguishes an antique bottle from an old bottle, and either from a new bottle. Quite often, new collectors assume that any old bottle is an antique and that if a bottle isn't old it is not a collectible. By collectible, I mean a relatively rare and/or valuable bottle, or one that holds special interest for the collector (for its historical value, perhaps). This is not necessarily the case. In the antique world, an antique is defined as any article more than 100 years old. But you will see quite a number of bottles listed in this book that are less than 100 years old and are in fact just as valuable, perhaps more so, than those that are antiques. I'm referring to bottles made between 1900 and 1950. As we discussed earlier, the history, origin, background, use, and rarity of the bottle can possibly gain more points with the bottle collector than how close the bottle comes to the 100-year mark.

The number and variety of old and antique bottles is greater than the new collectible items in today's market. On the other hand, the Jim Beams, Ezra Brooks, Avons, and recent Coke bottles, and other types of figurals manufactured more recently, are very desirable and collectible and are in fact made for that purpose. If you decide you want to collect new bottles, the best time to buy is when the first issue comes on the market. When the first issues are gone, the collectors' market is the only available source, and limited availability will drive prices up considerably. In mid-1992, the Coca-Cola Company reissued the 8-ounce junior-size Coke bottle in the Los Angeles area in an attempt to garner attention in a marketplace full of cans. This 8-ounce bottle has the same contour as the 6½-ounce bottle that was a Coke standard from the 1920s into the 1950s. (The 6½-ounce bottle is still available in a few parts of the United States, most noticeably in Atlanta, where Coca-Cola has its headquarters.) When the 8-ounce bottles were issued in Los Angeles, the "heavy-duty collectors" literally paid in advance and picked up entire case lots from the bottling operations before they hit the retail market.

For the beginning collector, and even the old-timer, books, reference guides, magazines, and other similar literature are readily available at libraries and bookstores. I still make it a point to read as much as possible since someone is always discovering something new. As a help, there is a bibliography in this book of various types of literature since clubs pool numerous sources of information as well as offer occasional digging expeditions. Various bottle clubs and dealers are also listed at the end of this book, beginning on page 422.

Now, get out to the antique shops, flea markets, swap meets, and antiques and bottle shows. Pick up those bottles and handle that glass. Ask questions, and soon you will be surprised by how much you have learned, not to mention how much fun it is.

Bottle Facts

In order for a new bottle collector to understand the hobby better, there are certain specifics such as age identification, bottle grading, labeling, and glass imperfections and peculiarities that are very important to familiarize yourself with.

As mentioned in the introduction, usually the first question from a novice is "How do you know how old a bottle is?" or "How can you tell that it is really an antique bottle?" Two of the most common methods for determining the age are by the mold seams and the color variations. Also, details on the lip, or top of the bottle, will provide some further clues.

Mold Seams (Figure 5)

Prior to 1900, bottles were manufactured with a blowpipe using the free-blown method or with a mold (in use after 1860). In either process, the mouth or lip of the bottle was formed last and applied to the bottle after completion (applied lip). An applied lip can be discerned by examining the mold seam, which will run from the base up to the neck and near the bottom of the lip. In the machine-made bottle, the lip is formed first and the mold seam runs over the lip. Therefore, the closer to the top of the bottle the seam extends, the more recent the bottle.

For the earliest bottles, manufactured before 1860, the mold seams will end low on the neck or at the shoulder. On bottles made between 1860 and 1880, the mold seam stops right below the mouth, which makes it easy to detect that the lip was formed separately. Around 1880, the closed mold was utilized, wherein the neck and lip were mechanically shaped and the glass had to be severed from the blowpipe. The ridge that resulted was evened off by hand sanding or filing. This mold seam usually ends within ¼ inch from the top of the bottle. After 1900, the seam extends

19

Age Identification Mold Seams of Bottles
Figure 5

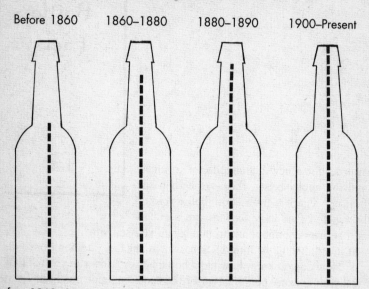

Before 1860   1860–1880   1880–1890   1900–Present

Before 1860: Seams extend to just over the shoulders.
1860–1880: Seams go most of the way up the neck of the bottle.
1880–1890: Seams continue through the top but not through or over the lip.
1900–present: Seams extend the full length of the bottle and over the lip.

clear to the top. Since the lips, or tops, were an integral part of the bottle-making process, it is important to understand some of that process.

Lips and Tops (Figures 6 and 7)

One of the best ways to identify bottles manufactured prior to 1840 is the presence of a "sheared lip." This type of lip was formed by cutting, or snipping, the glass free of the blowpipe with a pair of shears, a process that leaves it with a stovepipe look. Since hot glass can be stretched, some of these stovepipes have a very distinctive appearance. Around 1840, bottle manufacturers began to apply a glass ring around the sheared lip, forming a "laid-on-ring" lip. Between 1840 and 1880, numerous variations of lips or tops were produced by utilizing a variety of different tools. After 1880, manufacturers started to pool their processing information, resulting in a more evenly finished and uniform top. As a rule, the more uneven and crude the lip or top, the older the bottle.

Neck-Finishing Tools
Figure 6

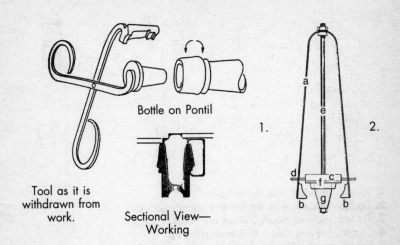

Bottle on Pontil

1.

2.

Tool as it is
withdrawn from
work.

Sectional View—
Working

1. The line drawings were developed from a description that appeared in the seventh edition (1842) of the *Encyclopaedia Britannica,* vol. X, p. 579: "The finisher then warms the bottle at the furnace, and taking out a small quantity of metal on what is termed a ring iron, he turns it once round the mouth forming the ring seen at the mouth of bottles. He then employs the shears to give shape to the neck. One of the blades of the shears has a piece of brass in the center, tapered like a common cork, which forms the inside of the mouth, to the other blade is attached a piece of brass, used to form the ring." This did not appear in the sixth edition (1823), though it is probable the method of forming collars was practiced in some glasshouses at that time.

2. The exact period in which neck-finishing tools evolved having metal springs with two jaws instead of one, to form collars, is undetermined. It doubtless was some time before Amosa Stone of Philadelphia patented his "improved tool," which was of simpler construction, as were many later ones. Like Stone's, "the interior of the jaws [was] made in such shape as to give the outside of the nozzle of the bottle or neck of the vessel formed the desired shape as it [was] rotated between the jaws in a plastic state . . ." U.S. Patent Office. From specifications for (A. Stone) patent No. 15,738, September 23, 1856.

Closures/Stoppers (Figure 8)

As discussed earlier, the Romans used small stones rolled in tar as stoppers. Later centuries saw little advancement in the methods of closure. For most of the fifteenth and sixteenth centuries, the closure consisted of a sized cloth tied down with heavy thread or string. Beneath

Bottle Lips/Tops Identification
Figure 7

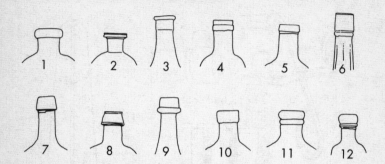

1. Tooled, rounded, rolled-over collar
2. Tooled, flanged, with flat top and squared edges
3. Tooled, rounded above ¾-inch flat band
4. Tooled, flat ring below thickened plain lip
5. Tooled, narrow beveled fillet below thickened plain lip
6. Tooled, broad sloping collar above beveled ring
7. Tooled, plain broad sloping collar
8. Tooled, broad sloping collar with beveled edges at top and bottom
9. Tooled, broad flat collar sloping to heavy rounded ring
10. Tooled, broad flat vertical collar with uneven lower edge
11. Tooled, double rounded collar, upper deeper than lower, neck slightly pinched at base of collar
12. Tooled, board round collar with lower level

English ink bottles depicting the "sheared lip," 1830–1840.

S.A. Whitney, Bottle Stopper
No. 31,046 Patented January 1, 1861
Figure 8

Drawing 1

Drawing 2

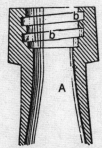

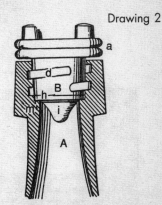

From Samuel A. Whitney's specifications for his "Bottle Stopper," patent No. 31,046, January 1, 1861. Drawing 1 shows the grooves in neck of the bottle. Drawing 2, on which "h" is a cork washer, shows the stopper in place. "The stopper is formed by pressing or casting the molten . . . glass in molds of the desired shape. . . . Although . . . applicable to a variety of bottles and jars, it is especially well adapted to and has been more especially designed for use in connection with mineral-water bottles, and such as contain effervescing wines, malt liquors, &c., the corks used in this class of bottles, if not lost, being generally so mutilated as to be unfit for second use when the bottles are refilled." (U.S. Patent Office.)

the cover was a stopper made of wax or bombase (cotton wading). Cotton wool was also dipped in wax to be used as a stopper, along with coverings made of parchment, paper, or leather. Corks and glass stoppers were still used in great numbers. The cork was sometimes tied or wired down for use with effervescent liquids. When the "close mold" came into existence, however, the shape of the lip was more accurately controlled, which made it possible to invent and manufacture many different capping devices.

One of the most unique was developed in 1873 when a British inventor, Hiram Codd, invented a bottle with a glass marble confined inside its neck so that when it was used with an effervescing liquid, the pressure of the gas forced the marble to the top of the neck, sealing the bottle. From 1879 to the early 1900s, the Hutchinson stopper became a common bottle closure. It used a heavy wire loop to control a rubber

Glass stoppers,
1850–1900.

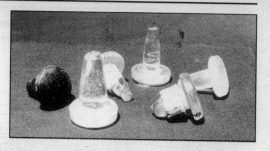

Glass stoppers, 1850–1900.

gasket that stayed inside the neck of the bottle. The Lighting stopper, used from 1880 to the early 1900s, was a porcelain or rubber plug anchored to the outside of the bottle by means of a permanently attached wire. The wire formed a bar that controlled the opening and closing of the bottle.

In 1897, William Painter invented the crown cap, which revolutionized the soft drink and beer bottling industry. A crown cap was formed from a circular tin plate crimped on the outer edge to fit tightly over the rolled lip of the bottle. The inside of the cap was filled with a cork disk that created an airtight seal. A modified version of this cap is still used on beer and soft drink bottles today.

Finally, in 1902, threads were manufactured on the outside of the lip to enable a threaded cap to be screwed onto the mouth of the bottle. This was not a new idea. Early glassblowers had produced bottles with inside and outside screw caps long before bottle-making machines came along. Early methods of production were so complex, however, that screw-top bottles produced before the 1800s were considered specialty bottles. They were expensive to replace and today are considered rare and quite collectible. In fact, the conventional screw-top bottle did not become common until after 1924, when the glass industry standardized the threads.

Dumfries Ale (English) depicting inside threads.

Dumfries Ale (English), full-bottle view depicting inside threads.

Glass Color

The next most common method for determining the age of a bottle is by examining the color of the glass. The basic ingredients for glass production (sand, soda, and lime) have remained the same for 3,000 years. These ingredients, when mixed together, are collectively called the "batch." When the batch is heated to a molten state, it is referred to as the "metal." In its soft or plastic stage, the metal can be molded into objects that when cooled become the solid material we know as glass.

Producing colored and perfectly clear glass were major challenges for glass manufacturers for centuries. In the thirteenth and fourteenth centuries the Venetians produced clear glass by using crushed quartz in place of sand. In 1668, the English tried to improve on this process by using ground flint to produce clear glass, and by 1675, an Englishman named George perfected lead glass. Today, this lead glass is referred to as "Flint glass." Prior to 1840, intentionally colored or colorless glass was reserved for fancy figured flasks and vessels. The coloration of bottles was considered unimportant until 1880, when food packers began to demand clear glass for preserved food products. Since most glass produced prior to this time was green, glass manufacturers began using manganese or delenium to bleach out the green tinge produced by the iron content of the sand. Only then did the clear bottle become common.

Iron slag was used up to 1860 and produced a dark olive-green or olive-amber glass that has become known as "black glass" and was used for wine and beverages that needed protection from light. Colors natural to bottle glass production are brown, amber, olive-green, and aqua.

The true blue, green, and purple colors were produced by metallic oxides added to the glass batch. Cobalt was added for blue glass, sulfur for yellow and green, manganese and nickel for purple, nickel for brown, copper or gold for red, and tin or zinc for milky colored glass (for apothecary vials, druggist bottles, and pocket bottles). Since these bright colors were expensive to produce, they are very rare and are sought after by most collectors.

"Purple glass" is the product of a number of imposed and natural forces and many collectors prize it above other colored glasses. As discussed earlier, the iron contained in sand caused glass to take on a color between green and blue. Glass manufacturers used manganese, which counteracted iron's blue effect and produced clear glass. Glass with this manganese content, which was most common in bottle production between 1880 and 1914, takes on a rich purple color when exposed to ultraviolet rays. This "purple glass" has come to be known as "desert glass" or "sun-colored glass" since the color is actually a result of exposure to the sun. One last note, glass that was produced between 1914 and 1930 is most likely to change to an amber or straw color.

Imperfections

Imperfections and blemishes are also clues to how old a bottle is and often add to the charm and value of an individual piece. Blemishes usually show up as bubbles or "seeds" in the glass. In the process of making glass, air bubbles form and rise to the surface, where they pop. As the "fining out" or elimination process became more advanced (around 1920), these bubbles or seeds were eliminated.

Another peculiarity of the antique bottle is uneven thickness of the glass. Often one side of the base has a 1-inch-thick side that slants off to paper thinness on the opposite edge. This imperfection was eliminated with the introduction of the Owens bottle-making machine in 1903. In addition, the various marks of stress and strain, sunken sides, twisted necks, and whittle marks (usually at the neck, where the wood mold made impressions in the glass) also give clues to indicate that a bottle was produced before 1900.

Labeling and Embossing

While embossing and labeling were a common practice in the rest of the world before 1850, American bottle manufacturers did not adopt the inscription process until 1869. These inscriptions included information about the contents, manufacturer, distributor, and slogans, or other messages advertising the product. Raised lettering on various bottles was produced with a plate mold, sometimes called a "slug plate," which was fitted inside the casting mold. This plate created a sunken area, and these bottles are of special value to collectors. Irregularities such as a misspelled name add to the value of the bottle, as will any name embossed with hand etching or another method of crude grinding. These bottles are very old, very collectible, and very valuable.

Inscription and embossing customs came to an end with the production of machine-made bottles (1903) and the introduction of paper labels. In 1933, with the repeal of Prohibition, the only letter embossing on bottles, usually those containing alcohol, is "Federal Law Forbids Sale or Re-Use of this Bottle."

Bottle Sources

Antique or collectible bottles can be found in a variety of different locations and sometimes where you least expect them. Excluding digging for bottles, which we'll discuss later in detail, the following sources comprise what I think is a good list for potential hiding places of that much sought after bottle.

Flea Markets, Swap Meets, Thrift and Secondhand Stores, Garage Sales, Salvagers

For the beginning collector, these sources will likely be the most fun (next to digging) and yield the most bottles at the best prices. As we discussed earlier, a little bit of homework can result in opportunities to purchase bottles of endless variety for an extremely low cost. As a rule, the majority of bottles found at these sources will fall into the common or common but above average category.

When looking around at flea markets, swap meets, and thrift stores, be sure to target household goods. It's a good bet that people selling household goods will have some type of bottle. When looking through the paper for garage sales, try to concentrate on the older areas of town, since the items being presented for sale will be noticeably older, more collectible, and more likely to fall into a rare category. Salvage stores or salvage yards are great places to search for bottles since these businesses deal with companies that have contracts to demolish old houses, apartments, and businesses, and on occasion, will come across treasures. One New York salvage company that contracted to clean out some old storage buildings came across an untouched illegal Prohibition setup complete with bottles and unused labels. What a find!

Local Bottle Clubs and Collectors

By joining a local bottle club or working with other collectors, you will find yet another source for your growing collection. Members will usually have quantities of unwanted or duplicate bottles that they will sell very reasonably, trade, or sometimes simply give away, especially to an enthusiastic new collector. In addition, bottle clubs are always a good source of information about digging expeditions.

Bottle Shows

Bottle shows not only expose you to bottles of every type, shape, color, and variety but provide you with the opportunity to talk with many experts in specialized fields. In addition, there are usually publications for sale relating to all aspects of the bottle-collecting hobby. Bottle shows can be a rewarding learning experience for the beginning collector in particular but also for the veteran collector.

One last note: Make sure to look under the tables at these weekend shows. The vendor may consider these duplicates as less attractive items, but a real bargain could be lurking there.

Auctions and Estate Sales

Auction houses have become a good source of bottles and glassware over the last 10 years. Try to find one that specializes in antiques and estate buyouts. To promote and provide buyers with a better idea of what will be for sale, the house usually publishes a catalog that provides bottle descriptions, conditions, and photographs. Auctions are fun and can be a very good source of bottles at economical prices. I do recommend, however, that you visit an auction first as a spectator to learn a little about how the whole process works before you decide to participate and buy at one. When buying, be sure of the color and condition of the bottle and terms of the sale.

Estate sales by themselves, apart from an auction, are a great source for bottles if the items for sale are from a home in a very old neighborhood or a section of the city that has historical significance. These sales are a lot of fun, especially when people running the sale let you browse, look over, and handle the contents. Prices are usually good and always subject to downward negotiation.

Knife and Gun Shows

What, bottles at a knife and gun show? Quite a number of gun and knife enthusiasts are also great fans of the West and keep an eye open for related artifacts. Every knife and gun show I've attended, or sold at, has had at least 10 dealers with bottles on their tables (or under the tables) for sale. And the prices were right since they were more interested in selling knives and guns than bottles. In addition, these dealers will often provide information on where they made their finds, which you can put to good use later.

Retail Antiques Dealers

This grouping includes those dealers who sell bottles at or near full-market prices. Buying from a dealer has its upside as well as its downside. Dealers usually have a large selection and will provide helpful information and details about the bottles. It is a safe bet that bottles for sale are authentic and have been priced in accordance with the true condition of the bottle.

On the other hand, to try to build up a collection from these dealers can be very expensive. But their shops are good places to browse, learn, and try to fill out a collection.

General Antique and Specialty Shops

The differences between a general shop and a retail dealer are usually the selection (more limited with a general shop) and the pricing, which is happily much lower. This is in part because these dealers are not as knowledgeable about bottles and therefore may incorrectly identify one, overlooking critical areas that determine the value. If a collector can become knowledgeable, these general dealers create the opportunity to acquire quality underpriced merchandise.

Digging
for
Bottles

There are many ways to begin your search for collectible bottles, but as I have mentioned before, there are few searches as satisfying and fun as digging up bottles yourself. While the goal is to find a bottle, the adventure of the hunt is as exciting as the actual find. From a beginner's viewpoint, digging is a relatively cheap and excellent way to start a collection. The efforts of individual and bottle club digging expeditions have turned up numerous important historical findings. These digs surfaced valuable information about the early decades of our country and the history of bottle and glass manufacturing in the United States. The following discussion of how to plan a digging expedition covers the essentials: locating the digging sites, equipment and tools, general rules, and helpful hints, as well as a section on privy/outhouse digging for the real adventurer.

Locating the Digging Site

Prior to any dig, you will need to learn as much as possible about the area you plan to explore. Do not overlook valuable resources in your own community. Chances are, you can collect important information from your local library, local and state historical societies, various types of maps, and city directories (useful for information about people who once lived on a particular piece of property). The National Office of Cartography in Washington, D.C., and the National Archives are also excellent resources.

In my experience, old maps are the best guides for locating digging areas with good potential. These maps depict what the town looked like in an earlier era and provide clues about where stores, saloons, hotels, red light districts, and the town dump were located. All are ripe for exploring. The two types of maps that will prove most useful are Plat maps and Sanborn Fire Insurance maps. A Plat map, which will show every home and business in the city or area where you wish to dig, can be compared to current maps to identify the older structures or determine where they once stood. The Sanborn Insurance maps are the most detailed, accurate, and helpful of all for choosing a digging site. These maps, which have also been published under other names, provide detailed information on each lot illustrating the location of houses, factories, cisterns, well, privies, streets, and property lines. These maps were produced for nearly every city and town in the country between 1870 and 1920 and are dated so that it's possible to determine the age of the sites you're considering. Figure 9 depicts an 1890 Sanborn Perris map section of East Los Angeles. This map section was used to locate an outhouse in East Los Angeles that dated between 1885 and 1905. A dig on that site turned up more than fifty bottles. Knowing the appropriate age of the digging site also helps to determine the age and types of bottles or artifacts you find there.

The local chamber of commerce, law enforcement agencies, and residents who have lived in the community for a number of years can be very helpful in your information search. Another great resource for publications about the area's history are local antiques and gift shops, which often carry old books, maps, and other literature on the town, county, and surrounding communities.

Since most early settlers handled garbage themselves, buried bottles can be unearthed almost anywhere, but a little thinking can narrow the search to a location that's likely to hold some treasures. Usually, the garbage was hauled and dumped within 1 mile of the town limits. Often, settlers or store owners would dig a hole about 25 yards out from the back of their home or business for garbage and refuse. Many hotels and saloons had a basement or underground storage area where empty bottles were kept.

Ravines, ditches, and washes are also prime digging spots because heavy rains or snow melt often washed debris down from other areas. Bottles can quite often be found beside houses and under porches. Residents would store or throw their bottles under their porches when porches were common building features in the late nineteenth and twentieth centuries. Walk down abandoned roads where houses or cabins once stood, investigate old wagon trails, railroad tracks, and sewers. If it is legal, and you should check first, old battlegrounds and military encamp-

Figure 9

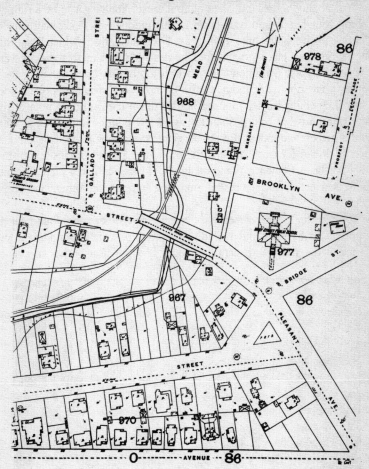

ments are excellent places to dig. Cisterns and wells are other good sources of bottles and period artifacts.

The first love of this bottle hound, and high on the list of most collectors, is an expedition to a ghost town. It's fun—and a lesson in history. The best places to conduct a search in ghost towns are near saloons, trade stores, the red light district, train stations, and the town dump (prior to 1900). The Tonopah, Nevada, town dump was the start of my digging experiences and is still a favorite spot.

Privy/Outhouse Digging

"You've dug bottles out of an old outhouse? You've got to be kidding!" Telling your family and friends about this unique experience will usually kick the conversation into high gear. I'm quite serious when I say that one of the best places to find old bottles—old bottles that can be very rare and in great condition—is in an old outhouse. Prior to 1870, most bottles were not hauled out to the dump. Why would people bother when they could simply toss old bottles down the outhouse hole in the back of a house or business? In fact, very few pontil-age (pre–Civil War) bottles are ever found in dumps. At that time people either dug a pit in their backyard for trash or used the outhouse. These outhouses, or priv-ies, have been known to yield all kinds of other artifacts such as guns, coins, knives, crockery, dishes, marbles, pipes, and other household items.

To develop a better sense of where privies can be found, it is important to have an understanding of their construction and uses. The privies of the nineteenth century (you'll find the best bottles in privies

Tim Blair, Los Angeles Historical Bottle Club, digging out an outhouse in East Los Angeles (circa 1885–1905).

that date from the nineteenth century) were deep holes lined with wood slats or brick, called "liners." You'll find privy holes were dug in a variety of shapes: square, round, rectangular, and oval. (The table following summarizes the different types of privy holes, their locations, and their depth.)

In general, privies in cities are fairly deep and usually provide more bottles and artifacts. Privies in rural areas are shallower and do not contain as many bottles. Farm privies are very difficult to locate and digs often produce few results.

How long was an outhouse used? Well, the life span of a privy is anywhere from ten to twenty years. It was possible to extend its useful life by cleaning it out or relining it with new wood, brick, or stone. In fact, nearly all older privies show some evidence of cleaning.

At some point, old privies were filled and abandoned. The fill materials included ashes, bricks, plaster, sand, rocks, building materials, or soil that had been dug out when a new or additional privy was added to the house. Often, bottles or other artifacts were thrown in with the fill. The depth of the privy determined the amount of the fill required. In any case, the result was a privy filled with layers of various materials. The bottom layer being the "use" layer or "trash" layer as shown in Figure 10.

It is possible to locate these old outhouses owing to the characteristic differences in density and composition of the undisturbed earth. Because of the manner of construction, it is fairly easy to locate them by probing the area with a metal rod or "probe."

As I mentioned earlier, your own community is a great place to begin the hunt for a privy or outhouse. A good starting point is to find an old house. Those built between 1880 and 1920 usually had a least one privy in the backyard. Try to locate a small lot with few buildings or obstructions to get in the way of your dig. First look for depressions in the ground. Since materials used to fill privy holes have a tendency to settle, a subtle depression may indicate where a septic tank, well, or privy was once located. In addition, like most household dumps, outhouses were usually located between 15 and 30 yards behind a residence or business. Another good indicator of an old privy site is an unexpected grouping of vegetation, such as bushes or trees, which flourishes above the rich fertilized ground. Privies were sometimes located near old trees for shade and privacy.

The most common privy locations were (1) directly outside the back door, (2) along a property line, (3) in one of the back corners or centered

TYPES OF PRIVIES

Construction	Shape	Location	Depth
brick	oval, round, rectangular, square	big towns and cities, behind brick buildings	not less than 6 feet deep
stone	round, square, rectangular	Limestone often used in area where stone is common.	rectangular, less than 10 feet, round holes often 20 feet or more
wood	square or rectangular	farms, small towns; may be first privy on lot	not more than 10 to 15 feet, often very shallow
barrel	round	cities and towns	8 to 12 feet

Older Privies
Figure 10

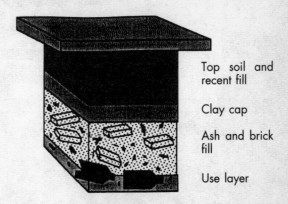

Top soil and recent fill

Clay cap

Ash and brick fill

Use layer

Older privies usually have a number of different layers.

near the back property line and (4) the middle of the yard. Figure 11 graphically depicts patterns of typical outhouse locations.

Now that you've located a privy (with luck it's full of great bottles), it's now time to get down and dirty and open up the hole. The approximate dimensions of the hole can usually be determined with your probe. If you know, or even think, that the hole is deeper than you are tall, it is extremely important to avoid a cave-in by opening up the entire hole. Never attempt to dig only a portion of the lined area in the hopes of getting to the trash layer quicker. Remember that the fill is looser than the surrounding ground and could come down on you. Also, always dig to the bottom and check the corners carefully. Privies were occasionally cleaned out but very often the unlucky person stuck with the job missed bottles and artifacts in the corners or on the sides. If you are not sure whether you've hit the bottom, check with the probe. It's easier to determine if you can feel the fill below what you may think is the bottom. In brick- and stone-lined holes, if the wall keeps going down, you are not on the bottom. Quite often it is difficult to date a privy without the use of detailed and accurate maps.

But it is possible to determine the age of the privy by the type and age of items found in the hole. The table on page 41 lists some types of bottles you might find in a dig and shows how their age relates to the age of the privy.

Ed Kuskie, Los Angeles Historical Bottle Club, digging out an outhouse in East Los Angeles (circa 1885–1905).

While finding a prized bottle is great, digging and refilling the hole can be hard work and very tiring. To help make this chore easier, lay a tarp on the ground surrounding the hole and as you dig, shovel the dirt onto the tarp. Then shovel the dirt off the tarp and fill 5-gallon plastic buckets. The first benefit of this method is the time and energy you'll save filling the hole. The second benefit, and maybe the biggest, is that you'll leave no mess. This becomes important for building a relationship with the property owner. The less mess the more likely you'll get permission to dig again. Also, your dig will be safer and easier if you use a walk board. Take an 8-foot-long 2 × 8 plank and place it over the hole. The digger, who is standing on the board pulling up buckets of dirt (let's all take turns), can do so without hitting the sides. This also reduces the risk of the bucket man falling in or caving in a portion of the hole. Setting up a tripod with a pulley over the hole will help to save time and prevent strain on the back.

The few short paragraphs I've presented are really just an outline of privy/outhouse digging. There are two publications that discuss the subject in greater detail, and people interested in privy/outhouse digging should locate them: *The Secrets of Privy Digging* by John Odell and *Privy Digging 101* by Mark Churchill. Information on how to purchase both of

Typical privy configurations
Figure 11

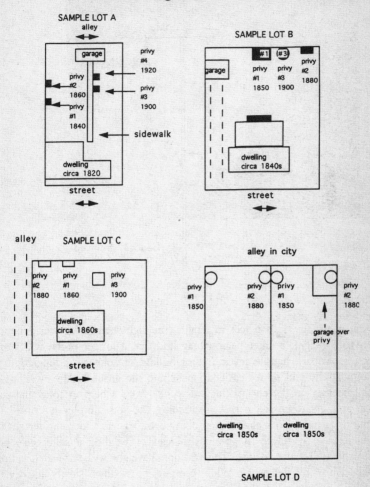

these fine publications can be found in the Bibliography. Now, let's have some "outhouse" fun.

The Probe

Regardless of whether you are digging in outhouses, old town dumps, or beneath a structure, a probe is an essential tool. The basic probe is actually a very simple device as shown in Figure 12.

Bottle probe
Figure 12

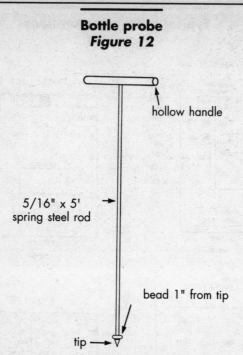

hollow handle

5/16" x 5'
spring steel rod

bead 1" from tip

tip

It is usually 5 to 6 feet in length (the right length for you depends on your height; a taller person may find that a longer probe will work better), with a handle made out of hollow or solid pipe tapered to a point at the end so it's easier to penetrate the ground. Also, welding a ball bearing on the end of the rod will serve as a help in collecting soil samples. As discussed earlier, examining the soil samples is critical to finding privies. To make your probing a bit easier, add some weight to the handle by filling the pipe with lead or welding a solid steel bar directly under the handle. The additional weight will reduce the effort needed to sink the probe. While probing, press down slowly and try to feel for differences in the consistency of the soil. Unless you are probing into sand, you should reach a point at which it becomes difficult to push, a natural bottom. If you find you can probe deeper in an adjacent spot, you may have found an outhouse. When this happens, pull out the probe and plunge it in again, this time at an angle to see if you feel a brick or wood line. After some practice, you'll be able to determine what type of material you are hitting. Glass, brick, crockery, and rocks all have their own distinctive sound and feel. While there are a number

Derek Abrams, digging out an outhouse in San Francisco, CA.

Selection of bottles and other artifacts found while Derek Abrams was digging the San Francisco outhouse.

DATING DIGGING SITES BY THE BOTTLES YOU FIND

Material	1920+	1900–19	1880–1900	1860–80	1840–60	Pre–1840
crown tops	yes	yes	no	no	no	no
screw tops	yes	yes	no	no	no	no
aqua glass	yes	some	yes	yes	yes	yes
clear glass	all	most	some	some	some	some
ground lip fruit jar	no	rare	yes	yes	rare	no
hinge mold	no	no	no	yes	yes	no
pontiled	no	no	no	yes	yes	yes
free blown	no	no	no	no	no	yes
historical flasks	no	no	no	yes	yes	yes
stoneware (crockery)	no	no	yes	yes	yes	yes

Comstock archaeology site (circa 1880), Virginia City, NV.

Wine bottle found in the Comstock archaeology site, Virginia City, NV (bottle circa 1890).

of places where you can purchase probes, you might want to have one custom made to conform to your body height and weight for more comfortable use.

Digging Equipment and Tools

When I first started digging, I took only a shovel and my luck. After a few broken bottles, I learned I was doing things the hard way. Since then, I've refined my list of tools and equipment. The following list includes those items that I've found useful; they are often recommended by other veteran diggers as well.

GENERAL DIGGING EQUIPMENT
  probe
  long-handled shovel
  short-handled shovel
  long-handled potato rake
  small hand rake
  old table knives
  old spoons
  hard- and soft-bristle brushes
  gloves, boots, eye protection, hat, and durable clothing
  insect repellent, snakebite kit, first-aid kit
  extra water
  dirt sifter (for coins or other items, a 2 × 2-foot wooden frame with
    chicken wire)
  hunting knife
  boxes for packing and storing bottles

PRIVY/OUTHOUSE DIGGING EQUIPMENT
  long-handled shovel
  5-foot probe
  slam probe*
  pick
  root cutters
  short-handled scratcher*
  1-inch × 15-foot or more rope with clip
  tripod with pulley*
  walk board
  short-handled shovel

10-foot probes*
posthole digger
pry bar
ax
5-gallon buckets
heavy tarps
hardhat and gloves

*Indicates optional item.

General Rules and Helpful Hints

I know I said there were no rules, but there is something you should always do: Always be responsible and ask for permission to dig. As a safety precaution, do not leave any holes open overnight. Do not damage shrugs, trees, or flowers unless the owner approves. When the digging is complete, always leave the site looking better than it was when you started. I can't stress this enough. That means filling in all holes and raking over the area. Remove your trash as well as trash left by previous prospectors or others. Always offer to give the owner some of the bottles. They may not want any, but they will appreciate the gesture. If you adhere to these few rules, the community or owner will thank you and future bottle diggers will be welcomed.

Try not to go out on a dig alone. But if you do be sure to tell someone where you're going and for how long you expect to be gone. When digging an outhouse, my recommendation is to go with no fewer than three people.

When you start to dig, don't be discouraged if you don't find any bottles. If you unearth other objects such as coins, broken dishes, or bottle tops, continue to dig deeper and in a wider circle. If you don't find any bottles, move to another spot. Always work from the edge to the center of the hole. Don't get discouraged! Even the very best have come home with empty bags and boxes, but never without the memory of a good time.

When you do find a bottle, stop your digging and remove the surrounding dirt a little at a time with a small tool, brush, or spoon. Handle the bottle very carefully since old bottles are very fragile.

Now that you know how to do it, what are you waiting for? Grab those tools, get those maps, and get started making the discoveries of a lifetime.

Bottle Handling

While selling bottles and listening to buyers at various shows, I am inevitably asked questions about cleaning, handling, and storing old bottles. Some collectors believe that cleaning a bottle diminishes its collectible value and desirability. Leaving a bottle in its natural state—as it was found—can be special. Others prefer to remove as much dirt and residue as possible. The choice rests with the owner. The following information will provide some help with how to clean, store, and take care of those special finds.

Bottle Cleaning

First off, never attempt to clean your new find in the field. In the excitement of the moment, it's easy to break the bottle or otherwise damage the embossing. With the exception of soda and ale bottles, glass bottles manufactured prior to 1875 usually have very thin walls. But even the bottles with thicker walls should be handled very carefully. The first step is to remove as much loose dirt, sand, or other particles as possible with a brush or a quick warm-water rinse. Then, using a warm-water solution and bleach (stir the mixture first), soak the bottles for a number of days (depending upon the amount of caked-on dirt). This should remove most of the excess grime. Other experienced collectors use cleaning mixtures of straight ammonia, kerosene, lime-a-away, and chlorine borax bleach. Do not use mixtures that are not recommended for cleaning glass.

After soaking, clean bottles with a bottle brush, steel wool, an old toothbrush, or any semistiff brush. At this point, you may want to soak the bottles again, this time in lukewarm water to remove any traces of cleaning materials. Either let the bottles air-dry or dry them with a soft towel. If the bottle has a label, the work will become more painstaking since soaking is not a cleaning option.

One last note: Do not clean your bottles in a dishwasher. While the hot water will produce a very clean bottle, the extreme heat could crack or even shatter fragile old bottles. A better option is the specialist who will clean your rare bottles with special tumbling machines. These machines, which leave the bottle with a clean polished look, can also be purchased for personal use.

Bottle Display

Now that you have clean, beautiful bottles, display them to their best advantage. My advice is to arrange your bottles in a cabinet rather than on wall shelving or randomly around the house. While the last two options are more decorative, they also leave the bottles more susceptible to damage. When choosing a cabinet, try to find one with glass sides since this will provide more light and better viewing. As an added touch, a light fixture sets off your collection beautifully. If you have picked up any other goodies from your digging, such as coins or gambling chips, scatter them around the bottles for a little Western flavor.

Bottle Protection

Because of the increased earthquake activity of the last three years, most notably the January 17, 1994, Northridge, California, earthquake, bottle collectors across the country are now taking added steps to protect their valuable pieces.

Since most of us have our collections in some type of display cabinet, it's important to know how to secure it best. First, fasten the cabinet to wall studs with brackets and bolts. If you are working with dry wall and it's not possible to secure the cabinet to a stud, butterfly bolts will provide a tight hold. Always secure the cabinet at both the top and bottom for extra protection.

Next, lock or latch the cabinet doors. This will prevent the doors from flying open. If your cabinet has glass shelves, be sure to not overload them with too many bottles. In an earthquake, the glass shelving can break under the stress of excess weight.

Finally, it's important to secure the bottles to the shelves with some type of adhesive, wax, or double-sided tape. There are a number of adhesives available at home-improvement centers and hardware stores. Two of the most commonly used are microcrystalline wax and Quake Secure.

Bottle Storage

For those bottles you've chosen not to display, the best method for storing them is empty liquor boxes with cardboard dividers (which prevent bottles from knocking into each other). As added protection, you might want to wrap the individual bottles in paper.

Record Keeping

Last but not least, it's a good idea to keep records of your collection. Use index cards detailing where the bottle was found or purchased, including the dealer's name and price you paid. Also, assign a catalog number to each bottle, record it on the card, and then make an index. Many collectors keep records with the help of a photocopy machine. If the bottle has embossing or a label, put the bottle on the machine and make a copy of it. Then type all the pertinent information on the back of the image and put it in a binder. When you are trading and selling your bottles, this kind of record keeping will be invaluable.

I first met Fred Holabird in 1983 during a Western gun and knife show where he was selling (what else?) bottles. After talking with him for a while, I bought a book he had written, and of course ended up buying a few bottles. It was the start of a great friendship. Fred has been collecting bottles since 1973, when he found his first embossed Pumpkin Seed Whiskey bottle in an old prospector's pit.

Fred has been in the mining industry for more than seventeen years as a geologist and mining company executive. In 1983, he founded a company specializing in Western Americana documents and glass. Since then he has been involved with numerous auctions, including the 1987 sale of Mel Fisher's Atocha treasure at Caesars Palace in Las Vegas. He is currently working as a consultant on Western Americana historical projects for numerous museums and auctions houses. Fred is also in the process of updating and rewriting his book of Nevada embossed bottles which is due to be published in October 1997.

I feel honored that Fred has taken time to tell us about the history and value of the bottles of Nevada.

Collecting embossed bottles from Nevada became a passion of mine over twenty years ago. It began as a hobby, as an outreach of my new home in Nevada. It became something of an obsession after I watched the market value climb regularly in the mid-1970s. Just when I thought the market had peaked, it would steady and take off again. So, I jumped in. . . .

Two books and numerous magazine articles later, I became a recognized "expert" on the subject. Not by design, but because of the enthusiasm I had developed after researching many of the merchants who bottled

McCullough's Pharmacy, Reno, NV, 1891–1932.

F. J. Steinmetz, Druggist, Carson City, NV, 1893–1910.

their products in glass containers. It was like a giant mystery novel. I was continually digging up "new" information on merchants that I couldn't seem to find through the normal channels of researching in directories, newspapers, and tax records.

One of my favorite stories comes from an autograph session at a local bookstore. In walked a well-dressed elderly gentleman who introduced himself as John Shier's grandson (Shier had a drugstore in the little mining camp of Delamar, now a ghost town). I had been particularly stymied in my research on Shier's drugstore because of a lack of records. It seemed that very little had survived. Then in walked his grandson with the best stories you could imagine, complete with photographs.

Collecting soon became fun because of the people. I enjoyed not only the folks involved in research, but the families I met, the people at research institutions, the folks who let us dig in their backyards, and the wild-goose chases after elusive rare bottles. The hobby was fresh and there were a lot of collections to find.

While I began logging collections, the discovery of quite a few very beautiful bottles from Nevada came as a small surprise. In the mid-1970s, the common perception was that embossed bottles from Nevada were quite plain. Since Nevada was undeveloped until modern historical times, 1860s to 1870s, most people thought bottles from Nevada were "plain." Most of the Nevada bottles known to the collecting world of the 1970s were drugstores and a few plain whiskeys and sodas without any fancy colors. But the idea that Nevada bottles were nothing but plain was soon dismissed. As I looked at more and more collections, I noticed there were quite a few striking color variations of otherwise plain bottles. Some of the most beautiful bottles are, of course, quite rare (one or two known). Among these are the amber Higgings Ink and the Morrill Apothecary, both from Virginia City.

One of the great Nevada bottles today is the W. S. Wright soda from Virginia City. While the bottle carries only the proprietor's name, it is the only true example of a merchant's bottle from the Nevada territorial period (pre-October 1864). Manufactured by the San Francisco Glass Works, this soda exhibits all the traits of early crude Western glassmaking. Colors range from emerald and grass-green to aqua to

A. M. Cole, Apothecary, Virginia City, NV, 1861–1908.

W. A. Perkins, Virginia City, NV, 1875–1882.

R. E. Queen, Reno, NV, 1878–1881.

shades of blue. As I collected color variations and displayed them at shows, I found people were as excited about the colors as they were about this newly discovered collectible.

One day I received an excited call from one of my digging friends in Virginia City. "We hit Wright's outhouse!" he exclaimed. In a hole about 15 feet deep, they found several feet of broken glass . . . probably several thousand broken bottles. Only two or three mint Wright bottles made it through, one of which is the crudest dark green-aqua glass peppered with charcoal bits and pieces. About twenty-five whole bottles were found with cracks. Most of these were seriously flawed, with large pieces of charcoal or "pot stones," resulting in cracks. I kept a good cross section to show the variation in flawed bottles.

Other popular "ghost town" bottles include the crown-top soda from the Eagle Bottling Company, of Goldfield (exceptionally rare), and drugstore bottles from Ruby Hill, Tuscarora, and Seven Troughs. The Seven Troughs bottle has a large owl on the front, a symbol of the Owl Drug store but unrelated to the Owl Drug Company. Seven Troughs was a small mining camp in the high desert located up a canyon. Unfortunately for the folks of Seven Troughs, the canyon drained after it became a populated community. As providence would have it, a horrendous flood washed away part of the town about the same time the mines began to peter out. Today nothing is left except a few rusty cans.

Sometimes collecting bottles in small towns that are all but vanished isn't all that easy since it's illegal in many areas. So the only hope of acquiring one of these rare bottles is buying from a collection or traveling to a neighboring town in the hope that digging there will uncover one of these rarities. The Seven Troughs bottle in my collection was dug from a deep hole in Lovelock, a town about 10 miles from Seven Troughs. With its 16-ounce capacity, it remains the largest known example.

Digging in Nevada has been quite an experience. While nowhere near as experienced as some of my friends, I have dug my share of holes, probably a thousand or so. But this amounts to about 10 percent of what my fanatical and very successful friends have dug. My "rule of thumb" is that one hole in ten will have bottles and only one in ten of those will have a "good" bottle.

J. F. Myers, Druggist, Reno, NV, 1878–1882.

John Shier, Pharmacist, Delamar, NV, 1893–1908.

Once, while working in a small mining town, a nice lady let us dig in her backyard after she came home from work. We located the privy and began digging. As bottles began to fly out of the hole, she came out, dangled her feet over the edge, and said she hoped we would find her father's broken plate, which she was told had been thrown out long before she was born. It was apparently the only missing piece in a set of china generations old. Fifteen minutes later, out came both pieces unstained. We made her day and she made ours.

The goal I've had over the past fifteen years has been to assemble a complete collection of Nevada merchant bottles. Considering widespread bottle production, this would be an insurmountable task with most states. But in Nevada, a state lightly populated compared to others, the task is

Henry F. Schuldt, Pharmacist,
Tusgarora, NV, 1878–1879.

A. M. Cole, Virginia City, NV,
1865–1870.

The Pioneer Drug Company,
Goldfield, NV, 1906–1918.

much easier. I am now only one bottle short of my original goal. The
Nevada collection offers a spectacular array of colors, sizes, and shapes.
But one prominent nationally collected color is missing from the ranks
of the Nevada embossed bottles—cobalt. The only cobalt bottles from
Nevada known to exist are two seltzers, both from Reno. For years I had
heard stories about a cobalt Delamar bottle. After some research I tracked
down an exceptionally kind lady in Panaca who showed me her
collection. And there they were. Two cobalt Delamar drugstore bottles.
She had made them both herself using glazed pottery. We laughed over
the stories based on those recreations that had circulated and grown. She
had made a number of unique ceramic bottles that the Las Vegas Bottle
Club gave away as prizes for displays, of which I have a few.

And there's always a story behind these ghost town bottles; for
instance, the history of various merchants is quite fascinating. Sometimes
the merchants would last only a few years in one town, moving on to
another when the gold dried up. Such was the case with Henry Schuldt

Lewis Drug Company, Ely, NV,
1906–1911.

F. J. Schneider, Druggist, Eureka,
NV, 1880–1890.

of Tuscarora, who moved to Grass Valley, California. More of his Tuscarora drug bottles have been dug there than in Tuscarora. George Thaxter moved from Carson City to Redlands, and W. H. Stowell moved from Eureka to Spokane. Bottles bearing these merchants' names have been discovered in both towns. Other merchants such as A. B. Stewart started "franchising." A. B. Stewart stores operated nearly simultaneously in Virginia City, Gold Hill, Silver City, Bodie, Seattle, and later Exeter.

Collecting anything today is both an investment and a hobby and I've enjoyed all aspects of the hobby. Because of my passion, the investment has been worthwhile as well. Because antique bottles are aesthetically pleasing and their shapes and colors are an art form, we've seen their entrance into art auction markets. Once this move was made, collecting bottles as an investment became legitimized and has proven to be both fun and profitable.

When considering a bottle purchase as an investment, the following factors, listed in descending order of importance, will influence the decision:

1. Demand—Is there sufficient demand for the bottle to support the price indefinitely? A number of factors such as bottle color, clarity,

State Hygienic Laboratory,
Reno, NV, 1910.

Clark's Drug Store, Ely-
McGill, 1908–1909.

H. G. Heidtmann, Becker's, Reno,
NV, 1900–1918.

Frank Adadie, Wholesale Liquors,
Eureka, NV, 1884–1886.

Sam Johnson's Bar, Reno, NV,
1909–1914.

crudeness, age, and collecting category all affect this demand. Major collecting categories are figurals, historical flasks, bitters, sodas, whiskeys, and medicines.

2. Market—Is the market for the bottle national, regional, or local? And does this market support the perceived demand? A national market means a broad support base with more collectors, therefore greater investment stability. Regional or local markets may be substantial enough to support a market long-term. The bottom line, though, is the number of collectors. The more collectors, the more competition, the more stable the price.

3. Condition—Is the condition of the bottle good enough to ensure an easy sale? Broken, chipped, or cracked bottles are often hard to sell unless they have an exceptional demand. Initially, when bottles first became valuable collectibles, the only acceptable investment condition was "mint." True "mint" used to be defined as a bottle with no scratches, discoloration, potstones, stains, chips, cracks, or blemishes. Now the term "mint" applies to any bottle that has no chips or scratches. A minor stain is okay. Recently, rarity has become a significant factor. If a bottle is sufficiently rare the condition will affect the price, but the bottle still remains marketable and in high demand.

4. Guarantee—Will the dealer or collector selling the bottle guarantee its original and condition? Will he or she give you your money

back if you are not satisfied? Investment guarantee may be the stickiest negotiating point in a sale. When a bottle sold to a collector is warranted in a specific condition, it should be in just that condition. One popular West Coast dealer has often overlooked small chips on some of the bottles he has sold through the mail, but he has never hesitated to refund money if the customer is not satisfied.

In summary, use good judgment when buying bottles as investments. Know the market, how to buy and sell, and understand the key factors affecting bottles as investments. If you are in doubt of investment criteria, be sure to check with a Certified Public Accountant (CPA) or the Internal Revenue Service (IRS). The thing to remember about collecting and investing is that it should be fun. I've had more than my share of fun doing this and if you share my passion for bottles, I'm sure you'll do the same.

Old Bottles

Old Bottles: Pre-1900

The bottles listed in this section have been broken down into individual categories by physical type and/or by the original contents of the bottle. For most categories, the trade names can be found in alphabetical order if they exist. Note that in the case of certain early bottles, such as flasks, a trade name does not appear on the bottle. These bottles have been listed according to the embossing or other identification on the bottle itself.

Since it is impossible to list every bottle available, I've tried to provide a good cross section of bottles in various price ranges and categories rather than listing only the rarest or most collectible pieces.

The pricing shown reflects the value of the particular bottle listed. Similar bottles could have values higher or lower than the items specifically listed in this book. This listing will still provide a good starting point for determining a price range.

Bottle Grading

Pricing, or putting a value on an old bottle, is dependent upon a number of variables, as well as on reliable sources. The guidelines below detail variables that are most often used by dealers and collectors to determine a value and are consistent with the methods that I have used over the years. These variables break down into the following three groups:

1. Rarity and demand for the specific bottle
2. Bottle type based on the original function
3. Unique features
   - embossing

- labeling
- pontil scars
- whittle marks
- imperfections in the glass
- colors
    - purple (amethyst)
    - cobalt blue
    - milk glass
    - black glass

Bottles are then categorized into one of the following conditions.

Mint—An empty or full bottle (preferably full) with a label or embossing. Clear in color, clean, with no chips, scrapes, or wear. If there is a box, it must be in good condition.

Extra Fine—An empty bottle with the label (slight wear) or embossing. Clear in color, clean, no chips, no scrapes, some wear. Usually there is no box or the box is not in very good condition.

Very Good—Bottle reflects some wear and label is usually missing or not very visible. Most likely these is no embossing and no box.

Good—Bottle reflects additional wear and label is completely absent. Color is usually faded and bottle is dirty. It's common to see some scrapes and minor chips. Most likely there will be no box.

Fair or Average—Bottle shows much wear, the label is missing, and there is no embossing. The color is very faded and the piece has numerous scrapes and some chips or even cracks. Definitely no box.

Even with the above guidelines, it is important to have some additional resources for grading those rare or unique bottles that give the collector a real challenge and fun. The bibliography in this book will provide some additional references. And remember to ask other collectors or dealers for help. They're a valuable resource.

Ale
and
Gin

Since ale and gin bottles are almost identical in style and similar in other ways, it becomes difficult to determine what the bottle originally contained unless information is provided on the bottle itself. Ale bottles should not be confused with beer bottles, a common mistake because of the similarities in shape.

Ale was a popular beverage at a time when available wines were not as palatable. Even the very best ale was not expensive to make or buy so it's easy to understand the demand for it. The bottles used by colonial ale makers were made of pottery and imported from England. When searching out these bottles, keep in mind that the oldest ones had a matte or unglazed surface.

In the seventeenth century, a Dutch physician named Francesco De La Bor prepared gin as a medical compound for the treatment of kidney disease. While its effectiveness in purifying the blood was questionable, gin drinking became very popular. It became so popular that many chemists decided to go into the gin-brewing business full-time to meet the growing demand. During the nineteenth century, gin consumption in America increased at a steady rate.

The design of the gin bottle, which has a squat body, facilitated packing in cases by preventing shifting and possible damage in shipping. The first case bottles had very short necks and were octagonal. Designs that came later featured longer necks. Bottles with tapered collars are dated to the nineteenth century. Case bottles vary in size from a half pint to multiple gallons. The early bottles were crudely made and have distinct pontil scars.

Gordon's London Dry Gin, clear.

E. P. Shaw Limited Ale, Wakefield, England, early 1880s.

A. C. A. Nolet, Schiedam, Aromatic, Schnapps
Olive green, 4⅝ in., smooth base, applied mouth $65–85
Dutch 1870–1880

A. M. Bininger & Co., No. 19 Broad Street, New York, Old London Dock—Gin
Medium amber, 8 in., smooth base, applied mouth.................$100–150
American 1860–1870

A. M. Bininger & Co., No. 19 Broad Street, New York, Old London Dock—Gin
Medium olive green, 9½ in., smooth base, applied mouth........$75–150
American 1860–1870

A. M. Bininger & Co., No. 17 Broad Street, New York, Old London Dock—Gin
Yellow olive, 9¾ in., smooth base, applied mouth $150–300
American 1860–1880 (note the rare "No. 17" on one panel)

A. M. Bininger and Company,
No. 19, Broad St., NY, Old
London Dock Gin, 1885.

Rectangular Case Gin
Deep greenish aqua, 9¼ in., pontil base, flared lip................$200–$300
Continental 1770–1800

Case Gin
Medium olive-amber, 9¾ in., pontil base, rolled lip..................$75–125
Dutch 1780–1810

Case Gin
Emerald green, 10¼ in., pontil base, rolled lip.........................$125–175
Dutch 1780–1810 (scarce in this color)

Dip Mold Case Gin
yellow olive green, 11 in., pontil base, applied mouth.............$100–120
Dutch 1770–1790

Large Case Gin
Yellow-amber, 12¾ in., pontil base, applied mouth.................$250–325
Dutch 1770–1810

Large Case Gin
Medium olive-amber, 15½ in., pontil base, rolled lip............,....$200–250
Dutch 1780–1810 (scarce in this large size)

Oversize Case Gin
Yellow olive green, 16¾ in., pontil base, rolled lip.................$450–750
Dutch 1770–1790 (scarce in this large size)

Champion, P & C, Scotch Ale
Amber, 6⅞ in., smooth base, applied mouth $175–300
American 1855–1865 (rare)

Cosmopoliet (man holding gin bottle), J. J. Melchers WZ, Schiedam
Olive-amber, 10½ in., smooth base, applied mouth $175–275
Dutch 1860–1870

Cream Ale, D-I-E-H-L-&-L-O-R-D, N-A-S-H-V-I-L-L-E-T-N
Amber, 7⅜ in., smooth base, applied mouth $250–350
American 1870–1880 (rare)

D. E. Landers, Albany Ale
Medium green, half-pint, smooth base, applied heavy collared
mouth $250–500
American 1860–1880 (rare)

Dr. Cronk Gibbons & Co., Superior Ale, Buffalo, N.Y.
Emerald green, 6¾ in., iron pontil, applied mouth $600–725
American 1840–1855

Dr. Girard's, London, Ginger Brandy
Yellow-amber, 9¼ in., pontil base, applied mouth...................$225–300
American 1860–1870

E. N. Cooke & Co., Distillers, Buffalo, N.Y.
Amber Case Gin, 9¾ in., smooth base, applied mouth $125–175
American 1875–1885

Ginter Co, Importers; Boston, Mass.; Contents 32 ounces; The Ginter Co., Registered
Yellow-green, 10⅛ in., smooth base, tooled lip............................$50–65
American 1870–1890

Holland's Gin
Olive green, 4⅝ in., smooth base, applied mouth $65–85
Dutch 1870–1880

W. C. Peacock and Company,
Honolulu, HI, 1885.

Club House Gin, London Jockey,
1865–1875.

Louis Meeus, Anvers Gin
Olive green, 5 in., smooth base, applied mouth $65–85
Dutch 1870–1880

Simon Rynbende & Zonen, Schiedam
Olive-amber, 10¼ in., smooth base, applied mouth $50–75
Dutch 1820–1880

W. C. Peacock & Co. LTD, Honolulu, T. H.
Clear, 8½ in., gin, smooth base, tooled lip $100–150
Territory of Hawaii 1890–1900 (rare)

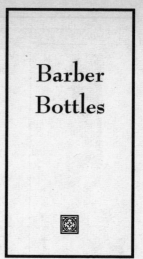

Barber Bottles

Starting in the mid-1860s and continuing to 1920, barbers in America used colorful decorated bottles filled with various tonics and colognes. The finish of these unique and colorful pieces originated when the Pure Food and Drug Act of 1907 restricted the use of alcohol-based ingredients in unlabeled or refillable containers.

Very early examples will have rough pontil scars with various types of ornamentation such as fancy pressed designs, paintings, and labels under glass. The bottles were usually fit with a cork, metal, or porcelain-type closure.

Barber Bottle, A. H. Seely Bay Rum
Cobalt blue, 10¾ in., heavy multicolored enamel and gold floral decorations, smooth base, rolled lip $250–350
American 1885–1925

Barber Bottle Label under Glass, Bay Rum, H. M. Pownall
Milk glass, 9½ in., multicolored label showing a bust of a pretty woman, smooth base, ground lip $175–250
American 1890–1920

Barber Bottle, Dog chasing a Deer in the Brush
Milk glass, 11 in., multicolored enamel, smooth base, rolled lip $225–300
American 1885–1925 (rare)

Barber Bottle, Fox and Hound Scene
Opalescent milk glass, 7½ in., multicolored, pontil base, smooth lip $120–160
American 1885–1925

American Barber Bottles, 1880–1910.

Barber Bottle, Frank Bell, Bay Rum, W. T. & Co.
Milk glass, 9½ in., floral decorations, smooth base, ground
lip $150–225
American 1885–1925

Barber Bottle, Hobnail Pattern
Yellow with amber tone, 7¼ in., smooth base, tooled lip $60–90
American 1890–1920

Barber Bottle, Label under Glass, J. V. Rice Tonic, W. T. & Co.
Clear glass, 7⅝ in., multicolored label with bust of a pretty woman,
smooth base, tooled lip..$275–375
American 1885–1925

**Barber Bottle, Label under Glass, LeVarn's Rose Hair Tonic and
Dandruff Cure Manufactured by The Mettowee Toilet Specialty Co.,
Granville, N.Y.**
Clear glass, 7⅝ in., white, black, gold label, smooth base, tooled
mouth $75–125
American 1885–1925

Barber Bottle, Mary Gregory Tennis Player
Green with yellow tone, 7⅝ in., vertical rib pattern with white enamel,
pontil base, rolled lip...$200–300
American 1885–1925

Barber Bottle, Mary Gregory Tennis Player
Deep cobalt, 8⅛ in., white enamel, pontil base, rolled lip $175–250
American 1885–1925

Wildroot Hair Tonic, Wildroot Chemical Company, Buffalo, NY, 1900–1920.

Barber Bottle, Shampoo
Opalescent milk glass, 7 in., red, yellow, green, black, and gold enamel, pontil base, rolled lip..$150–250
American 1885–1925

Barber Bottle, Vegederma
Purple amethyst, 7¾ in., white enamel, pontil base, rolled lip $250–325
American 1885–1925

Barber Bottle, Witch Hazel
Opalescent milk glass, 9⅛ in., multicolored enamel, pontil base, rolled lip..$175–275
American 1885–1925 (rare)

Barber Bottle
Clear glass, 6½ in., starburst pattern, smooth base, rolled lip.....$60–90
American 1885–1925

Barber Bottle
Deep cobalt blue, 6¾ in., vertical rib pattern with green, yellow, and white enamel, pontil base, tooled lip $125–200
American 1885–1925

Kokens Tonique De Luxe, The
Liquid Head Rest, hair tonic,
1890–1920.

Barber Bottle
Opalescent turquoise blue, 6⅞ in., stars and stripes pattern, pontil
base, rolled lip..$200–$300
American 1885–1925

Barber Bottle
Opalescent cranberry, 6⅝ in., hobnail pattern, polished pontil,
rolled lip..$80–120
American 1885–1925

Barber Bottle
Purple amethyst, 7 in., hobnail pattern, smooth base, rolled
lip $80–120
American 1885–1925

Barber Bottle
Opalescent cranberry, 7⅛ in., stripe and swirl pattern, smooth base,
flared lip...$50–75
American 1885–1925

Barber Bottle
Frosted turquoise blue, 7¾ in., rib pattern, Art Nouveau floral
decoration, pontil base, rolled lip..$250–350
American 1885–1925

Barber Bottle
Milk glass, 7⅞ in., brown and white enamel floral decoration, smooth base, tooled lip...$125–175
American 1885–1925 (rare)

Barber Bottle
Clear glass, 8 in., rib pattern, frosted jade color, Art Nouveau decoration, pontil base, smooth lip $200–300
American 1885–1925

Barber Bottle
Yellow-green, 8¼ in., yellow and orange enamel, pontil base, rolled lip $75–125
American 1885–1925

Barber Bottle
Turquoise blue, 8½ in., rib pattern, smooth base, rolled lip.....$80–120
American 1885–1925

Barber Bottle
Deep cobalt blue, 8¾ in., elongated bell form, white and gold enamel, pontil base, rolled lip..$150–200
American 1885–1925 (rare)

Barber Bottle
Fiery opalescent milk glass, 8¾ in., thumbprint pattern, polished pontil, rolled lip...$125–175
American 1885–1920

Brilliantine Bottle
Deep ruby red, 3⅞ in., smooth base, tooled lip $90–125
American 1885–1925 (rare)

Brilliantine Bottle
Deep ruby red, 4 in., smooth base, tooled lip...........................$225–325
American 1884–1925 (rare)

Beer Bottles

Attempting to find an American beer bottle made before the mid-nineteenth century is a difficult task, since up until that time most of the bottles used for beer and spirits were imported. The majority of these imported bottles were black glass pontiled bottles made in three-piece molds and rarely embossed. There are four types of early beer bottles: the porter, which is the most common, was used from 1820 to 1920; the ale from 1845 to 1850; the early lager used from 1847 to 1850 (rare), and the late lager from 1850 to 1860.

In spite of the large amounts of beer consumed in America before 1860, beer bottles were very rare and all have pontiled bases. Most of the beer manufactured during this time was distributed and dispensed from wooden barrels, or kegs, and sold to local taverns and private bottlers. Collectors often ask why the various breweries did not bottle the beer they manufactured. During the Civil War, the federal government placed a special tax, which was levied by the barrel, on all brewed beverages. This taxing system prevented the brewery from making the beer and bottling it in the same building. Selling the beer to taverns and private bottlers was much simpler than erecting another building just for bottling. This entire process changed after 1890 when the federal government revised the law to allow breweries to bottle the beer straight from the beer lines. The following list reflects the age and rarity of beer bottles made between 1860 and 1940.

YEAR	RARE	SCARCE	SEMI-COMMON	COMMON
1860–1870	X			
1870–1880		X		
1880–1890			X	
1890–1930				X

Embossed bottles marked "ale" or "porter" were first manufactured between 1850 and 1860. In the late 1860s, the breweries began to emboss their bottles with names and promotional messages. This practice continued into the twentieth century. It is interesting to note that Pennsylvania breweries made most of the beer bottles during the second half of the nineteenth century. By 1890, beer was readily available in bottles around most of the country.

The first bottles used for beer in the United States were made of pottery, not glass. Glass did not become widely used until after the Civil War (1865). A wholesaler for Adolphus Busch named C. Conrad sold the original Budweiser beer from 1877 to 1890. The Budweiser name was a trademark of C. Conrad, but in 1891, it was sold to the Anheuser-Busch Brewing Association. Up until the 1870s, beer bottles were sealed with cork stoppers. Late in the nineteenth century the lighting stopper was invented. It proved a convenient way of sealing and resealing blob-top bottles. In 1891, corks were replaced with the "Crown Cork Closure," invented by William Painter. This made use of a thin slice of cork within a tight-fitting metal cap. Once these were removed, they couldn't be used again.

Up until the mid-1930s, beer came in green glass bottles. After Prohibition, brown glass came into use since it was thought to filter damaging rays of the sun and to preserve freshness.

P. B. Milwaukee, Ticoulet and Beshorman, blob-top beer, 1895–1906.

A. B., San Francisco
Yellow with a green hue, quart, applied top.............................$200–400
American 1880–1885

Aberdeen Brewing Co., Aberdeen, Wash.
Amber, 9¼ in., smooth base, blob top...$25–35
American 1880–1900

Augusta Brewing Co., Augusta, Ga.
Aqua, 9¼ in., smooth base, crown top..$15–20
American 1885–1900

Bay View Brewing Co., Seattle, Wash., Not to Be Sold
Yellowish olive green, smooth base, tooled lip............................$75–100
American 1890–1910

Beadleston & Woerz, Excelsior Empire Brewery, New York
Aqua, 9 in., smooth base, applied top $25–30
American 1895–1910

Blatz, Val Brewing Co., Milwaukee
Amber, 12 in., smooth base, blob top $15–20
American 1895–1910

Boca Bob Beer
Amber, 11¾ in., smooth base, applied mouth $75–100
American 1880–1890 (Boca was an early mining town in Nevada
County, Calif.)

Brady Bros., Hartford, Conn., Registered 30 ounces
Cream color glaze, stoneware beer, 10½ in., metal closure $75–100
American 1880–1900

**Compliments of A. A. Codd Nevada Short Line Silver Belt Route (In
Belt Around Locomotive), XMas 1914, Lower Rochester, Nevada, MH
(In a Diamond) on base**
White glazed ceramic, 8¾ in. $2,000–3,000
American 1914 (Commemorates the first extension of the railroad,
which was completed on Christmas 1914.)

C. S. Knickerbocker, 1846
Brown slip glaze, 9¾ in., stoneware beer......................................$50–75
American 1855–1875

Dukehart & Co Maryland Brewery, Baltimore
Amber, 7⅞ in., smooth base, applied mouth $125–175
American 1875–1885

Eagle Brewing Co., San Francisco
Amber, 11⅝ in., stoneware beer, smooth base, tooled lip $100–150
American 1880–1910

F. Sandkuhler's Trade Mark Registered Superior Weiss Beer Brewery, 109 N. Collington Avenue, Baltimore
Tan glaze, 7¼ in., stoneware beer $25–35
American 1880–1900

Finley Brewing Co., Toledo, Ohio, Trade Mark (F in Diamond) on Bottom
Aqua, 10¾ in., smooth base, blob top $30–35
American 1885–1920

Fulton Street National Bottling Works, Trade (Eagle) Mark, San Francisco, Calif., Not to Be Sold
Amber, 11¾ in., smooth base, tooled lip $75–125
American 1880–1910

G. E. Twitchel Successor to C. Whittemore
Brown slip glaze, 8⅞ in., stoneware beer $50–75
American 1855–1875

Geappel & Litchfield
Light gray glaze, 10 in., stoneware beer..$50–90
American 1855–1875

Geo. S. Ladd & Co. Liquor Dealers, 19 S. Hunter Street, Stockton, Calif., Return Bottle & Get 5 cents
Light amber, 13½ in., smooth base, tooled top $200–400
American 1885–1895

Gold Edge Bottling Works
Amber, 8 in., smooth base, tooled top..$15–25
American 1900–1915

Grace Bros. Brewing Co., GBEC (Monogram) Santa Rosa, Calif., This Bottle Is Not to Be Sold
Amber, pint, smooth base, tooled lip $40–60
American 1890–1910

Blob-top beer bottle,
1880–1890.

H. Howard
Cream color, 10⅞ in., stoneware beer $70–100
American 1850–1870

H. Mehlmann S.L.O., Calif.
Amber, 11¼ in., smooth base, tooled lip $40–80
American 1890–1910

H. Sproat, Toronto
Medium cobalt blue, 12-sided, iron pontil, applied
mouth $2,000–3,000
Canadian 1845–1860 (rare)

H. Sproat, Toronto
Cobalt blue, 12-sided, 7⅜ in., smooth base, applied
mouth $1,000–1,500
Canadian 1855–1870

H. W. Miller
Light glaze, 9¾ in., stoneware beer $50–75
American 1855–1875

Henry-Brown Co., Glendale, Calif., Trade Mark Brand, Sierra Club, Ginger Beer, Contents 10 ounces
Brown and cream glaze, 6¾ in., stoneware beer...........................$50–75
American 1880–1900

Independent Brewing Co., of Pittsburgh
Light amber, 9 in., smooth base, crown top..................................$30–40
American 1885–1920 (scarce, Pittsburgh misspelled)

Indianapolis Brewing Co. (Winged Lady Motif) Trade Mark, Indianapolis, Ind., U.S.A.
Amber, 7⅜ in., smooth base, tooled top.......................................$15–20
American 1900–1915

J. B. Ferste, Ashland, Wis.
Gray glaze, 7½ in., stoneware beer..$30–50
American 1855–1870

J. S. Donner & Co.
Gray glaze, 7½ in., stoneware beer..$30–50
American 1855–1870

J. Smith & Co., Neshannock, Penna.
Aqua, 9⅜ in., smooth base, applied mouth...................................$60–90
American 1875–1885 (rare)

John Wieland's Export Beer, S.F.
Red amber, 7½ in., smooth base, tooled top $20–40
American 1890–1895

Koppitz-Melchers Brewing Co., Trade Mark (Star in Center) Reg., Detroit, Mich. (in a circle Slug Plate)
Aqua, 11¼ in., smooth base, blob top $15–25
American 1890–1910

Latter's Home Brewed Ginger Beer, Sacramento, Calif.
Two-tone stoneware, 7¾ in., smooth base, crown top..............$50–100
American 1855–1875 (scarce)

Los Angeles Brew Co. (Motif of Eagle and Shield)
Amber, 11⅜ in., smooth base, tooled lip $60–90
American 1880–1910

Rainier Beer, Bottling
Works, Reno, NV.
1905–1918.

**North Star Bottling Works, Trademark Carl Tornberg, Prop.,
S. F., Calif., Bottle Not to Be Sold**
Medium amber, 12 in., smooth base, tooled top........................$50–200
American 1890–1900

Otto & Layer, Berlin, White Beer, Philada
Pure olive green, 8-sided, 8 in., smooth base, applied
mouth $200–300
American 1855–1865

Peter Mugler Brewer, Sisson, Calif.
Yellowish amber, quart, smooth base, tooled lip $80–100
American 1890–1910

Rainier Beer, Seattle, U.S.A.
Amber, 5³⁄₈ in., smooth base, tooled lip.....................................$75–125
American 1880–1910 (rare miniature beer)

Reno Brewing Co., Reno, Nev.
Amber, 11⅛ in., smooth base, tooled lip $40–60
American 1890–1910

R. Green, Toronto
Sapphire blue, 12-sided, 10 in., smooth base, applied
mouth $2,500–3,500
Canadian 1855–1870

Rycroft-Arctic Soda Co., Ltd, Honolulu, T.I., Rycroft's Old Fashioned Ginger Beer, Net Contents 9 Fluid Oz.
Brown and cream glaze, 7 in., stoneware beer $50–75
American 1880–1885

S
Aqua, quart, smooth base, tooled top $75–125
American 1880–1885

Sonoma Brewing Co., SBCO, Sonoma, Calif.
Amber, half-pint, smooth base, tooled top....................................$40–60
American 1890–1910

Stockton Wholesale Liquor Co., Stockton, Calif. (SWL monogram)
Medium amber, 13½ in., smooth base, tooled top $150–300
American 1880–1890 (rare)

The Mathie Brewing Co. Means Quality, Los Angeles, Calif.
Yellowish amber, 11⅜ in., smooth base, tooled lip......................$40–80
American 1900–1905

This Bottle, B.B. Co., Not to Be Sold, Buffalo Brewing Co.
Clear, quart, smooth base, applied top...$50–75
American 1880–1885

This Bottle, B.B. Co., Not to Be Sold, Buffalo Brewing Co.
Clear, pint, smooth base, applied top $50–75
American 1880–1885

This Bottle, Buffalo Br'G Co. Sacramento, Not to Be Sold
Amber, 12⅛ in., smooth base, applied mouth $60–90
American 1880–1910

Ticoulet & Beshorman, Sac., Cal., "PCCW" on Base
Medium amber, 9 in., smooth base, tooled top............................$30–50
American 1885–1910

W. B. Co. S. F. Trade Mark
Deep bluish aqua, 6¼ in., smooth base with kickup, tooled
top $500–1,000
American 1875–1885 (rare, only five to ten known)

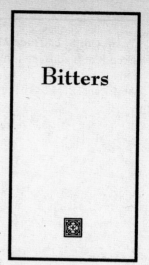

Bitters

When looking at antique bottles as collectibles, bitters bottles have long been favorites. Because of their unique form, bitters bottles were saved in large numbers, giving the collector of today some great opportunities to build very special collections.

Bitters, which originated in England, is a type of medicine made from roots or herbs named for their bitter taste. During the eighteenth century, bitters were added to water, ale, or spirits with the intent of curing all types of ailments. Because of the pretense that these mixtures had some medicinal value, bitters became very popular in America, since Colonists could import them from England without paying the liquor tax. While most bitters had a low alcohol content, some brands were labeled as high as 120 proof, higher than most hard liquor available at the time. As physicians became convinced bitters did have some type of healing value, the drink became socially acceptable. This thought process promoted sales to people who normally weren't liquor drinkers and also provided upstanding citizens a good excuse for having liquor in the home (for medicinal purposes, of course).

The best known among the physicians who made their own bitters for patients was Dr. Jacob Hostetter. After his retirement in 1853, he gave permission to his son David to manufacture it commercially. Hostetters Bitters was known for its colorful and dramatic advertisements. While Hostetters said it wouldn't cure everything, the list of ailments it claimed to alleviate with regular use covered most everything: indigestion, diarrhea, dysentery, chills, fever, liver ailments, and pains and weakness that came with old age (at that time, a euphemism for impotence). Despite these claims, David Hostetter died in 1888 from kidney failure, which could supposedly be cured by his bitters.

Most of the bitters bottles, over 1,000 types, were manufactured between 1860 and 1905. The more unique shapes, called "figurals," were in the likenesses of cannons, drums, pigs, fish, and ears of corn. In addition, a variety of other forms produced bottles that were round, square, rectangular, barreled-shaped, gin-bottle-shaped, twelve-sided, and flask-shaped. The embossed varieties are the most collectible, older, and more valuable.

These bottles were most commonly amber (pale golden yellow to dark amber-brown), frequently aqua (light blue), and sometimes green or clear glass. The rarest and most collectible colors are dark blue, amethyst, milk glass, and puce (a purplish brown).

Acorn Bitters
Golden amber, 9 in., smooth base, tooled sloping mouth........$175–350
American 1870–1890 (extremely rare)

Ageno Nerve & Stomach Bitters, Columbus, Ohio, Label Only
Amber, 9 in., smooth base, tooled mouth................................$125–175
American 1890–1900

Prussian Bitters, 1855–1865.

Alpine Herb Bitters, 1888.

Altvater's Magen Bitter, Label Only
Light orange-amber, 13 in., smooth base, tooled collared
mouth $150–300
American 1870–1890 (extremely rare)

American Stomach Bitters Co., Buffalo, N.Y., U.S.A.
Amber, 10½ in., smooth base, applied mouth $150–250
American 1885–1895

Ayala Mexican Bitters, M. Rothenberg & Co., San Francisco, Calif.
Medium yellow-amber, 9½ in., smooth base, tooled lip $150–200
American 1910–1911 (rare)

Argyle Bitters, E. B. Wheelock/N.O., C.I. & Sons
Yellow-olive, 9⅛ in., smooth base, applied mouth...................$120–150
American 1870–1875 (rare)

Bancroft's Bitters, D. W. Bancroft, Marshfield, VT
Aqua, 8⅞ in., smooth base, applied mouth.............................$150–180
American 1870–1875 (rare)

Barley Malt Bitters Co., Cincinnati, Ohio
Reddish amber, 10 in., smooth base, tooled lip $300–450
American 1870–1880 (rare)

Bavarian Bitters, Hoffheimer Brothers
Amber, 9⅜ in., smooth base, applied mouth $130–150
American 1870–1880

Botanic Stomach Bitters, Bach Meese & Co., San Francisco
Medium yellowish amber, 9 in., smooth base, applied
mouth $450–600
American 1885–1889 (rare)

Byrne & Castree, Salutaris Bitters
Dark puce-amber, 9¼ in., smooth base, applied mouth $500–1,200
American 1863–1868 (rare)

Bryant's Stomach Bitters
Medium olive-green, 12⅝ in., pontil base, applied
mouth $5,000–7,000
American 1860–1865 (extremely rare)

California Wine Bitters, W. M. Ritmeier's
Medium reddish amber, 9 in., smooth base, applied mouth....$150–250
American 1885–1895

Catawba Wine Bitters (motif of bunch of grapes)
Bright blue-green, 9½ in., iron pontil base, applied base $600–800
American 1860–1866

Celebrated Crown Bitters, F. Chevalier & Co., Sole Agents
Amber, 9 in., smooth base, large applied mouth.....................$225–325
American 1880–1885

Celebrated Nectar Stomach Bitters and Nerve Tonic, The Nectar Bitter Co., Toledo, Ohio Bottle
Yellowish green, 9¼ in., smooth base, tooled mouth...............$350–750
American 1880–1900 (extremely rare)

Chartreuse Damiana Bitters Bottle
Deep golden amber, 9¼ in., smooth base, applied mouth $100–200
American 1860–1880

Damiana Bitters, Baja
California, 1890.

Clifford & Fernald's Original Indian Vegetable Bitters Bottle
Aquamarine, 6⅞ in., pontil base, applied mouth $200–400
American 1840–1850 (extremely rare)

Clotworthy's Oriental Tonic Bitters Bottle
Light golden amber, 10 in., smooth base, applied mouth........$125–250
American 1860–1880 (extremely rare)

Deutenhoff's Swiss Bitters, G. M. Heidt, Savannah, Ga.
Dark amber, 9¼ in., smooth base, applied mouth...................$200–300
American 1870–1890 (extremely rare)

Dittmar's Stomach Bitters
Olive-amber, 10 in., smooth base, tooled mouth......................$500–850
American 1860–1880

Dr. Ball's Vegetable Stomachic Bitters, Northboro, Mass.
Aqua, 6¾ in., pontil base, applied mouth $150–200
American 1840–1855

Dr. C. W. Robacks, Stomach Bitters, Cincinnati, Ohio
Amber, 9⅛ in., smooth base, applied mouth $125–150
American 1860–1870

Dr. C. H. Smith's American Stomach Bitters, Albany, N.Y.
Clear, 7¾ in., smooth base, tooled mouth $125–175
American 1890–1900 (extremely rare)

Dr. Gillmore's Laxative Kidney & Liver Bitters
Medium amber, 10¼ in., smooth base, tooled mouth $75–150
American 1880–1890

Dr. J. Hostetter's Stomach Bitters
Amber, 8¾ in., smooth base, tooled mouth.............................$100–150
American 1905–1910

Dr. J. Hostetter's Stomach Bitters
Yellow with olive tone, 8⅞ in., smooth base, applied mouth....$80–120
American 1860–1870

Dr. J. Hostetter's Stomach Bitters
Medium amber, 9 in., smooth base, applied mouth.................$100–150
American 1870–1875

Dr. Jacob's Bitters, S. A. Spencer, New Haven, Conn.
Aqua, 8 in., pontil base, applied mouth $60–100
American 1870–1880

Dr. Hutington's Golden Tonic Bitters Bottle
Aquamarine, 9⅛ in., smooth base, applied mouth...................$150–300
American 1860–1880 (extremely rare)

Dr. Mowe's Vegetable Bitters Bottle
Aquamarine, 10 in., smooth base, applied mouth $100–200
American 1860–1880 (rare)

Dr. Sims's Anti-Constipation Bitters (Sample Bitters)
Amber, 7 in., smooth base, tooled mouth................................$175–275
American 1885–1895 (rare)

Dr. Stanley's South American Indian Bitters
Dark amber, 8⅞ in., smooth base, applied mouth...................$125–175
American 1885–1895

Dr. Stephen Jewett's Celebrated Health Restoring Bitters Bottle
Blue-green, 7⅛ in., pontil base, applied mouth $75–150
American 1840–1860

Dr. Tompkins's Vegetable Bitters Bottle
Blue-green, 9 in., smooth base, applied mouth.........................$100–200
American 1860–1880 (rare)

Dr. Wise's Olive Bitters, Cincinnati O
Clear glass, 10½ in., bell form, smooth base, tooled
mouth $125–150
American 1890–1910 (rare)

Dr. Wonser's U.S.A. Indian Root Bitters
Yellow-amber, 10¾ in., smooth base, applied mouth $200–400
American 1872–1874

Dr. Wonne's Gesundheits Bitters Bottle
Yellow-amber, 8⅞ in., smooth base, tooled mouth..................$150–250
American 1870–1890 (rare)

Eagle Angostura Bark Bitters (Sample Bitters)
Amber, 3⅞ in., smooth base, tooled mouth..............................$150–250
American 1885–1895

E. Bull's Luxury Bitters Bottle
Golden amber, 9⅛ in., smooth base, applied mouth.................$75–150
American 1860–1880

Eclipse Bitters, Stewart & Kiel, Sole Proprietors
Amber, 8¾ in., smooth base, applied mouth $125–175
American 1860–1880 (extremely rare)

E. J. Rose's Magador Bitters for Stomach, Kidney & Liver, Superior Tonic Cathartic and Blood Purifier
Amber, 8⅝ in., smooth base, tooled mouth $80–120
American 1860–1880

Empire State Drug Co. Laboratories, Buffalo, N.Y.
Amber, 9½ in., smooth base, tooled mouth $100–150
American 1870–1890

Excelsior Bitters
Amber, 9⅛ in., smooth base, applied mouth $400–600
American 1860–1866

Ferro Quina Stomach Bitters, Blood Maker, Doglaini Italia, D. P. Rosse, 1400 Dupont Str. S. F., Sole Agent, U.S.A. and Canada
Amber, 9⅛ in., smooth base, tooled lip $70–100
American 1895–1900

Fitzpatrick's CE 50 NT, Stomach Bitters
Clear, 8⅛ in., coffin flask form, smooth base, tooled
mouth $120–150
American 1885–1895

Geo Benz & Sons, Appetine Bitters Bottle
Deep reddish amber, 8 in., smooth base, tooled mouth...........$200–400
American 1880–1900

Genl. Frank Cheatham's Bitters, Nashville, Tenn.
Reddish amber, 10 in., smooth base, applied mouth $2,000–3,000
American 1870–1875 (extremely rare)

G. N. Morison's Invigorating Bitters, G. N. Morison, New Orleans
Amber, 9¼ in., smooth base, applied mouth $70–90
American 1865–1875 (rare)

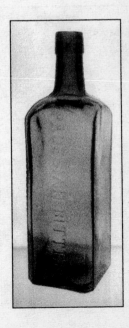

Mack's Sarsaparilla Bitters,
1875–1890.

H. N. Winfree's Aromatic Stomach Bitters, Chester, Va.
Greenish aqua, 6½ in., smooth base, tooled lip $80–120
American 1890–1910 (rare)

Hartwig Kantorowicz, Berlin
Deep olive green, 6⅞ in., smooth base, applied mouth...........$175–300
American 1880–1900

Hibernia Bitters
Medium yellowish amber, 9¾ in., smooth base, tooled lip $125–150
American 1886–1890

Heilbron's Aromatic Bitters
Aqua, 9⅜ in., smooth base, applied mouth..............................$125–150
English 1885–1895

Mack's Sarsaparilla Bitters, Mack & Co., Pro'rs, San Francisco
Amber, 9¼ in., smooth base, applied mouth $300–500
American 1884–1887 (scarce)

Mahan Bitters, St. Louis, Mo.
Aquia, 8½ in., smooth base, applied mouth..............................$80–100
American 1875–1885 (rare)

Old Sachem Bitters and
Wigwam Tonic, 1855–1865.

Old Homestead Wild Cherry
Bitters, 1855–1865.

McKee's Bitters Bottle
Yellow-amber 8⅜ in., smooth base, applied mouth $100–200
American 1860–1880 (extremely rare)

Mills' Bitters Bottle
Golden amber, 11¼ in., smooth base, applied mouth.............$300–500
American 1860–1880

Mills' Bitters A.M. Gilman Sole Proprietor
Light amber, 11¾ in., smooth base, applied mouth $2,000–3,000
American 1874 (less than 10 known)

National Bitters
Yellow, 12⅜ in., smooth base, applied mouth $600–800
American 1867–1875

O'Hare Bitters Co., Pittsburgh, Pa.
Yellow-amber, 9½ in., smooth base, tooled mouth $100–150
American 1890–1910 (scarce)

Orolo Bitters Bottle
Amber, 9 in., smooth base, applied mouth...............................$150–250
American 1860–1880 (extremely rare)

John Moffat Phoenix Bitters, NY, 1870–1880.

Prickly Ash Bitters Co.
Medium yellowish amber, 9¼ in., smooth base, tooled lip $50–75
American 1880–1890

Phoenix Bitters, John Moffat, New York, Price $1.00
Aqua, 5⅜ in., pontil base, rolled lip..$50–75
American 1870–1880

Rose's Orange Bitters Bottle
Lime green, 10¼ in., smooth base, applied mouth..................$125–250
England 1860–1880 (extremely rare)

S. B. Rothenberg, Sole Agent, U.S. Pat Applied For
Milk glass, 8⅞ in., smooth base, applied mouth......................$100–175
American 1891–1896

Seaworth Bitters Co., Cape May, New Jersey, U.S.A. (Sample Bitters)
Amber, 6⅜ in., smooth base, tooled mouth......................$2,500–3,500
American 1885–1895 (most desirable of sample bitters bottles)

Sir Robert Edgar's English Life Bitters, G. E. Graves Proprietor, Rutland, Vt., U.S.A.
Amber, 8¾ in., smooth base, applied mouth $250–350
American 1875–1885

Solomons' Strengthening & Invigorating Bitters, Savannah, Ga.
Blue, 9⅝ in., smooth base, applied mouth $300–500
American 1875–1880

Steketee's Blood Purifying Bitters (Sample Bitters)
Amber, 6⅝ in., smooth base, tooled mouth $175–275
American 1885–1895

The Fish Bitters, W. H. Ware, Patented 1866
Amber, 11⅝ in., smooth base, applied mouth $100–150
American 1866–1870

Uncle Tom's Bitters, Thomas Fould & Co., Trevorton, Pa.
Yellowish amber, 10 in., smooth base, applied mouth $150–200
American 1870–1880 (rare)

William Allen Congress Bitters Bottle
Aquamarine, 10¼ in., smooth base, applied mouth.................$125–150
American 1860–1880 (rare)

Wood's Ginger Bitters Bottle
Yellowish golden amber, 8¾ in., smooth base, applied
mouth $125–250
American 1870–1890 (extremely rare)

Wormser Bros., San Francisco
Amber, 9⅝ in., smooth base, applied mouth $2,500–3,500
American 1865–1870 (rare)

Whites Stomach Bitters
Golden amber, 9½ in., smooth base, applied mouth $100–150

Zingari Bitters Bottle
Golden amber, 12 in., smooth base, applied mouth.................$150–300
American 1860–1880

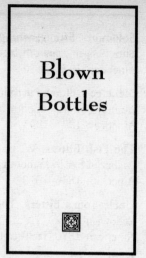

Blown Bottles

As mentioned earlier, free-blown bottles, also called simply blown bottles, were made without the use of molds and were shaped by the glassblower. It is difficult to attach ages and origins to them, since many were produced in Europe and the United States for a long time before records were kept.

Another type of blown bottle, the blown three-mold, was formed in a three-piece mold. These bottles were manufactured between 1820 and 1840 in Europe and the United States, and it is quite difficult to distinguish bottles from different sides of the Atlantic. Since blown three-mold and pressed three-mold are similar, it is important to know how to differentiate between them. With blown glass, the mold impression can be felt on the inside, while pressed glass impression can only be felt on the outside. Most blown three-mold bottles came in amethyst (purple), sapphire blue, and a variety of greens.

Case Gin Bottle
Yellow-olive, 9½ in., pontil base, applied mouth $50–100
American 1780–1830

Case Gin Bottle
Yellow-olive, 9¼ in., pontil base, applied mouth $50–100
American 1780–1830

Case Gin Bottle
Medium yellow-olive, 14 in., pontil base, rolled lip $250–500
American 1780–1830

Chestnut Flask, Pattern Molded
Clear, 4¾ in., pontil base, sheared/tooled lip, 10-diamond
pattern $250–350
American 1825–1835

Chestnut Flask, Pattern Molded
Medium purple amethyst, 6½ in., pontil base, sheared/tooled lip,
16 vertical rib pattern $200–300
European 1840–1860

Chestnut Flask
Yellowish amber, 5⅛ in., pontil base, sheared lip....................$200–300
American 1825–1835

Chestnut Flask
Olive, 5⅜ in., pontil base, applied mouth...............................$125–175
American 1790–1810

Chestnut Flask
Olive green, 5⅜ in., pontil base, rolled lip...............................$100–150
American 1780–1820

Chestnut Flask
Orangish amber, 5½ in., pontil base, applied string lip...........$175–225
American 1840–1850

Chestnut Flask
Medium olive-amber, 5⅝ in., pontil base, rolled mouth..........$125–175
American 1790–1810

Chestnut Flask
Deep cobalt blue, 6⅝ in., smooth base, applied string lips.....$150–200
French 1850–1880

Chestnut Flask
Golden amber, 6¾ in., pontil base, applied mouth $125–150
American 1800–1820

Chestnut Flask
Olive-amber, 7 in., pontil base, applied mouth $80–120
American 1780–1810

Free-blown globular bottle (rare), 1800–1820.

Chestnut Flask
Yellow-olive, 8 in., pontil base, applied double-collared
mouth $150–200
American 1790–1810

Chestnut Flask
Yellowish olive green, 8⅛ in., pontil base, applied mouth $150–200
American 1790–1810

Chestnut Flask
Yellow, 10 in., pontil base, rolled mouth...................................$175–225
American 1790–1810

Globular Bottle
Light yellowish olive, 9 in., pontil base, rolled lip $125–175
European 1790–1820

Globular Bottle
Deep aqua, 9 in., pontil base, rolled lip $60–85
American 1825–1835

Globular Bottle
Aqua, 9¼ in., pontil base, applied mouth $30–50
American 1800–1830

Midwestern Swirl, Pattern Molded
Bluish aqua, 8 in., pontil base, applied mouth, 24-rib swirled
pattern $150–250
American 1820–1835

Black Whiskey/Ale
Bottles, Hohann Hoff,
1870–1890.

Black Whiskey Bottle, three-
piece mold, 1820–1850.

Midwestern "Grandfathers" Flask
Medium amber, 8⅛ in., pontil base, sheared lip, 24 vertical rib
pattern $800–1,500
American 1825–1835

Nailsea Flask
Dark reddish amber, 4¾ in., pontil base, sheared lip................$75–150
English 1800–1840

Nailsea Flask
Canary yellow, 6¾ in., pontil base, sheared lip $200–300
English 1800–1840

Pitkin Flask
Amber, 6½ in., pontil base, sheared lip, 32 broken-rib pattern
swirled to left $200–300
American 1815–1825

Power Horn Figural
Golden amber, 13 in., pontil base, sheared lip........................$100–200
American 1840–1860

Saddle Flask
Bright yellow-olive, 13 in., smooth base, sheared lip, flattened
oval form with long neck..$100–200
American 1750–1850

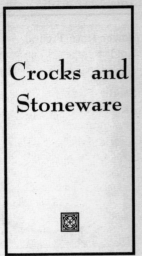

Crocks and Stoneware

While crocks are made of pottery and not glass, many bottle collectors also have crock collections since they have been found wherever bottles are varied. Crock containers were manufactured in America as early as 1641 and were used extensively in the sale of retail products during the nineteenth and early twentieth centuries. Miniature stoneware jugs were often used for advertising as were some stoneware canning jars. Store owners favored crocks since they kept beverages cooler and extended the shelf life of certain products. Crocks appeal to collectors because of their interesting shapes, painted and stenciled decorations, lustrous finishes, and folk art value.

In the late 1800s, the discovery of microbes in disease-causing bacteria prompted many medicine makers to seize a profitable if not unethical opportunity. An undocumented number of fraudulent cures were pushed on gullible and unsuspecting customers. The most infamous of these so-called cures were produced and sold in pottery containers by William Radam. He was given a patent for his "Microbe Killer" in 1886 and stayed in business until 1907, when the Pure Food and Drug Act ended his scheme. His "cure" was nothing but watered-down wine (wine comprised only 1 percent of the total contents).

With the invention of the automatic bottle machine in 1903, glass bottles became cheaper to make and hence more common. The production and use of pottery crocks and containers began a steady decline.

California Cough Balm, Price 10 Cents, Dose Teaspoonsful, Children Half
Cream and brown, 3¼ in., miniature advertising jug $150–200
American 1890–1915

Common early crock for beverage
(possibly whiskey), 1890–1910.

Crock—Strong, Cobb and Company,
Wholesale Druggist (rare),
1890–1910.

Carpenter & Co., 60 Broad St., Boston, Mass.
Gray with cobalt floral decoration, 12¾ in., applied handles, 3-
gal. saltglaze..$150–250
American 1870–1890

C. Crolius Manufacturer, New York
Gray with cobalt floral decoration, 12⅝ in., 2-gal. ovoid
jug..$500–1,000
American 1795–1830

C. F. Hetzel & Co., Cumberland, Md.
Gray with cobalt stenciling, 8⅛ in., canning jar $200–300
American 1870–1890

Centennial Jug 1876
Dark brown, 3 in., miniature jug, applied handle.....................$80–120
American 1876

Compliments of The Maraman Bros. Co. Groceries and Liquor, 702 and 704 W. Market St., Louisville, Ky.
Cream and brown, 3 in., miniature advertising jug.................$125–175
American 1890–1915

D. W. & H. E. Richards, 362 and 364 Broad St., Newark, N.J.
Gray with cobalt decoration, 13½ in., handled jug.................$175–250
American 1875

Dominick Fry, Pure Rye Whiskey, Manor Station, Pa.
Dark gray, 14 in., 2-gal. handled jug...$250–350
American 1870–1890

Excelsior Works Isaac Hewitt, Jr., Rices Landing, Pa.
Dark gray, 8½ in., stoneware canning jar................................$275–350
American 1870–1890

From Jacob Roemer, Clarington, Ohio
Gray glazed, 6⅛ in., stoneware canning jar.............................$250–350
American 1870–1890

Galloway's Everlasting Jar Patd. Feg. 8th and Pat. App for 1870
Gray, 6 in., qt., stoneware canning jar...$40–70
American 1870–1890

Grahan & Stone Gen. Merchandise, Jackson C.N., W. Va.
Drak gray, 7½ in., stoneware canning jar................................$250–350
American 1870–1890

H. Glazer, Huntington, Pa.
Gray, 7¾ in., 1-gal. saltglaze crock...$375–450
American 1865–1880

H. Schuler Paris, Ont.
Tan-gray, 11¼ in., 1-gal. handled jug $125–150
Canadian 1865–1880

I. M. Mead & Co.
Gray, 9½ in., saltglaze ovoid crock...$150–250
American 1840–1860

Jas. Benjamin Wholesale Stoneware Depot., No. 14 Water St., Cincinnati, Ohio
Tannish gray, 8⅛ in., stoneware canning jar...........................$200–250
American 1870–1890

Kramers Korner Kash Grocery and Marker, Athens, Pa.
Brown, 9 in., stoneware jug...$175–225
American 1875–1890

Nelden-Judson Drug Co., Salt Lake City, Utah
Gray, 9⅞ in., stoneware jug, applied handle............................$125–150
American 1895–1915

Norton & Fenton, Bennington, Vt.
Light gray, 13 in., 2-gal. stoneware ovoid jug.........................$200–300
American 1843–1847

S. R. Engerman, 140 Hamilton St., Allentown, Pa.
Dark gray, 12 in., stoneware handled jug................................$250–325
American 1870–1890

Steinhardt Bro., 315 Bowery, N.Y.
Gray, 11¼ in., stoneware handled jug.......................................$75–90
American 1855–1885

Stoneware Crock
Gray with cobalt decoration, 7 in., applied handles...................$70–90
American 1870–1890

Crocks—Vihno Verde, Do Lavradoe; Pullnaier
Bitters Wasser, Genende Pullna (European),
1860–1880.

Crocks—Herrington's Fluid
Beer—Purest on Earth,
1890–1900.

Stoneware Crock
Gray, 7⅛ in., cobalt bands going halfway around crock..............$80–90
American 1870–1890

Stoneware Crock
Gray, 8⅜ in., cobalt bands going halfway around crock..............$80–90
American 1870–1890

Three-Gallon Crock
Gray, 13½ in., floral decoration..$150–200
American 1870–1880

Cosmetic Bottles

This category includes those bottles that originally contained products to improve personal appearances, including treatments for skin, teeth, scalp (hair grooming and restoring agents), and perfumes. The most popular of these are the hair and perfume bottles.

Hair bottles are popular as collectible items because of their distinctive colors, such as amethyst and various shades of blue. The main producer of American-made perfume bottles in the eighteenth century was Casper Wistar, whose clients included Martha Washington. Another major manufacturer of that time was Henry William Stiegel. While most of Wistar's bottles were plain, Stiegel's were decorative and are more appealing to collectors.

In the 1840s, Solon Palmer started to manufacture and sell perfumes. By 1879, his products were being sold in drugstores around the country. Today, Palmer bottles are sought after for their brilliant emerald green color.

Alfred Wright, Perfumer, Rochester, N.Y.
Cobalt, 7½ in..$25–30

Ayer's Hair Vigor
Cobalt blue, 6½ in., smooth base, tooled mouth.........................$70–90
American 1885–1900

Bunker Hill Monument Cologne
Opalescent milk glass, 9¼ in. $50–70
American 1860–1870

Cameron's Kephalia for the Hair
Aqua, 7⅜ in., open pontil, applied mouth $200–300
American 1835–1845 (rare)

C. A. P. Mason Alpine Hair Balm
Olive green, 6⅞ in., open pontil, applied mouth $3,000–4,000
American 1855–1865 (rare)

Cologne Bottle
Purple amethyst, 4½ in., 8-sided, smooth base, rolled lip $400–500
American 1860–1870

Cologne Bottle
Deep cobalt blue, 4¾ in., 12-sided, smooth base, rolled lip $120–150
American 1860–1870

Cologne Bottle
Turquoise blue, 5½ in., rope-style corners, smooth base, tooled
lip $300–400
American 1865–1875 (extremely rare)

Phalon Perfumer, NY,
1859–1863.

Dr. Cambell's Hair Invigorator, Aurora, NY, 1859–1863.

Phalon's Chemical Hair Invigorator, Number 617 and 197, 1849–1859.

Cologne Bottle
Milk glass, 5¾ in., rib with dot pattern, smooth base, tooled
lip $100–300
American 1865–1875

Cologne Bottle
Medium cobalt blue, 6 in., 12-sided, smooth base, tooled
lip $200–300
American 1860–1870

Cologne Bottle
Medium pinkish amethyst, 7⅜ in., smooth base, tooled lip $200–300
American 1865–1875

Cologne Bottle
Milk glass, 10⅞ in., rib with dot pattern, smooth base, tooled
lip $175–275
American 1865–1875

Dodge Brothers, Melanine, Hair Tonic
Deep purple amethyst, 7¼ in., smooth base, applied
mouth $200–300
American 1865–1885

Dr. Tebbetts Physiological Hair Regenerator
Deep purple amethyst, 7½ in., smooth base, applied
mouth $150–200
American 1865–1875

Eau De Cologne
Clear, multicolored label showing pretty woman, pontil base,
flared lip $200–300
American 1890–1910 (rare)

E. N. Lightner & Co., E. N. L. & Co., Detroit, Mich.
Milk glass, 6¼ in., cologne, smooth base, tooled lip $125–150
American 1890–1910

Hall's Hair Renewer
Deep teal blue, 6⅜ in., smooth base, tooled lip.........................$60–100
American 1885–1900

Hurd's Hair Restorer
Aqua, 8⅛ in., pontil base, applied mouth $90–150
American 1840–1855 (rare)

J. L. Giofray & Co. Hair Renovator, Rockland, Me.
Reddish amber, 8⅛ in., smooth base, applied mouth........$1,200–1,500

Lightner's Heliotrope Perfumes, Detroit, Mich.
Milk glass, 6½ in.,...$25–35

Lightner's Jockey Club Perfumes, Detroit, Mich.
Milk glass, 6½ in.,...$25–35

Sandwich Cologne
Cobalt blue, 4⅝ in., 12-sided, smooth base, rolled lip............$125–175
American 1860–1870

Sallie Cologne
Clear, 7½ in., cologne, pontil base, flared lip $150–200
American 1880–1890

Scent Bottle
Purple amethyst, 2⅝ in., smooth base, ground lip......................$65–80
American 1860–1870

Solon Palmer, Perfumer
Opalescent green, 1⅞ in., smooth base, tooled lip......................$15–25

Velvetina, Goodrich Drug Co., Omaha
Milk glass, 5¼ in..$30–40

Victorian White Rose Perfumes
Clear, 8 in., smooth base, tooled lip..$150–250
American 1890–1910

Victorian Jockey Club Perfumes
Clear, 8⅛ in., smooth base, tooled lip.....................................$150–225
American 1880–1910

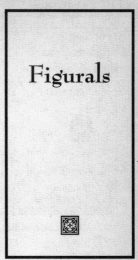

Figurals

Figural bottles were produced in large numbers in the late nineteenth and early twentieth centuries. These whimsical bottles were made in the shapes of animals, people, boots, and books, among other things. They came in a wide variety of colors and sizes and were quite popular among the very rich and the aristocrats of the time.

Atterbury Duck Bottle
Milk glass, 11½ in., smooth base, ground lip $300–450
American 1875–1880

Baby in Egg
Milk glass, 2½ in., smooth bases, ground lip..........................$140–180
American 1890–1920

Baby Face Bottle
Milk glass, 2⅝ in., smooth base, ground lip $175–275
American 1885–1900

Basket Decanter
Clear, 6¼ in., smooth base, tooled lip......................................$100–150
American 1885–1900 (rare)

Cabin Bottle
Amber, 9⅝ in., smooth base, applied mouth $100–200
American 1860–1880

Castle Bottle
Clear, 12 in., pontil base, tooled flared lip...............................$120–160
American 1890–1910

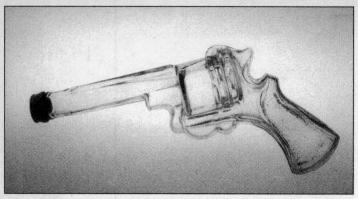

The Colonial Bar, Mello and Burns (shape of gun), 1900.

Columbus Column Bottle
Milk glass, 18½ in., smooth base, ground lip..........................$600–900
American 1893–1900 (Patented by Julius Librowicz, Jan. 17, 1893.)

Dice Bottle
Opalescent milk glass, 5⅛ in., smooth base, ground lip..........$120–160
American 1880–1910

Three Dice Bottle
Milk glass, 8⅞ in., smooth base, ground lip................................$70–90
American 1910–1920

Elephant Seated on Drum
Frosted clear glass, 9¾ in., smooth base, ground lip...............$100–150
German 1885–1900 (rare)

Elk's Tooth Flasks
Milk glass, 4 in., smooth base, ground lip...................................$75–100
American 1890–1910

Eye Opener Flask
Milk glass, 5⅛ in., smooth base, ground lip.............................$80–120
American 1890–1910

Good (Motif of Man in Night Cap) Night
Milk glass, 4 in., smooth base, ground lip.................................$120–160
American 1890–1910 (scarce)

Grandfather Clock
Milk glass, 12¼ in., smooth base, tooled lip............................$300–500
American 1885–1910 (rare)

Grant's Tomb Bottle
Milk glass, 8 in., smooth base, tooled lip $175–275
American 1893–1900

Grim Reaper (Decanter and Shot Glasses)
Bisque with brown, black, and silver enamel, "Made in Japan" stamped
on bases, four glasses...$100–175
Japan 1900–1925

Hand Holding Bottle
Milk glass, 6⅝ in., smooth base, tooled lip..................................$30–60
American 1890–1910

Joan of Arc
Clear glass, 13½ in., pontil base, tooled lip $75–100
French 1885–1900

Klondyke Nugget Flask
Milk glass, 5⅞ in., smooth base, ground lip $75–100
American 1890–1910

Kummel Bear
Black amethyst, 11⅛ in., smooth base, tooled mouth..............$100–150
American 1890–1910

La Tsarine
Milk glass, 13¼ in., tin base, ground mouth $150–300
French 1880–1900

Life Preserver
Milk glass, 5½ in., smooth base, tooled mouth........................$200–300
American 1890–1910

Lorraine Lady Bottle
Milk glass, 13 in., smooth base, tooled flared lip.....................$140–180
French 1900–1915

Man's Shoe
Black glass, 3½ in., smooth base, ground lip.............................$80–120
American 1890–1910

German sailors, 1960s.

Negro Waiter
Frosted clear glass with pink milk glass head, 14¼ in., smooth
base, ground lip $150–200
American 1880–1900

Nugget Pocket Flask
Milk glass, 5⅞ in., smooth base, ground lip $80–120
American 1890–1910

Oriental Atomizer Perfume Bottle
Milk glass, 5½ in., smooth base, ground lip $175–250
American 1890–1920

Polar Bear
Milk glass, 11 in., smooth base, tooled mouth.........................$100–150
French 1880–1910

Statue of Liberty Bottle
Milk glass, 13¾ in., smooth base, ground lip $200–300
American 1893–1900

Tear Drops Flasks
Milk glass, 3⅞ in., smooth base, ground lip $80–120
American 1890–1910

Owl Jar
Milk glass, 6 in., smooth base, ground lip...................................$45–60
American 1900–1910

Pistol
Bright yellowish green, 17 in., long $35–45
Italian (Barsottini) 1890–1910

Fire Grenades

Fire grenades are a highly prized item among bottle collectors and represent one of the first modern improvements in fire fighting.

A fire grenade is a bottle about the size of a baseball that was filled with water. Its use was simple. When thrown into a fire, it would break and spread its contents, hopefully extinguishing the flames.

The first American patent on a fire grenade was issued in 1863 to Alanson Crane of Fortress Monroe, Virginia. The best-known manufacturer of these highly specialized bottles was the Halden Fire Extinguisher Company in Chicago, which was awarded a patent in August 1871.

These grenades were manufactured in large numbers by companies with names as unique as the bottles themselves: Dash-Out, Diamond, Harkness Fire Destroyer, Hazelton's High Pressure Chemical Firekeg, Magic Fire, and Y-Burn. The fire grenade became obsolete with the invention of the fire extinguisher in 1905. Many of these grenades can still be found with the original closures, contents, and labels.

American Fire Extinguisher Co., Hand Grenade
Clear glass pint, 6⅜ in. (h), tooled top, smooth base..............$350–450
American 1860–1890 (rare)

Babcock Hand Grenade, Nonfreezing, 325–331 S. Des Plaines St., Chicago—"Manf'd by Fire Extinguisher Mfg. Co."
Deep cobalt blue, 7½ in. (h), ground lip, smooth base...$1,000–1,500
American 1880–1890

Babcock Hand Grenade, Nonfreezing, 325–331 S. Des Plaines St., Chicago—"Manf'd by Fire Extinguisher Mfg. Co."
Yellowish amber, 7½ in. (h), ground lip, smooth base........$700–1,000
American 1880–1890

Barnum's Hand Held Fire Extinguisher, Diamond, Pat'd June 26th, 1869
Medium yellow with olive tone, 5⅞ in. (h), tooled top...........$500–700
American 1870–1880 (very rare in this color)

Descours & Co. Fire Watcher, Hand Fire Grenade
Clear glass, 5¼ in. (h)..$200–275
English 1890–1910 (very rare)

Firex Fire Grenade (Unembossed)
Cobalt blue, 4 in. (h)..$50–100
English 1890–1910

Grenade—Prevoyante—Extincteur
Medium yellowish amber, 5⅝ in. (h), ground lip...................$400–600
French 1890–1910

Harden Star Hand Grenade—Fire Extinguisher—Patented No. 1, Aug. 8, 1871, Aug. 14, 1888
Turquoise blue, 6¼ in., ground lip, smooth base $35–45
American 1885–1895

Harden Star Hand Grenade—Fire Extinguisher—This Bottle Pat. May 27 84
Turquoise blue, 6⅝ in., sheared lip, smooth base........................$50–90
American 1885–1895

Harden Star Hand Grenade—Fire Extinguisher
Turquoise blue, 6⅝ in., sheared lip, smooth base........................$50–90
American 1885–1895

Harden Star Hand Grenade—Fire Extinguisher
Pale clear green, 6¾ in. (h), ground lip, smooth base.............$200–400
English 1885–1895 (very rare)

Harden Star Hand Grenade—Fire Extinguisher
Deep cobalt blue, 6¾ in. (h), ground lip, smooth base...........$200–400
English 1885–1895

Harkness Fire Destroyer
Deep cobalt blue, 6 in. (h), ground lip, smooth base $350–500
American 1880–1885

Hayward Hand Grenade Fire Extinguisher, No. 407 Broadway, N.Y.
(Base—Design H. Patent)
Amber, 5⅞ in., tooled lip, smooth base $400–600
American 1875–1890 (rare in this color)

Hayward's Hand Fire Grenade—Patented Aug. 8, 1871, S. F.
Hayward 407 Broadway, N.Y.
Cobalt blue, 6 in. (h), ground lip, smooth base $200–250
American 1875–1885

Hayward's Hand Fire Grenade—Patented Aug. 8, 1871, S. F.
Hayward 407 Broadway, N.Y.
Yellow-olive, 6⅛ in. (h), rolled lip, smooth base $175–250
American 1875–1885

Hayward's Hand Fire Grenade—N.Y.
Aqua, 6⅜ in., tooled lip, smooth base....................................$125–175
American 1880–1885

Hayward's Hand Fire Grenade—Patented Aug. 8, 1871, S. F.
Hayward 407 Broadway, N.Y.
Clear glass, 6¼ in. (h), smooth base $175–250
American 1875–1885 (Hayward Grenades are not often seen in clear glass)

Sulfuric Acid, 4 oz. line, Childs Fire Extinguisher, Utica, N.Y.
Aqua, 6⅛ in., tooled lip...$35–45
American 1890–1900

W. D. Allen Manufacturing Company, Chicago, Illinois (Motif of Crescent Moon)
Clear glass, 8¼ in., sheared lip, smooth base............................$500–700
American 1870–1890 (very rare)

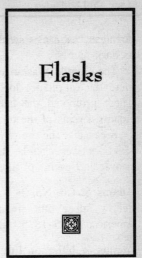

Flasks

Flasks have become a most popular and prized item among collectors owing to the variety of decorative, historical, and pictoral detail featured on many pieces. The outstanding colors have had a major effect on the value of these pieces, more so than with most other collectible bottles.

Early history documents that American flasks were first manufactured by the Pitkin Glasshouse in Connecticut around 1815, and quickly spread to other glasshouses around the country. Early flasks were free-blown and represent some of the better craftsmanship with more intricate designs. By 1850, approximately 400 designs had been used that produced black graphite pontil marks. The pontils were coated with powdered iron, which allowed the flasks' bottoms to break away without damaging the glass. The flasks made between 1850 and 1870 had no such markings because of the widespread use of the newly invented snap-case.

Since flasks were designed to be refilled with whiskey or other spirits, more time and effort was expended in the manufacturing process than for most other types of bottles. Flasks soon became a popular item for use with all types of causes and promotions. Mottos were frequently embossed on flasks and included a number of patriotic sayings and slogans. One of the more controversial flasks was the Masonic flask, which bore the order's emblem on one side and the American eagle on the other. Public feelings were high against this representation but the controversy soon passed. Masonic flasks are now a specialty item for collectors.

Also highly collectible are the Pitkin-type flasks, named for the Pitkin Glassworks where they were exclusively manufactured. While Pitkin-type flasks and ink bottles are common, the bottles, jugs, and jars are very rare. German Pitkin flasks are heavier and straight-ribbed, while the

American pattern is swirled or broken-ribbed with unusual colors such as dark blue.

The George Washington depiction was a popular face on flasks, as were the candidates for the presidential elections of 1824 and 1828. These promoted the likenesses of Andrew Jackson and John Quincy Adams. Events of the time also were reflected on these flasks.

Because of the use of flasks for the promotion of various political and special interest agendas, they represented a major historical record of the people and events of those times.

Adams & Co. No. 3
Yellow amber, pint, smooth base, ground lip $80–120
American 1865–1875 (rare—Pittsburgh District Glasshouse Marking)

Adams & Jefferson July 4 A.D. 1776, General Washington, Kensington Glass Works Philadelphia, E. Pluribus Unum, Eagle, T.W.D. (In Oval)
Light greenish aqua, pint, pontil base, sheared lip $200–275
American 1840–1860

A Merry Christmas and a Happy New Year—Rooster
Amber, 5¾ in., smooth base, tooled lip $200–300
American 1875–1885

A. Weinberg, AW Monogram, Tacoma, W.T.
Clear, 5¾ in., pint, smooth base, tooled lip.............................$500–700
American 1880–1889 (rare)

B. F. Jellison Washoe Exchange, 544 California St.
Amber, 5¼ in., smooth base, tooled lip $100–300
American 1880–1900

Bust of Grant, Eagle Union
Aqua, pint, smooth base, applied mouth $120–160
American 1865–1875 (scarce)

Bust of Taylor, Rough and Ready—Major, Bust of Ringold, Ringold
Grayish clear, pint, pontil base, sheared lip..............................$150–200
American 1830–1835

Bust of Washington—Bust of Taylor
Yellow-green, pint, pontil base, applied mouth..........................$400–500
American 1850–1855

Hunter-Fisherman, 1850–1880.

For Pike's Peak, Old Rye, Pittsburg,
PA, 1870–1880.

Braunschweiger & Co, Importers, S. F.
Clear, half-pint, smooth base, tooled and rolled lip, pumpkinseed
flask $125–150
American 1885–1912

Chas. F. Holton, CH Monogram, Olympia, W.T
Clear, pint, smooth base, tooled lip, coffin flask $600–900
American 1886–1889 (extremely rare)

Clasped Hands, Union—Eagle, C.I. & Sons
Medium yellow-green, smooth base, applied mouth.................$400–700
American 1860–1870 (very rare)

Clasped Hands—Eagle
Amber, half-pint, smooth base, applied mouth.........................$125–175
American 1860–1870

Clyde Glass Works, N.Y.
Golden amber, pint, smooth base, applied mouth....................$100–150
American 1875–1885

Western Hotel, Santa Rosa,
1904–1918.

Cluster of Grapes—Sheaf of Wheat
Aqua, half-pint, pontil base, sheared lip....................................$150–225
American 1825–1835 (scarce)

Coffin & Hay, Stag, Hammonton—Eagle
Aqua, half-pint, pontil base, sheared lip....................................$250–325
American 1825–1835

Coffin & Hay, Flag, Hammonton—Eagle
Light citron, quart, pontil base, sheared lip..............................$200–300
American 1825–1835

Cornucopia—Urn
Yellowish olive-amber, half-pint, pontil base, sheared lip...........$80–120
American 1825–1835

Cornucopia—Urn
Medium yellow-green, half-pint, pontil base, sheared lip........$175–250
American 1835–1845

Corn for the World, Ear of Corn—Monument, Baltimore
Aqua, pint, pontil base, sheared lip...$150–250
American 1825–1835

McDonough's, San Francisco, CA, 1885–1895.

Hardie and Amos, 1881.

Crystal Palace, 1890–1898.

Mint Saloon, 1906–1918.

Dancer, Chapman—Soldier, Baltimore, Md.
Olive green, pint, smooth base, applied mouth $800–1,200
American 1865–1875

Dan Donahoe Mint Saloon, Marysville
Clear, 5¼ in., smooth base, tooled lip, pumpkinseed..............$200–400
American 1882–1897

Deer, Good, Game—Willow Tree
Aqua, pint, pontil base, sheared lip..$150–250
American 1825–1835

E. Pluribus Unum One of Many, Eagle, T.W.D.—Kensington Glass Works, Philadelphia, Cornucopia
Aqua, half-pint, pontil base, sheared lip.....................................$300–400
American 1825–1830

Eagle—Eagle
Bluish aqua, pint, pontil base, sheared lip $175–250
American 1825–1835

Eagle—Cornucopia
Aqua, pint, pontil base, sheared lip..$175–250
American 1825–1835

Eagle—Liberty Tree
Amber, half-pint, pontil base, sheared lip $1,000–1,500
American 1825–1830 (Charter Oak flask)

Eagle, Pittsburgh, Pa.—Eagle
Olive green, pint, smooth base, applied mouth $175–250
American 1865–1875

Elk Pool Hall, Elko, Nev. (Token Flask)
Emerald green, 5¼ in., smooth base, tooled lip......................$250–275
American 1900–1910 (rare)

Ensign Saloon, No. 1 Market St., San Francisco
Clear, 6½ in., smooth base, tooled lip, coffin flask..................$300–600
American 1890–1900

For Pike's Peak, Prospector—Eagle
Deep olive-amber, quart, smooth base, applied mouth.............$500–800
American 1865–1875 (rare)

Pike's Peak Old Rye, 1857.

Phoenix Old Bourbon, Naber Alfs and Brune, San Francisco, 1875.

For Pike's Peak, Prospector, Old Rye—Eagle, Pittsburgh, Pa.
Aqua, quart, smooth base, applied mouth $70–90
American 1865–1875

For Pike's Peak, Prospector—Eagle, "Ceredo"
Yellowish green, quart, smooth base, applied mouth................$325–450
American 1870–1875

Genr. LaFayette, Bust of Lafayette—Eagle
Deep greenish aqua, pint, pontil base, sheared lip $1,800–2,800
American 1825–1835 (rare)

General Washington, Bust of Washington
Aqua, quart, smooth base, applied mouth $275–350
American 1825–1835

Geo. W. Robinson, No. 75, Main St., W. Va.
Aqua, quart, smooth base, applied mouth $125–150
American 1870–1880

Portrait of Washington and sheaf of rye on crossed rake and pitch fork, 1840–1860.

G. Z. Taylor
Aqua, pint, open pontil, sheared lip..$50–70
American 1825–1835

H. G. Tobin, Walla Walla, Saloon, Walla Walla, W.T.
Clear, half-pint, smooth base, tooled lip, pumpkinseed......$1,200–1,800
American 1885–1889 (extremely rare)

H. P. Brickwadel & Co., Wholesale, Liquor Dealers, 208 & 210, Front Street, S.F.
Yellowish golden amber, 7¼ in., smooth base, tooled lip........$450–600
American 1880–1883

Hunter—Grape Vine
Aqua, half-pint, smooth base, sheared lip......................................$60–90
European 1850–1870

Hunter—Olive Branches
Clear, half-pint, pontil base, applied mouth...................................$60–90
European 1850–1870

Hunter—Hound
Amber, quart, pontil base, sheared lip $400–500
American 1855–1870

Jenny Lind Fisler Ville Glass Works,
1855–1865.

Summer Tree-Winter Tree,
1850–1865.

Isabella, Anchor Glass Works, Sheaf of Grain
Aqua, half-pint, pontil base, sheared lip.....................................$250–350
American 1855–1860

J. F. Cutter, Extra Trade, Old Bourbon
Amber, 7⅜ in., pint, smooth base, applied mouth $600–900
American 1870–1880

Jenny Lind, Bust of Jenny Lind—Glass Factory, Glass House
Aqua calabash, pint, iron pontil, applied mouth.......................$125–150
American 1855–1860

**Jesse-Moore & Co., Louisville, Ky., G. H. Moore, Old Bourbon &
Rye, Moore Hunt & Co., Sole Agents**
Yellowish amber, 7⅜ in., smooth base, applied mouth......$5,000–7,000
American 1878–1882 (scarce)

**Kensington Glass Works, Philadelphia, Masonic Arch, "Franklin"—
Free Trade and Sailor's Rights, Ship**
Aqua, pint, pontil base, sheared lip...$250–325
American 1825–1830

"Lafayette," Bust of Lafayette, "S & C"—"Dewitt Clinton," Bust of Dewitt Clinton, C-T
Yellow-olive, half-pint, pontil base, sheared lip...................$1,000–1,500
American 1820–1825 (rare)

Lion—Cluster of Grapes
Deep cobalt blue, pint, pontil base, sheared lip........................$175–250
European 1850–1860

Log Cabin—Hard Cider
Aqua, 6⅜ in., pint, open pontil, sheared lip......................$2,500–3,500
American 1840–1843 (rare and important political flask)

Louis Kossuth, Bust of Kossuth and Flags—Paddlewheel Schooner, U.S. Steam Frigate, Mississippi
Aqua calabash, pint, iron pontil, applied mouth......................$200–300
American 1850–1860

Louisville, Ky. Glass Works
Aqua, pint, smooth base, applied mouth $75–150
American 1870–1880

Louis Taussig, 26 & 28 Main Street, S.F
Yellowish amber, 5⅞ in., half-pint, smooth base, tooled lip....$400–600
American 1884–1886

Major Bust of Ringold, Ringold—Bust of Ringold, Rough and Ready
Aqua, pint, pontil base, sheared lip...$125–175
American 1830–1835

Masonic Arch—Eagle
Olive-amber, pint, pontil base, sheared lip $175–250
American 1825–1835

Miller's Extra Trade, E. Martin & Co, Old Bourbon
Yellowish amber, 7¼ in., pint, smooth base, applied
mouth $400–600
American 1871–1879

Murphy—Briggs & Co, Wholesale and Retail, Liquor Dealers, Needles, Calif.
Deep amethyst, 6⅞ in., smooth base, tooled mouth..................$80–100
American 1900–1910

Edward L. Christin, Importer, 1899–1903.

Double Eagle Flasks, 1855.

Nevada Saloon, Goldfield, Nevada (Token Flask)
Emerald green, 6⅞ in., smooth base, tooled lip........................$150–225
American 1890–1920

Old Valley Whiskey, AAA, G MC M F (Inside Cross)
Yellowish gold, 7⅞ in., smooth base, applied mouth.........$1,000–1,500
American 1870–1880

Ortion & Cerhardt Wines & Liquors, 149 Powell St., S.F.
Clear, 5⅜ in., smooth base, tooled lip, pumpkinseed..............$150–225
American 1895–1898

Phoenix Naber, Alfs, & Brune, S.F.
Clear, 5¼ in., smooth base, tooled lip, pumpkinseed..............$350–500
American 1890–1900

Prospector—Eagle, Arsenal Glass Works, Pittsburgh, Pa.
Yellow-green, pint, smooth base, applied mouth $700–1,000
American 1870–1875 (scarce)

Rampant Lions—Cluster of Grapes
Cobalt blue, pint, pontil base, sheared lip $125–175
American 1850–1870

Scroll Flask
Lavender, quart, pontil base, sheared lip..............................$600–1,000
American 1840–1850

Scroll Flask
Amber, half-pint, pontil base, sheared lip $400–700
American 1830–1840

Smoke Ambrosia Cigars
Clear, 5½ in., smooth base, tooled lip, pumpkinseed..............$100–150
American 1900

Spring Garden, Anchor Glass Works, Log Cabin
Aqua, half-pint, smooth base, applied mouth $80–120
American 1860–1870

Success to the Railroad, Horse Pulling Cart
Emerald green, pint, open pontil, sheared lip...........................$175–275
American 1825–1835

Success to the Railroad, Locomotive—Success to the Railroad
Aqua, pint, pontil base, sheared lip...$225–350
American 1830–1834

Sunburst Flask, Keen—P & W
Yellowish amber, half-pint, pontil base, sheared lip.................$275–375
American 1810–1830

The Father of His Country, Bust of Washington
Medium teal blue, quart, pontil base, sheared lip.....................$200–300
American 1850–1860

The Father of His Country, Bust of Washington—Dyottville Glass Works Philadelphia, Gen. Taylor Never Surrenders, Bust of Taylor
Medium cobalt blue, quart, pontil base, sheared lip..............$800–1,000
American 1850–1855

The Father of His Country,
General Taylor Never
Surrenders, 1850–1860.

The Father of His Country, Bust of Washington—Gen. Z. Taylor, Bust of Taylor
Black glass, quart, smooth base, applied mouth $500–800
American 1850–1860

The Murphy Wine & Liquor Co., 308–310 Pike St., Seattle, Wash.
Clear, 6¾ in., smooth base, tooled lip..$50–75
American 1895–1910

The Noble Buffet, Beltink & Ritter, Oakland, Calif.
Clear, 6¼ in., smooth base, tooled lip.......................................$80–120
American 1906–1915

The Log Cabin, 3rd St., Portland, Ore., Billy Winters Pro.
Clear, pint, smooth base, tooled lip, pumkinseed.....................$650–950
American 1903–1915 (rare in pint size)

The Waldorf Cafes 10 oz., Becker Bros. Inc., San Francisco, Los Angeles, San Diego, 1915
Clear, 7⅝ in., smooth base, tooled lip..$60–90
American 1915

AAA Old Valley Whiskey,
1870–1880.

Traveler's Companion—Railroad Guide
Light blue-green, half-pint, pontil base, sheared lip..................$275–400
American 1850–1860

Traveler's Companion—Ravenna, Glass Co.
Golden amber, pint, iron pontil, applied mouth......................$500–800
American 1855–1870

Theodore Gier, Oakland, Calif.
Clear, 5¾ in., pint, smooth base, tooled lip..............................$80–120
American 1892–1910

Tree-Tree
Deep emerald, quart, pontil base, sheared lip....................$1,200–1,800
American 1845–1860

W. Ihmsen's Eagle Glass—Agriculture, Sheaf of Wheat and Crossed Tools
Deep greenish aqua, pint, pontil base, sheared lip.............$1,200–1,500
American 1825–1835

Willington Glass Co., West Willington, Conn.—Liberty Eagle
Olive green, half-pint, smooth base, applied mouth.................$125–175
American 1860–1870

Variety of Whiskey "Warranted Flask," 1870–1890.

Zanesville City Glass Works
Aqua, pint, smooth base, applied mouth $125–175
American 1870–1880

Zanesville Eagle, Ohio, J. Shepard & Co. Masonic Arch
Golden amber, pint, pontil base, sheared lip............................$400–600
American 1825–1835

Food and Pickle Bottles

Food bottles are one of the largest and most diverse categories in the field of collectible bottles. They were made for the commercial sale of a wide variety of food products excluding beverages except milk. Food bottles are an ideal specialty for the beginning collector since as a group they are so readily available. Many collectors are attracted to food bottles for their historical value. Nineteenth- and early twentieth-century magazines and newspapers contained so many illustrated advertisements for food products that many collectors keep scrapbooks of ads as an aid to dating and pricing the bottles.

Prior to the introduction of bottling, food could not to be transported long distances or kept for long periods of time on account of spoilage. The bottling of foodstuffs revolutionized the industry and began a new chapter in American business merchandising and distribution. With the glass bottle producers were able to use portion packaging, save labor, and sell from long distances.

Suddenly local producers faced competition from great distances and many interesting bottles were created specifically to distinguish them from others. Pepper sauce bottles, for instance, were made in the shape of Gothic cathedrals with arches and windows (green and clear); mustard jars and chili sauce bottles had unique embossing; cooking oil bottles were made tall and slim, and pickle bottles had large mouths. The pickle bottle is one of the largest of the food bottles, with a wide mouth and a square or cylindrical shape. While the pickle bottles were often unique in shape and design, their colors were almost exclusively aqua, although occasionally you will find a multicolored piece. When looking through ghost town dumps and digging behind older pioneer homes, you are

134

sure to find them in great numbers since pickles were a common and well-liked food, especially in the mining communities.

Two of the more common food bottles are the Worcestershire sauce bottles distributed by Lea & Perrins and the Heinz sauce bottles. The Worcestershire sauce in the green bottle was in high demand during the nineteenth century and is quite common. Henry J. Heinz introduced his sauces in 1869 with the bottling of horseradish but didn't begin bottling ketchup until 1889.

A. Doufour & Co., Bordeaux, Pour La Prune
Apple green, 4¾ in., pontil base...$75–125
French 1875–1890

CHs Bernard, San Francisco
Deep turquoise-aqua, 6½ in., spice, smooth base, applied
mouth $30–60
American 1880–1890

Keyhole Sauce (emerald green, extremely rare), 1845–1855.

Munger Brothers Company, Phoenix, AZ, 1900–1906.

Food bottle assortment—Curtice Brothers Preserves, Rochester, NY; Monogram Salad Oil, Swift and Company, U.S.A.; H. J. Heinz Company, 1900–1920.

Dodson-Hills, St. Louis
Aqua, 8⅝ in., cathedral pepper sauce, smooth base, tooled mouth $80–100
American 1885–1895

Cathedral Pickle Jar, E.H.V.B.
Deep aqua, 9¼ in., 6-sided, iron pontil, rolled lip $250–350
American 1850–1860

Cathedral Pepper Sauce
Aqua, 8¼ in., smooth base, applied top.......................................$25–50
American 1850–1860

Cathedral Pepper Sauce
Aqua, 8½ in., 6-sided, pontil base, applied mouth...................$80–120
American 1840–1855

Cathedral Pepper Sauce
Aqua, 9 in., smooth base, applied double-roll collar...................$40–80
American 1850–1860

Cathedral Pickle
Light blue-aquamarine, 9 in., open pontil, applied top............$100–200
American 1840–1855

Food bottle assortment—First three bottles common;
fourth bottle, A–1 Sauce, 1900–1920.

Cathedral Pickle/Pepper Sauce
Light blue-aquamarine, 11 in., smooth base, applied top.........$100–300
American 1850–1860

**Flaccus Bros., Steer (Motif of Steer's Head) Head, Table
Delicacies, Wheeling, W. Va.**
Clear, half-pint, smooth base, ground lip....................................$80–120
American 1890–1910

Gerkins from W. K. Lewis & Bros., Boston, Mass., Cathedral Pickle
Light green, 13 in., smooth base, rolled lip.............................$175–225
American 1855–1865

Giessen's Union Mustard, N.Y. (Spread-Winged Eagle)
Clear, 4⅞ in., pontil base, applied mouth....................................$50–75
American 1857–1865

Globe Tobacco Company, Detroit, Pat. Oct. 10, 1882
Yellow-amber 7¼ in., smooth base, ground lip..........................$70–100
American 1882–1895

Globe, Patented, May 25, 1886
Yellowish amber, quart, smooth base, ground lip..........................$60–90
American 1886–1895

Cathedral Pickle Jar,
1860–1880.

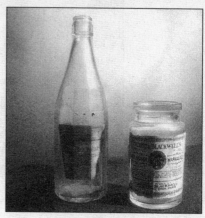

Apple Cider Vinegar, Safeway
Stores; Crosse and Blackwell's
Pure Orange Marmalade,
1910–1930.

Lea & Perrins Worcester Shire Sauce, 1870–1900.

Cathedral Pickle Jar with star on shoulder, 1875.

Globe, Patented, May 25, 1886
Amber, quart, smooth base, ground lip...$60–90
American 1886–1895

Holman's Baking Power, Buffalo, N.Y.
Deep bluish aqua, 5¾ in., smooth base, tooled lip....................$50–100
American 1890–1900

Horlick's Malted Milk, Original-Genuine Horlick's Malten Milk Trade M. M. Mark (Label under Glass Display Bottle)
Clear, 6¾ in., smooth base, tooled lip.......................................$250–350
American 1890–1910

Horlick's Malted Milk, Horlick's Malted Milk Trade, M. M. Mark, "That's Meat and Drink to Me" Hot or Cold (Label under Glass Display Bottle)
Clear, 8⅛ in., smooth base, tooled lip.......................................$350–500
American 1890–1910

J. A. Folger & Co., San Francisco
Clear, 2 in., smooth base, tooled lip...$35–50
American 1885–1900

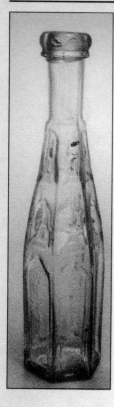

Cathedral Pepper Sauce Bottle,
1870.

Cathedral Pickle/Sauce Bottle,
1870.

Jesse H. Lippincott, Pittsburgh, Peppersauce Bottle
Aqua, 8½ in., smooth base, applied mouth....................................$40–70
American 1855–1880 (rare)

John W. Stout & Co., X, New York
Aqua, 8½ in., smooth base, applied mouth....................................$40–60
American 1860–1865

Landsdale & Bro, Cathedral Pickle
Aqua, 8⅞ in., pontil base..$350–450
American 1845–1860

Lime Juice
Olive-amber, 10⅜ in., smooth base, applied mouth $100–200
American 1860–1870 (blown in three-piece mold)

Heinz's Trieste Mustard—hand blown in Heinz glass factory, Sharpsburg, PA, 1885–1910.

Heinz's Preserved Sweet Pickles—hand blown in Heinz glass factory, Sharpsburg, PA, 1893–1905.

Mustard Jar, Maine and Morro Castle Embossing
Clear, smooth base, ground lip...$90–140
American 1893–1900

Pepper Sauce, Ribbed
Aqua, 10½ in., pontil base, rolled mouth....................................$50–75
American 1857–1865

Product Jar, Pat. Glass, Boston, Mass., June 2, 1889
Sapphire blue, 4½ in., smooth base..$300–400
American 1889–1905

T. B. Smith & Co., Philada, Cathedral Pickle
Aqua, 9¼ in., pontil base, tooled mouth...................................$175–250
American 1855–1865

This Trade Mark Registered, Maple SAP and Boiled Cider, Vinegar, The C. I. Co. Ltd, East Ridge, N.H.
Cobalt blue, 11⅜ in., smooth base, tooled mouth................$700–1,000
American 1885–1895

Heinz's Tabasco Pepper Sauce—hand blown in Heinz glass factory, Sharpsburg, PA, 1889–1899.

Heinz's Table Sauce—hand blown in Heinz glass factory, Sharpsburg, PA, 1895–1909.

Wm. L. Haller, Carlisle, Pa.
Aqua, half-gallon, smooth base, applied mouth $250–350
American 1870–1880

W. M. & P., N.Y. Pickle Jar
Aqua, 7¾ in., pontil base...$35–50
American 1885–1900

Wm. White, Newport Garden, Pepper Sauce
Aqua, 11 in., pontil base, applied mouth $40–70
American 1855–1880

Wendell & Espy—Mince Meat—152 So. Front, Philadelphia
Aqua, 8⅛ in., pontil base, rolled lip...$500–800
American 1845–1860 (rare)

Heinz's Keystone Ketchup—produced in Heinz glass factory, Sharpsburg, PA, 1889–1913.

Heinz Mince Meat—hand blown in Heinz glass factory, Sharpsburg, PA, 1893–1905

Assortment of Heinz products, 1885–1915.

Fruit Jars

Unlike food bottles, fruit jars were sold empty for use in home preservation of many different types of food. The use of fruit jars was predominant in the 1800s, when food-stuffs were not available prepackaged and home canning was the only option. Though fruit jars carry no product or advertising, they aren't necessarily common or plain since the bottle manufacturers' name is usually embossed in large lettering along with the patent date. The manufacturer whose advertising campaign gave fruit jars their name was Thomas W. Dyott, who was in the market early, selling fruit jars by 1829.

With respect to closures, the most common of those used in the first fifty years was a cork sealed with wax. In 1855, an inverted saucerlike lid was invented that could be inserted into the jar to provide an airtight seal. The Hero Glassworks invented the glass lid in 1856 and improved upon it in 1858 with a zinc lid invented by John Landis Mason, who also produced fruit jars. Because the medical profession warned that zinc could be harmful, Hero Glassworks developed a glass lid for the Mason jar in 1868. Mason eventually transferred his patent rights to the Consolidated Fruit Jar Company, which let the patent expire. In 1880, the Ball Brothers began distributing Mason jars, and in 1898 the use of a semiautomatic bottle machine increased the output of the Mason jar until the automatic machine was invented in 1903.

Fruit jars come in a wide variety of sizes and colors, commonly aqua and clear. It's more difficult to find blues, ambers, blacks, milk glass, greens, and purples.

A. G. W. L. Pitts. Pa.
Aqua, half-gal. $35–45
American 1865–1885

A. G. Smalley & Co
Amber, quart $20–25
American 1895

Anchor Mason's Patent
Clear, quart..$25–40
American 1915

Anchor Mason's Patent
Clear, pint $15–25
American 1915

A. Stone & Co., Philada
Aqua, pint, smooth base, applied mouth $1,000–1,500
American 1860–1870 (extremely rare)

**A. Stone & Co., Philada Manufactured by Cunninghams & Co.,
Pittsburgh, Pa.**
Aqua, quart, iron pontil...$300–400
American 1855–1865 (rare)

Atlas E-Z Seal
Blue, quart...$15–25
American 1915–1930

Atlas E-Z Seal, Trade Mark Reg.
Blue, quart...$15–25
American 1915–1930

Atlas E-Z Seal fruit jar,
1890–1920.

Assortment of Atlas fruit jars, 1885–1920.

Atlas Strong Shoulder Mason
Light olive green, half-gal. $20–30
American 1915–1925

BBGM Co., Ball Bro's Glass MF'G Co., Buffalo
Aqua, midget, smooth base, ground lip $400–600
American 1870–1885 (rare)

Ball
Aquamarine, quart..$75–125
American 1920–1930

Ball Perfect Mason
Deep aqua, quart, smooth base $25–30
American 1820–1930

Ball Perfect Mason
Medium yellowish green, quart..$25–35
American 1920–1930

Ball Sure Seal
Deep blue, pint $25–30
American 1908–1910

Ball Ideal and Ball Perfect
Mason, 1915–1930.

Bennett's No. 2, Bennett's Patent Feb. 6, 1866, A. Kline Patd., Oct. 21, 1863
Aqua, quart, smooth base with six molded "feet"......................$500–700
American 1866–1870 (rare with molded feet)

Boyd's Perfect Mason
Blue, quart..$15–25
American 1925–1935

Cohansey Glass Mf'g. Co., Pat. Mar. 20, 77
Aqua, quart barrel..$75–125
American 1877–1890

Crown (Motif of Crown) Imperial
Clear, half-pint $15–20
American 1920

Cunningham & Co., Pittsburgh, Pa.
Cornflower blue, half-gallon, smooth base, applied mouth $75–125
American 1880–1890

Decker's Victor Mason City, Iowa
Clear, quart..$20–30
American 1920–1940

Decker Dependable Food
Clear, pint $20–30
American 1920–1940

Flaccus Brothers steerhead fruit
jar, 1890–1900.

Drey Perfect Mason
Clear, half-pint $15–25
American 1920–1930

Drey Square Mason
Clear, pint $10–15
American 1915–1925

Excelsior Improved, Patd. Feb. 12, 56, Nov. 4, 62, Dec. 6, 64, June 9, 68 Sep 8, 88
Aqua, quart..$35–50
American 1856–1890

Flaccus Bros Steer (Motif of Steer's Head) Head, Table Delicacies Wheeling, W. Va.
Clear, half-pint, smooth base, ground lip....................................$75–100
American 1890–1910

Franklin Fruit Jar
Aqua, half-gal., smooth base, ground lip.......................................$35–50
American 1880–1885

Friedley & Cornman's Patent Oct. 25, 1859, Ladies Choice
Aqua, half-gal., smooth base, ground lip....................................$750–900
American 1859–1865

Gilberds Improved (Over Star) Jar
Aqua, quart, smooth base, ground lip $150–225
American 1885–1890

Globe
Light golden amber, quart $50–100
American 1885–1910

Hartell's Fruit Jar
Yellow-green, quart, smooth base, ground lip $50–100
American 1858–1890

Hartell's Glass Air-Tight Cover—Patented Oct. 19, 1858
Deep aqua, half-gal., smooth base, ground lip $35–50
American 1860–1870

Hartell & Letchworth, Patent May 22, 1866
Aqua, quart, smooth base, ground lip $75–100
American 1866–1870

J & B Fruit Jar Pat'd. June 14, 1898
Aqua, pint $35–50
American 1898–1905

J & B Fruit Jar Pat'd. June 14, 1898
Aqua, quart $35–50
American 1898–1905

J. C. Lefferts Patented Feb. 15, 1859, Manufacturer
Cast iron, quart $300–400
American 1859–1880

J. P. Smith, Son & Co.—Pittsburgh, Pa.
Aqua, quart, smooth base $50–100
American 1860–1880

Kerr Self Sealing Mason
Clear, half-pint $15–20
American 1920–1935

Knox (K Inside Keystone) Mason
Clear, half-pint $15–25
American 1915–1925

Mason Brothers common,
Trademark, Mason's Improved,
1875–1880.

LaFayette (Bust of LaFayette)
Aqua, quart, smooth base, applied mouth $500–700
American 1885–1895

L'Ideale Brevetee S.G.D.G.
Aqua, half-pint $30–50
American 1880–1890

Mason
Amber, pint $30–45
American 1870–1880

Mason's Patent, Nov. 30, 1858
Clear, quart..$40–50
American 1870–1880

Mason's Patent, Nov. 30, 1858
Yellow-amber, half-gal., smooth base, ground lip $125–175
American 1880–1890

Mason's (Keystone) Patent, Nov. 30, 1885
Aqua, pint..$40–50
American 1880–1890

Mason's C.F.J. Co. (Monogram) Patent, Nov. 30, 1858
Light green, pint, smooth base, ground lip..................................$40–50
American 1880–1890

Mason's Patent November 30th, Amber, 1880.

Mason fruit jar, amber, 1905–1920.

Mason's 404 Patent, Nov. 30, 1858
Aqua, midget, smooth base, ground lip $120–150
American 1870–1875 (scarce)

Mason's Patent, Nov. 30, 1858, Dupont (Inside circle)
Aqua, half-gal., smooth base, ground lip....................................$125–225
American 1880–1890 (scarce)

Mason's (Cross) Patent Nov. 30, 1858
Light yellow-green, half-gal., smooth base, ground lip $70–100
American 1870–1880

Mason's (Cross) Patent, Nov. 30, 1858
Olive green, quart, smooth base, ground lip.................................$35–45
American 1890–1910

McMechen's Always the Best Old Virginia, Wheeling W. Va. U.S.A. (Around Woman Holding a Box)
Clear, 5 in., smooth base, tooled mouth......................................$40–60
American 1890–1910

Millville Atmospheric Fruit Jar—Whitall's Patent June 18, 1861
Aqua, pint, smooth base $50–100
American 1860–1890

Moore's Patent, Dec. 3, 1861
Aqua, quart..$35–45
American 1861–1880

NE Plus Ultra Air Tight Fruit Jar Made by Bodine & Bros.
Wms'Town, N.J. For Their Patented Glass Lid
Deep aqua, pint, iron pontil, applied mouth $600–800
American 1855–1865

Packed by M. H. Davis & Son, Milford, Del., Cohansey Glass Co.
Philadelphia
Aqua, quart..$50–90
American 1885–1895

Pacific San Francisco Glass Work—Patd FEBY 9th 1864, Victory
Reisd June 22D 1867
Aqua, half-gal., smooth base, ground lip....................................$150–200
American 1868–1870

Perfect Seal
Clear, half-pint $25–35
American 1920

Pine Deluxe Jar
Aqua, pint...$10–15
American 1915–1925

Presto Supreme Mason
Clear, half-pint $15–20
American 1920–1935

Royal (Inside a Crown) Trade Mark, Full Measure Registered Quart
Green, quart $20–25
American 1895

Spratt's Patent, July 18, 1854, Pat'd. April 5, 1851
Clear, 5⅛ in., metal can..$300–400
American 1851–1855

Sun Trade Mark
Aqua, pint...$35–45
American 1880–1895

Standard
Amber, quart, smooth base...$250–350
American 1875–1885 (rare in this color)

Stark Jar Patented
Clear, quart, smooth base $50–75
American 1910–1915

The Eagle, M. S. Burr & Co., Boston, Trade Mark (Around Eagle in Circle)
Clear, quart..$50–75
American 1885–1895

The Empire, Pat. Feb. 13, 1866
Aqua, half-gal., ground lip...$40–60
American 1865–1885

The Haserot Co., Cleveland, Mason Patent
Aqua, quart..$25–40
American 1880–1910

The Hero
Deep aqua, half-gal. $40–50
American 1875–1885

The Howe Jar, Scranton PA, Pat, Feb 28/88
Clear, quart, ground lip $40–75
American 1890–1910

The Leader
Aqua, quart..$25–35
American 1885–1895

The Mason's (Ghosted "The Mascot") Improved
Medium amber, half-gal., smooth base, ground lip $125–150
American 1880–1910

The Salem Jar—Holz Clark & Taylor, Salem, N.J.
Aqua, quart, smooth base, ground lip......................................$800–1,200
American 1865–1875 (rare)

The Van Vliet Jar of 1881
Aqua, quart, smooth base, ground lip.......................................$300–400
American 1881–1885

Trade Mark Lightning, Patd. Apr. 25, 82, Patd. Jan. 5, 75 Reisd June 5, 1877
Golden amber, quart, smooth base, ground lip $60–90
American 1877–1885

Trade Mark, VR, Lightning
Deep purple amethyst, quart, smooth base, ground lip............$125–150
American 1880–1900

Trade Mark Lightning, Patd Apr 25, 82 Patd Jan. 5 75 Reisd June 5, 77
Golden amber, half-gal., smooth base, ground lip....................$120–160
American 1880–1900

Whitall's Patent June 18, 1861, W.T & Co.
Aqua, pint, smooth base $250–350
American 1861–1870 (extremely rare)

Winslow Jar, Patented Nov. 29, 1870, Patented Feb. 25, 1873
Aqua, half-gal., smooth base..$75–100
American 1870–1880

Winslow Jar., Patented Nov. 29, 1870, Patented Feb. 25, 1873
Aqua, quart, smooth base $70–90
American 1870–1880

Wm. L. Haller, Carisle, Pa.
Aqua, half-gal., smooth base, applied mouth $275–325
American 1870–1880

Woodbury Improved, W.G.W., Woodbury Glass Works, Woodbury, N.J.
Aqua, quart..$25–35
American 1885–1895

Hutchinson Bottles

The Hutchinson bottle was developed in the late 1870s by Charles A. Hutchinson. What is most interesting about his development is that the stopper, and not the bottle itself, differentiated the design from others. The stopper, which Hutchinson patented in 1879, was intended as an improvement to cork stoppers since they eventually shrank and allowed air to seep into the bottle.

The new stopper consisted of a rubber disk that was held between two metal plates attached to a spring stem. The stem was in the form of a figure eight, with the upper loop larger than the lower to prevent the stem from falling into the bottle. The lower loop could pass through the bottle's neck and push down the disk to permit the filling or pouring of the bottle's contents. A refilled bottle was sealed by pulling the disk up to the bottle's shoulder, where it made a tight fit. When opened, the spring was hit, which made a popping sound. Thus, the Hutchinson bottle was the source of the phrase "pop bottle" and the story behind how carbonated drinks came to be known as "pop."

Hutchinson stopped producing bottles in 1912, when warnings about metal poisoning were issued. As collectibles, Hutchinson bottles rank high on the curiosity and price scales, but pricing varies quite sharply by geographical location, compared to the relatively stable prices of most other bottles.

Hutchinson bottles carry abbreviations of which the following three are the most common:

tbntbs—"This bottle not to be sold"
TBMBR—"This bottle must be returned"
TBINS—"This bottle is not sold"

Anchor Steam (Motif of Anchor) Bottling Works, Shawnee, O.T.
Aqua, 6⅝ in., smooth base, tooled lip......................................$100–175
American 1890–1907 (rare, Oklahoma Territory)

Arizona Bottling Works, Phoenix, Arizona
Aqua, 6¾ in., smooth base, tooled top..$20–35
American 1900–1915

C. A. Werle, Mok. Hill
Aqua, 6⅜ in., smooth base, tooled lip.......................................$75–125
American 1890–1900 (rare)

California Bottling Works
Aqua, 6¾ in., smooth base, tooled top...$15–20
American 1890–1906

Chr. Wiegand, Las Vegas, N.M.
Clear, 7¼ in., smooth base, tooled lip.......................................$400–600
American 1890–1900 (extremely rare)

C. Schnerr & Co., Sacramento, Cal., Capital Soda Works
Aqua, 6¾ in., smooth base, tooled top..$25–50
American 1890–1905

E. & J. Lodtmann, Santa Cruz Co., Cal, (Gravitating Stopper Made by John Matthews, N.Y., Pat. Oct. 11, 1864 on Base)
Aqua, 7⅛ in., smooth base, applied mouth.................................$80–120
American 1880–1890

EWA Bottling Works, H.T.
Aqua, 7¾ in., smooth base, tooled mouth $75–125
American 1890–1910 (scarce, Hawaiian Territory)

Excelsior Soda Works, Los Angeles, Calif.
Aqua, 7 in., smooth base, tooled top...$50–60
American 1890–1900

Forster & Polhemus, Poughkeepsie, N.Y.
Dark amethyst, 6⅞ in., smooth base, tooled top......................$75–125

G.G. Gilmore, Roswell, N.M.
Aqua, 6¾ in., smooth base, tooled mouth $450–550
American 1890–1900

Ginger Ale Co., S.F. Diamond Trade (D in Diamond Motif) Mark
Aqua, 6¾ in., smooth base, tooled top.......................................$75–100
American 1890–1905

G. Norris & Co. City Bottling Works, Detroit, Mich., C. & Co. Lim.
Cobalt blue, 6¾ in., smooth base, tooled mouth.....................$275–350
American 1885–1900

G. Norris & Co. City Bottling Works, Detroit, Mich.
Medium cobalt blue, 6⅞ in., smooth base, applied mouth......$200–300
American 1890–1900

Golden West Soda Works, San Francisco, Cal
Medium blue-aquamarine, 6¾ in., smooth base, tooled top......$50–125
American 1885–1900

Golden West Soda Works, San Francisco, Cal
Aqua, 6⅞ in., smooth base, tooled lip...$50–80
American 1885–1900 (rare mug base Hutch)

Guyette & Company, Registered, Detroit, Mich., This Bottle Is Never Sold
Medium cobalt blue, 7 in., smooth base, tooled lip.................$150–200
American 1890–1910

H. Aman, Cheyenne, Wyo.
Aqua, 6½ in., smooth base, tooled top.......................................$120–150
American 1890–1900

H. & B. (M'Ville on base)
Aqua, 7⅛ in., smooth base, applied mouth..............................$150–200
American 1885–1895 (extremely rare)

H. Denhalter & Son, Salt Lake City U.T.
Aqua, 6⅝ in., smooth base, applied mouth.................................$90–140
American 1885–1890 (scarce)

Henry J. Postel, Sacramento, Cal
Aqua, 7 in., smooth base, tooled top..$25–50
American 1880–1900

Hollister and Company,
Honolulu, HI, 1895.

Hawaiian Soda Works, Honolulu, H.I.
Aqua, 7¾ in., smooth base, tooled lip..$60–90
American 1895–1910

Hennessy & Nolan, Albany, N.Y., Empire State Trade Mark (Motif of Capitol Building) Mineral Water
Clear, 7⅛ in., smooth base, tooled lip......................................$50–100
American 1880–1900

Hygeia Soda Works, Kahului, H.T.
Aqua, 8 in., smooth base, tooled lip...$100–150
American 1900–1910 (rare, Hawaiian Territory)

Humboldt Artesian Mineral Water, Eureka, Cal., City
Aqua, 6¾ in., smooth base, tooled top...$45–50
American 1895–1905

J. Esposito, 812 & 814 Koca Nola, Trade Mark, Washington Ave., Philadelphia
Yellow with olive tone, 7¾ in., smooth base, tooled
mouth $1,000–1,500
American 1890–1910 (rare)

J. P. Dostal, Iowa City, Iowa
Yellow-olive, 6⅜ in., smooth base, applied mouth....................$80–120
American 1855–1865

John Mitchell, Nanaimo, B.C.
Light bluish aqua, 7 in., smooth base, tooled top........................$40–80
American 1885–1900

Lahaina Ice Co., Ltd. Lahaina, Maui
Aqua, 8 in., smooth base, tooled top...$20–30
American 1900–1910

Livermore Soda Works, Livermore, Cala
Aqua, 6⅝ in., smooth base, tooled top....................................$250–350
American 1880–1890 (extremely rare)

Lytton Springs (Motif of Pelican) Sweet Drinks, P.M.H. Co., San Francisco, C.H.B. Label reads "Imitation Orange Cider, Nevada City Soda Works, Nevada City"
Aqua, 6⅞ in., smooth base, tooled lip......................................$100–150
American 1880–1900

M. Cronan, 230 K. Street, Sacramento, "Sac Soda Works"
Aqua, 6⅞ in., smooth base, tooled top...$40–80
American 1880–1890

Maui Soda Works, W on Base
Aqua, 7¾ in., smooth base, tooled top...$25–45
American 1890–1900

Maui Soda Works
Aqua, 8 in., smooth base, tooled top...$20–30
American 1900–1910

McManus & Meade Bottlers, Nasonville, R.I., Registered
Aqua, 6⅝ in., smooth base, tooled top......................................$600–800
American 1890–1910 (scarce—State of Rhode Island)

Martinelli, Watsonville
Bluish aqua, 6¾ in., smooth base, applied top $75–100
American 1880–1890

Meamber Bros., Yreka
Aqua, 7 in., smooth base, tooled top...$40–80
American 1890–1910

Milwaukee Bottling Co., Spokane Falls, W.T.
Aqua, 6¾ in., smooth base, tooled lip......................................$350–550
American 1885–1889 (rare, Washington Territory)

Mokelumne Hill Soda Works, W on Base
Light greenish aqua, 6½ in., smooth base, tooled top...............$50–100
American 1890–1910 (scarce)

Mokelumne Hill Soda Works, W on Base
Bluish aqua, 7 in., smooth base, tooled top................................$50–70
American 1890–1910

Monroe Cider & Vinegar Co., Ferndale Cal.
Aqua, 6⅞ in., smooth base, tooled top......................................$75–150
American 1895–1905

Mt. Shasta Soda Works, Sisson, Cal.
Aqua, 7 in., smooth base, tooled top...$40–80
American 1890–1900

New Liberty Soda W. Co., Trade (Bust of Liberty) Trade Mark S.F.
Aqua, 6½ in., smooth base, tooled top......................................$50–100
American 1885–1895 (rare)

O. Tullman's Mineral Water Works, S.L.O.
Aqua, 7 in., smooth base, tooled top...$45–65
American 1885–1895

Pacific & Puget Sound Soda Works, Seattle, W.T. (A in Diamond)
Aqua, 7 in., smooth base, tooled top...$150–200
American 1880–1885

Pioneer Trade (Motif of Anchor) Mark, Soda Works, P.O. MC & D on Smooth Base
Deep aqua, 6¼ in., smooth base, tooled top................................$60–90
American 1890–1900

Popular Soda Water Co. PoP.
Aqua, 6⅞ in., smooth base, tooled top...$25–50
American 1890–1905

Prescott Bottling Works, Prescott, A.T.
Aqua, 6¼ in., smooth base, tooled top......................................$225–250
American 1890–1900 (rare, Arizona Territory)

Pacific Soda Works, 1895.

Prescott Bottling Works, Arizona
Territory, 1885–1895.

R.W. Black Bottler, Oklahoma, Ter., R.W.W. on Smooth Base
Aqua, 6⅝ in., smooth base, tooled top......................................$150–250
American 1890–1907

S.L.O. Bottling Works, L. Albert, I.G. Co. 33 on Base
Aqua, 6½ in., smooth base, tooled top...$50–75
American 1885–1895

Slogan Bottling Works, Charles J. Kaslo B.C.
Aqua, 7 in., smooth base, tooled top..$40–80
American 1890–1900

South Mcalester Bottling Works, South Mcalester, Ind. Ter.
Aqua, 6⅜ in., smooth base, tooled lip......................................$150–220
American 1890–1907 (rare, Indian Territory)

Standard Bottling Co., Fort Bragg
Aqua, 6½ in., smooth base, tooled top...$45–65
American 1900–1905

Alameda Soda Water Comp., 1897.

Home Soda Works, Arizona Territory, 1885–1895.

Standard Bottling Works, Minneapolis, Minn.
Deep amber, 6⅝ in., smooth base, tooled top $125–175
American 1890–1910

Star Soda Works (Four-Pointed Star) Gribble & Co., Nevada City
Aqua, 7 in., smooth base, tooled top...$50–90
American 1890–1900

Steam Soda Works, Bottle Is Not Sold
Aqua, 6½ in., smooth base, tooled top..$25–50
American 1890–1900 (rare)

Stephens & Jose, Virginia City, Nevada (SJ Monogram), Gravitating Stopper Made by John Matthews, New York Pat. Oct. 11, 1864 on Base
Deep aqua, 7⅛ in., smooth base, applied mouth.....................$300–500
American 1875–1990 (rare, Virginia City, Nevada)

Pearson Brothers, Bodie,
1881–1887.

The Northrop & Sturgis Company, Portland, Ore.
Aqua, 6⅜ in., smooth base, tooled top..$40–60
American 1890–1900

W. E. Deamer Nevada Soda Water Co., Grass Valley, Nevada Co. Calif.
Deep blue-aqua, 7¼ in., smooth base, tooled top........................$40–80
American 1885–1900

Woodland Soda Works
Aqua, 7 in., smooth base, tooled top..$50–100
American 1890–1900 (extremely rare)

WM Aylmer, Fargo, D.T.
Deep blue-aqua, 6⅜ in., smooth base, tooled top...................$400–600
American 1885–1889

W. H. Boyer, Kingston, Pa.
Aqua, 5½ in., smooth base, applied mouth................................$50–100
American 1885–1890 (rare, stubby)

Wm. A. Kearney, Shamokin, Pa., This Bottle Never Sold
Deep amber, 6⅞ in., smooth base, tooled top $350–450
American 1885–1895

X L C R Soda (Star & Shield Motif) Works
Aqua, 7 in., smooth base, applied top $50–100
American 1880–1885 (rare)

Ink
Bottles

Ink bottles are unique because of their centuries-old history, which provides collectors today with a wider variety of designs and shapes than any other group of bottles. People often ask why a product as cheap to produce as ink was sold in such decorative bottles. While other bottles were disposed of or returned after use, the ink bottle was usually displayed openly on desks in dens, libraries, and studies. It's safe to assume that even into the late 1880s people who bought bottles considered the design of the bottle as well as the quality of its contents.

Prior to the eighteenth century, most ink was sold in brass or copper containers. The very rich would refill their gold and silver inkwells from these storage containers. Ink that was sold in glass and pottery bottles in England in the 1700s had no brand-name identification and, at best, would have a label identifying the ink and/or its manufacturer.

In 1792, the first patent for the commercial production of ink was issued in England, twenty-four years before the first American patent was issued. Molded ink bottles appeared in America around 1815 or 1816. The blown three-mold variety was in use through the late 1840s. The most common shaped ink bottle, the umbrella, is a multisided conical that can be found with both pontiled and smooth bases. One of the more collectible ink bottles is the teakettle, identified by the neck, which extends upward at an angle from the base.

As the fountain pen grew in popularity between 1885 and 1890, ink bottles gradually became less decorative.

A. M. & Co., N.Y. (Sample Cabin Ink)
Clear glass cabin, 3⅝ in., smooth base, tooled lip $200–300
American 1890–1900

Cone Ink, Dessauer's,
1880–1890.

Umbrella Ink, Gibb, 1860–1870.

Alling's—Patd. Apl. 25, 1871
Blue green, 1¾ in., smooth base, smooth lip $25–40
American 1871–1875

Alling's—Patd. Apl. 25, 1871
Clear, 1¾ in., smooth base, smooth lip.......................................$25–40
American 1871–1875

Barrel Form Ink, Pat. Oct. 19, 1865
Clear, 2⅛ in., smooth base, tooled lip...$20–35
American 1870–1890

Barrel Form Ink
Greenish aqua, 3 in., smooth base, flared lip $15–20
English 1870–1880

Bertinguiot Ink
Deep olive amber, 2¼ in., open pontil, sheared lip.................$100–200
European 1845–1855

Blackwood's Patent London
Aqua, 2 in., smooth base, sheared lip...$75–125
English 1870–1880

Blown Three-Mold Geometric Ink
Yellow olive-amber, 1¾ in., pontil base, tooled mouth............$120–160
American 1815–1825

Umbrella Ink, Carlton,
1870–1880.

Bust of Ben Franklin Teakettle Ink
Pale aqua, 4 in., long, smooth base, ground lip $140–200
French 1885–1895

Butler's Ink, Cincinnati
Aqua, 2⅜ in., 12-sided, open pontil, rolled lip........................$100–150
American 1845–1860

Butler's Ink Cincinnati
Pale apple green, 2¼ in., 12-sided, open pontil, rolled lip......$150–250
American 1840–1855

Cabin Ink
Clear, glass log cabin, 2½ in., smooth base, tooled lip............$300–500
American 1880–1890

Cabin Link
Aqua, 2½ in., smooth base, tooled lip.....................................$350–500
American 1880–1890

Cone Ink, unembossed, 1890–1910.

Carter's Cathedral Master Ink
Cobalt blue, 6¼ in., smooth base...$90–125
American 1920–1925

Carter's Cathedral Master Ink
Cobalt blue, 9¾ in., smooth base...$100–125
American 1920–1925

China Pottery Teakettle Ink
Tan with mottled white-and-brown glaze, 2⅛ in......................$200–300
European 1885–1900

David's Writing Fluid
Cobalt blue, 9 in., smooth base, tooled top.................................$40–80
American 1885–1890

E. Waters, Troy, N.Y.
Aqua, 6¾ in., master ink, pontil base, applied mouth.............$400–600
American 1840–1855

Estes, N.Y.—Ink
Aqua, 6¾ in., master ink, 8-sided, pontil base, applied
mouth...$250–400
American 1845–1855

F. Kidder—IM Provd—Indelible Ink
Aqua, 2⅜ in., open pontil, rolled lip...$80–120
American 1835–1850

G. A. Miller, Quincy, Ill.
Aqua with yellow olive, 2½ in., 8-sided, smooth base.............$175–275
American 1865–1875

Gesetzkich, Geschutzt, Figural German Soldier's Helmet Inkwell
Black glass, 3¼ in., smooth base, ground lip............................$100–175
German 1885–1910

Golden Treasure
Aqua barrel ink, 4⅞ in., smooth base, applied mouth..............$80–130
American 1855–1865

H. G. Hotchkiss, Lyons, N.Y.
Sapphire blue, 9⅝ in., smooth base, applied mouth.................$80–130
American 1880–1890 (rare)

Schoolhouse Ink, 1860–1870.

Bertinquiot Inkwell, 1855.

Hover, Phila
Medium emerald green, 9 in., master ink, pontil base............$500–800
American 1845–1855

Harrison's Columbian Ink
Aqua, 2 in., 8-sided, pontil base, rolled lip..............................$120–160
American 1840–1855

Harrison's Columbian Ink
Deep cobalt blue, 2⅛ in., pontil base, rolled lip.....................$350–450
American 1835–1855

Harrison's Columbian Ink
Aqua, 7⅛ in., pontil base, applied mouth..................................$80–120
American 1840–1855

Ink for Boot and Shoemakers, E. Packard & Co., Quincy, Mass.
Olive-amber, 7⅝ in., smooth base, applied mouth..................$175–275
American 1855–1870

J. & I.E.M. Igloo Ink
Light green, 2¼ in., smooth base, sheared lip............................$75–125
American 1840–1855 (rare)

J. M. & S
Aqua, 1⅝ in., smooth base, ground lip..$70–90
American 1870–1880

J.S. Dunham
Bluish aqua, 2½ in., deep open pontil, rolled lip....................$175–275
American 1840–1855

James S. Mason & Co.
Aqua, 2⅜ in., 8-sided, open pontil, rolled lip..........................$200–300
American 1840–1855

J. S. Mason, Philadelphia
Medium emerald green, 4⅜ in., pontil base, flared lip............$350–500
American 1840–1855

J.W. Ely, Cincinnati
Aqua, 2⅝ in., pontil base, rolled lip...$250–450
American 1845–1855 (extremely rare)

Kirtland's Ink W & H
Bluish aqua, 2 in., smooth base, sheared lip, turtle ink............$150–225
American 1875–1895

Levinson's Inks, St. Louis
Amber, 2½ in., amber cabin ink, smooth base, tooled lip.........$90–150
American 1880–1890 (scarce)

L. H. Thomas Ink
Aqua, 2⅛ in., cone ink, smooth base, sheared lip.......................$40–60
American 1875–1895 (rare)

M. & C. Ltd.
Medium emerald green, 2⅞ in., smooth base, tooled lip.........$200–300
English 1880–1890

S. S. Stafford Ink, made in USA,
This Bottle Contains One Full
Quart, cobalt-blue,
1890–1909.

Miscellaneous inks, 1890–1910.

Carters Ink, 8½"; Carter 8-sided Ink, 1880–1900.

N. J. Simonds, Lawrence, Mass.
Bluish aqua, 8 in., 12-sided, pontil base, applied
mouth $1,400–1,800
American 1845–1855 (rare)

Opdyke Bros. Ink
Aqua barrel, 2½ in., smooth base, tooled lip $175–250
American 1870–1880

Paris—Depose—NA
Medium cobalt blue, 2¾ in., smooth base, ground lip $175–275
French 1885–1895

Patterson's Excelsior Ink
Aqua, 2⅝ in., 8-sided, pontil base, rolled lip $300–500
American 1840–1855 (rare)

Paul's Ink—New York, Chicago
Cobalt blue, 9¼ in., master ink, smooth base, tooled lip $80–120
American 1890–1910

S. O. Dunbar, Taunton
Aqua, 2⅜ in., 8-sided, open pontil, rolled lip $125–175
American 1840–1855

Stafford's Ink
Teal green, 9½ in., smooth base, applied top $50–150
American 1890–1910

Superior Black Steel Pen Ink Prepared by George A. Moss
Medium blue-green, 2½ in., 8-sided, pontil base, rolled lip....$120–180
American 1840–1855 (umbrella ink)

Teakettle Ink
Pale aqua, 1⅞ in., smooth base, sheared lip $275–375
American 1875–1895

Teakettle Ink
Medium teal blue, 2 in., smooth base, ground lip $125–175
American 1875–1895

Teakettle Ink
Milk glass, 2 in., smooth base, ground lip................................$350–500
American 1875–1895

Teakettle Ink
Deep cobalt blue, 2¼ in., smooth base, ground lip.................$375–500
American 1875–1895

Water's Ink, Troy, N.Y.
Aqua, 2⅝ in., 6-sided, open pontil, rolled lip........................$700–900
American 1845–1860 (rare, umbrella ink)

The Western Ink Co., Bloomington, Ill.
Aqua, 3⅛ in., smooth base, applied mouth................................$90–140
American 1875–1885

Turtle Ink
Cobalt blue, 1¾ in., smooth base, ground lip....................$1,500–2,200
American 1875–1895 (extremely rare)

Coventry Ink, 1875.

R. F. Ink, 1870.

Miscellaneous inks (middle ink has a sheared lip), 1850–1870.

Turtle Ink
Amber, 1⅝ in., smooth base, ground lip....................................$175–275
American 1875–1895 (rare)

Turtle Ink
Deep amber, 2 in., smooth base, ground lip $175–250
American 1875–1895

Umbrella Ink, Stoddard Glass Works
Deep olive-amber, 2 in., 16-sided, pontil base, rolled lip $250–350
American 1840–1855

Umbrella Ink
Medium cobalt blue, 2½ in., 8-sided, open pontil, rolled
lip $375–500
American 1840–1855

Umbrella Ink
Light apple green, 2⅝ in., 8-sided, smooth base, rolled lip $275–400
American 1860–1870 (rare)

Underwood's Inks
Medium cobalt blue, 9¾ in., smooth base, tooled top................$40–80
American 1880–1910

Water's Ink, Troy, N.Y.
Aqua, 2⅝ in., six-sided, open pontil, rolled lip $700–900
American 1845–1860

W. E. Bonney
Aqua barrel, 2⅝ in., smooth base, rolled lip $70–90
American 1855–1865

Willis Ton's Superior Indelible
Aqua, 2½ in., open pontil, flared lip $175–275
American 1835–1850 (rare)

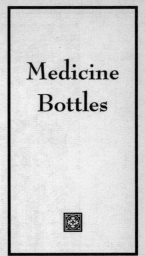

Medicine Bottles

The medicine bottle group includes all pieces specifically made to hold patent medicines. Bitters bottles and cure bottles, however, are excluded from this category because the healing powers of these mixtures were very questionable.

A patent medicine was one whose formula was registered with the U.S. Patent Office, which opened in 1790. Not all medicines were patented, since the procedure required the manufacturer to reveal the medicine's contents. After the passage of the Pure Food and Drug Act of 1907, most of these patent medicine companies went out of business after they were required to list the ingredients of the contents in the bottle. The public demand quickly diminished as consumers learned that most medicines consisted of liquor diluted with water and an occasional pinch of opiates, strychnine, and arsenic. I have spent many enjoyable hours reading the labels on these bottles and wondering how anyone would survive after taking the recommended doses.

One of the oldest and most collectible medicine bottles was manufactured in England from 1723 to 1900, the embossed Turlington "Balsam of Life" bottle. The first embossed U.S. medicine bottle dates from around 1810. When searching out these bottles, always be on the lookout for embossing and original boxes. Embossed "Shaker" or "Indian" medicine bottles are very collectible and valuable. Most embossed medicines made before 1840 are clear and aqua, the embossed greens, ambers, and blues are much more collectible and valuable.

A. Grandjeans Composition for the Hair
Clear, 3 in., pontil base, flared lip $150–225
American 1845–1855

175

The Cuticura System of Curing
Constitional Humors, Potter
Drug and Chemical Company,
Boston, MA, USA, 1880–1885.

Abel's White Pine Balsam, Los Angeles, Calif.
Light aqua, 4½ in., smooth base, tooled lip.................................$30–60
American 1895–1899

Alexander Silameau
Medium cobalt blue, 6¼ in., pontil base, applied mouth........$500–800
American 1840–1855

A. M. Cole Apothecary, Virginia, Nev.
Clear, 4¼ in., smooth base, flared lip..$25–50
American 1865–1870

A. M. Cole, Virginia City, Nev.
Bluish aqua, 8½ in., smooth base, applied top........................$300–600
American 1865–1870

A. T. & S F. Chemical Dept.
Clear, 10¾ in., smooth base, tooled lip...$70–90
American 1890–1900 (Atchison Topeka & Santa Fe Railroad)

Baker's Vegetable Blood & Liver Cure, Look Out Mountain Medicine Co. Manufacturers & Proprietors, Greenville, Tenn.
Medium amber, 9¾ in., smooth base, tooled lip.....................$200–300
American 1880–1890 (scarce)

Trunk Brothers, Denver, CO,
1880–1890.

Bear's Oil
Light greenish aqua, 2⅝ in., open pontil, rolled lip $175–250
American 1830–1840

Bohmansson Druggist, Arcata, Calif.
Green 4½ in., smooth base, tooled top $50–100
American 1880–1890

Budd's Wound Nerve and Bone Liniment, Prepared by Jas.
Delamater, Sole Proprietors
Aqua, 5⅜ in., pontil base, applied mouth...............................$300–400
American 1840–1855

By A. A. Cooley, Hartford, Conn.
Olive-amber, 4½ in., open pontil, sheared lip.........................$150–200
American 1845–1860

Carters Spanish Mixture
Olive-amber, 8½ in., iron pontil, applied mouth $250–350
American 1845–1860

Carters Spanish Mixture
Yellowish olive green, 8¼ in., iron pontil, applied mouth.......$275–375
American 1845–1860

Catarrh Dr. Kilmer's Cough Cure Consumption Oil, Specific
Aqua, 8⅞ in., smooth base, tooled mouth $300–400
American 1885–1900

C. C. Pendleton's Tonic
Amber, 9½ in., smooth base, applied mouth $110–170
American 1875–1885 (rare)

Clark's Drug Store Ely McGill
Clear, 4½ in., smooth base, applied mouth..................................$25–75
American 1908–1909

Coleman's Blood Searcher Stomach Tonic Coleman Medicine Co., 125 Market Street, Camden, N.J. (Labeled Medicine)
Medium cobalt blue, 7¾ in., smooth base, tooled lip..................$35–70
American 1880–1900

Crane & Brigham, San Francisco (In a Leaf)
Gold with amber tone, 10 in., smooth base, applied flat collar ring
mouth $750–1,250
American 1865–1875 (rare bay rum)

U.S.A. Hospital Department
6¾"; 2¾"; 1861–1865.

Owl Drug Company, cobalt-blue
(extremely rare), 1900–1910.

Owl Drug Company, milk
glass, 1895–1900.

D. Mitchell's Tonic for the Hair, Rochester, N.Y.
Deep bluish aqua, 6¼ in., pontil base, applied mouth............$125–150
American 1840–1855

Dr. B. Sherman
Medium amber, 9⅝ in., smooth base, applied mouth $80–120
American 1875–1885 (rare)

Dr. E. Champlain Ligneous Extract Patented
Medium bluish aqua, 5½ in., smooth base, applied top............$50–100
American 1865–1870 (scarce)

D. Evans Camomile Pills
Light greenish aqua, 3 in., pontil base, flared lip.........................$25–50
American 1840–1855 (scarce)

Dr. Campbell's Hair Invigorator, Aurora, N.Y.
Light blue-gray aqua, 6 in., pontil base, double-ring collar........$50–100
American 1859–1865

Dr. Carter's Compound Pulmonary Balsam
Light green-aqua, 5¼ in., pontil base, flared lip $50–75
American 1850–1860

Churchill's Drugstore, Yreka, CA, 1880–1890.

Florida Water, Davis Brother's, San Francisco, 1875–1885.

Dr. Culver's Malarial Germ Destroyer, Cleveland, Ohio, Johnston, Eckert and Co.
Medium amber, 8 in., smooth base, tooled lip with pour
spout...$150–200
American 1880–1885 (very rare)

Dr. Davis's Depurative
Medium emerald green, 9⅝ in., smooth base, applied
mouth..$800–1200
American 1855–1865 (rare pontiled period medicine)

Dr. H. B. Skinner, Boston
Yellowish olive-amber, 5⅞ in., pontil base, applied mouth.....$200–300
American 1840–1850 (rare colored medicine)

Dr. J. Hedges, Fever & Ague Annihilator, New York
Aqua, 7¼ in., pontil base, applied mouth...............................$150–175
American 1840–1855

Dr. J. S. Wood's Elixir, Albany, N.Y.
Deep emerald green, 8¾ in., iron pontil, applied $275–400
American 1840–1855

Dr. Larookah's Indian Vegetable Pulmonic Syrup
Aqua, 8⅝ in., smooth base, applied mouth.............................$125–150
American 1870–1880

Dr. Liebig's Wonderful German Invigorator, No. 1 400 Geary St., S.F., Cal
Light bluish aqua, 7 in., smooth base, applied top $200–300
American 1883–1897

Dr. McMunn's Elixir of Opium
Bright green, 4 in., open pontil, flared lip.................................$50–100
American 1840–1855

Dr. Murray's Magic Oil S.F., Cal
Medium blue-aqua, 6¼ in., smooth base, applied top.............$100–200
American 1874 (rare)

Dr. Perry's Lastchance Liniment
Aqua, 5¾ in., smooth base, applied top.....................................$50–100
American 1885–1895 (scarce)

Dr. R. C. Flower's Scientific Remedies, Manufactured by the R.C. Flower Medical Co., Boston, Mass. U.S.A.
Amber, 9⅛ in., smooth base, tooled mouth...............................$80–120
American 1880–1900

Dr. S. F. Stowe's Ambrosial Nectar (Motif of Stemmed Glass) Patented
Light yellow-green, 8 in., smooth base, applied mouth............$100–150
American 1866–1870 (scarce in this coloration)

Duff Gordon Sherry Medical Department U.S.A.
Deep olive-green, 9¾ in., smooth base, applied top $300–500
American 1855–1865

Dunbar & Co.'s Wormwood Cordial, Boston
Greenish aqua, 9½ in., smooth base, applied mouth...............$200–300
American 1860–1870

Searby's Florida Water, 1875–1885.

Julius Deetken Registered Pharmacist, Deadwood, SD, 1885.

Dustin Brothers Pharmacy, Blackfoot, Idaho

Light amethyst, 6½ in., smooth base, tooled top..........................$25–50
American 1885–1895

Edwin W. Joy & Co. 852 Market St., San Francisco, Cal

Amber, 4¼ in., smooth base, tooled top......................................$30–60
American 1900–1910 (scarce)

Empire State Drug Co. Laboratories, Buffalo, N.Y.

Aqua, 9½ in., smooth base, tooled top.......................................$75–150
American 1890–1900 (Label reads "Mrs. Fowler's special compound for the cure of all weaknesses and diseases peculiar to women").

Ethereal Cough Syrup, The Holden Drug Co., Stockton, Calif.

Light greenish aqua, 5¾ in., smooth base, tooled top.................$25–50
American 1885–1900 (scarce)

Federal Tonic Brownlow & Raymond

Deep cobalt blue, 10¼ in., smooth base, applied top...........$500–1,000
American 1865–1870 (rare)

Selection of miniature medicine bottles, 1860–1890.

F. F. Muller, Elko, Nev.
Clear, 3½ in., smooth base, tooled top...$50–100
American 1876–1888 (scarce, only one pattern is known)

F. J. Schneider Druggist, Eureka, Nev.
Clear, 4¼ in., smooth base, tooled top...$25–75
American 1872–1915

F. J. Steinmetz Druggist Opposite Post Office, Carson City, Nev.
Clear, 5¼ in., smooth base, tooled top...$25–50
American 1893–1910

Forces Asth-Manna, Trade Mark Reg., Asthma, Bronchitis, Colds, Etc., S.B. Force M'F'G. Chemist, San Francisco, Calif.
Amber, 8¾ in., smooth base, tooled lip $75–125
American 1895–1910 (scarce)

Friends Rheumatic Dispeller, Buffalo, N.Y.
Aqua, 6¼ in., open pontil, applied mouth..................................$70–90
American 1840–1855

Friedenwald's Buchu-Gin—Buchu-Gin for All Kidney & Liver Troubles, J. H. Friedenwald & Co., Baltimore, M.D.—Friedenwald's Buchu-Gin
Deep yellowish green, 9⅞ in., smooth base, tooled lip............$125–150
American 1890–1900

From the Laboratory of G. W. Merchant Chemist, Lockport, N.Y.
Emerald green, 5½ in., open pontil, applied mouth................$175–250
American 1850–1860

H. H. Watkins Pioneer Druggist,
Kingman, AZ, 1888–1890.

Dustin Brothers Pharmacy,
Blackfoot, ID, 1880–1900.

Gargling Oil, Lockport, N.Y.
Emerald green, 7⅛ in., smooth base, applied mouth...............$100–150
American 1865–1875 (scarce in this larger size)

Geo. W. Hoyt, Pharmacist, Cheyenne, W.T.
Clear, 4⅛ in., smooth base, tooled lip..$70–90
American 1885–1890 (scarce Wyoming Territory bottle)

Graefenberg Co. Dysentery Syrup, N.Y.
Light greenish aqua, 4¾ in., open pontil, hand-tooled rolled
lip $25–75
American 1845–1860

Grecian Fancheronian Drops, J. S. Fancher, New York
Aqua, 7⅝ in., iron pontil, applied mouth $150–250
American 1850–1860

G. W. Merchant, Chemist, Lockport, N.Y.
Medium emerald green, 7⅜ in., iron pontil, applied
mouth $175–250
American 1850–1860

Citrate of Magnesia, Goldfield
Drug and Jewlers, NV,
1890–1900.

Kuhlmann Brothers Drugs,
Bodie, CA, 1880–1890.

G.W. Merchant, Chemist, Lockport, N.Y.
Deep blue-green, 7¼ in., smooth-base, applied mouth............$175–250
American 1860–1870

G. W. Stone's Cough Elixir, Boston, Mass.
Aqua, 6¼ in., open pontil, applied mouth..................................$90–125
American 1840–1855

Guinn's Pioneer Blood Renewer, Macon Medicine Co., Macon, Ga.
Amber, 10⅞ in., smooth base, applied mouth.........................$150–250
American 1875–1885

Gun Wa's Chinese Remedy, Warranted Entirely Vegetable and Harmless
Bright medium yellow, ⅛ in., smooth base, applied mouth....$350–500
American 1880–1888 (scarce female remedy)

Atlas Baby Syrup, 1890–1900.

Hall's Pulmonary Balsam, J.R., Gates & Co., Proprietors, San Francisco
Aqua, 6½ in., smooth base, applied top....................................$50–100
American 1880–1885

H. Bowman Druggist, 262J Street, Sacramento
Medium bluish aqua, 7¼ in., smooth base, applied top............$50–100
American 1875–1885 (scarce)

Henry F. Schuldt Pharmacist, Cor. Weed & Main Sts., Tuscarora, Nev.
Clear, 5¼ in., smooth base, tooled top.................................$500–1,000
American 1878–1879 (rare, less than ten known)

Henley's Royal Balsam
Clear, 7 in., smooth base, applied top (laid on ring top) $600–1,200
American 1866–1869 (rare)

H. H. Watkins
Light amethyst, 10½ in., smooth base, tooled top $50–100
American 1880–1885 (scarce)

Higby & Stearns, Detroit, Mich.
Medium sapphire blue, 7¼ in., smooth base, applied
mouth $200–300
American 1865–1875 (extremely rare)

Hyatt's Infallible Life Balsam, N.Y.
Medium yellowish green, 9½ in., iron pontil, applied
mouth $375–500
American 1845–1855

I. Covert Balm of Life
Olive green, 5⅝ in., pontil base, applied mouth.....................$500–700
American 1840–1855

Indian Cough Syrup, Warm Springs, Ore.
Clear, 7 in., smooth base, tooled top..$25–50
American 1855–1865

Jaffe's Electric Pain Expeller
Light green-aqua, 5½ in., smooth base, applied top $25–75
American 1880–1890

J. Lipman, San Francisco
Deep blue-aqua, 6½ in., smooth base, tooled top.........................$25–75
American 1880–1890

Jamestown Drug Store, Jamestown, Cal
Clear, 5 in., smooth base, tooled top..$30–60
American 1885–1900

Jelly of Pomegranate Prepared by Dr. Gordak Only
Aqua, 7 in., open pontil, flared top $75–150
American 1855–1865

Jensen the Druggist, Butte, Mont.
Clear, 7 in., smooth base, tooled top..$40–75
American 1880–1890

J. F. Myers Druggist, Reno, Nev.
Clear, 4 in., smooth base, tooled top..$50–150
American, 1878–1882

J. H. & Co., "Hull" (on Reverse)
Medium lime green, 5¾ in., open pontil, rolled top $75–150
American 1855–1865

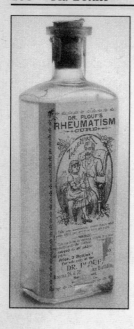

Dr. J. E. Plouf's Rheumatism Cure, 1880–1890.

Bronson and Lighthall Druggists, 1885–1890.

JJ (Monogram) J. Jones Jr., Goldhill, Nev.
Clear, 3½ in., smooth base, tooled lip..$70–90
American 1885–1890

John Gilbert & Co. Druggists, 177 North 3rd St., Philad. (All in slugplate)
Light greenish, aqua, 7½ in., open pontil, applied flanged lip....$50–75
American 1845–1855

John Moffat Price, $1.00 Phoenix Bitters, New York
Light grayish green, 5½ in., open pontil, laid on ring top..........$50–75
American 1845–1855

John Shier Pharmacist, Delamar, Nevada
Clear, 6 in., smooth base, tooled top.......................................$400–750
American 1893–1908 (fewer than 12 known)

Julius Deetken Registd. Pharmacist, Deadwood, S.D.
Clear, 7½ in., smooth base, flared lip...$50–100
American 1885–1895

J. W. Bull's Compound Pectoral, Baltimore
Aqua, 5½ in., open pontil, applied mouth $100–150
American 1840–1855 (rare)

Kickapoo Indian Pills Pure Vegetable Certain and Effective
Amber, 5⅛ in., smooth base, tooled top $100–200
American 1898–1900

Kuhlmann Bro. Drugs, Bodie, Cal
Clear, 6 in., smooth base, tooled top $50–150
American 1875–1885

Lewis Drug Co., Ely, Nevada
Clear, 4½ in., smooth base, tooled top...$25–75
American 1906–1911

L. Q. C. Wishart's, Trade (Motif of Pine Tree) Mark, Pine Tree, Tar Cordial, Philadelphia
Rich bluish green, 10¼ in., smooth base, applied mouth........$125–175
American 1890–1900

Louden & Co's Indian Expectorant, Philada
Aqua 7½ in., pontil base, applied mouth $100–150
American 1835–1855

Lyon's Power—B & P, N.Y.
Deep burgundy-puce, 4¼ in., open pontil, rolled lip $100–150
American 1840–1855

Lyon's Power—B & P, N.Y.
Olive green, 4¼ in., open pontil, rolled lip...............................$100–150
American 1840–1855 (rare)

McCullough's Pharmacy, Reno, Nevada
Clear, 4¾ in., smooth base, tooled top...$25–50
American 1891–1932

Missisquoi a Springs
Deep bluish green, 9½ in., smooth base, applied mouth...........$90–150
American 1865–1870

Mrs. A. L. Cook's Prescription Drugstore, Pocatello, Idaho
Clear, 5½ in., smooth base, tooled top...$50–75
American 1865–1875 (scarce)

Nowill's Pectoral Honey of Liverwort, 1870–1885.

Mrs. E. Kidder Dysentery Cordial, Boston
Aqua, 7⅜ in., open pontil, applied mouth $125–175
American 1840–1850

Myer's Rock Rose, New Haven
Aqua, 9 in., pontil base, applied mouth $200–300
American 1845–1855

Nelson's Extract of Roses and Rosemary H.P., Wakelee Sole Agent
Pale cobalt blue, 6¾ in., smooth base, applied top $50–100
American 1875–1885 (extremely rare)

Nowill's Pectoral Honey of Liverwort
Clear, 4¾ in., open pontil, flange top $25–50
American 1840–1850

Oregon Blood Purifier, Wm. Funder & Co., Portland, Ore.
Medium amber, 7½ in., smooth base, tooled top $25–50
American 1879–1881 (scarce)

Professor Woods' Hair Restorative Depots, 1854.

Duff Gordon Sherry Medical Department, USA, 1865.

Owl Pharmacy, W. H. Davis, Prop., Everett, Wash.
Clear, 6¾ in., smooth base, tooled top..$25–50
American 1900–1915 (scarce)

Owl Bottle (Whiskey Top) One Winged
Amber, 11½ in., smooth base, tooled top $100–150
American 1900–1905 (scarce owl variant)

Pala Verda Balsam
Amber, 8⅜ in., smooth base, applied mouth $125–175
American 1875–1885 (name of a western tree)

Perrine Apple Ginger, Phila—Perrine's (Motif of Apple), Ginger—Depot, No. 37 Front St., Philada
Amber, 10 in., smooth base, tooled mouth...............................$150–200
American 1880–1890

Phelp's Arcanum, Worcester, Mass.
Olive-amber, 8½ in., pontil base, applied mouth..................$700–1,000
American 1840–1855

Spirit of Nitrate, Goldfield, NV, 1890.

Phelp's Arcanum, Worcester, Mass.
Deep olive-amber, 8¾ in., pontil base, applied
mouth $1,000–1,500
American 1840–1855

Plank's Chill Tonic Co. (Bust of Mr. Plank), Chattanooga, Tenn.
Pinkish amethyst, 6⅜ in., smooth base, tooled mouth $80–120
American 1890–1910

P. M. Cohen & Co. (Motif of Mortar and Pestle), Charleston, S.C.
Aqua, 9⅝ in., pontil base, applied mouth................................$250–350
American 1845–1855

Assortment of miniature and medium-size common medicines, 1870–1900.

Lamplough's Effervescing Pyretic Saline, 1880.

Pond's Pain Destroyer
Aqua, 3⅜ in., pontil base, then flared lip..................................$150–200
American 1845–1855 (rare)

Pratt's Abolition Oil for Abolishing Pain
Aqua, 5¾ in., smooth base, tooled top...$40–80
American 1885–1895

Professor Woods Hair Restorative Depots, St. Louis & New York
Deep bluish aquamarine, 7 in., open pontil, applied tapered
collar..$50–100
American 1854–1860 (rare)

Reed & Cutler Druggists, Boston
Light greenish aqua, 7½ in., open pontil, applied top...............$50–100
American 1845–1855

Reinhardt's German Vegetable Bitter Exlixir
Aqua, 3⅞ in., open pontil, rolled lip...$80–120
American 1845–1855

R. E. Queen, Reno, Nev.
Clear, 5 in., smooth base, tooled top $75–100
American 1878–1881 (rare)

Roberts Drug Store, Goldfield, Nevada
Clear, 5 in., smooth base, applied top $50–150
American 1905–1906 (rare)

Rohrer's Wild Cherry Tonic Expectoral, Lancaster, PA
Medium amber, 10⅝ in., iron pontil, applied top $200–275
American 1855–1870

Schenck's Pulmonic Syrup
Blue aqua, 7 in., open pontil, applied top $75–150
American 1855–1865

Scholtz Established 1881, Denver, The Scholtz Rx Bottle
Clear, 9½ in., smooth base, tooled top......................................$50–100
American 1881

Scott's Red Oil Liniment, Phila
Light greenish aqua, 4¾ in., open pontil, tooled rolled lip $25–50
American 1845–1855

Selden's Magic Fluid, New York
Aqua, 7⅜ in., pontil base, applied mouth..................................$80–120
American 1840–1855

Shaker Fluid Extract Valerian
Aqua, 3¾ in., pontil base, flared lip...$125–175
American 1835–1850

Assortment of miniatures, 1870–1890.

Carnrick's Soluble Food for
Infants and Invalids, 1900.

Shaker Cherry Pectoral Syrup, Canterbury, N.H.
Aqua, 5½ in., open pontil, applied mouth..............................$125–175
American 1840–1855

State Hygienic Laboratory, Reno, Nevada
Clear, 3½ in., smooth base $25–100
American 1910 (rare)

Stewart & Holmes Drug Co. Optimus, Seattle, Wash.
Light greenish aqua, smooth base, tooled top..............................$25–50
American 1885–1900 (scarce)

The Adam's Sanatorium, Cure for the Tobacco Habit, Mexico, Mo.
Cobalt blue, 5¼ in., smooth base, tooled lip $275–400
American 1885–1895

The Blood, Dr. Kilmer's Ocean Weed Heart Remedy Specific
Aqua, 8½ in., smooth base, tooled mouth $70–100
American 1885–1895

The Craig Kidney Cure Company
Amber, 9½ in., smooth base, applied mouth $150–225
American 1880–1885

The Imperial Blood & Liver Tonic, the King of All Tonics, Dr. R. Drake, Sole Proprietor, La Grange, Ind.
Yellowish amber, 9 in., smooth base, tooled mouth.................$150–250
American 1880–1885

Assortment of medium-size medicine bottles, 1870–1900.

In Business for Your Health, the Pioneer Drug Co., Goldfield, Nev.
Clear, 6 in., smooth base, tooled top...$50–150
American 1906–1918 (scarce)

The Original Balm of Thousand Flowers, Jules Hauel Philadelphia
Clear, 4⅞ in., open pontil, flanged lip $50–150
American 1840–1850

The River Swamp, Chill and Fever Cure, Augusta, Ga.
Amber, 6¼ in., smooth base, tooled mouth...........................$400–600
American 1880–1890

Thompsonian Appetizer, Trade (Motif of Fat Man) Mark, Prepared by J. J. Vogt & Co., Cleveland, O
Yellowish amber, 9 in., smooth base, applied mouth...............$375–475
American 1865–1875 (rare)

Townsend's Phosphated Cereal Tonic
Orangish amber, 10⅛ in., smooth base, applied mouth..........$120–180
American 1870–1880 (rare)

Trade Mark Spark's Perfect Health for Kidney & Liver Diseases, Camden, N.J.
Deep amber, 9⅜ in., smooth base, tooled lip $100–175
American 1885–1895

U.S.A. Hosp. Dept.
Sapphire blue, 2½ in., smooth base, tooled lip........................$400–600
American 1875-1895 (extremely rare in this small size)

U.S.A. Hosp. Dept.
Deep cobalt blue, 9 in., smooth base, tooled lip......................$600–900
American 1860–1870

U.S.A. Hosp. Dept.
Yellowish olive green, 9⅞ in., smooth base, applied mouth....$275–375
American 1860–1870 (Bottle created during the Civil War for the Federal
Medical Corps.)

Warranted Cod Liver Oil, Pure Medicinal
Deep bluish aqua, 10½ in., iron pontil, applied mouth $80–120
American 1840–1855

Owl Pharmacy, W. H. Davis
Prop., Everett, WA, 1900.

Jensen the Druggist, Butte, MT,
1885.

Web's Liver and Kidney, A No. 1 Cathartic Tonic
Amber, 8⅝ in., smooth base, tooled mouth $175–275
American 1880–1890 (rare—triangular)

W. E. Hagan & Co., Troy, N.Y.
Medium cobalt blue, 6¾ in., smooth base, applied mouth........$80–120
American 1860–1870

Worm Mixter Stabler
Clear, 3⅝ in., pontil base, rolled lip...$90–120
American 1845–1855 (rare)

W. W. C., Woodridge Wonderful Cure Co., Columbus, Ca W.W.C.
Amber, 8¼ in., smooth base, applied mouth $125–175
American 1880–1885

W. W. Huff's Liniment
Emerald green, 6 in., open pontil, applied mouth.................$800–1,200
American 1840–1855 (rare in this larger size)

W. Pfrunder Druggist, Portland, Ore.
Medium yellow-amber, 6¼ in., smooth base, tooled lip $200–275
American 1890–1910 (rare)

Milk
Bottles

In recent years, many collectors have taken a
renewed interest in collecting milk bottles. The
first patent for a milk bottle was issued in January 1875 to the "Jefferson Co. Milk Assn."
The bottle itself featured a tin top with a spring clamping device. The
first known standard-shaped milk bottle (pre-1930) had a patent date of
March 1880 and was made by the Warren Glass Works of Cumberland,
Maryland. In 1884, A. V. Whiteman patented a jar with a domed tin
cap to be used along with the patent of the Thatcher and Barnhart
fastening device for a glass lid. There is no trace, however, of a patent
for the bottle itself. Among collectors today, the Thatcher milk bottle is
one of the most prized. There are several variations on the original. Very
early bottles were embossed with a picture of a Quaker farmer milking
his cow while seated on a stool. "Absolutely Pure Milk" is stamped into
the glass on the bottle's shoulder.

An important development in the design of the milk bottle was the
patent issued to H.P. and S. L. Barnhart for their methods of capping
and sealing. Their invention involved the construction of a bottle mouth
adapted to receive and retain a wafer disk or cap. It was eventually
termed the milk bottle cap and revolutionized the milk bottling industry.
Between 1900 and 1920, there were not many new patents on bottles.
With the introduction of the Owens Semiautomatic and Automatic Bottle
Machines, milk bottles were mass-produced. Between 1921 and 1945,
the greatest number of milk bottles were manufactured and used. After
1945, square milk bottles and paper cartons were commonly used.

Of all the milk bottles, there are two types that are of particular
interest to the collector. These are the "babytops," which had an embossed baby's face on the upper part of the neck, and the "cop-the-

cream," which had a policeman's head and cap embossed into the neck. Both of these clear-colored bottles, along with their tin tops, are very rare and valuable.

Babytops

Associated Dairies, Los Angeles
Orange and green babytop, quart $100

Bomgardener
Orange babytop, quart $75

Dickson City Dairy
Red babytop, quart $75

Fairyland Farms
Red babytop, quart $75

Fox Dairy, Fostoria, OH
Red babytop, ½ pint $75

Green's Dairy, Ashland, PA
Green babytop, quart $100

Hoffman's, Telford, PA
Red babytop, quart $100

McIntire Dairy, Bridgewater, MA
Orange babytop, quart $75

Ohio Child Conservation League, Mt Vernon, OH
Red babytop, half-pint $75

Orchard Farm Dairy, Schenectady, N.Y.
Orange babytop, quart $75

Page's
Orange babytop, quart $75

Parkdale Dairy, Washington, NJ
Orange babytop, quart $100

Pecora's Hazleton, PA
Black babytop, quart $75

Purity Dairy Co.
Green babytop quart $100

Mann's Sunny Acres, Dairy Farm, Chepachet, RI, quart, 1940s; Hennessey's Fruit Hill Stock Farm, North Providence, RI, quart, 1940s.

Riviera Dairy, Santa Barbara, Ca
Green babytop, quart $100

Sunbury Dairy
Orange babytop, quart $100

Twin's Farm Dairy
Black babytop, quart $75

Borden Milk Bottles

The Borden Milk Company was started by Gail Borden in 1857. The Civil War marked the turning point of the business since the Union Army contracted for most of Borden's output of condensed milk. After the war Borden took the American Bald Eagle as his trademark and named the product "Eagle Brand." Borden began selling fluid milk in 1875, and in 1885 started selling milk in bottles. At the 1939 World's Fair, Elsie the Cow was introduced.

Borden's Golden Crest
Brown and red, quart... $25

Borden's Golden Crest
Pint $25

Borden's Golden Crest
Half-pint $25

Cleveland Dairy Farm, Orange, VA, quart, 1945–1950.

Borden's N.Y. World's Fair
Gray and red, half-pint $25

Borden's Elsie
Red, quart $25

Borden's Elsie
Creamtop quart $50

Elsie Says—If It's Borden's
Half-pint $25

Borden's 1857–1937
Quart $50

Borden's Grove City, Pa.
Red and gold modern top pint $50

Borden's Gold and Red
Quart $25

Borden's Guernsey Farms
Orange, quart $25

Crop-the-Cream
Alameda Dairy, Alameda, CA
Orange, quart $100

America-First-Last-Always, quart, 1942–1945; Food Fights Too, Plan All Meals for Victory, 1942–1945.

Belmont Dairy, Warren, OH
Red, quart.. $100

Bentley's Dairy, Fall River, MA
Orange, quart $100

Collier's Meadow Crest Farm
Red, quart.. $100

Crombie Guernsey Dairy, Joliet, IL
Red, quart.. $100

Diamond Rock Creamery, Troy, NY
Red, quart.. $100

Fountain Head Dairy, Hagerstown, MD
Orange, quart $100

Frozen Gold State Milk, Sheboygan, WI
Black, half-pint $150

Glenside Dairy, Deep Water, NJ
Brown, quart.. $100

Green Acre Dairy, Newport, RI
Green, quart $75

Hillside Dairy, Whately, MA
Black, quart $100

Krueger's Dairy
Red, quart $100

Losten Dairy, Chesapeake City, MD
Orange, quart $100

Orchard Farm Dairy, Dallas, PA
Square, quart $45

Robert's Jersey Farm, Norway, ME
Quart $75

Royal Farm's Dairy, Baltimore, MD
Red, quart $100

West End Dairy, Jeanette, PA
Red, quart $100

Wolles Dairy, Sioux City
Red, quart $100

Cream Separators
Ideal Dairy, Fresno, CA
Orange, quart $75

Mission Creamery, Daly City, CA
Black, quart $75

One-Quarter Pints
Bentley Renckens, Dunkirk, NY
Red $20

Ceases Food Service
Red $25

Hygienic Dairy Co.
Red $15

Zenda Farms, Clayton, NY
Orange $15

Half-Pints
Arden Milk
Red, modern top $25

Beacon Dairies, Deland-Sanford, Fl
Orange $15

Carnation Dairy Reg. Cal (Unusual Milk Can Shape)
Red.. $25

Grant's Milk, Maine, East Aroostook Potatoes
Red.. $10

Harrisburger Hotel, Harrisburg, PA
Red.. $12

I.O.O.F. Home
Red.. $25

Jane Alden
Red.. $10

Mahelona Hospital, Kapaa, Kauai T.H.
Red.. $15

Missouri Pacific Line
Red.. $20

Onondaga Col. Home, Syracuse, N.Y.
Orange $15

Park Cafeteria
Green $10

Rosedale Dairy, Brampton-Ontario, Canada
Red.. $25

Taylor's Milk Electric Milk Truck
Red.. $25

Square Quarts
Broguiere's Dairy, Montebello, CA
Black and red, Desert Storm set $25

Brook Hill Farms, Acidolphilus Milk
Maroon $15

Dairylea
Red.. $6

Round Hill Dairy, Perfect Ice
Cream, quart, 1945–1950;
Coltsfood Farm, Cornwall, CT,
quart, 1945–1950.

Deerfoot Farms, Newton, MA
Red.. $6

Duncan's Dairy, Catskill, NY
Orange $5

Famous American Pioneers, Daniel Boone
Red.. $25

General Mills, Larro Feeds Advertising Bottle
Blue and orange $25

Harrisburg Dairy, 25th Birthday
Red, brown, and bluish green $10

Heatherwood Farms
Black, red, green $25

Jersey Dairy, 4-H Clubs
Green $25

McAnally's Dairy, Coyle, OK
Black $10

McCue's Dairy, Long Branch, NJ
Red.. $6

Model Dairy, Huron, SD
Red.. $20

Rutland Hill Co-op, Watertown NY
Orange $5

Sheyenne Valley Brand Milk, Cooperstown, ND
Red.. $15

Super Swiss, Sterling, MA
Brown $15

Woodlawn Square Dancers
Red.. $10

Woodland Farm Dairy, Boy Scouts of American, Founded Feb 8, 1910
Green $25

Square Ambers
  The square amber milk bottle was used by dairies to contain a special vitamin D milk. The quart size was the most common, with the pint, half-pint, and half-gallon being more rare.

Arthur Rochalau & Sons, St. Albans, VT
White, quart $10–12

Borden's with Elsie
White, quart $10–15

Co-op Dairy, Phoenix, AZ
White, quart $20–25

Assorted milk bottles one-fourth to one-half pints, 1880–1890.

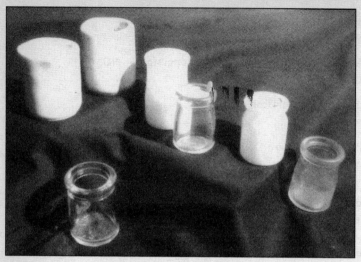

Coffee Creamers, 1880–1890.

Darigold Milk, Portland, OR
White, quart $10–12

Giacoruzzi Dairy, El Rio, Ca
White, quart $10–12

Iowa Golden Dairies
White, quart $10–12

Lady Pamela Dairy, Horseheads, NY
White, quart $10–12

Lancaster Creamery, Lancaster, MA
White, quart $12–15

Nehl's Dairy
White rectangle, 2-quart $8–12

Portage Co-op Creamery, Portage, WI
White rectangle, 2-quart $8-12

Sanitary's Best by Test Milk
White, quart $10–12

Sunshine Dairy, KY
Yellow and white, quart..$10–15

Winder Milk, Salt Lake City, UT
Yellow, quart $12–15

Witherell's Dairy, Rochester, NH
White, quart $12–15

Miscellaneous
High-Ground Dairy Co. (Motif of Stag's Head), Brooklyn, N.Y. 5 cents Store Bottle, One Quart, Registered "Store" Bottle (on base)
Clear, quart...$35–45

F. Buzzelli & Sons, Baby Top Patent Design, Niagara Falls, N.Y.
Clear, 9¼ in., quart..$50–80

One Quart, Mason Products Company
Clear, quart...$125–175
American 1900–1920 (rare, Elko, Nevada)

One Quart, Registered, Wm. Weckerle & Sons, W. 806 Jefferson St.
Amber, 9¼ in. quart..$50–80

Property of the N.Y. Condensed Milk Co., This Bottle Warranted to Contain One Full Quart
Clear, quart...$35–45

Half-pint milk, Tonopah, NV, 1900–1920.

Store Bottle, Pershing Creamery, Phone 42 (in a pattern with flower at side), Lovelock, Nevada
Clear, quart, green-painted label..$25–45

Try Miners Dairy Fresh Milk Pasteurized Compare the Flavor, Our Seal on Hood Gives You Extra Protection, No Hands Touch Pouring Lip of Bottle Until You Break the Seal and Remove Hood
Clear, quart, orange-and-red-painted label $25–40

Valley Dairy Phone 367 (In a Crest), Yerington, Nev. Drink Milk for Health and Energy
Clear, quart, magenta and red-painted label $25–40

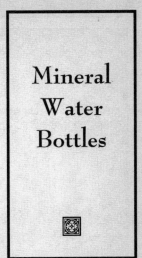

Mineral Water Bottles

The drinking of water from mineral springs was very popular for a full century, with the peak period falling between 1860 and 1900. The majority of collectible bottles were produced during these years. Although the shapes and sizes of mineral water bottles are not very creative, the lettering and design, both embossed and paper, are bold and interesting. Mineral water bottles can range in size from 7 to 14 inches. Most were cork-stopped, manufactured in a variety of colors, and embossed with the name of the glasshouse manufacturer and an eagle.

A. D. Schnackenberg & Co., Mineral Water, Brooklyn, N.Y.
Amber, 7¾ in., smooth base, applied mouth $300–400
American 1870–1880

Adirondack Spring, Whitehall, N.Y.
Emerald green, 7⅞ in. smooth base, applied mouth................$150–200
American 1865–1875

Artesian Spring Co., Ballston, N.Y., Ballston Spa, SA Mineral Water
Medium blue-green, 7¾ in., smooth base, applied mouth...........$65–85
American 1870–1880

B & G San Francisco Superior Mineral Water
Medium cobalt blue, 6½ in., pontil base, applied mouth........$200–400

B & G San Francisco
Medium blue, 6¾ in., pontil base, blob top.............................$400–800
American 1852–1856

W. Lant and Company.
Coventry—Registered; Tolenas
Soda Springs, Natural Mineral
Water, 1885–1910.

Boardman
Deep cobalt blue, 7⅛ in., iron pontil, applied mouth $125–175
American 1840–1855

B. B. Lippincott Stockton Superior Mineral Water, Union Glass Works
Medium cobalt blue, 7 in., pontil base, blob top $1,000–2,000
American 1852–1858

Buffman's Sarsaparilla & Lemon, Mineral Water, Pittsburgh
Medium cobalt blue, 7 in., iron pontil, applied mouth............$350–500
American 1840–1855

Burgess Mineral Waters—N.O.
Cobalt blue, 7¼ in., iron pontil, applied mouth...................$800–1,200
American 1845–1855 (extremely rare, New Orleans)

C. A. Reiners & Co. 723 Turk Street, S.F., Improved Mineral Water
Deep green-aqua, 7¼ in., pontil base, applied mouth $50–100
American 1875–1882

C. B. Hale, Camden, N.J.
Yellow–olive green, 6½ in., smooth base, applied mouth............$70–90
American 1855–1865

C. A. Reiners and Company,
723 Turk Street, San Francisco,
Improved Mineral Water,
1875–1882.

Champion Spouting Spring, Saratoga Mineral Spring, C.S.S. Limited Saratoga, N.Y., Champion Water
Aqua, 7 in., smooth base, applied mouth................................$125–150
American 1870–1880

Champion Spouting Spring Saratoga, N.Y., Champion Water
Aqua, 7⅞ in., smooth base, applied mouth.............................$200–300
American 1865–1875

Chase & Co. Mineral Water, San Francisco, Stockton & Marysville Calif.
Medium emerald green, 7¼ in., pontil base, blob top..........$500–1,000
American 1853–1855

Chas. Grove, Cola, Pa.
Medium emerald green, 7⅛ in., iron pontil............................$100–150
American 1840–1855

Clark & White, C, New York
Olive-amber, 7½ in., smooth base, applied mouth.....................$50–75
American 1855–1865

Congress & Empire Spring Co., Hotchkiss' Sons, C, New York, Saratoga, N.Y.—Congress Water
Medium olive green, 7⅝ in., smooth base, applied mouth......$100–150
American 1870–1875

Columbia Soda Works, S.F. C.C. Dall
Aqua, 7¼ in., smooth base, applied mouth..............................$200–300
American 1879–1881

D. A. Knowlton, Saratoga, N.Y.
Deep olive green, 7½ in, smooth base, applied mouth...............$70–90
American 1861–1863

Darien Mineral Springs, Tifft & Perry, Darien Centre, N.Y.
Aqua, 7⅝ in., smooth base, applied mouth........................$250–350
American 1870–1880

Deep Rock Spring, Trade, Deep Rock Mark, Oswego, N.Y.
Aqua, 7¼ in., smooth base, applied mouth.............................$175–250
American 1865–1880

Dr. Cronk—B&C
Sapphire blue, 10 in., iron pontil, applied mouth..............$2,500–3,500
American 1855–1870

Mills Seltzer Springs, 1874–1885.

Eagle in Slugplate
Light bluish green, 6¾ in., iron pontil, blob top $100–200
American 1860–1880

E. Harley, West Market St., Dyottville Glass Works, Philad
Emerald green, 7¼ in., iron pontil, applied top.......................$100–200
American 1855–1870

Empire Water
Emerald green, 9⅜ in., smooth base, applied mouth..................$50–75
American 1865–1880

E. Roussel's Mineral Waters Phila. Patent
Aqua, 6½ in., pontil, applied top $300–500
American 1855–1880

Geo. Gemenden, Savannah, Geo (Eagle, Shield, and Flags)
Deep emerald green, 7 in., iron pontil, applied mouth............$100–150
American 1840–1855

Ghirardelli's Branch, Oakland
Medium blue, 7½ in., smooth base, applied mouth $75–150
American 1863–1869 (scarce)

Golden Gate
Medium green, 7¼ in., smooth base, applied mouth.................$75–150
American 1850–1860

Guilford Mineral, Guilford, Vt.
Yellow-green, quart, smooth base, applied mouth $40–60
American 1865–1875

G. W. Weston & Co., Saratoga, N.Y.
Deep olive-amber, 7½ in., smooth base, applied mouth..........$100–150
American 1860–1870

H. Mau & Co., Eureka, Nevada
Medium bluish aqua, 7 in., smooth base, blob top..................$100–200
American 1882–1886 (scarce)

H. Brand & Co., Toledo, Ohio
Cornflower blue, 7¼ in., smooth base, blob top.......................$75–150
American 1885–1887 (scarce)

H. Rickett's & Co Glass Works, Bristol
Deep yellow-amber, 7¾ in., pontil base, applied mouth $60–80
England and American 1825–1840

Haas Brothers' Natural Mineral Water, Napa Soda, 1873–1877.

H. Sproatt, Toronto
Cobalt blue, 10 in., smooth base, applied mouth...............$2,500–3,500
Canadian 1855–1870 (extremely rare)

Hanbury Smith's Mineral Water
Yellow-olive, 8⅛ in., smooth base, applied mouth......................$50–75
American 1855–1875

Italian Soda Water Manufactory, San Francisco
Medium teal, 7¼ in., iron pontil, applied mouth $200–300
American 1856–1863

J. J. Sprenger, Holidaysburgh, PA
Deep sapphire blue, 7⅜ in., iron pontil, applied mouth $200–300
American 1840–1855 (rare)

John Clarke, New York
Yellow-olive-amber, 7⅜ in., pontil base, applied mouth...........$90–140
American 1850–1860

John H. Gardener & Son, Sharon Springs, N.Y., Sharon Sulphur Water
Teal blue, 7½ in., smooth base, applied mouth.......................$250–350
American 1865–1875

L. J. Miday & Co., Canton, Ohio
Aqua, quart, smooth base, applied mouth $50–80
American 1870–1880

Lynch & Clarke, New York
Yellow-olive-amber, 7⅛ in., pontil base, applied mouth..........$250–350
American 1845–1855

Lynde & Putman Mineral Waters, San Francisco, CAL, Union Glass Works Philadelphia
Teal blue, 7¼ in., iron pontil, applied top................................$300–500
American 1850–1851

Meinke & Ebberwein, 1882, Savannah
Cobalt blue, 7⅞ in., smooth base, applied mouth $50–75
American 1870–1880

Middletown Healing Springs, Grays & Clark, Middletown, VT
Yellow amber, 9½ in., smooth base, applied mouth................$500–800
American 1865–1875 (rare)

Minnequa Water, Bradford, Co., PA
Aqua, 9⅝ in., smooth base, applied mouth..............................$250–350
American 1875–1885 (rare)

Missisquoi, A. Springs
Deep bluish green, 9½ in., smooth base, applied mouth...........$90–150
American 1865–1870

Morgan Bros. & Co, New York—Superior Mineral Water, Union Glass Works, Philadelphia
Teal, 7¼ in., iron pontil, applied mouth...................................$150–200
American 1840–1855 (scarce)

New Century Mineral Water
Light greenish aqua, 7 in., smooth base, tooled top...................$50–100
American 1904–1910 (rare)

Oak Orchard, Acid Springs—H.W. Bostwick, Agt. No. 574, Broadway New York
Amber, 9 in., smooth base, applied mouth...............................$100–150
American 1865–1875

The Excelsior Water,
1850–1860

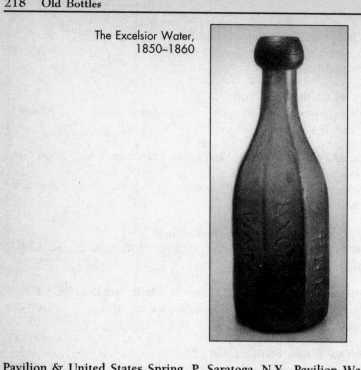

Pavilion & United States Spring, P, Saratoga, N.Y., Pavilion Water
Deep bluish green, 7½ in., smooth base, applied mouth.........$275–375
American 1865–1875 (scarce)

Star Spring Co. (Five-Pointed Star), Saratoga, N.Y.
Yellow-amber, 7⅝ in., smooth base, applied mouth $120–150
American 1865–1875

St. Regis, Water, Massena Springs
Medium bluish green, 9⅞ in., smooth base, applied mouth....$125–175
American 1870–1880 (scarce)

Washington Spring, Saratoga, N.Y.
Emerald green, 8 in., smooth base, applied mouth $250–325
American 1865–1875 (scarce)

Wm. Betz & Co., Pittsbg Mineral Water
Deep aqua, 7⅞ in., pontil base, applied mouth $125–200
American 1840–1855

Pattern-Molded Bottles

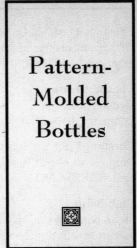

A pattern-molded bottle is one that is blown into a ribbed or otherwise pattern mold. This group includes globular and chestnut flasks. One of these, the Stiegel bottle, manufactured during the late eighteenth century, is considered very rare and valuable. The two types of Stiegel bottles manufactured at the Stiegel Glass Factory are the Diamond daisy and Hexagon designs.

Since pattern-molded bottles are among the more valuable and rare pieces, collectors need to familiarize themselves with the types, sizes, colors, and the various manufacturers of these bottles.

Chestnut Flask
Light blue-green, 4¾ in., pontil base, rolled mouth, 24 vertical ribs...$75–150
American 1820–1840

Chestnut Flask
Golden yellow, 4¾ in., pontil base, sheared mouth, 24 ribs swirled to left...$150–300
American 1820–1840

Chestnut Flask
Aqua, 4¾ in., pontil base, sheared lip, 10-diamond pattern....$225–350
American 1825–1835

Chestnut Flask
Yellowish amber, 5⅛ in., pontil base, sheared lip.................$200–300
American 1825–1835

Chestnut Flask
Orange amber, 5½ in., pontil base, applied string lip $175–225
American 1840–1850

Chestnut Flask
Medium amethyst, 6½ in., pontil base, sheared lip $200–300
European 1840–1860

Chestnut Flask
Deep cobalt blue, 6⅝ in., smooth base, applied lip................$150–200
French 1850–1880

Club Bottle
Bluish aqua, 7½ in., pontil base, applied mouth, 24-rib pattern
swirled to left $265–375
American 1820–1830

Globular Bottle
Yellow-amber, 7¾ in., pontil base, rolled mouth $200–400
American 1820–1840

Globular Bottle
Aquamarine, 8¼ in., pontil base, applied mouth $100–200
American 1820–1840

Freeblown Chestnut Bottle
Aquamarine, 9 in., pontil base, applied mouth...........................$50–100
American 1820–1850

Freeblown Chestnut Bottle
Aquamarine, 11 in., pontil base, applied mouth.........................$50–100
American 1820–1850

Freeblown Club Bottle
Yellow-olive, 8⅛ in., pontil base, rolled lip.............................$100–125
American 1790–1830

Freeblown Creamer
Medium cobalt blue, 4¾ in., pontil base...............................$800–1,200
American 1810–1830

Freeblown Globular Bottle
Aqua, 9¼ in., pontil base, rolled mouth......................................$30–50
American 1800–1830

Globular Bottle
Deep aqua, 9 in., pontil base, rolled mouth $60–80
American 1825–1835

Globular Storage/Utility Bottle
Medium yellow-olive, 9 in., pontil base, rolled lip..................$125–175
European 1790–1820

Jacobs & Brown, Hamilton, Ohio
Aqua, 5¾ in., pontil base, applied mouth....................................$70–90
American 1820–1830

Molded Bottle
Aquamarine, 6¾ in., pontil base, applied mouth with string rim, 18
vertical ribs...$100–200
American 1820–1840

Molded Midwestern Swirl
Bluish aqua, 8 in., pontil base, applied mouth, 24 ribs swirled to
right pattern $150–250
American 1820–1835

Midwestern Grandfather's Flask
Deep amber, 7¾ in., pontil base, sheared lip, 24 broken-rib pattern
swirled to right..$1,000–1,500
American 1820–1830

Midwestern Grandfather's Flask
Medium amber, 8⅛ in., pontil base, sheared lip, 24 vertical-rib
pattern $800–1,500
American 1825–1835

Midwestern Chestnut Flask
Light yellow, 5¾ in., pontil base, sheared lip, 16 vertical-rib
pattern $275–375
American 1820–1830

Midwestern Chestnut Flask
Yellow-olive, 4¾ in., pontil base, sheared lip, 24 vertical-rib
pattern $400–500
American 1820–1830

Midwestern Chestnut Flask
Deep reddish amber, 5 in., pontil base, sheared lip, 24 broken-rib
pattern swirled to left..$400–600
American 1820–1830 (rare)

Midwestern Chestnut Flask
Medium amber, 5⅛ in., pontil base, sheared lip, 18-rib pattern
swirled to right...$150–250
American 1820–1830

Midwestern Chestnut Flask
Yellow-olive, 6⅞ in., pontil base, sheared lip, 20 vertical broken-rib
pattern $450–550
American 1820–1830

Midwestern Club Bottle
Yellow-green, 7⅞ in., pontil base, applied mouth, 24 broken-rib
pattern $100–125
American 1790–1830 (rare color)

Midwestern Club Bottle
Deep greenish aqua, 7⅝ in., pontil base, rolled lip, 18 vertical-rib
pattern $100–125
American 1790–1830

Midwestern Globular Swirl Bottle
Medium yellow-green, 7½ in., pontil base, rolled lip, 24-rib pattern
swirled to right...$400–700
American 1820–1830

Midwestern Globular Bottle
Medium amber, 8⅛ in., pontil base, rolled lip.........................$275–350
American 1820–1830

Midwestern Globular Bottle
Medium amber, 9⅛ in., pontil base, rolled lip.........................$275–400
American 1820–1830

Midwestern Pitkin Flask
Medium green, 6⅝ in., pontil base, sheared lip, 32 broken-rib pattern
swirled to right...$300–450
American 1810–1830

Midwestern Pitkin Flask
Medium olive-green, 5⅛ in., pontil base, sheared lip, 36 broken-rib
pattern swirled to right $275–375
American 1790–1810

Pitkin Flask
Yellow with olive tone, 6¾ in., pontil base, sheared lip, 36 broken-rib
pattern swirled to right $300–400
American 1790–1810

Stiegel Type Flask
Deep purple amethyst, 5¾ in., pontil base, sheared lip, 20 vertical-
rib pattern $1,500–2,000
American 1780–1800

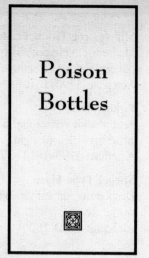

Poison Bottles

Poison bottles are a unique category for collecting by the very nature of their contents. While most people assume that poison bottles are plain, the fact is that most are very decorative in order to make them easily identifiable as containers of toxic substances. Around 1853, the American Pharmaceutical Association recommended laws for identification of all poison bottles. In 1872, the American Medical Association also recommended that poison bottles be identified with a rough surface on one side and the word *poison* on the other. As so often happened during that era, passing of these laws was very difficult and the manufacturers were left to do whatever they wanted. Because a standard wasn't established, a varied group of bottle shapes, sizes, and patterns were manufactured, including the skull and crossbones, or skulls, leg bones, and coffins.

These bottles were manufactured with quilted or ribbed surfaces and diamond/lattice-type patterns for identification by touch. Colorless bottles are very rare since most poison bottles were produced in dark shades of blue and brown, another identification aid. When collecting these bottles, caution must be exercised since it is not uncommon to find a poison bottle with its original contents. If the bottle has the original glass stopper the value will greatly increase.

Poison AEC
Amber, 9⅛ in., tooled lip, ground glass stopper.........................$30–50
American 1890–1910

Poison-Poison, Patent Applied For, Bears Oil Sold by Thomas Hollis Company, Boston, Mass.
Cobalt blue, 5 in., smooth base, tooled lip...............................$100–150
American 1890–1910

Poison—H. K. Mulford
Company, Chemist,
Philadelphia, cobalt-blue,
1900–1910.

Poison, Bowker's Pyrox
Clear, 4⅛ in., smooth base $30–50
American 1890–1910

Carbolic Acid Kirwin-Porter Drug Co. (Lattice & Diamond Pattern)
Clear, 4⅜ in., smooth base, tooled lip...$35–60
American 1890–1910

**Champion Embalming Fluid, The Champion Chemical Co.,
Springfield, Ohio—Poison (56 oz. graduation)**
Clear, 10¾ in., smooth base, tooled lip......................................$90–125
American 1890–1920

Poison-Poison, C.L.C. & Co., Pat. Appl'd For
Cobalt blue, 3⅜ in., smooth base, tooled lip $75–100
American 1890–1910

Poison-Poison, C.L.C. & Co., Pat. Appl'd For
Cobalt blue, 4⅞ in., smooth base, tooled lip $75–100
American 1890–1910

Poison-Poison, C.L.C. & Co., Pat. Appl'd For
Moss green, 5½ in., smooth base, tooled lip............................$125–175
American 1890–1910

Poison-Poison, Diamond Antiseptics Bernarys, Eli Lily and Co.
Yellow-amber, 10⅛ in., smooth base, tooled mouth $175–250
American 1890–1910 (scarce in this large size)

Assortment of various poisons, 1900–1920.

Poison (Skull and Crossed Bones) DP—Poison
Medium cobalt blue, 2⅞ in., smooth base, tooled lip..............$600–900
American 1890–1910 (coffin-shaped poison)

Poison (Skull and Crossed Bones) DP—Poison
Cobalt blue, 3 in., smooth base, tooled lip...............................$500–700
American 1890–1910 (coffin-shaped poison)

Dodge—Poison (64 oz. graduation)
Clear, 11½ in., smooth base, tooled lip......................................$75–100
American 1890–1920

Poison, Durfee Embalming Fluid Co., Grand Rapids, Mich. (60 oz. graduation)
Clear, 11 in., smooth base, tooled lip..$90–125
American 1890–1920

Poison, Excelsior Preservative, Prepared by Prof. E. Crane, Kalamazoo, Mich.
Clear, 6⅝ in., smooth base, tooled lip......................................$100–175
American 1890–1910 (rare)

Poison (Skull and Crossed Bones) H. K. Mulford Co., Chemist, Philadelphia (Skull and Crossed Bones) Poison
Cobalt blue, 3⅛ in., smooth base, tooled lip...........................$100–150
American 1890–1910

Poison, J.T.M. & Co.
Clear, 2½ in., smooth base, tooled lip.......................................$275–425
American 1890–1910 (rare in clear, usually found in amber)

Poison, J.T.M. & Co., Mercury Bichloride, Abbott Laboratories, North Chicago
Amber, 5 in., smooth base, tooled lip.......................................$500–800
American 1890–1910 (rare in this size)

Poison-Jacob's Bichloride—Tablets (Skull and Cross Bones) Poison
Amber, 2¼ in., smooth base, tooled lip $600–900
American 1890–1910 (extremely rare)

Jacob Julle—Not To Be Taken—Strychnine
Cobalt blue, 5¾ in., smooth base, tooled lip $20–30
English 1890–1920

Jacob Julle—Not To Be Taken—Strychnine
Amber, 5¾ in., smooth base, tooled lip $20–30
English 1890–1920

McCormick & Co., Balto (In Circle around Bee), Patent Applied For
Cobalt blue, 2⅛ in., smooth base, tooled lip $15–20
American 1890–1915

Poison, N.B. & Co., Pat. App'd For
Amber, 2½ in., smooth base $150–250
American 1890–1910 (Scarce)

Poison-Poison, P.D. & Co.
Clear, 2⅝ in., smooth base, tooled lip..$35–60
American, 1890–1910

Ser-C-Sol Elliott Poison—Poison—Not To Be Taken—Ser-C-Sol, Elliot—Not To Be Taken
Golden yellow-amber, 5¼ in., smooth base, rolled lip, triangular shape
with indented panels..$150–200
American 1890–1910 (extremely rare)

Sharpe & Dohme—Baltimore
Amber, 2¼ in., smooth base, tooled lip $10–20
American 1890–1910

Gift—poison bottle (German), 1900–1910.

Strychnia Poison
Clear, 2½ in., smooth base, tooled lip..$60–80
American 1890–1910

The Imperial Fluid Company, Poison, Syracuse, N.Y.
Clear, 8⅝ in., smooth base, tooled lip...$75–100
American 1890–1920

The Owl Drug Co—Poison
Cobalt blue, 2¾ in., smooth base $35–60
American 1890–1910

The Owl Drug Co—Poison
Cobalt blue, 3¼ in., smooth base $35–60
American 1890–1910

The Owl Drug Co—Poison
Cobalt blue, 3⅞ in., smooth base, tooled lip $100–150
American 1890–1910

The Owl Drug Co—Poison
Amber, 3¼ in, smooth base, tooled lip $100–150
American 1890–1910

Poison—The Sun Drug Co—Poison
Yellow-green, 3⅜ in., smooth base, tooled lip..........................$100–150
American 1890–1910

Poison—Triloids
Cobalt blue, 1⅝ in., smooth base, tooled lip $20–30
American 1890–1915

Sarsaparilla was advertised as a "cure-all" elixir, which actually makes these bottles a subset of the "Cures" or "Bitters" category. In the seventeenth century, sarsaparilla was touted as a blood purifier and later as a cure for the dreaded venereal disease, syphilis. As time passed, sarsaparilla was recognized as nothing more than the "snake oil" sold at the medicine shows. As you can see from the image of "The Red Root of Jamaica" label (below), the bottle labels were unique and very ornate. One of the most popular brands among collectors is Doctor Townsend, which was advertised as "The Most Extraordinary Medicine in the World." Usually, these bottles are aqua or green. Blues and other dark colors are rarer.

Dr. Guystott's Yellow Dock and Sarsaparilla, 1862.

Buffum's Sarsaparilla & Lemon Mineral Water, Pittsburgh
Deep cobalt blue, 7⅝ in., iron pontil, applied mouth $700–900
American 1840–1855

Dr. Guystott's Yellow Dock & Sarsaparilla, Cincinnati
Aqua, 10 in., iron pontil, applied top $50–150
American 1862–1865

Hall's Sarsaparilla, J. R. Gates & Co., Proprietors San Francisco
Medium green, 9½ in., applied top $75–150
American 1855–1865

Dr. Henry's Sarsaparilla
Medium bluish aqua, 9½ in., applied top $50–150
American 1850–1860

Dr. J. Dennis's Georgia Sarsaparilla, Augusta, Ga.
Aqua, 10¼ in., iron pontil, applied mouth $800–1,500
American 1845–1855 (extremely rare)

Halls Sarsaparilla, 1855.

Dr. Henry's Sarsaparilla, 1890.

Dr. J. S. Felger, Ashland, Ohio
Amber, 8⅞ in. $100–150
American 1885–1900 (rare)

Dr. King's Sarsaparilla, Dr. King Remedy Company, Proctorville, Ohio, Chicago, Ill., U.S.A.
Aqua, 9¼ in..$100–150
American 1885–1900 (rare)

Dr. Meyers Vegetable Extract Sarsaparilla Wild Cherry Dandelion, Buffalo, N.Y.
Medium bluish aqua, 9¼ in., iron pontil, applied top.............$150–300
American 1850–1860

Dr. Townsend's Sarsaparilla, Albany, N.Y. (Sample)
Aqua, 4½ in., smooth base, tooled mouth $150–225
American 1880–1890

Dr. Townsend's Sarsaparilla, Albany, N.Y.
Yellow-amber, 9 in., smooth base, applied mouth....................$275–375
American 1855–1865 (extremely rare)

Dr. Townsend's Sarsaparilla, Albany, N.Y.
Teal blue, 9¼ in., smooth base, applied mouth.......................$150–200
American 1855–1865

Dr. Townsend's Sarsaparilla, Albany, N.Y.
Olive green, 9½ in., pontil base, applied mouth......................$175–275
American 1845–1855 (rare in this color)

Indian Sarsaparilla, J. J. Mack & Co.
Aqua, 9 in., smooth base, double-collared lip...........................$150–225
American 1865–1885

Irwin M. Gray & Co., Gray's Sarsaparilla, Montrose, Pa.
Aqua, 8½ in., smooth base, tooled lip..$75–150
American 1880–1900

J. & T. Hawk's Masury's Sarsaparilla Compound, Rochester, N.Y.
Aqua, 11¼ in., smooth base, applied mouth............................$250–350
American 1860–1870

Kennedys Sarsaparilla
Aqua, 9½ in., smooth base, double-collared lip.......................$150–180
American 1880–1900

Log Cabin Sarsaparilla, Rochester, N.Y.
Amber, 8⅞ in., smooth base, applied mouth...........................$150–200
American 1880–1890

Turners Sarsaparilla, Buffalo, N.Y.
Deep aqua, 12 in., smooth base, applied mouth......................$300–400
American 1880–1900

Wetherells Sarsaparilla
Aqua, 9⅜ in., smooth base, applied mouth...............................$75–100
American 1885–1900

Snuff was basically composed of tobacco mixed with ingredients of salt, different scents, and flavors such as cinnamon and nutmeg. It was usually mixed in a powder form, and inhaling snuff was much more fashionable than smoking or chewing tobacco. It was yet another substance touted as a cure-all, in this case for sinus problems, headaches, and numerous other problems.

Most of the snuff bottles from the eighteenth and early nineteenth centuries were embossed, dark brown or black, with straight sides. They were either square or rectangular in shape, with beveled edges and narrow bodies with wide mouths. In the latter part of the nineteenth century, the bottles were colorless or aqua and rectangular or cylindrical, with occasional embossing and possibly labels.

Doct. Marshalls Snuff
Aqua, 3⅓ in., labeled $50–75

E. Roome, Troy, N.Y.
Olive green, 4½ in...$150–175

E. Roome, Troy, N.Y.
Olive-amber, 4½ in...$150–200

E. Roome, Troy, N.Y.
Pale blue-green, 4¼ in..$550–750

Garrett Snuff Co.
Brown, 4 in., blown mouth $5–7

Hockin Duke St., London
Dark olive green, 4 in., pontil, applied top $150–250
English 1840–1860

E. Roome, Troy, NY, 1845.

Levi Garrett & Sons
Amber, 4³⁄₈ in. $175–225

Otto Landsberg & Co., Celebrated Snuff
Cobalt, 5 in. $20–25

Railroad Mill Snuff
Amber, 4½ in. $10–15

Rectangular, with Beveled Edges
Olive-amber, 6¼ in..$30–40

Square Snuff Bottle
Yellow-amber, 4 in. $125–150

True Cephalic Snuff by the Kings Patent
Aqua, 3³⁄₄ in...$150–200

True Cephalic Snuff by the Kings Patent
Deep aqua, 3½ in. $150–175

Wymans Copenhagen Snuff
Amber, quart $60–80

Snuff
Medium olive green, 4¹⁄₈ in., sheared top, open pontil................$30–50
American 1850–1860

Soda
Bottles

After years of selling, buying, and trading, I think that the soda bottle supports one of the largest collector groups in the United States. Even collectors who don't normally seek out soda bottles always seem to have a few on their tables for sale (or under the table).

Soda bottles, as a rule, are not unique in design since the manufacturers had the task of producing bottles as cheaply as possible to keep up with demand. The only way to distinguish among bottles is by the lettering, logos, embossing, or labels (not very common).

Soda is basically artificially flavored or unflavored carbonated water. In 1772, an Englishman named Joseph Priestley succeeded in defining the process of carbonation. Small quantities of unflavored soda were sold by Professor Benjamin Silliman in 1806. By 1810, New York druggists were selling homemade seltzer as a cure-all for stomach problems. By 1881, flavoring was included in these seltzers.

The first commercially sold soda was Imperial Inca Cola, its name inspired by the Native American Indian, which promoted medical benefits. The first truly successful cola drink was developed in 1886 by Dr. John Styth Pemberton of Atlanta, Georgia. It's known today as Coca-Cola. Carbonated water was added to Coca-Cola in 1887. By 1894, bottled Coca-Cola was taking off. The familiar configuration of the Coke bottle as we now know it was designed in 1915 by Alex Samuelson. Numerous inventors attempted to ride on the coattails of Coke's success. The most successful of these inventors was Caleb Bradham, who started Brad's drink in 1890, and in 1896 changed it name to Pep-Kola. In 1898, it was changed to Pipi-Cola, and by 1906 to Pepsi-Cola. The taste war goes on today.

Pacific Congress Water, blob-top soda, 1869–1876.

Non Pareil Soda Water Company (rare), 1881–1887.

With the advent of the soda bottle and the use of carbonation, the age of closure inventions set in. Various entrepreneurs developed the Hutchinson-type wire stoppers, lighting stoppers, and cod stoppers.

A. P. Smith, Charleston, S.C.
Deep cobalt blue, 7½ in., iron pontil, applied top $200–400
American 1865–1875

A.R. Cox, Norristown, PA
Medium emerald green, 7¼ in., iron pontil, applied
mouth $100–140
American 1840–1860

Backus & Pratt, Binghampton, N.Y.
Blue, 7⅝ in., iron pontil, applied mouth....................................$75–100
American 1840–1860

Baldwin Tuthill & Co., 112 Warren St., New York
Medium emerald green, 7 in., iron pontil, applied mouth...........$50–65
American 1840–1860

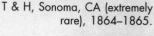

T & H, Sonoma, CA (extremely rare), 1864–1865.

A. J. Wintle and Sons, Bill Mills, N. R. Ross, 1880–1900 (European).

Big Chief, Modesto, CA
Green glass, 10 oz., head of Indian chief with headress $250–300
American 1956

Big Chief, Long Pine, NB
Clear glass, 8 oz., face of Indian chief with headress.................$10–15
American 1950s

Big Ten, Pleasant City, Oh
Clear glass, 10 oz., football player..$10–15
American 1957

Black Kow, Columbus, OH
Amber glass, 12 oz., cow face with tongue hanging out..............$15–25
American 1951

Blue Rock, Chicago, IL
Clear glass, 12 oz., Statue of Liberty..$25–30
American 1949

Breig & Schafer S.F. (Picture of Fish)
Bluish aqua, 7 in., smooth base, blob top $100–300
American 1879–1890 (scarce)

Bremenkampf & Regli, Eureka, Nev.
Light lime green, 7 in., smooth base, applied top $300–500
American 1878–1885

Bum's Root Beer, Los Angeles, Calif.
Amber glass, 8 oz., Bum's face with cigar.....................................$75–100
American 1942

Burr & Waters—Bottlers—Buffalo, N.Y., This Bottle to Be Returned
Cobalt blue, 7⅜ in., iron pontil, applied mouth................$1,000–1,500
American 1840–1855 (rare)

California Soda Works, H. Ficken, San Francisco (Picture of Eagle on reverse)
Deep lime green, 7 in., smooth base, applied top $700–1,200
American 1878–1879 (rare)

Canada Dry, Lyndon B. Johnson, TX
Clear glass, 7 oz . Vice-President's seal.......................................$150–200
American 1964

C. B. Hale & Co., Camden, N.J.
Emerald green, 6¾ in., iron pontil, applied mouth $150–200
American 1840–1855

Champagne Mead
Medium lime green, 7¼ in., smooth base, blob top $300–400
American 1871–1872 (rare)

C & K Eagle Works, Sac City
Cobalt blue, 7¼ in., smooth base, blob top $50–125
American 1858–1866

Coca-Cola Bottling Works, Phoenix, Ariz.
Aqua, 8 in., crown top $100–125
American 1900–1910

Coca-Cola, Trade Mark Registered, Rome, Ga.
Amethyst, 7½ in., crown top $80–100
American 1900–1910

Lancaster Glass Works, NY,
1850–1860.

C & L Eagle Works,
1858–1866.

Coca-Cola, Knoxville, Tenn.
Amber, 7½ in., crown top..$75–100
American 1905–1910

Columbia Soda Works, San Francisco DD Dall (Seated Liberty)
Medium bluish aqua, 7 in., smooth base, blob top.................$200–400
American 1879–1881 (rare)

Comstock Cove & Co., 139 Friend St., Boston, C. G. & Co.
Medium green, 6¾ in., smooth base, blob top $50–150
American 1855–1865 (scarce)

Cottle Post & Co., Portland, Ore.
Amber, 7 in., smooth base, tooled top...................................$600–1,400
American 1877–1887 (extremely rare)

Craven—Union Glass Works, Philadelphia
Peacock blue, 7⅜ in., pontil base, applied mouth $75–100
American 1840–1855

Cross
Medium green, 7¼ in., graphite pontil, blob top....................$200–400
American 1855–1865 (rare, may have held Holy water)

Crystal Soda Water Co., Patented Nov. 12, 1872, Taylor's USPT
Deep greenish aqua, 7¾ in., smooth base, applied top.............$50–150
American 1873–1886

Dr. Pepper Bottling Works, Edna, Tex.
Clear glass, 8 oz., 100 percent embossed.....................................$35–50
American 1930

D. O. Kane—Dyottville Glass Works, Philadelphia
Deep green, 7 in., iron pontil, applied mouth..............................$50–60
American 1840–1860

D. S. & Co. San Francisco
Deep blue, 6¾ in., smooth base, applied top...........................$200–400
American 1861–1864

D. S. & Co. San Francisco
Deep blue-turquoise, 7¼ in., smooth base, blob top $500–1,500
American 1861–1864 (rare color)

D. S. Rahn, Perkiomenville
Medium blue-green, smooth base, applied mouth....................$300–400
American 1860–1870

E. A. Post, Portland, Ogn
Blue aqua, 7 in., smooth base, applied top...............................$200–400
American 1881–1883 (rare)

Empire Soda Works, San Francisco
Green, 7 in., smooth base, applied top.....................................$200–400
American 1861–1871 (rare in this color)

Empire Soda Works D&M, San Francisco
Deep aqua, 7½ in., smooth base, applied top............................$50–150
American 1864–1865 (scarce)

F. Dusch, This Bottle Never Sold
Medium cobalt blue, iron pontil, applied mouth.....................$125–175
American 1845–1855

Luke Bear, 1860–1867.

Fields—Superior—Soda Water, Charleston, S.C.
Cobalt blue, 7¼ in., iron pontil, applied mouth..................$800–1,200
American 1845–1855

Gardner & Co., Hackettstown, N.J.
Sapphire blue, 6¾ in., smooth base, applied mouth................$300–400
American 1855–1865

Hass Bro's Natural Mineral Water, Napa Soda
Deep blue-aqua, 6¾ in., smooth base, applied top..................$100–200
American 1873–1877

H. Knebel, 458 Fourth St., New York, Union Glass Works, Improved Mineral Water
Bluish aqua, 7 in., graphite pontil, applied top...........................$75–150
American 1845–1855 (scarce)

Haddock & Sons
Yellowish olive, 6⅞ in., pontil base, rolled lip.........................$750–850
American 1820–1830 (torpedo shaped)

H. L. & J. W. Brown, Hartford, Ct.
Dark olive-amber, 6⅜ in., iron pontil, applied mouth.............$175–230
American 1840–1860

E. Wideman and J. Chappaz (bitters) 1861–1863; Dr. Henley's Wild Grape Root, IXL Bitters 1868; Pride of Kentucky Old Bourbon, Livingston and Company Sole Agents 1874–1879; J.F. Cutter, Extra Old Bourbon 1870–1875.

Collection of early Rexall store medicines 1885–1900.

Dr. S.S. Fitch medicine collection 1850–1860.

Hale's Honey of Horehound and Tar;
Vegetable Pulmonary Balsam; London;
Umbrella Ink 1850–1865.

OS Good's India
Cholagogue; Dr. Wistar's
Balsam of Wild Cherry;
Mrs. S.A. Allen's Worlds
Hair Balsam 1850–1875.

Case gin grouping: TJAP
TOEWANE. KIDELEN;
BB.A.J. WITHTKAM PF
Schiedam; Sealed Gin with
Insignia 1860–1870.

John Ryan mineral and soda collection: John Ryan 1852; John Ryan 1866; John Ryan Ginger Ale 1852; John Ryan Gravitating Stopper; John Ryan Excelsior Union Glass Works 1852–1877.

Hawaii soda water bottles: Maui; Kurtistown; LaHaina; Kohala 1865–1907.

Collection of soda bottles 1865–1885.

Owl Drug Store Poison
1890–1900.

Cottle Post and Company,
Portland, Ore. 1877–1887.

Log Cabin Hops and
Buchu Remedy 1880.

Climax Bitters,
San Francisco 1875.

D.A. Knowlton
Saratoga, N.Y. 1865–1880.

Wm. H. Keith and Company
Apothecaries, San Francisco
1851–1857.

The Fish Bitters, W.H. Ware Patented 1866; Royal Imperial Gin London 1875; National Bitter, Patent 1867; Stafford Ink 1880; Medicine (Picture of Owl with Trademark) 1885; Cathedral Pickle 1875.

Fish's Infallible Hair Restorative 1863; J. Moore Old Bourbon, E. Chielovigh and Company Sole Agents 1877; Miller's Extra E Martin and Company Old Bourbon 1871–1874; Dr. Henley's Wild Grape Root IXL Bitters 1868–1872; Old Sachem Bitters and Wigwam Tonic 1860–1865; Keyhole Sauce 1845–1855.

Selection of bitters, whiskeys, medicines, mineral water, sodas, and inks.

Selection of Dr. J. Hostetter's Stomach Bitters 1875.

Liberty-Freedom-Equality Half-Pint 1942–1945; Kusel Dairy Equipment Company, Watertown, Wis. 1945.

Larsen Cognac, Invincible (Sixteen Different Colors) Miniature 1980s.

Stewart's Trade Wind,
Jamaica Rum Miniature 1950s.

Uncle Sam on the Barrel, "What We
Want", Miniature early 1900s.

Mount Gay Eclipse Rum; Black Heart
Demerara Rum Miniature 1950s.

Frontier Beverages; Aspinock Beverages 1942–1945.

Selection of soda bottles with applied labels 1940–1950.

Hogan & Thompson, San Francisco, Cal., Union Glass Works Philadelphia
Medium deep cobalt, 7¼ in., graphite pontil, applied
top $2,000–4,000
American 1854–1860 (rare)

J. Monier & Co., CL FR Na
Blue-green, 7 in., graphite pontil, blob top...............................$200–600
American 1856–1858 (rare)

J. Lake, Schenectady, N.Y.
Deep sapphire blue, 7½ in., iron pontil, applied mouth $425–525
American 1840–1860

J. T. Brown, Chemist, Boston Double Soda Water
Deep cobalt blue, 8¾ in., smooth base, applied mouth...........$750–850
American 1860–1870 (torpedo shaped)

J. Tweddle Jr.'s Celebrated Soda of Mineral Waters—Barclay Street 41, New York
Medium blue-green, 7½ in., iron pontil, applied mouth $90–120
American 1840–1855

J. Wise, Allentown, Pa., This Bottle Belongs to James Wise
Medium cornflower blue, 6¾ in., smooth base, blob top..........$50–150
American 1850–1860 (scarce)

Jackson's Napa Soda Springs, Natural Mineral Water F. M. Vallejo
Medium bluish aqua, 7 in., smooth base, blob top.................$300–800
American 1890–1905 (rare)

John Seedorf, Charleston, S.C., Soda Water
Cobalt blue, 7½ in., iron pontil, applied mouth......................$225–275
American 1840–1855

Keys, Burlington, N.J.
Medium blue-green, 7 in., iron pontil, applied mouth.............$350–375
American 1840–1860

Knicker Bocker Soda Water, 18S. S52
Deep sapphire blue, 7⅝ in., iron pontil, applied mouth $175–200
American 1840–1860

Owen Casey Eagle Soda
Works, 1867–1871.

J. D. Stellmenn, Palmyra, NY; Ashland
Bottling Works, Ashland, WI; John
Howell, Buffalo, NY; 1885–1900.

Lancaster Glass Works, New York

Light blue, 7¼ in., iron pontil, blob top $50–150
American 1845–1860

L. C. Smith

Deep cobalt blue, 7¼ in., iron pontil, applied mouth $140–170
American 1840–1860

Mr. Sacrimento, Union Glass Works, Philadelphia

Bluish green, 7 in., graphite pontil, blob top $1,000–2,000
American 1851–1863 (rare, misspelling on Sacramento)

Mr. Sacramento, P.C.

Deep cobalt blue, 7¼ in., graphite pontil, blob top $500–1,200
American 1851–1863

Napa Soda Natural Mineral Water

Deep sapphire blue, 7¼ in., smooth base, applied mouth.......$250–300
American 1860–1865

Napa Soda Phil Caduc Natural Mineral Water

Medium cobalt blue, 7 in., smooth base, applied mouth $300–500
American 1873–1881 (scarce)

Owen Casey Eagle Soda Works, SAC City
Deep sapphire blue, 7¼ in., smooth base, applied mouth...........$55–65
American 1860–1870

Owen Casey Eagle Soda Works, SAC City
Medium green, 7½ in., smooth base, applied mouth...............$200–400
American 1867–1871 (rare in this color)

P. Conway Bottler Philadelphia, No. 8 Hunter St. & 108 Filbert St.
Cobalt blue, 7 in., iron pontil, applied mouth $90–110
American 1840–1850

P. B. Colusa, Calif.
Aqua, 7 in., smooth base, blob top...$200–400
American 1887–1888 (rare)

Pearson Bros. Bodie
Aqua, 7¼ in., smooth base, applied top................................$800–1,500
American 1881–1887 (extremely rare, less than 10 known)

Soda bottles: Drink Clown Brand Beverages; Raaz's Better Beverages; Club Soda Sparkling Water; Chester Club Quality Beverages; 1945–1968.

Soda bottles: Big Boy Quality Beverages; Barr's Soda; Springtime Anytime; Nezi N Scot Beverages; 1945–1955.

Pepsi-Cola, Darlington, S.C.
Light amethyst, 8½ in., tooled top...$50–75
American 1900–1910

Pepsi-Cola, Charlottesville, VA, Pepsi-Cola, Registered
Aqua, 8¼ in., crown top...$50–75
American 1910–1920

Phoenix Glass Works, Brooklyn
Pale green, 7⅛ in., iron pontil, applied mouth........................$350–400
American 1840–1855

Pioneer Brown & Co.
Blue-aqua, 7¼ in., smooth base, blob top...............................$300–600
American 1866–1869

Polar Pak, San Diego, CA
Clear glass, 7 oz., bear sitting on iceberg.................................$20–30
American 1944

This Bottle is the Property of O'Neil Brothers, North Fitzroy; A. J. Wintle and Sons, Bill Mills, N. R. Ross; 1880–1900 (European).

Premium, Newton, New York
Emerald green, 7 in., iron pontil, applied mouth.........................$50–70
American 1840–1860

S. Smith, Auburn, N.Y.
Cobalt blue, 7½ in., smooth base, applied mouth $275–350
American 1855–1865 (round bottom)

San Francisco Glass Works
Deep green, 7 in., smooth base, applied mouth $300–600
American 1870–1876 (rare in green)

Seitz & BR Easton, Pa, "S" on Back
Medium cobalt blue, 7¼ in., smooth base, applied mouth......$100–200
American 1840–1860

Seymour & Co., Buffalo, N.Y.
Cobalt blue, 7⅛ in., iron pontil, applied mouth......................$300–400
American 1840–1855

Snappy, Los Angeles, CA
Green glass, 6½ oz., Eastern woman, radio tower, globe.........$200–225
American 1937

Sparks Bottling Company, Sparks, Nevada
Greenish aqua, 10 in., smooth base, crown top $300–700
American 1905–1907 (extremely rare, less than 10 known)

San Francisco Glass Works,
1870–1876.

Solon Spring Water Beverages,
12 ounces, 1940.

Steinke & Kornahrens Soda Water, Return This Bottle, Charleston, S.C.
Cobalt blue, 8 in., iron pontil, applied mouth $500–700
American 1845–1855 (rare)

Stephens & Jose, Virginia City, Nevada
Light blue–aquamarine, 7¼ in., gravitating stopper $1,500–2,000
American 1874

Southwick & Tupper, New York
Deep cobalt blue, 7⅜ in., iron pontil, applied mouth $275–350
American 1840–1860

The Excelsior Water
Medium green, 7¼ in., iron pontil, applied mouth $50–150
American 1845–1855

Nevada City Soda Works, L. Seibert, 1885.

Pioneer Soda Water, San Francisco, 1897–1906.

Tonopah Soda Works, Nev.
Light greenish aqua, 6¾ in., smooth base $800–1,600
American 1902–1905 (extremely rare, only 15 known)

Tower Root Beer, Charleston, MA
Amber glass, 7 oz., small picture of castle tower......................$100–125
American 1955

Tweddles Celebrated Soda Mineral Waters, Courtland Street 38, New York
Medium green, 7¼ in., iron pontil, applied top......................$100–200
American 1840–1860

Uncle Tom's Root Beer, San Bernardino, CA
Clear glass, 28 oz., black waiter $400–450
American 1952

King Cotton, Fine Flavors, 1955–1960.

Union Lava Conshohocken, Patented 1852
Deep cobalt blue, 7¼ in., iron pontil, applied top $50–150
American 1852–1860

Valley Spring, Phoenix
Clear glass, 32 oz., prospector in desert with donkey..................$10–15
American 1949

Valentine & Vreeland, Newark, N.J., Supr. Soda Water, Union Glass Works, Philadelphia
Cobalt blue, 7⅜ in., iron pontil, applied mouth......................$125–150
American 1845–1855

Williams & Severance, San Francisco, Calif., Soda and Mineral Waters
Medium green, 7¼ in., graphite pontil, applied mouth..........$200–400
American 1852–1854

Yankee Doodle Root Beer, Los Angeles, Calif.
Clear glass, 29 oz., Minuteman playing fife $40–50
American 1949

Eagle in Slug Plate, 1895.

Pioneer Soda Works, San
Francisco, 1897–1905.

CHRONOLOGY OF THE GLASS PACKAGE FOR COCA-COLA
1894 ——— 1975

Archives
The Coca-Cola Company
Atlanta, Georgia

Chronology of Coca–Cola Bottles, 1894–1975.

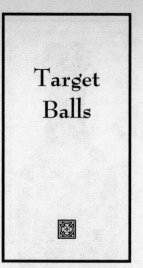

Target Balls

Target balls, which are small rounded bottles, were filled with confetti, ribbon, and other items. They were used for target practice from the 1850s to the early 1900s. They gained considerable popularity during the 1860s and 1870s with the Buffalo Bill Cody and Annie Oakley Wild West shows. Around 1900, clay pigeons started to be used in lieu of target balls. Because they were made to be broken, they are unfortunately extremely difficult to find, and are very rare, collectible, and valuable.

Boers & CP Delft Flesschenfabriek
Light green, 2¾ in., sheared opening $1,000–1,500
Dutch 1880–1890 (extremely rare)

Bogardus Glass Ball, Patd. April 10, 1877
Olive green, 2⅝ in., sheared opening $300–400
American 1880–1890

Charlottenburg Glasshutten F. W. Otte Jun
Clear, 2⅝ in., sheared opening $400–600
German 1885–1895 (extremely rare)

E. E. Eaton Guns & C. 53 State St., Chicago
Golden yellow-amber, 2⅝ in., sheared opening $800–1,400
American 1880–1890 (rare)

Gurd & Son, 185 Dundas Street, London, Ont.
Amber, 2¾ in., sheared opening...$400–600
Canadian 1880–1890 (scarce)

Ira Paine's Filled Ball, Pat. Oct. 23, 1877
Light yellow, 2⅝ in., sheared opening......................................$350–450
American 1880–1890

L. Jones Gunmaker Blackburn Lancashire
Cobalt blue, 2⅝ in., sheared opening......................................$200–300
English 1880–1890

L. Jones Gunmaker Blackburn Lancashire
Light sapphire blue, 2¾ in., sheared opening..........................$150–200
English 1880–1890

N. B. Glass Works Perth
Aqua, 2⅝ in., smooth base, sheared opening............................$80–110
English 1880–1890

N. B. Glass Works Perth
Cobalt blue, 2⅝ in., smooth base, sheared opening..................$80–120
English 1880–1890

Patent Applied For
Yellow-amber, 2½ in., sheared opening, hobnail
pattern $1,000–1,500
American 1880–1890 (rare)

Patd Sept 16th 1877
Light olive green, 2⅝ in., sheared opening........................$1,800–2,800
American 1877–1885 (rare, Whitail Tatum Company of South Jersey)

Sophienhutte in Ilmenau (Thur.)
Amber, 2⅝ in., sheared opening...$350–450
German 1885–1895 (rare)

Van Gutsem—A St.-Quentin
Light cobalt blue, 2½ in., sheared opening..............................$250–350
French 1880–1890

Van Gutsem—A St.-Quentin
Deep cobalt blue, 2½ in., sheared opening..............................$175–275
French 1880–1890

W. W. Greener St. Marys Works, Brimm & Haymarket, London
Cobalt blue, 2⅝ in., sheared opening...$80–120
English 1880–1890

W. W. Greener St. Marys Works, Brimm & Haymarket, London
Light pinkish amethyst, 2⅝ in., sheared opening.....................$275–375
English 1880–1890

Target Ball
Cobalt blue, 2¾ in., sheared opening, diamond pattern..........$250–350
American 1880–1885

Target Ball
Aqua, 2¾ in., sheared opening, blown in three-piece mold $200–300
American 1880–1890 (rare)

Target Ball
Deep cobalt blue, 2¾ in., sheared opening, diamond
pattern $200–300
French 1880–1890 (scarce)

Target Ball (Motif of Man Shooting in Two Opposite Circles)
Medium pinkish amethyst, 2½ in., sheared opening................$250–350
American 1880–1890

Warner Bottles

The Warner bottle was named for H. H. Warner, who sold a number of remedies developed by a Dr. Craig. Warner developed his bottle for those and other cures and began producing great volumes and varieties (over twenty) in 1879 in Rochester, New York.

Warner bottles can frequently be found with their original labels and boxes, giving additional value to these already expensive and rare bottles.

H. H. Warner & Co., Tippecanoe, Pat. Nov 20 83, Rochester, N.Y.
Amber, 9 in., smooth base, applied mouth......................................$70–90
American 1875–1885

H. H. Warner & Co. Tippecanoe, Rochester, N.Y.
Amber, 9⅛ in., smooth base, applied mouth $50–75
American 1875–1885

Warner's Safe Diabetes Cure (Motif of Safe), London
Yellowish olive green, 9¼ in., smooth base, applied mouth....$275–350
English 1885–1890

Warner's Safe Diabetes Cure (Motif of Safe), Rochester, N.Y.
Amber, 9½ in., smooth base, applied mouth $120–170
American 1875–1885

Warner's Safe Diabetes Cure (Motif of Safe), London
Yellow with amber tone, 9⅜ in., smooth base, applied
mouth $120–170
English 1885–1895

Warner's Safe Diabetes Cure (Motif of Safe), Schutz Marke, Frankfurt A/Main
Red amber, 9⅜ in., smooth base, applied mouth......................$500–800
German 1880–1890 (extremely rare)

Warner's Safe Kidney & Liver Remedy (Motif of Safe), Rochester, N.Y.
Medium amber, 9½ in., smooth base, tooled mouth...................$35–50
American 1885–1895

Warner's Safe Kidney & Liver Cure (Motif of Safe), Rochester, N.Y.
Medium amber, 7½ in., smooth base, applied mouth.................$55–70
American 1880–1895

Warner's Safe Nervine (Motif of Safe), Rochester, N.Y.
Medium amber, 7½ in., smooth base, applied mouth.................$65–85
American 1885–1895

Warner's Safe Nervine (Motif of Safe) Trade Mark, Rochester, N.Y.
Amber, 9½ in., smooth base, applied mouth...............................$50–75
American 1885–1895

Warner's Safe Nervine, 1875.

Warner's Safe Tonic, Rochester, NY, 1875.

Log Cabin—Scalpine—Rochester, N.Y., Pat. Sept. 6, 87
Amber, 8⅝ in., smooth base, applied mouth $300–400
American 1887–1895 (rare)

Log Cabin—Scalpine—Rochester, N.Y. Pat. Sept. 6, 87
Amber, 9 in., smooth base, tooled mouth................................$300–400
American 1880–1890 (rare)

Warner's Safe Cure (Motif of Safe), London
Yellow-amber, 4⅝ in., smooth base, tooled mouth $350–450
English 1880–1890 (smallest of Warner bottles)

Warner's Safe Rheumatic Cure (Motif of Safe) Trade Mark, Melbourne, Aus.
Medium amber, 9½ in., smooth base, tooled mouth $125–175
Australian 1880–1890

Warner's Safe Cure (Motif of Safe), Frankfurt A/M
Deep olive green, 9⅛ in., smooth base, applied mouth...........$600–900
German 1880–1895

Warner's Safe Cure (Motif of Safe) Trade Mark, Frankfurt A/M
Red-amber, 9¼ in., smooth base, applied mouth.....................$400–600
German 1880–1895

Warner's Safe Cure (Motif of Safe) Schutz Marke, Pressburg
Red-amber, 9¼ in., smooth base, applied mouth.....................$600–800
European 1880–1900

Warner's Safe Cure (Motif of Safe), Rochester, N.Y., U.S.A., London, England, Toronto, Canada
Orange-amber, 9½ in., smooth base, tooled mouth...................$80–120
American 1885–1895

Warner's Safe Cure (Motif of Safe), London, Eng, Toronto, Canada, Rochester, N.Y.
Medium reddish amber, 11 in., smooth base, applied
mouth $400–600
American 1875–1890 (commonly referred to as the Animal Cure)

Warner's Safe Remedy (Motif of Safe), Rochester, N.Y.
Medium amber, 7½ in., smooth base, applied mouth $30–50
American 1885–1890

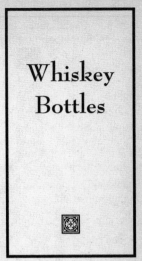

Whiskey Bottles

Whiskeys, sometimes referred to as spirits, come in an array of sizes, designs, shapes, and colors. The whiskey bottle dates back to the nineteenth century and the avid collector can acquire rare and valuable pieces.

In 1860, E. G. Booz manufactured a whiskey bottle in the design of a cabin embossed with the year 1840 and the words "Old Cabin Whiskey." One theory has it that the word *booze* was derived from his name to describe hard liquor. The Booz bottle is given the credit of being the first to emboss a name on whiskey bottles.

After the repeal of Prohibition in 1933, the only inscription that could be found on any liquor bottle was "Federal Law Forbids Sale or Re-use of This Bottle," which was continued through 1964.

Adolph Harris & Co. (Antlered Deer Head), San Francisco
Medium amber, 12 in., smooth base, tooled lip $300–500
American 1902–1906 (scarce)

Ahrens-Bullwinkle Co., Trade (Antlered Deer Standing) Mark, San Francisco, Calif.
Medium yellow-amber 11½ in., smooth base, tooled lip $900–1,300
American 1900–1910 (rare)

Altona, J. T., Gayen
Olive-amber, 9¼ in., smooth base, applied mouth $140–180
Dutch 1850–1870

A. M. Bininger & Co., New York
Amber, 9⅞ in., smooth base, applied mouth $75–125
American 1860–1870

Tea Cup Extra Old Bourbon, 1890–1910.

A. M. Bininger & Co., 19 Broad St., N.Y.
Yellowish amber, 12¼ in., smooth base, sheared lip $800–1,200
American 1860–1870

Bourbon Whiskey from A. P. Hotaling, Old Private Stock, San Francisco
Medium amber, 11⅞ in., smooth base, applied mouth $2,500–3,500
American 1879–1885 (scarce)

Barry & Patten 114 & 116 Montgomery Street, San Francisco
Medium olive-amber, 11¼ in., pontil base, blob top............$500–1,200
American 1855–1860

Bartletts Glass Ware, Whiskey Cylinder
Yellow-olive, 11¾ in., smooth base, applied mouth.................$150–200
American 1860–1875

Bear Grass Kentucky Bourbon, Braunschweiger N. Bumstead Sole Agents, S.F.
Medium amber, 11½ in., smooth base, tooled top $3,000–6,000
American 1881–1885 (rare)

Hotel Donnelly, Tacoma (rare),
1895–1900.

Washington Bar, Coleman and
Granger, Tonopah, NV,
1905–1906.

**Bear (Bear Head in a Triangle) Grass Bourbon, S.F.,
Braunscheweiger & Co**
Clear, 11¾ in., smooth base, tooled lip.....................................$300–500
American 1895–1905

**Bear Grass Kentucky Bourbon, Braunschweiger & Bumstead, Sole
Agents, San Francisco**
Amber, 12 in., smooth base, large applied mouth..............$3,500–5,500
American 1881–1885

Bennett & Carroll, No. 120 Wood St., Pittsburgh, Pa.
Yellow-amber, 8⅜ in., iron pontil, applied mouth...................$500–800
American 1855–1865

Bennett & Carroll, No. 120 Wood St., Pittsburgh, Pa.
Medium yellow-amber, 9½ in., iron pontil, applied mouth.....$400–600
American 1855–1865

**Bottled by J. Gundlach & Co., California Wine & Brandies, San
Francisco**
Clear, 11⅜ in., smooth base, applied mouth.........................$600–1,200
American 1880–1885 (scarce)

Bulkley, Fiske & Co., New York, B.F. & Co N.Y.
Tan and olive glaze, 7⅛ in., handled stoneware whiskey
flask $250–350
American 1860–1870

**Bininger's Old Kentucky Bourbon, 1849 Reserve, Distilled in 1848
A.M. Bininger & Co, No. 13 Broad St., N.Y.**
Medium amber, 9⅝ in., smooth base, applied mouth $120–160
American 1860–1870

**Bininger's Old Kentucky Bourbon, 1849 Reserve, Distilled In 1848
A. M. Bininger & Co., No. 19 Broad St., New York**
Medium orange-amber, 9¾ in., smooth base, applied
mouth $150–200
American 1860–1870

Bininger's Peep-O-Day, No. 19 Broad St.
Yellow-amber, 7¾ in., smooth base, applied lip.......................$300–500
American 1860–1870

**Bouquet Pure Rye Whiskey, Humphrey & Martin, Phila, Label Under
Glass Back Bar Bottle**
Clear, 9⅛ in., polished pontil, tooled and flared lip................$400–600
American 1890–1900 (extremely rare)

Buchanans Extract of Sugar Corn
Golden amber, 8¾ in., smooth base, tooled mouth...........$1,000–1,500
American 1875–1885 (rare)

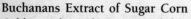

Old Kirk, A.P. Hotaling and
Company, Whiskey,
1900–1910.

Henry Campe and Company, Wholesale Liquor Dealers, San Francisco, CA, 1895–1900.

Quaker Club Old Rye, S. B. Rothenberg, 1895.

Buffalo Bourbon, Geo. E. Dierssen & Co., Sacramento, Cal
Light amber, 12 in., smooth base, tooled mouth.......................$300–800
American 1896–1909 (rare)

C. Sandheger, Peach & Honey, Label Under Glass Back Bar Bottle
Amber, 11¾ in., smooth base, applied mouth $375–475
American 1875–1885

Casper's Whiskey Made by Honest North Carolina People
Cobalt blue, 11⅞ in., smooth base, applied mouth $375–450
American 1880–1890

Casper's Whiskey Made by Honest North Carolina People
Cobalt blue, 12 in., smooth base, tooled mouth........................$350–450
American 1880–1895

Chestnut Grove Whiskey C.W.
Amber, 8⅝ in., pontil base, applied mouth...............................$150–200
American 1860–1870

Choice Old Cabinet Kentucky Bourbon, Crane Hastings & Co., Sole Agents, San Francisco
Light golden amber, 11½ in., smooth base, applied top.......$800–1,800
American 1878–1883

Cognac W. & Co. (On Applied Seal)
Medium amber, 5¾ in., pontil base, applied mouth...............$400–600
American 1860–1870 (rare)

Crown Distilleries Company
Red, 12 in., smooth base, embossed screw top $200–400
American 1899–1901

Daniel Schaeffer's Log Cabin Whiskey
Medium amber, smooth base, inside screw threads.................$400–800
American 1890–1900

Naber, Alfs and Brune
Wholesale Liquor Dealers, San
Francisco, 1880–1883.

Old J. H. Cutter Back Bar
Whiskey, 1890–1910.

Wicker Pattern Whiskey;
Malcolm Fraser & Co. Ancient
Liqueur; 1900–1920.

D. B. Lester Grocer, Savannah, Ga.
Amber, 9½ in., smooth base, applied mouth $150–200
American 1880–1890

Denver Club Whiskey Trademark with Insignia
Light greenish aqua, 10½ in., smooth base, applied top $300–800
American 1875–1885

Dougherty's Old Rye Whiskey, Label Under Glass Back Bar Bottle
Clear, 8¾ in., pontil base, tooled lip.......................................$175–275
American 1880–1900

**Dr. Miller's Ratafia Damiana. Siebe Bros. & Plagemann S.F. Sole
Agents, Pacific Coast**
Chocolate amber, 11¼ in., smooth base, applied top..............$300–700
American 1878–1879 (rare)

E. N. Cooke & Co Distillers, Buffalo, N.Y.
Amber, 9¾ in., smooth base, applied mouth $125–175
American 1875–1885

**Established 1793 Coates & Co.s Original Plymouth Gin, Black Friars
Distillery Plymouth, England, Back Bar Bottle**
Clear, 8½ in., polished pontil, flared lip $275–375
American 1890–1910

Teakettle Old Bourbon—Shea, Bocqueraz and McKee Agents, San Francisco, 1873–1885; J. H. Cutter Old Bourbon, C. P. Moorman Manufacturing, Louisville, KY, 1873–1879; Pure Rye Whiskey, Alfred Greenbaum and Company, Sole Agents, 1889–1892.

Evans & O'Brien, No. 222 Main St., Stockton
Light yellow-amber, 10¾ in., smooth base, applied mouth $2,000–3,000
American 1869–1875

Fine Old Brandy, Label Under Glass Back Bar Bottle
Clear, 9¼ in., polished pontil, tooled lip $375–475
American 1880–1910

Forest Lawn J.V.H.
Olive green, 7½ in., iron pontil, applied mouth $300–500
American 1860–1870

G. Ebberwein, Savannah Geo, Mineral G.E. Water
Light sapphire blue, 7½ in., smooth base, applied mouth...........$25–40
American 1875–1885

G. O. Blake's Bourbon Ky. Whisky, Moore, Reynolds & Co., Sole Agents for Pacific Coast
Medium yellowish amber, 12 in., smooth base, applied mouth $3,000–4,500
American 1875–1880

Good Samaritan Brandy, Gentry, Slote & Co., New York
Olive amber, 7 in., large iron pontil, applied mouth $375–500
American 1865–1875 (rare)

Griffith Hyatt & Co., Baltimore
Medium olive green, 7⅜ in., open pontil, applied mouth.......$700–900
American 1855–1865

H. Pharazyn, Phila, Right Secured
Yellow-amber, 12¼ in., smooth base, sheared lip $800–1,200
American 1870–1875 (scarce figural whiskey bottle)

H.A. Graef's Son, New York Canteen
Deep yellow–olive green, 6⅝ in., smooth base, applied
mouth $400–700
American 1875–1885 (rare in this coloration)

H. Ricketts & Co., Glass Works Bristol, Bininger (Cluster of Grapes), New York
Deep olive-amber, 11¼ in., pontil base, applied mouth $1,000–2,500
American 1855–1865

Henry Kuck, 1878, Savannah, Ga.
Emerald green, 7¼ in., iron pontil, applied mouth $25–40
American 1875–1885

Imperial Levee, J. Noyes, Hollywood, Miss.
Yellowish amber, 9⅜ in., iron pontil, applied mouth $1,200–1,800
American 1855–1870

Daniel Schaeffer's Log Cabin
Whiskey, 1897.

Imported by R. F. Nichols & Co., Camp St., New Orleans
Deep olive-amber, 11½ in., pontil base, applied mouth $600–900
American 1840–1860 (blown in a three-piece mold)

J.F.T. & Co., Philad
Golden yellowish amber, 7 in., pontil base, applied mouth.....$400–600
American 1855–1865

J. H. & C. F. Miller, 58 Varick & 17, 19, 21, and 23 Laigh St., N.Y.
Medium amber, 7½ in., smooth base, applied mouth $250–350
American 1865–1875 (coffin-type flask)

J. H. Cutter Old Bourbon, A. P. Hotling & Co., Sole Agents
Dark amber, 11¾ in., smooth base, applied top $300–400
American 1873–1880

J. H. Cutter Old Bourbon, A. P. Hotling, Sole Agents
Medium amber, 11⅞ in., smooth base, applied mouth $600–800
American 1877–1880

J. H. Cutter Extra Trade (Star Inside Shield) Mark, Old Bourbon
Medium yellowish amber, 12 in., smooth base, applied
mouth $80–120
American 1880–1891

J. H. Cutter Old Bourbon, E. Martin & Co., Sole Agents
Light amber, 12 in., smooth base, applied mouth....................$300–600
American 1874–1879

J. N. Kline & Cos, Aromatic Digestive Cordial
Amber, 5½ in., smooth base, applied mouth $300–400
American 1865–1875 (teardrop flask)

J. N. Kline & Cos, Aromatic Digestive Cordial
Deep cobalt blue, 5½ in., smooth base, applied mouth...........$375–475
American 1865–1875 (rare with these colors)

JNO. F. Horne, Knoxville, Tenn.
Golden amber, 9½ in., smooth base, tooled mouth.................$125–175
American 1880–1890

Jordan Giles & Co
Medium yellowish amber, 12 in., smooth base, applied
mouth $750–1,250
American 1873

Common Whiskey, glob-top,
1905–1915.

Common Whiskey, applied lip,
1900–1915.

Jos. Melczer & Co. Wholesale Liquor Dealers, San Francisco, Calif.
Clear, 11¼ in., smooth base, applied top.................................$300–600
American 1890–1910

Kane, O'Leary & Co, 221 & 223 Bush St. S.F.
Medium amber, 12⅛ in., smooth base, applied mouth $1,500–2,500
American 1879–1881

Kellogg's Nelson County Kentucky Bourbon
Light yellow, 11¾ in., smooth base, tooled top.......................$400–700
American 1889–1910 (inside screw threads)

L. Lyons Pure Ohio Catawba Brandy, Cini
Deep amber, 13⅜ in., smooth base, applied mouth $250–350
American 1870–1880

Lilienthal & Co (Crown over Monogrammed Shield) Distillers
Medium yellow-amber, 11¾ in., smooth base, applied
mouth $175–250
American 1874–1880

Kellogg's Nelson Country
Kentucky Bourbon,
1885–1905.

M. Rothenberg & Co, San Francisco, Calif.
Medium orange-amber, 11½ in., smooth base, tooled lip.....$750–1,250
American 1900–1910

Mohawk Whiskey, Pure Rye—Patented Feb. 11, 1868
Yellow-amber, 12⅜ in., smooth base, sheared lip and rolled
lip $1,800–2,800
American 1868–1875

**N. VanBergen & Co., Gold Dust Kentucky Bourbon, N. Van Bergen
Sole Props.**
Blue-aquamarine, 11¾ in., smooth base, applied top.........$1,200–2,000
American 1865–1885

Naber, Alfs & Brune, Wholesale Liquor Dealers, San Francisco
Medium amber, 11⅝ in., smooth base with high kick-up, tooled
lip $1,000–1,500
American 1880–1888

Naber Alfs & Brune, Wholesale Liquor Dealers, San Francisco
Medium amber, 11½ in., smooth base with high kick-up, applied
lip $2,000–3,000
American 1880–1888

O. K. Old Bourbon Castle Whiskey F. Chevalier & Co., Sole Agents
Medium amber, 11⅞ in., smooth base, applied top.................$300–600
American 1875–1880

Okolona Rye Whiskey, Label Under Glass Back Bar Bottle
Clear, 9⅛ in., polished pontil, tooled mouth $275–375
American 1885–1900

Old Wheat Whiskey, S.M. & Co
Amber, 11⅛ in., pontil base, applied mouth...........................$275–350
American 1860–1870

O. K. Old Bourbon Castle
Whiskey, 1875–1880.

Wolters Brothers and Company, 115 and 117, Front Street, San Francisco, 1886–1895.

Buffalo Old Bourbon, George E. Dierssen and Company, 1896–1909.

Orofino Portlando
Medium amber, 11¾ in., smooth base, applied mouth $800–2,000
American 1880–1885 (*oro fino* translates to "fine gold")

Oscar Sheuzac & Co. Bordeaux
Clear, 10½ in., open pontil, laid on ring on top $1,500–3,000
American 1845–1850

Pure Malt Whiskey, Bourbon Co., Kentucky
Amber, 8⅝ in., smooth base, applied mouth and handle $500–800
American 1865–1875 (rare)

R. B. Cutter, Louisville, Ky.
Amber, 8⅝ in., open pontil, applied mouth and handle $275–325
American 1860–1870

Relda Pure Rye, Back Bar Bottle
Clear, 11⅛ in., smooth base, tooled mouth $700–900
American 1885–1910

Russ Aromatic Schnapps, New York
Deep bluish aqua, 9⅞ in., iron pontil, applied mouth $200–300
American 1855–1865

R. B. Cutter Pure Bourbon
Medium pinkish puce, 8⅜ in., iron pontil, applied mouth $350–450
American 1860–1870

Simmond's Nabob
Yellow-amber, 10¾ in., smooth base, applied mouth $70–90
American 1880–1885

Simmond's Nabob
Medium amber, 10¾ in., smooth base, applied mouth $70–90
American 1880–1885

S. S. Smith, Jr., & Co., Cincinnati, O
Cobalt blue, 9⅝ in., smooth base, applied mouth $1,000–1,800
American 1870–1875 (extremely rare)

St. George Vineyard (Motif of St. George on Horse Spearing a Dragon), San Francisco, Calif.
Medium yellow-amber, 11⅛ in., smooth base, applied
mouth $125–175
American 1900–1906 (scarce)

Assortment of black glass whiskey bottles, 1870–1890.

Assortment of various types of whiskey bottles, 1870–1920.

O. K. Old Bourbon Castle
Whiskey, F. Chevalier and
Company, Sole Agents,
1875–1880.

Golden Eagle Distilleries, San
Francisco, CA, 1902–1910.

Spruance Stanley & Co. (In a Horseshoe) Wholesale Liquor Dealers, San Francisco
Medium amber, 11⅞ in., smooth base, applied mouth $275–325
American 1888–1895

Star Whiskey, New York, W. B. Crowell Jr
Golden yellow-amber, 8⅛ in., pontil base, applied mouth $350–450
American 1860–1870

The Campus Gossler Bros. Prop's, N.W. Cor. 104 Str. & Columbus Ave., N.Y.
Amber, 9¾ in., smooth base, applied mouth $125–150
American 1880–1890

T. J. Dunbar & Co
Olive-amber, 9⅜ in., iron pontil, applied tapered mouth $125–175
American 1845–1855 (rare)

The Old Mill, Whitlock & Co
Medium amber, 8⅛ in., pontil base, applied mouth................$250–350
American 1860–1870

Turner Brothers, New York
Medium olive green, 9¾ in., smooth base, applied
mouth $700–1,000
American 1860–1870 (rare in this color)

Dancing Lady, 1890–1900.

Dancing Lady, (reverse side of
bottle), 1890–1900.

Unembossed back bar whiskey barrel 8⅜", 1865–1875; Old Kentucky Reserve Bourbon 8", 1849–1850.

Udolpho Wolfe's Schiedam Aromatic Schnapps
Deep yellow–olive green, 9½ in., iron pontil, applied mouth....$90–140
American 1850–1860

Vidvard & Sheehan
Yellow-olive, 9¾ in., smooth base, applied mouth with pour spout and handle...$1,200–1,800
American 1865–1875

Collection of whiskey bottles, 1860–1890.

Collection of whiskey bottles, 1860–1890.

**W. A. Gaines, Frankfort, K.Y., S.F. Private Stock, Livingston & Co.
Sole Agents**
Deep medium amber, 12 in., smooth base, applied top...........$300–500
American 1876–1885

W. C. Peacock & Co., Honolulu, Hi, Wine & Liquor Merchants
Medium amber, 11 in., smooth base, tooled top......................$100–200
American 1885–1895

Weeks & Gilson So., Stoddard, N.H.
Olive-amber, 11⅞ in., smooth base, three-piece mold, applied
mouth, whiskey cylinder..$275–400
American 1865–1875 (rare)

Wharton's Whiskey Chestnut Grove
Medium cobalt blue, 5⅛ in., smooth base, applied mouth......$300–400
American 1860–1870

Whitney Glass Works
Olive-green, 11¼ in., smooth base, applied mouth, whiskey
cylinder...$80–120
American 1860–1875 (rare)

Wm. Daly—Sole Importer—New York
Olive-green, 9¼ in., pontil base, applied mouth, bell
shape..$500–800
American 1865–1875

Wolters Bros & Co., 221 California St. S.F.
Medium amber, 12 in., smooth base, glob top...................$2,000–3,000
American 1881–1885 (rare)

New Bottles

New Bottles: Post-1900

The bottles listed in this section have been broken down solely by characteristics of the bottles themselves. The contents of these groups hold little interest for the collector. New bottles covered in this section are valuable precisely for their decorative, appealing, and sometimes unique designs.

The goal of most new-bottle collectors is to collect a complete set of items designed and produced by a favorite manufacturer. As it is with the reproductions of old bottles such as Coca-Cola, or new items such as the Avon items, the right time to purchase is when the first issue comes out on the retail market, or prior to retail release if possible. As with the old bottles, I have provided a good cross section of new bottles in various price ranges and categories rather than listing only the rarest or most collectible pieces.

The pricing shown reflects the value of the particular item listed. Newer bottles are usually manufactured in limited quantities without any reissues. Since retail prices are affected by factors such as source, type of bottle, desirability, condition, and the possibility that the bottle was produced exclusively as a collectors' item, the pricing can fluctuate radically at any given time.

Bottle Grading

Pricing for new bottles is dependent upon a number of variables that break down into the following three categories:

1. Rarity and demand of the specific bottle
2. Type of bottle based on historical or event-oriented condition
3. Unique features

labeling
color
design
manufacturer's production errors

After the above variables have been determined, bottles are then categorized, just as the older bottles are, as falling into one of the following conditions:

1. **Mint**—An empty or full bottle (preferably full) with a label or embossing. Clear in color and clean, with no chips, scrapes, or evident wear. If there is a box, it must also be in good condition.
2. **Extra Fine**—An empty bottle with the label showing only slight wear, or embossing. Clear in color, clean, with no chips or scrapes, but some wear. Usually there is no box, or the box is not in very good condition.
3. **Very Good**—The bottle shows some wear and its label is usually missing or not very visible. Most likely there is no embossing and no box.
4. **Good**—Bottle reflects additional wear and label is completely absent. Color is usually faded and bottle is dirty. It's common to see some scrapes and minor chips, and most likely there will be no box.
5. **Fair or Average**—Bottle shows much wear, the label is missing, and there is no embossing. The color is very faded and the piece has numerous scrapes, chips, or even cracks. It will definitely come without an accompanying box.

Even with the preceding guidelines, it is important to have access to additional resources for grading rare and unusual bottles that present the collector with a real challenge—and a feeling of accomplishment when the collector does discover its origin. The bibliography of this book provides a listing of references I find very useful. Remember, too, that other collectors and dealers represent a wealth of unique information and experience. Use them!

Avon Bottles

The cosmetic empire known today as Avon began as the California Perfume Company, was the creation of D. H. McConnell, a door-to-door book salesman who gave away perfume samples to stop the doors from slamming in his face. As time went on, McConnell gave up on books and concentrated on selling perfumes. Although based in New York, the name Avon was used in 1929 along with the name California Perfume Company or C.P.C. After 1939, the company operated exclusively under the name Avon. Bottles embossed with C.P.C. are very rare and collectible owing to the small quantities issued and the even smaller quantity that have been well preserved.

Today Avon offers the collector a wide range of products in bottles shaped like cars, people, chess pieces, trains, animals, sporting items (footballs, baseballs, etc.), and numerous other objects. The most scarce pieces and sought-after are the pre–World War II figurals. They're very hard to find, but almost all are well preserved.

To those who collect Avon items, anything Avon related is considered collectible. That includes boxes, brochures, magazine ads, or anything else labeled with the Avon name. Since many people who sell Avon items are unaware of the individual piece value, a collector can find great prices at swap meets, flea markets, and garage sales. While this book offers an excellent detailed cross section of Avon collectibles, I recommend that serious collectors obtain Bud Hastings's new *14th Edition of Avon Products & California Perfume Co. (CPC) Collector's Encyclopedia,* which offers pricing and pictures on thousands of Avon & California Perfume Co. (CPC) products from 1886 to present.

A Man's World, Globe on stand 1969 ....$7–10

A Winner, Boxing gloves 1960 ....$20–25

Ballad Perfume, 3 drams, ⅜ ounce 1939 ....$100–125

Bath Urn, Lemon Velvet Bath Oil 1971–1973 ....$4–5

Beauty Bound Black Purse 1964..$45–55

Bell Jar Cologne 1973...$5–10

Benjamin Franklin, Wild Country After-shave 1974–1976..........$4–5

Big Game Rhino, Tai Winds After-shave 1972–1973 ....$7–8

Big Whistle 1972...$4–5

Bird House Power Bubble Bath 1969..$7–8

Bird of Paradise Cologne Decanter 1972–1974...........................$4–5

Blacksmith's Anvil, Deep Woods After-shave 1972–1973............$4–5

Bloodhound Pipe, Deep Woods After-shave 1976 ....$5–6

Blue Blazer After-shave Lotion 1964...$25–30

Blue Blazer Deluxe 1965 ....$55–65

Blue Moo Soap on a Rope 1972 ....$5–6

Blunderbuss Pistol 1976 ....$7–10

Bon Bon Black, Field and Flowers Cologne 1973 ....$5–6

Bon Bon White, Occur Cologne 1972–1973...............................$5–6

Bon Bon White, Topaze Cologne 1972–1973..............................$5–6

Boot Gold Top, Avon Leather After-shave 1966–1971................$3–4

Boot Western 1973..$4–5

Boots and Saddle 1968 ....$20–22

Brocade Deluxe 1967 ....$30–35

Buffalo Nickel, Liquid Hair Lotion 1971–1972..........................$4–5

Bulldog Pipe, Oland After-shave 1972–1973 ....$4–5

Bunny Puff and Talc 1969–1972 ....$3–4

American Buffalo 1975...$6–8

American Eagle Pipe 1974–1975 ....$6–8

American Eagle, Windjammer After-shave 1971–1972................$3–4

American Ideal Perfume,
California Perfume Company 1911 ....$125–140

American Schooner, Oland After-shave 1972–1973....................$4–5

Andy Capp Figural (England) 1970 ....$95–105

Angler, Windjammer After-shave 1970..$5–7

Apple Blossom Toilet Water 1941–1942..................................$50–60

Apothecary, Lemon Velvet Moist Lotion 1973–1976..................$4–6

Apothecary, Spicy After-shave 1973–1974..................................$4–5

Aristocrat Kittens Soap (Walt Disney)...$5–7

Armoire Decanter, Charisma Bath Oil 1973–1974 ....$4–5

Armoire Decanter, Elusive Bath Oil 1972–1975 ....$4–5

Auto Lantern 1973 ....$6–8

Auto, Big Mack Truck, Windjammer After-shave 1973–1975 .....$5–6

Auto, Cord, 1937 Model, Wild Country After-shave
1974–1975...$7–8

Auto, Country Vendor, Wild Country After-shave 1973 ....$7–8

Auto, Dusenberg, Silver, Wild Country After-shave
1970–1972...$8–9

Auto, Dune Buggy, Sports Rally Bracing Lotion 1971–1973......$4–5

Auto, Electric Charger, Avon Leather Cologne 1970–1972.........$6–7

Auto, Hayes Apperson, 1902 Model, Avon Blend 7 After-shave
1973–1974...$5–7

Auto, Maxwell 23, Deep Woods After-shave 1972–1974.............$5–6

Auto, MG, 1936, Wild Country After-shave 1974–1975.............$4–5

Auto, Model A, Wild Country After-shave 1972–1974................$4–5

Auto, Red Depot Wagon, Oland After-shave 1972–1973 ....$6–7

Auto, Rolls Royce, Deep Woods After-shave 1972–1975............$6–8

Auto, Stanley Steamer, Windjammer After-shave 1971–1972 .....$6–7

Auto, Station Wagon, Tai Winds After-shave 1971–1973............$7–8

Auto, Sterling 6, Spicy After-shave 1968–1970...........................$6–7

Auto, Sterling 6 II, Wild Country After-shave 1973–1974 ....$4–5

Auto, Stutz Bearcat, 1914 Model, Avon Blend 7 After-shave
1974–1977 ....$5–6

Auto, Touring T, Tribune After-shave, 1969–1970......................$6–7

Auto, Volkswagen, Red, Oland After-shave 1972 ....$5–6

Avon Calling, Phone, Wild Country After-shave
1969–1970...$15–20

Avon Dueling Pistol II, Black Glass 1972 ....$10–15

Avonshire Blue Cologne 1971–1974...$4–5

Baby Grand Piano, Perfume Glace 1971–1972............................$8–10

Baby Hippo 1977–1980..$4–5

Club Bottle, 5th Annual 1976..$25–30

Club Bottle, Bud Hastin 1974..$70–95

Club Bottle, CPC Factory 1974 ....$30–40

Collector's Pipe, Windjammer After-shave 1973–1974 ....$3–4

Colt Revolver 1851 1975–1976...$10–12

Corncob Pipe After-shave 1974–1975 ....$4–6

Corvette Stingray '65 1975...$5–7

Covered Wagon, Wild Country After-shave 1970–1971 ....$4–5

Daylight Shaving Time 1968–1970..$5–7

Defender Cannon 1966 ....$20–24

Dollar's 'N' Scents 1966–1967 ....$20–24

Dutch Girl Figurine, Somewhere 1973–1974 .... $8–10

Duck After-shave 1971 .... $4–6

Dueling Pistol 1760 1973–1974 .... $9–12

Dueling Pistol II 1975 .... $9–12

Eight Ball Decanter, Spicy After-shave 1973 .... $3–4

Electric Guitar, Wild Country After-shave 1974–1974 .... $4–5

Enchanted Frog Cream Sachet, Sonnet 1973–1976 .... $3–4

Fashion Boot, Moonwind Cologne 1972–1976 .... $5–7

Fashion Boot, Sonnet Cologne 1972–1976 .... $5–7

Fielder's Choice 1971–1972 .... $4–6

Fire Alarm Box 1975–1976 .... $4–6

First-Class Male, Wild Country After-shave 1970–1971 .... $3–4

First Down, Soap on a Rope 1970–1971 .... $7–8

First Down, Wild Country After-shave $3–4

First Volunteer, Tai Winds Cologne 1971–1972 .... $6–7

Fox Hunt 1966 .... $25–30

French Telephone, Moonwind Foaming Bath Oil 1971 .... $20–24

Garnet Bud Vase, To a Wild Rose Cologne 1973–1976 .... $3–5

Gavel, Island Lime After-shave 1967–1968 .... $4–5

George Washington, Spicy After-shave 1970–1972 .... $2–3

George Washington, Tribute After-shave 1970–1972 .... $2–3

Gold Cadillac 1969–1973 .... $7–10

Gone Fishing 1973–1974 .... $5–7

Grade Avon Hostess Soap 1971–1972 .... $6–8

Hearth Lamp, Roses, Roses, 1973–1976 .... $6–8

Hobnail Decanter, Moonwind Bath Oil 1972–1974 .... $5–6

Hunter's Stein 1972 .... $10–14

Indian Chieftain, Protein Hair Lotion 1972–1973 ....$2–3

Indian Head Penny, Bravo After-shave 1970–1972 ....$4–5

Inkwell, Windjammer After-shave 1969–1970 ....$6–7

Iron Horse Shaving Mug, Avon Blend 7 After-shave
1974–1976 ....$3–4

Jack-in-the-Box, Baby Cream 1974 ....$4–6

Jaguar Car 1973–1976 ....$6–8

Jolly Santa 1978 ....$6–7

Joyous Bell 1978...$5–6

King Pin 1969–1970...$4–6

Kodiak Bear 1977 ....$5–10

Koffee Klatch, Honeysuckle Foam Bath Oil 1971–1974...............$5–6

Liberty Bell, Tribute After-shave 1971–1972 ....$4–6

Liberty Dollar, After-shave 1970–1972 ....$4–6

Lincoln Bottle 1971–1972..$3–5

Lip Pop Colas, Cherry 1973–1974 ....$1–2

Lip Pop Colas, Cola 1973–1974 ....$1–2

Lip Pop Colas, Strawberry 1973–1974 ....$1–2

Longhorn Steer 1975–1976 ....$7–9

Looking Glass, Regence Cologne 1970–1972 ....$7–8

Mallard Duck 1967–1968 ....$8–10

Mickey Mouse, Bubble Bath 1969 ....$10–12

Mighty Mitt Soap on a Rope 1969–1972..$7–8

Ming Cat, Bird of Paradise Cologne 1971 ....$5–7

Minibike, Sure Winner Bracing Lotion 1972–1973 ....$3–5

Nile-Blue Bath Urn, Skin So Soft 1972–1974 ....$4–6

No Parking 1975–1976 ....$5–7

Old Faithful, Wild Country After-shave 1972–1973 ....$4–6

One Good Turn, Screwdriver 1976 ....$5–6

Opening Play, Dull Golden, Spicy After-shave 1968–1969.......$8–10

Opening Play, Shiny Golden, Spicy After-shave
1968–1969 ....$14–17

Owl Fancy, Roses, Roses 1974–1976 ....$3–4

Owl Soap Dish and Soaps 1970–1971 ....$8–10

Packard Roadster 1970–1972 ....$4–7

Pass Play Decanter 1973–1975 ....$6–8

Peanuts Gang Soaps 1970–1972 ....$8–9

Pepperbox Pistol 1976 ....$5–10

Perfect Drive Decanter 1975–1976 ....$7–9

Pheasant 1972–1974 ....$7–9

Piano Decanter, Tai Winds After-shave 1972 ....$3–4

Pipe, Full, Decanter, Brown, Spicy After-shave 1971–1972.........$3–4

Pony Express, Avon Leather After-shave 1971–1972 ....$3–4

Pony Post "Tall" 1966–1967 ....$7–9

Potbelly Stove 1970–1971 ....$5–7

President Lincoln, Tai Winds After-shave 1973.................$6–8

President Washington, Deep Woods After-shave 1974–1976......$4–5

Quail 1973–1974 ....$7–9

Rainbow Trout, Deep Woods After-shave 1973–1974.............$3–4

Road Runner, Motorcycle $4–5

Rook, Spicy After-shave 1973–1974............................$4–5

Royal Coach, Bird of Paradise Bath Oil 1972–1973............$4–6

Scent with Love, Elusive Perfume 1971–1972 ....$9–10

Scent with Love, Field Flowers Perfume 1971–1972.............$9–10

Ballantine bottles, which are brightly colored and ceramic, contain imported Scotch whiskey and usually read "Blended Scotch Whiskey, 14 Years Old." The majority of these bottles' designs are based on sporting or outdoor themes, such as ducks or fish-

Ballantine's Liqueur Blended Scotch Whisky, early 1950s.

ermen with their heads represented by the bottle cap. The more collectible items, however, are the older bottles (1930), which are non-figural and very decorative.

Charioteer	$5–10
Discus Thrower	$5–10
Duck	$8–10
Fisherman	$10–12
Gladiator	$5–10
Golf Bag	$8–10
Mallard Duck	$6–8
Mercury	$5–10
Old Crow Chessman	$9–10
Scottish Knight	$10–12
Seated Fisherman	$10–12
Silver Knight	$12–15
Zebra	$12–15

The Barsottini bottle, which is manufactured in Italy, does not use any American or nongeographic themes for the U.S. marketplace. These bottles are ceramic and come in gray and white to represent the brickwork of buildings, and usually represent European subjects such as the Eiffel Tower or the Florentine Steeple.

Alpine Pipe, 10 inches $8–12

Antique Automobile, Ceramic, Coupe................................$6–9

Antique Automobile, Open Car $6–9

Clock, with Cherub...$30–40

Clowns, Ceramic, 12 in. each $9–12

Eiffel Tower, Gray and White, 15 inches.........................$8–12

Florentine Cannon "L," 15 in. $14–20

Florentine Steeple, Gray and White.................................$9–12

Monastery Cask, Ceramic, 12 in. $14–20

Paris Arc de Triomphe, 7½ in. $10–12

Pisa's Leaning Tower, Gray and White.............................$10–12

Roman Coliseum, Ceramic $7–10

Trivoli Clock, Ceramic, 15 in. $12–15

Jim Beam Bottles

The James B. Beam distilling company was founded in 1778 by Jacob Beam in Kentucky and now bears the name of Colonel James B. Beam, Jacob Beam's grandson. Beam whiskey was very popular in the South during the nineteenth and early twentieth centuries but not produced on a large scale. Because of low production, the early Beam bottles are very rare, collectible, and valuable.

In 1953, the Beam company packaged bourbon in a special Christmas/New Year ceramic decanter, which was a rarity for any distiller. When the decanters sold well, Beam decided to redevelop its method of packaging, which led to production of a wide variety of different series in the 1950s. The first of these were the ceramics of 1953. In 1955 the executive series was issued to commemorate the 160th anniversary of the corporation. In 1955, Beam introduced the Regal China series to honor significant people, places, and events with a concentration on America and contemporary situations. In 1956, political figures were introduced with the elephant and the donkey as well as special productions for customer specialties, which were made on commission. In 1957, the trophy series came along to signify various achievements within the liquor industry. And, in 1958, the state series was introduced to commemorate the admission of Alaska and Hawaii into the Union. The practice has continued with Beam still producing decanters commemorating all fifty states.

In total, over 500 types of Beam bottles have been issued since 1953.

AC Spark Plug 1977
Replica of a spark plug in white, green, and gold.........................$22–26

Ahepa 50th Anniversary 1972
Regal China bottle designed in honor of AHEPA's (American Hellenic Education Progressive Association) 50th anniversary $4–6

Aida 1978
Figurine of character from the opera *Aida* $140–160

Akron Rubber Capital 1973
Regal China bottle honoring Akron, Ohio.....................................$15–20

Alaska 1958
Regal China, 9½ in., star-shaped bottle $55–60

Alaska 1964–1965
Reissue of the 1958 bottle $40–50

Alaska Purchase 1966
Regal China, 10 in., blue-and-gold bottle $4–6

American Samoa 1973
Regal China, reflects the seal of Samoa...$5–7

American Veterans..$4–7

Antique Clock..$35–45

Antioch 1967
Regal China, 10 in., commemorates diamond jubilee of Regal.........$5–7

Antique Coffee Grinder 1979
Replica of a box coffee mill used in mid-nineteenth century.......$10–12

Antique Globe 1980
Represents the Martin Behaim globe of 1492...................................$7–11

Antique Telephone (1897) 1978
Replica of an 1897 desk phone, second in a series.....................$50–60

Antique Trader 1968
Regal China, 10½ in., represents Antique Trader newspaper...........$4–6

Appaloosa 1974
Regal China, 10 in., represents favorite horse of the Old West..$12–15

Arizona 1968
Regal China, 12 in., represents the State of Arizona......................$4–6

Armadillo..$8–12

Armanetti Award Winner 1969
Honor's Armanetti, Inc., of Chicago as "Liquor Retailer of the
Year"..$6–8

Armanetti Shopper 1971
Reflects the slogan "It's fun to Shop Armanetti—Self-Service Liquor
Store," 11¾ in...$6–8

Armanetti Vase 1968
Yellow-toned decanter embossed with flowers................................$5–7

Bacchus 1970
Issued by Armanetti Liquor Stores of Chicago, 11¾ in. $6–9

Barney's Slot Machine 1978
Replica of the world's largest slot machine $14–16

Barry Berish 1985
Executive series $110–140

Barry Berish 1986
Executive series, bowl $110–140

Bartender's Guild 1973
Commemorative honoring the International Bartenders
Association...$4–7

Baseball 1969
Issued to commemorate the 100th anniversary of baseball $18–20

Beam Pot 1980
Shaped like a New England bean pot, club bottle for the New England
Beam Bottle and Specialties Club..$12–15

Beaver Valley Club 1977
A club bottle to honor the Beaver Valley Jim Beam Club of
Rochester $8–12

Bell Scotch 1970
Regal China, 10½ in., in honor of Arthur Bell and Sons.................$4–7

Beverage Association, NLBA..$4–7

The Big Apple 1979
Apple-shaped bottle with "The Big Apple" over the top.................$8–12

Bing's 31st Clambake Bottle 1972
Commemorates 31st Bing Crosby National Pro-Am Golf Tournament
in January 1972..$25–30

Bing Crosby National Pro-Am 1970 ....$4–7

Bing Crosby National Pro-Am 1971 ....$4–7

Bing Crosby National Pro-Am 1972 ....$15–25

Bing Crosby National Pro-Am 1973 ....$18–23

Bing Crosby National Pro-Am 1974 ....$15–25

Bing Crosby National Pro-Am 1975 ....$45–65

Bing Crosby 36th 1976..$15–25

Bing Crosby National Pro-Am 1977 ....$12–18

Bing Crosby National Pro-Am 1978 ....$12–18

Black Katz 1968
Regal China, 14½ in. $7–12

Blue Cherub Executive 1960
Regal China, 12½ in. $70–90

Blue Daisy 1967
Also known as Zimmerman Blue Daisy.................................$10–12

Blue-gill, Fish..$12–16

Blue Goose Order..$4–7

Blue Jay 1969...$4–7

Blue Goose 1979
Replica of blue goose, authenticated by Dr. Lester Fisher, director of
Lincoln Park Zoological Gardens in Chicago...........................$7–9

Blue Hen Club $12–15

Blue Slot Machine 1967..$10–12

Bobby Unser Olsonite Eagle 1975
Replica of the racing car used by Bobby Unser $40–50

Bob DeVaney..$8–12

Bob Hope Desert Classic 1973
First genuine Regal China bottle created in honor of the Bob Hope
Desert Classic $8–9

Bob Hope Desert Classic 1974 ....$8–12

Bohemian Girl 1974
Issued for the Bohemian Café in Omaha, Neb., to honor the Czech
and Slovak immigrants in the United States, 14½ in....................$10–15

Bonded Gold $4–7

Bonded Mystic 1979
Urn-shaped bottle, burgundy-colored $4–7

Bonded Silver..$4–7

Boris Godinov, with Base 1978
Second in opera series $350–450

Bourbon Barrel...$18–24

Bowling Proprietors..$4–7

Boys Town of Italy 1973
Created in honor of the Boys Town of Italy....................................$7–10

Bowl 1986
Executive series $20–30

Broadmoor Hotel 1968
To celebrate the 50th anniversary of this famous hotel in Colorado
Springs, Co., "1918—The Broadmoor—1968" $4–7

Buffalo Bill 1971
Regal China, 10½ in., commemorates Buffalo Bill............................$4–7

Bulldog 1979
Honors the 204th anniversary of the United States Marine
Corps $15–18

Cable Car 1968
Regal China, 4½ in. $4–6

Caboose 1980..$50–60

California Mission 1970
This bottle was issued for the Jim Beam Bottle Club of Southern
California in honor of the 20th anniversary of the California
Missions, 14 in. $10–15

California Retail Liquor Dealers Association 1973
Designed to commemorate the 20th anniversary of the California Retail
Liquor Dealers Association $6–9

Cal-Neva 1969
Regal China, 9½ in. $5–7

Camellia City Club 1979
Replica of the cupola of the State Capitol Building in
Sacramento $18–23

Cameo Blue 1965
Also known as the Shepherd Bottle..$4–6

Cannon 1970
Bottle issued to commemorate the 175th anniversary of the Jim Beam
Company. Some of these bottles have a small chain shown on the cannon
and some do not. Those without the chain are harder to find and more
valuable, 8 in.
  Chain $2–4
  No chain..$9–13

Canteen 1979
Replica of the exact canteen used by the armed forces...................$8–12

Captain and Mate 1980 ....$10–12

Cardinal (Kentucky Cardinal) 1968 ....$40–50

Carmen 1978
Third in the opera series..$140–180

Carolier Bull 1984
Executive series $18–23

Catfish..$16–24

Cathedral Radio 1979
Replica of one of the earlier dome-shaped radios.........................$12–15

Cats 1967
Trio of cats: Siamese, Burmese, and Tabby......................................$6–9

Cedars of Lebanon 1971
This bottle was issued in honor of the Jerry Lewis Muscular Dystrophy
Telethon in 1971...$5–7

Charisma 1970
Executive series $4–7

Charlie McCarthy 1976
Replica of Edgar Bergen's puppet from the 1930s........................$20–30

Cherry Hills Country Club 1973
Commemorating 50th anniversary of Cherry Hills Country Club $4–7

Cheyenne, Wyoming 1977..$4–6

Chicago Cubs, Sports Series $30–40

Chicago Show Bottle 1977
Commemorates 6th annual Chicago Jim Beam Bottle Show.........$10–14

Christmas Tree $150–200

Churchill Downs—Pink Roses 1969
Regal China, 10¼ in. $5–7

Churchill Downs—Red Roses 1969
Regal China, 10¼ in. $9–12

Circus Wagon 1979
Replica of a circus wagon from the late nineteenth century.........$24–26

Civil War North 1961
Regal China, 10¼ in. $10–15

Civil War South 1961
Regal China, 10¼ in...$25–35

Clear Crystal Bourbon 1967
Clear glass, 11½ in..$5–7

Clear Crystal Scotch 1966..$9–12

Clear Crystal Vodka 1967 ....$5–8

Cleopatra Rust 1962
Glass, 13¼ in...$3–5

Cleopatra Yellow 1962
Glass, 13¼ in., rarer than Cleopatra Rust.......................................$8–12

Clint Eastwood 1973
Commemorating Clint Eastwood Invitational Celebrity Tennis
Tournament in Pebble Beach $14–17

Cocktail Shaker 1953
Glass, Fancy Disp. Bottle, 9¼ in..$2–5

Coffee Grinder...$8–12

Coffee Warmers 1954
Four types are known: red, black, gold, and white........................$7–12

Coffee Warmers 1956
Two types with metal necks and handles $2–5

Coho Salmon 1976
Official seal of the National Fresh Water Fishing Hall of Fame is on
the back..$10–13

Colin Mead...$180–210

Cobalt 1981
Executive series $18–23

Collector's Edition 1966
Set of six glass famous paintings: *The Blue Boy, On the Terrace, Mardi
Gras, Austide Bruant, The Artist Before His Easel,* and *Laughing
Cavalier* (each) $2–5

Collector's Edition Volume II 1967
A set of six flask-type bottles with famous pictures: *George Gisze,
Soldier and Girl, Night Watch, The Jester, Nurse and Child,* and *Man
on Horse* (each)...$2–5

Collector's Edition Volume III 1968
A set of eight bottles with famous paintings: *On the Trail, Indian Maiden,
Buffalo, Whistler's Mother, American Gothic, The Kentuckian, The Scout,*
and *Hauling in the Gill Net* (each)..$2–5

Collector's Edition Volume IV 1969
A set of seven bottles with famous paintings: *Balcony, The Judge, Fruit Basket, Boy with Cherries, Emile Zola, The Guitarist Zouave,* and *Sunflowers* (each)...$2–5

Collector's Edition Volume V 1970
A set of six bottles with famous paintings: *Au Café, Old Peasant, Boaring Party, Gare Saint Lazare, The Jewish Bride,* and *Titus at Writing Desk* (each)..$2–5

Collector's Edition Volume VI 1971
A set of three bottles with famous art pieces: *Charles I, The Merry Lute Player,* and *Boy Holding Flute* (each)...$2–5

Collector's Edition Volume VII 1972
A set of three bottles with famous paintings: *The Bag Piper, Prince Baltasor,* and *Maidservant Pouring Milk* (each) $2–5

Collector's Edition Volume VIII 1973
A set of three bottles with famous portraits: Ludwig van Beethoven, Wolfgang Amadeus Mozart, and Frederic Francis Chopin (each).....$2–5

Collector's Edition Volume IX 1974
A set of three bottles with famous paintings: *Cardinal, Ring-Neck Pheasant,* and *The Woodcock* (each)...$3–6

Collector's Edition Volume X 1975
A set of three bottles with famous pictures: *Sailfish, Rainbow Trout,* and *Largemouth Bass* (each) $3–6

Collector's Edition Volume XI 1976
A set of three bottles with famous paintings: *Chipmunk, Bighorn Sheep,* and *Pronghorn Antelope* (each)...$3–6

Collector's Edition Volume XII 1977
A set of four bottles each with a different reproduction of James Lockhart on the front (each)..$3–6

Collector's Edition Volume XIV 1978
A set of four bottles with James Lockhart paintings: *Raccoon, Mule Deer, Red Fox,* and *Cottontail Rabbit* (each) $3–6

Collector's Edition Volume XV 1979
A set of three flasks with Frederic Remington paintings: *The Cowboy* (1902), *The Indian Trapper* (1902), and *Lieutenant S. C. Robertson* (1890) (each)..$2–5

Collector's Edition Volume XVI 1980
A set of three flasks depicting duck scenes: *The Mallard, The Redhead,* and *The Canvasback* (each)..$3–6

Collector's Edition Volume XVII 1981
A set of three bottles with Jim Lockhart paintings: *Great Elk, Pintail Duck,* and *The Horned Owl* (each)...$3–6

Colorado 1959
Regal China, 10¾ in..$20–25

Colorado Centennial 1976
Replica of Pike's Peak..$8–12

Colorado Springs $4–7

Computer, Democrat 1984 ....$12–18

Computer, Republican 1984...$12–18

Convention Bottle 1971
Commemorates the first national convention of the National Association of Jim Beam Bottle and Specialty Clubs hosted by the Rocky Mountain Club, Denver, Colo..$5–7

Convention Number 2, 1972
Honors the second annual convention of the National Association of Jim Beam Bottle and Specialty Clubs in Anaheim, Calif...............$20–30

Convention Number 3, Detroit 1973
Commemorates the third annual convention of Beam Bottle Collectors in Detroit, Mich. $10–12

Convention Number 4, Pennsylvania 1974
Commemorates the annual convention of the Jim Beam Bottle Club in Lancaster, Pa. $80–100

Convention Number 5, Sacramento 1975
Commemorates the annual convention of the Camellia City Jim Beam Bottle Club in Sacramento, Calif..$5–7

Convention Number 6, Hartford 1976
Commemorates the annual convention of the Jim Beam Bottle Club
in Hartford, Conn. $5–7

Convention Number 7, Louisville 1978
Commemorates the annual convention of the Jim Beam Bottle Club
in Louisville, Ky. $5–7

Convention Number 8, Chicago 1978
Commemorates the annual convention of the Jim Beam Bottle Club
in Chicago $8–12

Convention Number 9, Houston 1979
Commemorates the annual convention of the Jim Beam Bottle Club
in Houston, Tex. $20–30
    Cowboy, beige $35–45
    Cowboy, in color..$35–45

Convention Number 10, Norfolk 1980
Commemorates the annual convention of the Jim Beam Bottle Club at
the Norfolk Naval Base, Va...$18–22
    Waterman, pewter $35–45
    Waterman, yellow..$35–45

Convention Number 11, Las Vegas 1981
Commemorates the annual convention of the Jim Beam Bottle Club in
Las Vegas, Nev. $20–22
    Showgirl, blond $45–55
    Showgirl, brunette $45–55

Convention Number 12, New Orleans 1982
Commemorates the annual convention of the Jim Beam Bottle Club in
New Orleans, La...$30–35
    Buccaneer, gold $35–45
    Buccaneer, in color..$35–45

Convention Number 13, Saint Louis 1983 (stein)
Commemorates the annual convention of the Jim Beam Bottle Club in
St. Louis, Mo..$55–70
    Gibson girl, blue..$65–80
    Gibson girl, yellow $65–80

Convention Number 14, Florida, King Neptune 1984
Commemorates the annual convention of the Jim Beam Bottle Club
in Florida...$15–20
   Mermaid, blond $35–45
   Mermaid, brunette $35–45

Convention Number 15, Las Vegas 1985
Commemorates the annual convention of the Jim Beam Bottle Club in
Las Vegas, Nev. $40–50

Convention Number 16, Pilgrim Woman, Boston 1986
Commemorates the annual convention of the Jim Beam Bottle Club
in Boston, Mass. $35–45
   Minutemen, color $85–105
   Minutemen, pewter..$85–105

Convention Number 17, Louisville 1987
Commemorates the annual convention of the Jim Beam Bottle Club
in Louisville, Ky. $55–75
   Kentucky Colonel, blue...$85–105
   Kentucky Colonel, gray $85–105

Convention Number 18, Bucky Beaver 1988 ....$30–40
   Portland rose, red...$30–40
   Portland rose, yellow...$30–40

Convention Number 19, Kansas City 1989
Commemorates the annual convention of the Jim Beam Bottle Club in
Kansas City, Mo. $40–50

Cowboy 1979
Awarded to the collectors who attended the 1979 convention for the
International Association of Beam Clubs $35–50

CPO Open $4–7

Crappie 1979
Commemorates the National Fresh Water Fishing Hall of
Fame...$10–14

Dark Eyes Brown Jug 1978 ....$4–6

D-Day $12–18

Delaware Blue Hen Bottle 1972
Commemorates the State of Delaware $4–7

Delco Freedom Battery 1978
Replica of a Delco battery $18–22

Delft Blue 1963...$3–5

Delft Rose 1963 ....$4–6

Del Webb Mint 1970
Metal stopper..$10–12
China stopper $50–60

Devil Dog..$15–25

Dial Telephone 1980
Fourth in a series of Beam telephone designs...............................$40–50

Dodge City 1972
Issued to honor the centennial of Dodge City $5–6

Doe 1963
Regal China, 13½ in...$10–12

Doe—Reissued 1967 ....$10–12

Dog 1959
Regal China, 15¼ in...$20–25

Don Giovanni 1980
The fifth in the opera series $140–180

Donkey and Elephant Ashtrays 1956
Regal China, 12 in. (pair)..$12–16

Donkey and Elephant Boxers 1964 (pair) $14–18

Donkey and Elephant Clowns 1968
Regal China, 12 in. (pair)..$4–7

Donkey and Elephant Football Election Bottles 1972
Regal China, 9½ in. (pair)..$6–9

Donkey New York City 1976
Commemorates the National Democratic Convention in New York
City $10–12

Duck 1957
Regal China, 14¼ in. $15–20

Ducks and Geese 1955 ....$5–8

Ducks Unlimited Mallard 1974...$40–50

Ducks Unlimited Wood Duck 1975 ....$45–50

Ducks Unlimited 40th Mallard Hen 1977 ....$40–50

Ducks Unlimited Canvasback Drake 1979 ....$30–40

Ducks Unlimited Blue-winged Teal 1980
The sixth in a series, 9½ in. $40–45

Ducks Unlimited Green-Winged Teal 1981...............................$35–45

Ducks Unlimited Wood Ducks 1982...$35–45

Ducks Unlimited American Wigeon PR 1983 ....$35–45

Ducks Unlimited Mallard 1984...$55–75

Ducks Unlimited Pintail PR 1985...$30–40

Ducks Unlimited Redhead 1986 ....$15–25

Ducks Unlimited Blue Bill 1987...$40–60

Ducks Unlimited Black Duck 1989 ....$50–60

Eagle 1966
Regal China, 12½ in. $10–13

Eldorado 1978..$7–9

Election, Democrat 1988..$30–40

Election, Republican 1988 ....$30–40

Elephant and Donkey Supermen 1980 (pair)...........................$10–14

Elephant Kansas City 1976
Commemorates the National Republican Convention in Kansas
City $8–10

Elks $4–7

Elks National Foundation $8–12

Emerald Crystal Bourbon 1968
Green glass, 11½ in. $3–5

Emmett Kelly 1973
Likeness of Emmett Kelly as sad-faced Willie the Clown $18–22

Emmett Kelly, Native Son $50–60

Ernie's Flower Cart 1976
In honor of Ernie's Wines and Liquors of Northern California....$24–28

Evergreen, Club Bottle $7–10

Expo 1974
Issued in honor of the World's Fair held at Spokane, Wash. $5–7

Falstaff 1979
Second in Australian opera series, limited edition of 1,000
bottles $150–160

Fantasia Bottle 1971 ....$5–6

Father's Day Card $15–25

Female Cardinal 1973 ....$8–12

Fiesta Bowl, Glass $8–12

Fiesta Bowl 1973
The second bottle created to honor the Fiesta Bowl $9–11

Figaro 1977
Character Figaro from the opera *Barber of Seville* $140–170

Fighting Bull $12–18

Figi Islands $4–6

First National Bank of Chicago 1964
Commemorates the 100th anniversary of the First National Bank of
Chicago. Approximately 130 were issued, with 117 being given as
mementos to the bank directors and none for public distribution.
This is the most valuable Beam bottle known. Also, beware of
reproductions $1,900–2,400

Fish 1957
Regal China, 14 in. $15–18

Fish Hall of Fame..$25–35

Five Seasons 1980
Club bottle of the Five Seasons Club of Cedar Rapids honors the
State of Iowa $10–12

Fleet Reserve Association 1974
Issued by the Fleet Reserve Association to honor the Career Sea Service
on its 50th anniversary $5–7

Florida Shell 1968
Regal China, 9 in. $4–6

Floro de Oro 1976 ....$10–12

Flower Basket 1962
Regal China, 12¼ in. $30–35

Football Hall of Fame 1972
Reproduction of the new Professional Football Hall of Fame
Building $14–18

Foremost—Black and Gold 1956
First Beam bottle issued for a liquor retailer, Foremost Liquor Store
of Chicago $225–250

Foremost—Speckled Beauty 1956
The most valuable of the Foremost bottles $500–600

Fox 1967, Blue Coat $65–80

Fox 1971, Gold Coat $35–50

Fox, Green Coat $12–18

Fox, White Coat $20–30

Fox, on a Dolphin $12–15

Fox, Uncle Sam...$5–6

Fox, Kansas City, Blue, Miniature.......................................$20–30

Fox, Red Distillery $1,100–1,300

Franklin Mint..$4–7

French Cradle Telephone 1979
Third in the Telephone Pioneers of America series....................$20–22

Galah Bird 1979 .... $14–16

Gem City, Club Bottle $35–45

George Washington Commemorative Plate 1976
Commemorates the U.S. Bicentennial, 9½ in. $12–15

German Bottle—Weisbaden 1973 .... $4–6

German Stein $20–30

Germany 1970
Issued to honor the American armed forces in Germany $4–6

Glen Campbell 51st 1976
Honors the 51st Los Angeles Open at the Riviera Country Club in
February 1976 .... $7–10

Golden Chalice 1961 .... $40–50

Golden Jubilee 1977
Executive series $8–12

Golden Nugget 1969
Regal China, 12½ in. $35–45

Golden Rose 1978 .... $15–20

Grand Canyon 1969
Honors the Grand Canyon National Park's 50th anniversary $7–9

Grant Locomotive 1979 .... $55–65

Gray Cherub 1958
Regal China, 12 in. $240–260

Great Chicago Fire Bottle 1971
Commemorates the great Chicago fire of 1871 and salutes Mercy
Hospital, which helped the fire victims $18–22

Great Dane 1976 .... $7–9

Green China Jug 1965
Regal Glass, 12½ in. $4–6

Hank Williams, Jr. $40–50

Hannah Dustin 1973
Regal China, 14½ in. $10–12

Hansel and Gretel Bottle 1971..$4–6

Harley-Davidson 85th Anniversary Decanter.........................$110–150

Harley-Davidson 85th Anniversary Stein...............................$180–220

Harolds Club—Man-in-a-Barrel 1957
First in a series made for Harolds Club in Reno, Nev. $380–410

Harolds Club—Silver Opal 1957
Commemorates the 25th anniversary of Harolds Club.................$20–22

Harolds Club—Man-in-a-barrel 1958......................................$140–160

Harolds Club—Nev. (gray) 1963
Created for the "Nevada Centennial—1864–1964." This is a rare
and valuable bottle..$90–110

Harolds Club—Nev. (silver) 1964...$90–110

Harolds Club—Pinwheel 1965..$40–45

Harolds Club—Blue Slot Machine 1967....................................$10–14

Harolds Club—VIP Executive 1967
Limited quantity issued...$50–60

Harolds Club—VIP Executive 1968..$55–65

Harolds Club—Gray Slot Machine 1968.......................................$4–6

Harolds Club—VIP Executive 1969
This bottle was given as a Christmas gift to the casino's
executives..$260–285

Harolds Club—Covered Wagon 1969–1970..................................$4–6

Harolds Club 1970..$40–60

Harolds Club 1971..$40–60

Harolds Club 1972..$18–25

Harolds Club 1973..$18–24

Harolds Club 1974..$12–16

Harolds Club 1975..$12–18

Harolds Club VIP 1976..$18–22

Harolds Club 1977 ....$20–30

Harolds Club 1978 ....$20–30

Harolds Club 1979 ....$20–30

Harolds Club 1980 ....$25–35

Harolds Club 1982 ....$110–145

Harp Seal $12–18

Harrahs Club, Nevada—Gray 1963
This is the same bottle used for the Nevada Centennial and Harolds
Club $500–550

Harry Hoffman $4–7

Harveys Resort Hotel at Lake Tahoe $6–10

Hatfield 1973
The character of Hatfield from the story of the Hatfield and McCoy
feud $15–20

Hawaii 1959
Tribute to the 50th state $35–40

Hawaii—Reissued 1967 ....$40–45

Hawaii 1971 ....$6–8

Hawaii Aloha 1971 ....$6–10

Hawaiian Open Bottle 1972
Honors the 1972 Hawaiian Open Golf Tournament $6–8

Hawaiian Open 1973
Second bottle created in the honor of the United Hawaiian Open
Golf Classic $7–9

Hawaiian Open 1974
Commemorates the 1974 Hawaiian Open Golf Classic $5–8

Hawaiian Open Outrigger 1975 ....$9–11

Hawaiian Paradise 1978
Commemorates the 200th anniversary of the landing of Captain
Cook $15–17

Hemisfair 1968
Commemorates "Hemisfair 68—San Antonio".................................$8–10

Herre Brothers $22–35

Hobo, Australia $10–14

Hoffman 1969 ....$4–7

Holiday—Carolers...$40–50

Holiday—Nutcracker $40–50

Home Builders 1978
Commemorates the 1979 convention of the Home Builders $25–30

Hone Heke..$200–250

Honga Hika 1980
First in a series of Maori warrior bottles. Honga Hika was a war-chief
of the Ngapuke tribe...$220–240

Horse (Appaloosa) $8–12

Horse (black)...$18–22

Horse (black), reissued 1967 ....$10–12

Horse (brown)..$18–22

Horse (brown), reissued 1967...$10–12

Horse (mare and foal) $35–45

Horse (Oh, Kentucky) $70–85

Horse (pewter)...$12–17

Horse (white) $18–20

Horse (white), reissued 1967 ....$12–17

Horseshoe Club 1969...$4–6

Hula Bowl 1975 ....$8–10

Hyatt House—Chicago $7–10

Hyatt House—New Orleans...$8–11

Idaho 1963 ....$30–40

Illinois 1968
Honors the Sesquicentennial 1818–1968 of Illinois..........................$4–6

Indianapolis Sesquicentennial $4–6

Indianapolis 500 ....$9–12

Indian Chief 1979 ....$9–12

International Chili Society 1976..................................$9–12

Italian Marble Urn 1985
Executive series $12–17

Ivory Ashtray 1955..$8–10

Jackalope 1971
Honors the Wyoming jackalope.......................................$5–8

Jaguar $18–23

Jewel Tea Man—50th Anniversary $35–45

John Henry 1972
Commemorates the legendary "steel-drivin' man".........$18–22

Joliet Legion Band 1978
Commemorates the 26th national championship.............$15–20

Kaiser International Open Bottle 1971
Commemorates the 5th Annual Kaiser International Open Golf
Tournament $5–6

Kangaroo 1977..$10–14

Kansas 1960
Commemorates the "Kansas 1861–1961 Centennial"....$35–45

Kentucky Black Head—Brown Head 1967
   Black head $12–18
   Brown head $20–28
   White head $18–23

Kentucky Derby 95th, Pink, Red Roses 1969 ....$4–7

Kentucky Derby 96th, Double Rose 1970 ....$15–25

Kentucky Derby 97th 1971 ....$4–7

Kentucky Derby 98th 1972 ....$4–6

Kentucky Derby 100th 1974 ....$7–10

Key West 1972
Honors the 150th anniversary of Key West, FL.................................$5–7

King Kamehameha 1972
Commemorates the 100th anniversary of King Kamehameha
Day $8–11

King Kong 1976
Commemorates Paramount's movie release in December 1976 ......$8–10

Kiwi 1974 ....$5–8

Koala Bear 1973 ....$12–14

Laramie 1968
Commemorates the "Centennial Jubilee Laramie Wyo.
1868–1968" $4–6

Largemouth Bass Trophy Bottle 1973
Honors the National Fresh Water Fishing Hall of Fame $10–14

Las Vegas 1969
Bottle used for customer specials, casino series $4–6

Light Bulb 1979
Honors Thomas Edison...$14–16

Lombard 1969
Commemorates "Village of Lombard, Illinois—1869 Centennial
1969" $4–6

London Bridge...$4–7

Louisville Downs Racing Derby 1978 ....$4–6

Louisiana Superdome $8–11

LVNH Owl..$20–30

Madame Butterfly 1977
Figurine of Madame Butterfly, music box plays "One Fine Day"
from the opera $340–370

The Magpies 1977
Honors an Australian football team $18–20

Maine 1970 ....$4–6

Majestic 1966...$20–24

Male Cardinal...$18–24

Marbled Fantasy 1965..$38–42

Marina City 1962
Commemorates modern apartment complex in Chicago..............$10–15

Marine Corps $25–35

Mark Antony 1962 ....$18–20

Martha Washington 1976 ....$5–6

McCoy 1973
Character of McCoy from the story of the Hatfield and McCoy
feud...$14–17

McShane—Mother-of-pearl 1979
Executive series $85–105

McShane—Titans 1980 ....$85–105

McShane—Cobalt 1981
Executives series...$115–135

McShane—Green Pitcher 1982
Executive series $80–105

McShane—Green Bell 1983
Executive series $80–110

Mephistopheles 1979
Figurine depicts Mephistopheles from the opera *Faust*, music box
plays "Soldier's Chorus" $160–190

Michigan Bottle 1972 ....$7–9

Milwaukee Stein $30–40

Minnesota Viking 1973...$9–12

Mint 400 1970 ....$80–105

Mint 400 1970
Commemorates the annual Del Webb Mint 400................................$5–6

Mint 400 1971 ....$5–6

Mint 400 1972
Commemorates the fifth annual Del Webb Mint 400......................$5–7

Mint 400 1973
Commemorates the sixth annual Del Webb Mint 400......................$6–8

Mint 400 1974 ....$4–7

Mint 400 Seventh Annual 1976 ....$9–12

Mississippi Fire Engine 1978..$120–130

Model A Ford 1903 (1978) $38–42

Model A Ford 1928 (1980) $65–75

Montana 1963
Tribute to "Montana, 1864 Golden Years Centennial 1964" $50–60

Monterey Bay Club 1977
Honors the Monterey Bay Beam Bottle and Specialty Club $9–12

Mortimer Snerd 1976..$24–28

Mother-of-pearl 1979..$10–12

Mount St. Helens 1980
Depicts the eruption of Mount St. Helens....................................$20–22

Mr. Goodwrench 1978 ....$24–28

Musicians on a Wine Cask 1964..$4–6

Muskie 1971
Honors the National Fresh Water Fishing Hall of Fame $14–18

National Tobacco Festival 1973
Commemorates the 25th anniversary of the National Tobacco
Festival..$7–8

Nebraska 1967 ....$7–9

Nebraska Football 1972
Commemorates the University of Nebraska's national championship
football team of 1970–1971...$5–8

Nevada 1963 ....$34–38

New Hampshire 1967..$4–8

New Hampshire Eagle Bottle 1971...............................$18–23

New Jersey 1963..$40–50

New Jersey Yellow 1963..$40–50

New Mexico Bicentennial 1976...$8–12

New Mexico Statehood 1972
Commemorates New Mexico's 60 years of statehood $7–9

New York World's Fair 1964 ....$5–6

North Dakota 1965...$45–55

Northern Pike 1977
The sixth in a series designed for the National Fresh Water Fishing
Hall of Fame...$14–18

Nutcracker Toy Soldier 1978...$90–120

Ohio 1966 ....$5–6

Ohio State Fair 1973
In honor of the 120th Ohio State Fair...$5–6

Olympian 1960 ....$2–4

One Hundred First Airborne Division 1977
Honors the division known as the Screaming Eagles......................$8–10

Opaline Crystal 1969 ....$4–6

Oregon 1959
Honors the centennial of the state...$20–25

Oregon Liquor Commission $25–35

Osco Drugs..$12–17

Panda 1980..$20–22

Paul Bunyan $4–7

Pearl Harbor Memorial 1972
Honoring the Pearl Harbor Survivors Association $14–18

Pearl Harbor Survivors Association 1976 ....$5–7

Pennsylvania 1967 ....$4–6

Pennsylvania Dutch, Club Bottle $8–12

Permian Basin Oil Show 1972
Commemorates the Permian Basin Oil Show in Odessa, Tex..........$4–6

Petroleum Man..$4–7

Pheasant 1960 ....$14–18

Pheasant 1961, reissued; also 1963, 1966, 1967, 1968 ....$8–11

Phi Sigma Kappa (centennial series) 1973
Commemorates the 100th anniversary of this fraternity...................$3–4

Phoenician 1973 ....$6–9

Pied Piper of Hamlin 1974..$3–6

Ponderosa 1969
A replica of the Cartwrights of "Bonanza" TV series fame................$4–6

Ponderosa Ranch Tourist 1972
Commemorates the millionth tourist to the Ponderosa Ranch $14–16

Pony Express 1968..$9–12

Poodle—Gray and White 1970 ....$5–6

Portland Rose Festival 1972
Commemorates the 64th Portland, Ore., Rose Festival....................$5–8

Portola Trek 1969
Issued to celebrate the 200th anniversary of San Diego $3–6

Poulan Chain Saw 1979..$24–28

Powell Expedition 1969
Depicts John Wesley Powell's survey of the Colorado River............$3–5

Preakness 1970
Issued to honor the 100th anniversary of the running of the
Preakness $5–6

Preakness Pimlico 1975 ....$4–7

Presidential 1968
Executive series $4–7

Prestige 1967
Executive series $4–7

Pretty Perch 1980
Eighth in a series, this fish is used as the official seal of the National
Fresh Water Fishing Hall of Fame....................................$13–16

Prima Donna 1969...$4–6

Professional Golf Association............................$4–7

Queensland 1978...$20–22

Rabbit..$4–7

Rainbow Trout 1975
Produced for the National Fresh Water Fishing Hall of Fame $12–15

Ralph Centennial 1973
Commemorates the 100th anniversary of the Ralph Grocery
Company $10–14

Ralph's Market...$8–12

Ram 1958 ....$40–55

Ramada Inn 1976 ....$10–12

Red Mile Racetrack..$8–12

Redwood 1967 ....$6–8

Reflections 1975
Executive series $8–12

Regency 1972..$7–9

Reidsville 1973
Issued to honor Reidsville, N.C., on its centennial..........$5–6

Renee the Fox 1974
Represents the companion for the International Association of Jim
Beam Bottle and Specialties Club's mascot $7–9

Rennie the Runner 1974..$9–12

Rennie the Surfer 1975..$9–12

Reno 1968
Commemorates "100 Years—Reno" $4–6

Republic of Texas 1980..$12–20

Republican Convention 1972 ....$500–700

Republican Football 1972..$350–450

Richard Hadlee..$110–135

Richards—New Mexico 1967
Created for Richards Distributing Company of Albuquerque,
NM..$8–10

Robin 1969..$5–6

Rocky Marciano 1973..$14–16

Rocky Mountain, Club Bottle..$10–15

Royal Crystal 1959..$3–6

Royal Di Monte 1957..$45–55

Royal Emperor 1958 ....$3–6

Royal Gold Diamond 1964..$30–35

Royal Gold Round 1956 ....$80–90

Royal Opal 1957..$5–7

Royal Porcelain 1955 ....$380–420

Royal Rose 1963..$30–35

Ruby Crystal 1967..$6–9

Ruidoso Downs 1968
  Pointed ears $24–26
  Flat ears $4–6

Sahara Invitational Bottle 1971
In honor of the Del Webb 1971 Sahara Invitational Pro-Am Golf
Tournament $6–8

San Bear—Donkey 1973
Political series $1,500–2,000

Samoa..$4–7

San Diego 1968
Issued by the Beam Company for the 200th anniversary of its
founding in 1769 ....$4–6

San Diego—Elephant 1972 ....$15–25

Santa Fe 1960 ....$120–140

SCCA, etched..$15–25

SCCA, smoothed...$12–18

Screech Owl 1979...$18–22

Seafair Trophy Race 1972
Commemorates the Seattle Seafair Trophy Race................$5–6

Seattle World's Fair 1962...$10–12

Seoul, Korea 1988 ....$60–75

Sheraton Inn...$4–6

Short Dancing Scot 1963 ....$50–65

Short-Timer 1975..$15–20

Shriners 1975...$10–12

Shriners—Indiana $4–7

Shriners Pyramid 1975
Issued by the El Kahir Temple of Cedar Rapids, IA....................$10–12

Shriners Rajah 1977 ....$24–28

Shriners Temple 1972...$20–25

Shriners Western Association $15–25

Sierra Eagle $15–22

Stutz Bearcat 1914, 1977...$45–55

Submarine—Diamond Jubilee...$35–45

Submarine Redfin 1970
Issued for Manitowoc Submarine Memorial Association $5–7

Superdome 1975
Replica of the Louisiana Superdome.......................................$5–8

Swagman 1979
Replica of an Australian hobo called a swagman who roamed that
country looking for work during the Depression...........................$10–12

Sydney Opera House 1977 ....$9–12

Tall Dancing Scot 1964 ....$9–12

Tavern Scene 1959 ....$45–55

Telephone No. 1 1975
Replica of a 1907 phone of the magneto wall type.....................$25–30

Telephone No. 2 1976
Replica of an 1897 desk set...$30–40

Telephone No. 3 1977
Replica of a 1920 cradle phone...$15–20

Telephone No. 4 1978
Replica of a 1919 dial phone $40–50

Telephone No. 5 1979
Replica of a pay phone $25–35

Telephone No. 6 1980
Replica of a battery phone $20–30

Telephone No. 7 1981
Replica of a digital dial phone...$35–45

Tenpin 1980...$8–11

Texas Hemisfair $7–11

Texas Rose 1978
Executive series $14–18

Thailand 1969 ....$4–6

Thomas Flyer 1907, 1976B...$60–70

Tiffany Poodle 1973
Created in honor of Tiffany, the poodle mascot of the National
Association of the Jim Beam Bottle and Specialties Clubs............$20–22

Tiger—Australian...$14–18

The Tigers 1977
Issued in honor of an Australian football team...............................$20–24

Titian 1980...$9–12

Tobacco Festival $8–12

Tombstone $4–7

Travelodge Bear $4–7

Treasure Chest 1979...$8–12

Trout Unlimited 1977
To honor the Trout Unlimited conservation organization..............$14–18

Truth or Consequences Fiesta 194
Issued in honor of Ralph Edwards's radio and television
show $14–18

Turquoise China Jug 1966 ....$4–6

Twin Bridges Bottle 1971
Commemorates the largest twin bridge between Delaware and New
Jersey $40–42

Twin Cherubs 1974
Executive series..$8–12

Twin Doves 1987
Executive series $18–23

U.S. Open 1972
Honors the U.S. Open Golf Tourney at Pebble Beach, CA............$9–12

Vendome Drummers Wagon 1975
Honors the Vendomes of Beverly Hills, CA $60–70

VFW Bottle 1971
Commemorates the 50th anniversary of the Department of Indiana
VFW $5–6

Viking 1973 ....$9–12

Volkswagen Commemorative Bottle—Two Colors 1977
Commemorates the Volkswagen Beetle $40–50

Vons Market $28–35

Walleye Pike 1977
Designed for the National Fresh Water Fishing Hall of Fame......$12–15

Walleye Pike 1987 ....$17–23

Washington 1975
A state series bottle to commemorate the Evergreen State................$5–6

Washington—The Evergreen State 1974
The club bottle for the Evergreen State Beam Bottle and Specialties
Club $10–12

Washington State Bicentennial 1976 ....$10–12

Waterman 1980 ....$100–130

Western Shrine Association 1980
Commemorates the Shriners convention in Phoenix, Ariz...........$20–22

West Virginia 1963 ....$130–140

White Fox 1969
Issued for the second anniversary of the Jim Beam Bottle and
Specialties Club in Berkley, Calif. $25–35

Wisconsin Muskie Bottle 1971 ....$15–17

Woodpecker 1969 ....$6–8

Wyoming 1965 ....$40–50

Yellow Katz 1967
Commemorates the 50th anniversary of the Katz Department
Stores $15–17

Yellow Rose 1978
Executive series $7–10

Yellowstone Park Centennial...$4–7

Yosemite 1967..$4–6

Yuma Rifle Club $18–23

Zimmerman—Art Institute $5–8

Zimmerman Bell 1976
Designed for Zimmerman Liquor Store of Chicago..........................$6–7

Zimmerman Bell 1976...$6–7

Zimmerman—Blue Beauty 1969...$9–12

Zimmerman—Blue Daisy $4–6

Zimmerman—Cherubs 1968...$4–6

Zimmerman—Chicago $4–6

Zimmerman—Eldorado $4–7

Zimmerman—Glass 1969..$7–9

Zimmerman—Oatmeal Jug...$40–50

Zimmerman—The Peddler Bottle 1971...$4–6

Zimmerman Two-Handled Jug 1965..$45–60

Zimmerman Vase, Brown...$6–9

Zimmerman Vase, Green $6–9

Zimmerman—50th Anniversary $35–45

Automobile and Transportation Series

Chevrolet
1957 Convertible, Black, New...$85–95

1957 Convertible, Red, New $75–85

1957, Black..$70–80

1957, Dark Blue, Pa. $70–80

1957, Red $80–90

1957, Sierra Gold $140–160

1957, Turquoise...$50–70

1957, Yellow Hot Rod...$65–75

Camaro 1969, Blue..$55–65

Camaro 1969, Burgundy..$120–140

Camaro 1969, Green..$100–120

Camaro 1969, Orange..$55–65

Camaro 1969, Pace Car..$60–70

Camaro 1969, Silver...$120–140

Camaro 1969, Yellow, Pa. $55–65

Corvette 1986, Pace Car, Yellow, New $60–85

Corvette 1984, Black..$70–80

Corvette 1984, Bronze $100–200

Corvette 1984, Gold...$100–120

Corvette 1984, Red $55–65

Corvette 1984, White..$55–65

Corvette 1978, Black..$140–170

Corvette 1978, Pace Car...$135–160

Corvette 1978, Red $50–60

Corvette 1978, White..$40–50

Corvette 1978, Yellow...$40–50

Corvette 1963, Black, Pa. $75–85

Corvette 1963, Blue, N.Y. $90–100

Corvette 1963, Red $60–70

Corvette 1963, Silver $50–60

Corvette 1955, Black, New...$110–140

Corvette 1955, Copper, New $90–110

Corvette 1955, Red, New $110–140

Corvette 1954, Blue, New $90–110

Corvette 1953, White, New..$100–120

Dusenberg
Convertible, Cream $130–140

Convertible, Dark blue..$120–130

Convertible, Light blue $80–100

Convertible Coupe, Gray $160–180

Ford
International Delivery Wagon, Black.......................................$80–90

International Delivery Wagon, Green......................................$80–90

Fire Chief 1928 ....$120–130

Fire Chief 1934 ....$60–70

Fire Pumper Truck 1935 ....$45–60

Model A, Angelo's Liquor..$180–200

Model A, Parkwood Supply..$140–170

Model A 1903, Black...$35–45

Model A 1903, Red $35–45

Model A 1928 ....$60–80

Model A Fire Truck 1930...$130–170

Model T 1913, Black..$30–40

Model T 1913, Green...$30–40

Mustang 1964, Black...$100–125

Mustang 1964, Red...$35–45

Mustang 1964, White..$25–35

Paddy Wagon 1930 ....$100–200

Phaeton 1929 ....$40–50

Pickup Truck 1935...$20–30

Police Car 1929, Blue $75–85

Police Car 1929, Yellow $350–450

Police Patrol Car 1934..$60–70

Police Tow Truck 1935..$20–30

Roadster 1934, Cream, PA, New $80–90

Thunderbird 1956, Black..$60–70

Oldsmobile 1903..$25–35

Olsonite Eagle Racer $35–40

Police Patrol Car 1934, Yellow $110–140

Space Shuttle..$20–30

Stutz 1914, Gray $40–50

Stutz 1914, Yellow $40–50

Thomas Flyer 1909, Blue $60–70

Thomas Flyer 1909, Ivory $60–70

Vendome Wagon..$40–50

Volkswagen, Blue..$40–50

Volkswagen, Red..$40–50

Thunderbird 1956, Blue, PA $70–80

Thunderbird 1956, Gray..$50–60

Thunderbird 1956, Green..$60–70

Thunderbird 1956, Yellow..$50–60

Woodie Wagon 1929..$50–60

Mercedes
1974, Blue $30–40

1974, Gold $60–80

1974, Green..$30–40

1974, Mocha..$30–40

1974, Red $30–40

1974, Sand beige, PA $30–40

1974, Silver, Australia...$140–160

1974, White $35–45

Trains
Baggage car..$40–60

Boxcar, Brown..$50–60

Boxcar, Yellow $40–50

Bumper $5–8

Caboose, Gray..$45–55

Caboose, Red...$50–60

Casey Jones with Tender..$65–80

Casey Jones Caboose...$40–55

Casey Jones Accessory Set $50–60

Coal Tender, No Bottle...$20–30

Combination Car $55–65

Dining Car..$75–90

Flatcar..$20–30

General Locomotive...$60–70

Grant Locomotive $50–65

Log Car...$40–55

Lumber Car $12–18

Observation Car...$15–23

Passenger Car...$45–53

Tank Car $15–20

Track..$4–6

Turner Locomotive $80–100

Water Tower $20–30

Wood Tender $40–45

Wood Tender, No Bottle $20–25

Other
Ambulance $18–22

Army Jeep $18–20

Bass Boat $12–18

Cable Car $25–30

Circus Wagon $20–30

Ernie's Flower Cart $20–30

Golf Cart $20–30

HC Covered Wagon 1929...$10–20

Jewel Tea $70–80

Mack Fire Truck 1917 ....$120–135

Mississippi Pumper Fire Truck 1867 ....$115–140

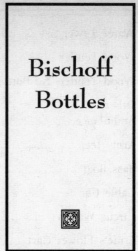

Bischoff Bottles

Bischoffs, which was founded in Trieste, Italy, in 1777, issued decorative figurals in the eighteenth century, long before any other company. The early bottles are rare because of the limited production and the attrition of extent bottles over the years. Modern-day Bischoffs were imported into the United States beginning in 1949. Collectors haven't shown intense interest in modern imports and since sales have not been made often enough to have establish values, prices are not included in this book. Three other types of Bischoffs will be covered: Kord Bohemian decanters, Venetian glass figurals, and ceramic decanters and figurals.

Kord Bohemian Decanters

These decanters were hand-blown and hand-painted glass bottles created in Czechoslovakia by the Kord Company, with a tradition of Bohemian cut, engraved, etched, and flashed glass. Stoppers and labels with the bottles are considered very rare and valuable today. The cut-glass and ruby-etched decanters were imported to the United States in the early 1950s. The ruby-etched is considered rare only if complete with the stopper.

In addition, most of these decanters have a matching set of glasses, which increases the value if the entire set is intact.

Amber Flowers 1952
A two-toned glass decanter, 15½ in., dark, amber stopper..........$30–40

Amber Leaves 1952
Multitoned bottle with long neck, 13½ in. $30–40

Anisette 1948–1951
Clear glass bottle with ground glass stopper, 11 in......................$20–30

Bohemian Ruby-Etched, 1949–1951
Round decanter, tapered neck, etched stopper, 15½ in..............$30–40

Coronet Crystal 1952
A round tall bottle, multitoned, with a broad band of flowers, leaves,
and scroll circles, 14 in. $30–40

Cut-Glass Decanter (blackberry) 1951
A geometric design, hand-cut overall, ground stopper,
10½ in. $32–42

Czech Hunter 1958
Round thick clear glass, heavy round glass base, 8½ in..............$18–26

Czech Hunter's Lady 1958
"Mae West"-shaped decanter of cracked clear glass,
10 in...$18–26

Dancing—Country Scene 1950
Clear glass hand-blown decanter with peasant boy and girl doing a
country dance beside a tree, 12¼ in. $25–35

Dancing—Peasant Scene 1950
Decanter of pale and amber glass, peasants in costume dancing to
music of bagpipes, 12 in. $25–35

Double—Dolphin 1949–1969
Fish-shaped twin bottles joined at the bellies, hand-blown clear
glass $20–30

Flying Geese Pitcher 1952
Green glass handle and stopper, glass base, 9½ in. $15–25

Flying Geese Pitcher 1957
Clear crystal handled pitcher, gold stopper, 9½ in. $15–25

Horse Head 1947–1969
Pale amber-colored bottle in the shape of a horse's head, round
pouring spout on top, 8 in. $15–25

Jungle Parrot—Amber Glass 1952
Hand-etched jungle scenes with a yellow-amber color,
15½ in. $25–35

Jungle Parrot—Ruby Glass 1952
Hand-etched jungle scenes with a ruby-colored body,
15½ in. $20–30

Old Coach Bottle 1948
Pale amber color, round glass stopper, 10 in. $25–35

Old Sleigh Bottle 1949
Glass decanter, hand-painted, signed, 10 in. $22–32

Wild Geese—Amber Glass 1952
Tall round decanter with tapering etched neck, flashed with a yellow-
amber color, 15½ in...$25–35

Wild Geese—Ruby Glass 1952
Tall round decanter with tapering etched neck, flashed with a ruby-red
color, 15½ in. $25–35

Venetian Glass Figurals

*These figurals are produced in limited editions by the Serguso Glass Company
in Morano, Italy, and are unique in design and color, with birds, fish, cats,
and dogs.*

Black Cat 1969
Glass black cat with curled tail, 12 in. long...............................$18–25

Dog—Alabaster 1966
Seated alabaster glass dog, 13 in. $33–45

Dog—Dachshund 1966
Alabaster dog with brown tones, 19 in. long..............................$40–50

Duck 1964
Alabaster glass tinted pink and green, long neck, upraised wings, 11
in. long..$42–52

Fish—Multicolor 1964
Round fat fish; alabaster glass; green, rose, yellow $18–25

Fish—Ruby 1969
Long, flat, ruby glass fish, 12 in. long $25–35

Ceramic Decanters and Figurals

These are some of the most interesting, attractive, and valuable of the Bischoff collection and are made of ceramic, stoneware, and pottery. Decanters complete with handles, spouts, and stoppers demand the highest value.

African Head 1962 .... $15–18

Bell House 1960 .... $30–40

Bell Tower 1960 .... $15–30

Boy (Chinese) Figural 1962 .... $30–40

Boy (Spanish) Figural 1961 .... $25–35

Clown with Black Hair 1963 .... $30–40

Clown with Red Hair 1963 .... $15–25

Deer Figural 1969 .... $20–25

Egyptian Dancing Figural 1961 .... $12–17

Egyptian Pitcher—Two Musicians 1969 .... $15–24

Egyptian Pitcher—Three Musicians 1959 .... $20–28

Floral Canteen 1969 .... $18–22

Fruit Canteen 1969 .... $13–19

Girl in Chinese Costume 1962 .... $30–40

Girl in Spanish Costume 1961 .... $30–40

Greek Vase Decanter 1969 .... $13–19

Mask—Gray Face 1963 .... $16–26

Oil and Vinegar Cruets—Black and White 1959 .... $18–25

Vase—Black and Gold 1959 .... $19–22

Watchtower 1960 .... $12–16

Borghini bottles, ceramics of modernistic style with historical themes, are manufactured in Pisa, Italy. These bottles vary greatly in price depending on distribution points. The lowest values are in areas closest to the point of distribution or near heavy retail sales. Recent bottles are stamped "Borghini Collection Made in Italy."

Cats
Black with red ties, 6 in. $11–15

Cats
Black with red ties, 12 in. $10–15

Female head
Ceramic, 9½ in. $11–15

Penguin
Black and white, 6 in. $8–11

Penguin 1969
Black and white, 12 in. $12–16

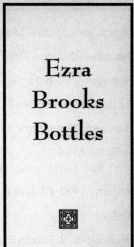

Ezra Brooks Bottles

The Ezra Brooks Distilling Company did not start to issue figurals until 1964, ten years after the Jim Beam company, and quickly became a strong rival owing to effective distribution, promotion techniques, original designs, and choice of subjects.

While many of the Brooks bottles depict the same themes as the Jim Beam series (sports and transportation), they also produced bottles based on original subjects. The Maine lobster looks good enough to put on anyone's dinner table. The most popular series depict antiques such as an Edison phonograph and a Spanish cannon. Yearly new editions highlight American historical events and anniversaries. One of my favorites is the Bucket of Blood (1970)—from the Virginia City, Nevada, saloon by the same name—in a bucket-shaped bottle.

While these bottles are still filled with Kentucky bourbon, most purchases of these figural bottles are made by collectors.

Alabama Bicentennial 1976 ....$12–14

American Legion 1971
Distinguished embossed star emblem from World War I.............$20–30

American Legion 1972
Salutes the Illinois American Legion's 54th National
Convention $45–55

American Legion 1973
Salutes Hawaii, which hosted the American Legion's 54th National
Convention $10–12

American Legion—Denver 1977 ....$19–22

American Legion—Miami Beach 1973............$8–12

Amvets—Dolphin 1974............$8–10

Amvets—Polish Legion 1973............$14–18

Antique Cannon 1969............$6–9

Antique Phonograph 1970............$8–12

Arizona 1969
Man with burro in search of Lost Dutchman Mine............$4–8

Auburn 1932 Classic Car 1978............$18–20

Badger No. 1 Boxer 1973............$9–11

Badger No. 2 Football 1974............$10–14

Badger No. 3 Hockey 1974............$9–12

Baltimore Oriole Wildlife 1979............$20–30

Bare-Knuckle Fighter 1971............$5–7

Baseball Hall of Fame 1973............$20–22

Baseball Player 1974............$14–16

Bear 1968............$5–9

Bengal Tiger Wildlife 1979............$20–30

Betsy Ross 1975............$8–12

Big Bertha
Nugget Casino's very own elephant with a raised trunk............$10–13

Big Daddy Lounge 1969
Salute to South Florida's state liquor chain and Big Daddy
Lounges............$4–6

Bighorn Ram 1973............$14–18

Bird Dog 1971............$12–14

Bordertown
Salutes the Borderline Club, on the border of California and
Nevada............$5–10

Bowler 1973............$4–6

Bowling Tenpins 1973 ....$9–12

Brahma Bull 1972 ....$10–12

Bucket of Blood 1970
Salutes the famous Virginia City, Nev., saloon; bucket-shaped
bottle $5–7

Bucking Bronco, Rough Rider 1973 ....$7–9

Bucky Badger, Football $20–25

Bucky Badger, Hockey 1975 ....$18–24

Bucky Badger No. 1 Boxer 1973 ....$9–12

Buffalo Hunt 1971 ....$5–7

Bulldog 1972
Mighty canine mascot and football symbol $10–14

Bull Moose 1973 ....$12–15

Busy Beaver $4–7

Cabin Still $20–35

Cable Car 1968 ....$5–6

California Quail 1970 ....$8–10

Canadian Honker 1975 ....$9–12

Canadian Loon Wildlife 1979 ....$25–35

Cardinal 1972 ....$20–25

Casey at the Bat 1973 ....$6–10

Ceremonial Indian 1970 ....$15–18

CB Convoy Radio 1976 ....$5–9

Charolais Beer 1973 ....$10–14

Cheyenne Shootout 1970
Honoring the Wild West and its Cheyenne Frontier Days $6–10

Chicago Fire 1974 ....$20–30

Chicago Water Tower 1969 ....$8–12

Christmas Decanter 1966 ....$5–8

Christmas Tree 1979...$13–17

Churchill 1970
Commemorating the "Iron Curtain" speech at Westminster College
by Churchill $5–9

Cigar Store Indian 1968 ....$4–6

Classic Firearms 1969
Embossed gun set consisting of derringer, Colt .45, Peacemaker, over-
and-under flintlock, and pepperbox $15–19

Clowns, Imperial Shrine 1978 ....$9–11

Clown Bust No. 1 Smiley 1979 ....$22–28

Clown Bust No. 2 Cowboy 1979..$20–25

Clown Bust No. 3 Pagliacci 1979 ....$15–22

Clown Bust No. 4 Keystone Kop..$30–40

Clown Bust No. 5 Cuddles $20–30

Clown Bust No. 6 Tramp $20–30

Clown with Accordion 1971 ....$15–18

Clown with Balloon 1973...$20–32

Club Bottle, Birthday Cake $9–12

Club Bottle, Distillery $9–12

Club Bottle 1973
The third commemorative Ezra Brooks Collectors Club bottle, in the
shape of America...$14–18

Clydesdale Horse 1973 ....$8–12

Colt Peacemaker Flask 1969 ....$4–8

Conquistadors
Tribute to the great drum and bugle corps...$6–9

Conquistadors Drum and Bugle 1972...$12–15

Corvette Indy Pace Car 1978...$45–55

Corvette 1957 Classic, 1976 ....$110–140

Court Jester $5–7

Dakota Cowboy 1975 ....$34–44

Dakota Cowgirl 1976 ....$20–26

Dakota Grain Elevator 1978 ....$20–30

Dakota Shotgun Express 1977 ....$18–22

Dead Wagon 1970
Made to carry gunfight losers to Boot Hill............................$5–7

Delta Belle 1969 ....$6–7

Democratic Convention 1976 ....$10–16

Derringer Flask 1969 ....$5–8

Distillery 1970
Reproduction of the Ezra Brooks Distillery in Kentucky $9–11

Dusenburg $24–33

Elephant 1973 ....$7–9

Elk
Salutes those organizations that practiced benevolence and
charity..$20–28

English Setter—Bird Dog 1971 ....$14–17

Equestrienne 1974 ....$7–10

Esquire, Ceremonial Dancer $10–16

Farthington Bike 1972 ....$6–8

Fire Engine 1971 ....$14–18

Fireman 1975 ....$18–23

Fisherman 1974 ....$8–12

Flintlock 1969 (two versions: Japanese and Heritage)
Japanese $7–9
Heritage..$12–16

Florida "Gators" 1973
Tribute to the University of Florida Gators football team...............$9–11

Foe Eagle 1978 ....$15–20

Foe Flying Eagle 1979 ....$20–25

Foe Eagle 1980 ....$25–40

Foe Eagle 1981 ....$18–28

Football Player 1974 ....$10–14

Ford Mustang...$20–30

Ford Thunderbird—1956, 1976...$70–80

Foremost Astronaut 1970
Tribute to a major liquor supermarket, Foremost Liquor Store $5–7

Fresno Decanter...$5–12

Fresno Grape with Gold...$48–60

Fresno Grape 1970...$6–11

Gamecock 1970..$9–13

Go Big Red, Football-Shaped Bottle
   No. 1 with football 1972 ....$20–28
   No. 2 with hat 1971...$18–22
   No. 3 with rooster 1972 ....$10–14

Golden Antique Cannon 1969
Symbol of Spanish power $5–7

Golden Eagle 1971 ....$18–22

Golden Grizzly Bear 1970 ....$4–6

Golden Horseshoe 1970
Salute to Reno's Horseshoe Club $7–9

Golden Rooster No. 1
Replica of solid-gold rooster on display at Nugget Casino in Reno,
Nev. $35–50

Gold Prospector 1969 ....$5–9

Gold Seal 1972 ....$12–14

Gold Turkey $35–45

Go Tiger Go 1973 ....$10–14

Grandfather Clock 1970 ....$5–7

Grandfather Clock 1970 ....$12–20

Greater Greensboro Open 1972 ....$16–19

Greater Greensboro Open 1972 ....$15–20

Greater Greensboro Open Golfer 1973 ....$17–24

Greater Greensboro Open Map 1974 ....$29–36

Greater Greensboro Open Cup 1975 ....$25–30

Greater Greensboro Open Club and Ball 1977 ....$20–25

Great Stone Face—Old Man of the Mountain 1970 ....$10–14

Great White Shark 1977 ....$8–14

Hambletonian 1971 ....$13–16

Happy Goose 1975 ....$12–15

Harolds Club Dice 1968 ....$8–12

Hereford 1971 ....$12–15

Hereford 1972 ....$12–15

Historical Flask Eagle 1970 ....$3–5

Historical Flask Flagship 1970 ....$3–5

Historical Flask Liberty 1970 ....$3–5

Historical Flask Old Ironsides 1970 ....$3–5

Historical Flask 1970 ....$3–5

Hollywood Cops 1972 ....$12–18

Hopi Indian 1970
Kachina doll $15–20

Hopi Kachina 1973 ....$50–75

Idaho—Ski the Potato 1973
Salutes the State of Idaho $8–10

Indianapolis 500 ....$30–35

Indian Ceremonial $13–18

Indian Hunter 1970 ....$12–15

Iowa Farmer 1977 ....$55–65

Iowa Grain Elevator 1978 ....$25–34

Iron Horse Locomotive $8–14

Jack O'Diamonds 1969 ....$4–6

Jayhawk 1969 ....$6–8

Jester 1971 ....$6–8

Jug, Old-time 1.75 Liters $9–13

Kachina Doll No. 1 1971 ....$80–100

Kachina Doll No. 2 1973 ....$10–60

Kachina Doll No. 3 1974 ....$50–60

Kachina Doll No. 4 1975 ....$20–25

Kachina Doll No. 5 1976 ....$30–40

Kachina Doll No. 6 1977 ....$25–35

Kachina Doll No. 7 1978 ....$35–45

Kachina Doll No. 8 1979 ....$50–60

Kansas Jayhawk 1969 ....$4–7

Katz Cats 1969
Siamese cats are symbolic of Katz Drug Company of Kansas City,
Kans. $8–12

Katz Cats Philharmonic 1970
Commemorating its 27th annual Star Night $6–10

Keystone Kops 1980 ....$32–40

Keystone Kops 1971 ....$25–35

Killer Whale 1972 .... $15–20

King of Clubs 1969 .... $4–6

King Salmon 1971 .... $18–24

Liberty Bell 1970 .... $5–6

Lincoln Continental Mark I 1941 .... $20–25

Lion on the Rock 1971 .... $5–7

Liquor Square 1972 .... $5–7

Little Giant 1971
Replica of the first horse-drawn steam engine to arrive at the Chicago
fire in 1871 .... $11–16

Maine Lighthouse 1971 .... $18–24

Maine Lobster 1970 .... $15–18

Man-o-War 1969 .... $10–16

M&M Brown Jug 1975B $15–20

Map, U.S.A. Club Bottle 1972 .... $7–9

Masonic Fez 1976 .... $12–15

Max "The Hat" Zimmerman 1976 .... $20–25

Military Tank 1971 .... $15–22

Minnesota Hockey Player 1975 .... $18–22

Minuteman 1975 .... $10–15

Missouri Mule, Brown 1972 .... $7–9

Moose 1973 .... $20–28

Motorcycle $10–14

Mountaineer 1971
One of the most valuable Ezra Brooks figural bottles $40–55

Mr. Foremost 1969 .... $7–10

Mr. Maine Potato 1973 .... $6–10

Mr. Merchant 1970 .... $6–10

Mule $8–12

Mustang Indy Pace Car 1979 .... $20–30

Nebraska—Go Big Red! $12–15

New Hampshire State House 1970 .... $9–13

North Carolina Bicentennial 1975 .... $8–12

Nugget Classic
Replica of golf pin presented to golf tournament participants $7–12

Oil Gusher $6–8

Old Capital 1971 .... $30–40

Old EZ No. 1 Barn Owl 1977 .... $25–35

Old EZ No. 2 Eagle Owl 1978 .... $40–55

Old EZ No. 3 Show Owl 1979 .... $20–35

Old Man of the Mountain 1970 .... $10–14

Old Water Tower 1969
Famous landmark, survived the Chicago fire of 1871 .... $12–16

Oliver Hardy Bust $12–18

Ontario 500 1970 .... $18–22

Overland Express 1969 .... $17–20

Over-Under Flintlock Flask 1969 .... $6–9

Panda—Giant 1972 .... $12–17

Penguin 1972 .... $8–10

Penny Farthington High-wheeler 1973 .... $9–12

Pepperbox Flask 1969 .... $4–6

Phoenix Bird 1971 .... $20–26

Phoenix Jaycees 1973 .... $10–14

Phonograph $15–20

Piano 1970 .... $12–13

Pirate 1971 ....$6–10

Polish Legion American Vets 1978..................................$18–26

Portland Head Lighthouse 1971
Honors the lighthouse that has guided ships safely into Maine
Harbor since 1791..$18–24

Potbellied Stove 1968 ....$5–6

Queen of Hearts 1969
Playing card symbol with royal flush in hearts on front of the
bottle..$4–6

Raccoon Wildlife 1978..$30–40

Ram 1973 ....$13–18

Razorback Hog 1969 ....$12–18

Razorback Hog 1979 ....$20–30

Red Fox 1979..$30–40

Reno Arch 1968
Honoring the "Biggest Little City in the World," Reno, Nev............$4–8

Sailfish 1971 ....$7–11

Salmon, Washington King 1971.......................................$20–26

San Francisco Cable Car 1968..$4–8

Sea Captain 1971 ....$10–14

Sea Lion—Gold 1972...$11–14

Senators of the United States 1972
Honors the senators of the United States of America $10–13

Setter 1974..$10–15

Shrine King Tut Guard 1979 ....$16–24

1804 Silver Dollar 1970 ....$5–8

Silver Saddle 1973...$22–25

Silver Spur Boot 1971
Cowboy-boot-shaped bottle with silver spur buckled on; "Silver Spur—
Carson City Nevada" embossed on side of boot $7–11

Simba 1971 ....$9–12

Ski Boot 1972 ....$5–7

Slot Machine 1971
A replica of the original nickel Liberty Bell slot machine invented by
Charles Fey in 1895..$18–24

Snowmobiles 1972..$8–11

South Dakota Air National Guard 1976 ....$18–22

Spirit of '76 1974 ....$5–7

Spirit of Saint Louis 1977, 50th Anniversary $6–11

Sprint Car Racer..$30–40

Stagecoach 1969 ....$10–12

Stan Laurel Bust 1976 ....$10–16

Stock Market Ticker 1970
A unique replica of a ticker-tape machine $8–11

Stonewall Jackson 1974 ....$22–28

Strongman 1974..$8–12

Sturgeon 1975...$20–28

John L. Sullivan 1970 ....$15–20

Syracuse, NY 1973 ....$11–16

Tank Patton 1972
Reproduction of a U.S. Army tank $16–20

Tecumseh 1969
Figurehead of the U.S.S. *Delaware*; this decanter is an embossed replica
of the statue of the United States Naval Academy...........................$5–6

Telephone 1971
Replica of the old-time upright handset telephone $16–19

Tennis Player 1972...$8–12

Terrapin, Maryland 1974...$14–16

Texas Longhorn 1971 ....$18–22

Ticker Tape 1970 ....$8–12

Tiger on Stadium 1973
Commemorates college teams who have chosen the tiger as their
mascot...$12–17

Tom Turkey $18–24

Tonopah 1972...$12–15

Totem Pole 1972 ....$10–14

Tractor 1971
A model of the 1917 Fordson made by Henry Ford......................$9–11

Trail Bike Rider 1972 ....$10–12

Trojan Horse 1974 ....$15–18

Trojans—USC Football 1973 ....$10–14

Trout and Fly 1970..$7–11

Truckin' and Vannin' 1977...$7–12

Vermont Skier 1972 ....$10–12

VFW—Veterans of Foreign Wars 1973.......................................$6–10

Virginia—Red Cardinal 1973 ....$15–20

Walgreen Drugs 1974 ....$16–24

Weirton Steel 1973 ....$15–18

Western Rodeos 1973 ....$17–23

West Virginia—Mountaineer 1971 ....$65–75

West Virginia—Mountain Lady 1972..$14–20

Whale 1972...$14–20

Wheat Shocker 1971
The mascot of the Kansas football team in a fighting pose.............$5–7

Whiskey Flask 1970
Reproduction of collectible American patriotic whiskey flask of the 1800s: Old Ironsides, Miss Liberty, American Eagle, Civil War Commemorative..$12–14

Whitetail Deer 1947...$18–24

White Turkey 1971 ....$20–25

Wichita $4–8

Wichita Centennial 1970 ....$4–6

Winston Churchill 1969 ....$6–10

Zimmerman's Hat 1968
A salute to "Zimmerman's—World's Largest Liquor Store"..............$5–6

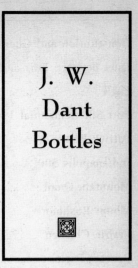

J. W. Dant Bottles

J.W. Dant Distilling Company also produces bottles similar to the Brooks and Beam bottles, and they likewise have strong collector appeal. These bottles usually depict American themes such as patriotic events and folklore in addition to various animals.

Because Dant has such a liking for American history and traditions, most of these bottles are decorated with historical scenes in full color. Some bottles carry an embossed American eagle and shield with stars. These bottles are all limited editions and the molds are not reused.

Garnier Bottles

Garnet Et Cie, a French firm founded in 1858, has long been given credit for being the pioneer of the modern collectible liquor bottle because they introduced the Garnier figural bottles in 1899. During Prohibition and World War II, there was a temporary halt in production but they quickly resumed manufacturing in the 1950s.

Those bottles manufactured prior to World War II are the most rare and valuable but are not listed in this book owing to the difficulty of establishing valid price levels. Among them are the Cat (1930), Clown (1910), Country Jug (1937), Greyhound (1930), Penguin (1930), and Marquise (1931).

Aladdin's Lamp 1963 ....$40–50

Alfa Romeo 1913, 1970 ....$20–30

Alfa Romeo 1929, 1969 ....$20–30

Alfa Romeo Racer 1969 ....$20–30

Antique Coach 1970..$25–30

Apollo 1969
Apollo spaceship, 13½ in. $17–22

Aztec Vase 1965 ....$15–20

Baby Foot—Soccer Shoe 1963
Black with white trim, 3¾ in. × 8½ in.......................................$10–20
1962 soccer shoe, large..$7–11

Baby Trio 1963 ....$7–10

Baccus Figural 1967 ....$20–25

Bahamas
Black policeman, white jacket and hat, black pants, red stripe, gold details..$15–24

Baltimore Oriole 1970 ....$10–16

Bandit Figural 1958 ....$10–14

Bedroom Candlestick 1967 ....$20–25

Bellows 1969 ....$14–21

Bird Ashtray 1958 ....$3–4

Bluebird 1970 ....$12–18

Bouquet 1966 ....$15–25

Bull (and Matador), Animal Figural 1963 ....$17–23

Burmese Man Vase 1965 ....$15–25

Canada $11–14

Candlestick 1955 ....$25–35

Candlestick Glass 1965 ....$15–25

Cannon 1964 ....$50–60

Cardinal State Bird—Illinois 1969 ....$12–15

Cat—Black 1962 ....$15–25

Cat—Gray 1962 ....$15–25

Chalet 1955 ....$40–50

Chimney 1956 ....$55–65

Chinese Dog 1965 ....$15–25

Chinese Statuette—Man 1970 ....$15–25

Chinese Statuette—Woman 1970 ....$15–25

Christmas Tree 1956...$60–70

Citroën 1922, 1970 ....$20–30

Classic Ashtray 1958 ....$20–30

Clock 1958..$20–30

Clown Holding Tuba 1955 ....$15–25

Coffee Mill 1966...$20–30

Columbine Figural 1968
    Female partner..$20–30
    Harlequin $30–40

Drunkard—Drunk on Lamppost $15–20

Duckling Figural 1956 ....$18–26

Duo 1954
Two clear glass bottles stacked, two pouring spouts $12–18

Egg Figural 1956 ....$70–80

Eiffel Tower 1951
    13½ in. $15–25
    12½ in. $14–20

Elephant Figural 1961...$20–30

Empire Vase 1962 ....$10–18

Fiat 500 1913, 1970
Yellow body...$20–30

Fiat Nuevo 1913, 1970
Blue body $20–30

Flask Garnier 1958..$9–12

Flying Horse Pegasus 1958 ....$50–60

Ford 1913, 1970..$20–30

Fountain 1964...$25–35

Giraffe 1961 ....$20–35

Goldfinch 1970 ....$12–16

Paris, French Policeman..$10–15

Paris Taxis 1960 ....$20–30

Partridge 1961 ....$25–35

Pheasant 1969 ....$25–35

Pigeon—Clear Glass 1958 ....$10–15

Pony 1961 ....$25–35

Poodle 1954 ....$12–15

Renault 1911, 1969 ....$20–30

Road Runner 1969..$10–15

Robin 1970...$10–15

Rocket 1958 ....$10–15

Rolls Royce 1908, 1970 ....$20–30

Rooster 1952 ....$15–25

Saint Tropez Jug 1961B $20–30

Scarecrow 1960...$25–35

Sheriff 1958..$15–25

Snail 1950 ....$58–68

Soccer Shoe 1962 ....$30–40

S.S. *France*—Large 1962 ....$80–130

S.S. *France*—Small 1962 ....$50–60

S.S. *Queen Mary* 1970..$25–35

Stanley Steamer 1907, 1970...$20–30

Teapot 1961 ....$15–25

Teapot 1935 ....$20–30

Trout 1967 ....$17–22

Valley Quail 1969..$8–12

Hoffman Bottles

The Hoffman bottles are considered limited editions since each issue is restricted in terms of quantity produced. When this set number is reached, the molds are destroyed, which quickly establishes these designs as very collectible, rare, and valuable.

While these bottles often reflect European figures in various occupations, they have also focused on American subjects. These include the 1976 Bicentennial bottle and the 1976 Hippie bottle.

Occupation Series

Mr. Bartender with Music Box
"He's a Jolly Good Fellow" $25–30

Mr. Charmer with Music Box
"Glow Little Glow Worm"..$10–15

Mr. Dancer with Music Box
"The Irish Washerwoman" $18–22

Mr. Doctor with Music Box
"As Long as He Needs Me"..$20–25

Mr. Fiddler with Music Box
"Hearts and Flowers"..$20–22

Mr. Guitarist with Music Box
"Johnny Guitar" $20–22

Mr. Harpist with Music Box
"Do-Re-Mi"..$10–15

Mr. Lucky with Music Box
"When Irish Eyes Are Smiling"..$15–20

Mrs. Lucky with Music Box
"The Kerry Dancer"...$12–15

Mr. Policeman with Music Box
"Don't Blame Me"..$30–35

Mr. Sandman with Music Box
"Mr. Sandman"..$10–20

Mr. Saxophonist with Music Box
"Tiger Rag"..$15–20

Mr. Shoe Cobbler with Music Box
"Danny Boy"..$15–20

Bicentennial Series ⅕-Quart Size

Betsy Ross with Music Box
"The Star-Spangled Banner"...$30–40

Majestic Eagle with Music Box
"America the Beautiful"..$60–80

C. M. Russell Series ⅕-Quart Size

Buffalo Man...$20–25

Flathead Squaw...$15–20

Last of Five Thousand...$14–18

Red River Breed...$23–30

The Scout...$30–40

The Stage Drive..$20–30

Trapper...$20–30

Japanese Bottles

While bottle making in Japan is an ancient art, the collectible bottles now produced are mainly for export purposes. Greater numbers of these bottles, now available in the American marketplace, have kept prices reasonable.

Daughter $12–18

Faithful Retainer $25–35

Golden Pagoda $12–18

"Kiku" Geisha, Blue, 13¼ in. $20–30

Maiden $12–18

Noh Mask $12–18

Okame Mask $50–70

Playboy $14–24

Princess $14–24

Red Lion Man $40–60

Sake God, Colorful Robe, Procelain, 10 in. ... $20–30

Sake God, White, Bone China, 10 in. $12–15

White Lion Man $35–50

White Pagoda $15–20

"Yuri" Geisha, Pink, Red Sash, 13¼ in. $35–45

House of Koshu

Angel, with Book, 7 ounces $5–10

Angel, Sitting on a Barrel, 17 ounces $5–10

Beethoven Bust, 7 ounces...$5–10

Centurian Bust, 7 ounces $5–10

Children, 7 ounces $7–10

Declaration of Independence...$4–6

Geisha, Blue...$40–45

Geisha, Cherry Blossom...$30–35

Geisha, Lily $25–35

Geisha, Violet...$30–40

Geisha, Wisteria $30–40

Geisha, Lavender with Fan...$45–50

Geisha, Reclining...$60–70

Geisha, Sitting...$45–50

Lion Man, Red $40–45

Lion Man, White $80–95

Pagoda, Green $25–30

Pagoda, White $20–25

Pagoda, Gold $15–20

Sailor with a Pipe...$6–10

Kamotsuru Bottles

Daokoru, God of Wealth $9–13

Ebisu, God of Fishermen...$10–15

Goddess of Art...$10–12

Hotei, God of Wealth...$7–10

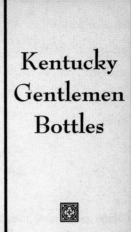

Kentucky Gentlemen Bottles

These bottles are similar in design to the Beam and Brooks bottles but are released less frequently. As a rule, these bottles reflect clothing of various periods of American history, most notably around the Civil War time frame.

Confederate Infantry
In gray uniform with sword, 13½ in. $10–15

Frontiersman (1969)
Coonskin cap, fringed buckskin, power horn, long rifle, 14 in. $12–15

Kentucky Gentlemen (1969)
Figural bottle, frock coat, top hat and cane; "Old Colonel," gray ceramic, 14 in. $12–15

Pink Lady (1969)
Long bustle skirt, feathered hat, pink parasol, 13¼ in. $20–32

Revolutionary War Officer
In dress uniform and boots, holding sword, 14 in. $12–16

Union Army Sergeant
In dress uniform with sword, 14 in. $9–13

Lionstone bottles, manufactured by Lionstone Distillery, reflect a great deal of realism in their designs in terms of components and details. Their "Shootout at O.K. Corral" work, for example, consists of three bottles with nine figures and two horses.

The Lionstone bottles are issued in series form and include a sport, circus, and bicentennial series. The most popular among collectors is the Western series. Since prices of these bottles have continued to be firm in the market, the collector should always be on the lookout for old, uncirculated stock.

Bar Scene No. 1	$125–140
Bartender	$18–22
Belly Robber	$12–16
Blacksmith	$20–30
Molly Brown	$18–25
Buffalo Hunter	$25–35
Calamity Jane	$18–23
Camp Cook	$13–17
Camp Follower	$9–12
Canadian Goose	$45–55
Casual Indian	$8–12

Cavalry Scout...$8–12

Cherry Valley Club $50–60

Chinese Laundryman..$12–15

Annie Christmas $10–15

Circuit Judge...$8–12

Corvette, 1.75 Liters $60–75

Country Doctor..$12–18

Cowboy..$8–10

Frontiersman $14–16

Gambels Quail $8–12

Gentleman Gambler...$25–35

God of Love $17–22

God of War...$17–22

Gold Panner $25–35

Highway Robber..$15–20

Jesse James $18–23

Johnny Lightning...$50–65

Judge Roy Bean..$20–30

Lonely Luke $45–60

Lucky Buck...$18–24

Mallard Duck $35–45

Miniatures—Western (six)..$85–110

Mint Bar with Frame...$700–900

Mint Bar with Nude and Frame...$1,000–1,250

Mountain Man...$15–20

Annie Oakley..$14–16

Pintail Duck $40–55

Proud Indian $10–14

Railroad Engineer $15–18

Renegade Trader $15–18

Riverboat Captain $10–15

Roadrunner $28–36

Saturday Night Bath $60–70

Sheepherder $25–35

Sheriff $10–12

Sodbuster $13–16

Squawman $20–30

Stagecoach Driver $45–60

STP Turbocar $40–50

STP Turbocar with Gold and Platinum (pair) $150–185

Telegrapher $15–20

Tinker $25–35

Tribal Chief $25–35

Al Unser No. 1 .... $15–20

Wells Fargo Man $8–12

Woodhawk $15–17

Bicentennial Series

Firefighters No. 1 .... $110–120

Mail Carrier $23–29

Molly Pitcher $10–12

Paul Revere $10–12

Betsy Ross $15–25

Sons of Freedom $25–34

George Washington $15–25

Winter at Valley Forge $16–20

Bicentennial Westerns

Barber...$30–40

Firefighter No. 3 ....$60–70

Indian Weaver...$20–24

Photographer $34–40

Rainmaker..$22–28

Saturday Night Bath $50–65

Trapper $30–36

Bird Series (1972–1974)

Bluebird—Eastern $18–24

Bluebird—Wisconsin $20–30

Bluejay $20–25

Peregrine Falcon $15–18

Meadowlark..$15–20

Mourning Doves...$50–70

Swallow...$15–18

Circus Series (miniatures)

The Baker $10–15

Burmese Lady...$10–15

Fat Lady..$10–15

Fire-eater..$10–15

Giant with Midget $10–15

Giraffe-Necked Lady...$10–14

Snake Charmer $10–15

Strong Man...$10–15

Sword Swallower..$10–15

Tattooed Lady..$10–15

Dog Series (miniatures)

Boxer..$10–15

Cocker Spaniel...$9–12

Collie...$10–15

Pointer..$10–15

Poodle..$10–15

European Worker Series

The Cobbler..$20–25

The Horseshoer..$20–35

The Potter..$20–35

The Silversmith...$25–35

The Watchmaker...$20–35

The Woodworker...$20–35

Oriental Worker Series

Basket Weaver...$25–35

Egg Merchant..$25–35

Gardener...$25–35

Sculptor..$25–35

Tea Vendor...$25–35

Timekeeper..$25–35

Sports Series

Baseball..$22–30

Basketball $22–30

Boxing $22–30

Football $22–30

Hockey $22–30

Tropical Bird Series (miniatures)

Blue-Crowned Chlorophoniá $12–16

Emerald Toucanet $12–16

Northern Royal Flycatcher $12–16

Painted Bunting $12–16

Scarlet Macaw $12–16

Yellow-headed Amazon $12–16

Miscellaneous Lionstone Bottles

Buccaneer $25–35

Cowgirl $45–55

Dance Hall Girl $50–55

Falcon $15–25

Firefighter No. 2 .... $80–100

Firefighter No. 3 .... $25–35

Firefighter No. 5, 60th Anniversary $22–27

Firefighter No. 6, Fire Hydrant $40–45

Firefighter No. 6, Gold or Silver $250–350

Firefighter No. 7, Helmet $60–90

Firefighter No. 8, Fire Alarm Box $45–60

Firefighter No. 8, Gold or Silver $90–120

Firefighter No. 9, Extinguisher $55–60

Firefighter No. 10, Trumpet $55–60

Firefighter No. 10, Gold $200–260

Firefighter No. 10, Silver...$125–175

Indian Mother and Papoose..$50–65

"The Perfesser" $40–45

Roses on Parade..$60–80

Screech Owls...$50–65

Unser-Olsonite Eagle $35–45

Miscellaneous Miniatures

Bartender $12–15

Cliff Swallow Miniature...$9–12

Dance Hall Girl Miniature..$15–22

Firefighter Emblem..$24–31

Firefighter Engine No. 8 ....$24–31

Firefighter Engine No. 10 ....$24–31

Horseshoe Miniature $14–20

Kentucky Derby Racehorse, Cannanade...........................$35–45

Lucky Buck...$10–12

Rainmaker...$10–15

Sahara Invitational No. 1..$35–45

Sahara Invitational No. 2..$35–45

Sheepherder..$12–15

Shootout at O.K. Corral, (set of 3) $250–300

Woodpecker $10–15

The Girolamo Luxardo bottle is made in Torreglia, Italy, and was first imported into the United States in 1930. The Luxardo bottle usually contained wine or liquors, as Luxardo also produces wine.

Luxardo bottles are well designed and meticulously colored, adding to the desirability of this line. Most of these bottles are figural and consist of historical subjects and classical themes. The most popular bottle, the Cellini, was introduced in the early 1950s and is still used. The names and dates of many of the earlier bottles are not known owing to lack of owners' records. Bottles in mint condition with the original label, and with or without contents, are very rare, collectible, and valuable. One of the rarer and more valuable of these bottles is the Zara, which was made prior to World War II.

Alabaster Fish Figural (1960–1968)..$30–40

Alabaster Goose Figural (1960–1968)
Green and white, wings..$25–35

Ampulla Flask (1958–1959)...$20–30

Apothecary Jar (1960)
Hand-painted multicolor, green and black......................$20–30

Assyrian Ashtray Decanter (1961)
Gray, tan, and black...$15–25

Autumn Leaves Decanter (1952)
Hand-painted, two handles...$35–45

Autumn Wine Pitcher (1958)
Hand-painted country scene, handled pitcher $30–40

Babylon Decanter (1960)
Dark green and gold $16–23

Bizantina (1959)
Gold-embossed design, wide body $28–38

Blue-and-Gold Amphora (1968)
Blue and gold with pastoral scene in white oval $20–30

Blue Fimmetta or Vermillian (1957)
Decanter..$20–27

Brocca Pitcher (1958)
White background pitcher with handle, multicolor flowers, green
leaves $28–37

Buddha Goddess Figural (1961)
Goddess head in green-gray stone $14–19
Miniature $11–16

Burma Ashtray Specialty (1960)
Embossed white dancing figure, dark green background..............$20–25

Burma Pitcher Speciality (1960)
Green and gold, white embossed dancing figure $14–19

Callypso Girl Figural (1962)
Black West Indian girl, flower headdress in bright color $20–25

Candlestick Alabaster (1961) $30–35

Cellini Vase (1958–1968)
Glass-and-silver decanter, fancy $14–19

Cellini Vase (1957)
Glass-and-silver-handled decanter with serpent handle................$14–19

Ceramic Barrel (1968)
Barrel-shaped with painted flowers...$14–19

Cherry Basket Figural (1960)
White basket, red cherries $14–19

Classical Fragment Specialty (1961)
Roman female figure and vase $25–33

Cocktail Shaker (1957)
Glass-and-silver decanter, silver-painted top $14–19

Coffee Carafe Specialty (1962)
Old-time coffeepot, white with blue flowers $14–19

Curva Vaso Vase (1961)
Green, green and white, ruby-red $22–29

Deruta Amphora (1956)
Colorful floral design on white $11–16

Deruta Cameo Amphora (1959)
Colorful floral scrolls and cameo head on eggshell white $25–35

Deruta Pitcher (1953)
Multicolor flowers on base perugia $11–16

Diana Decanter (1956)
White figure of Diana with deer on black $11–16

Dogal Silver and Green Decanter (1952–1956)
Hand-painted gondola $14–19

Dogal Silver Ruby (1952–1956)
Hand-painted gondola $14–18

Dogal Silver Ruby Decanter (1956)
Hand-painted Venetian scene and flowers $17–22

Dogal Silver Smoke Decanter (1952–1955)
Hand-painted gondola $14–19

Dogal Silver Smoke Decanter (1953–1954)
Hand-painted gondola $11–16

Dogal Silver Smoke Decanter (1956)
Hand-painted silver clouds and gondola $11–16

Dogal Silver Smoke Decanter (1956)
Hand-painted gondola, buildings, flowers $14–18

Dolphin Figural (1959)
Yellow, green, blue $42–57

"Doughnut" Bottle (1960)..$15–20

Dragon Amphora (1953)
Two-handled white decanter with colorful dragon and flowers....$10–15

Dragon Amphora (1958)
One handle, white pitcher, color dragon.....................................$14–18

Duck-Green Glass Figural (1960)
Green-and-amber duck, clear glass base..$35–45

Eagle (1970)...$45–55

Egyptian Specialty (1960)
Two-handled amphora, Egyptian design on tan and gold............$14–19

Etruscan Decanter (1959)
Single-handled black Greek design on tan background................$14–19

Euganean Bronze (1952–1955)...$14–19

Euganean Coppered (1952–1955)...$13–18

Faenza Decanter (1952–1956)
Colorful country scene on white single-handled decanter............$21–28

Fighting Cocks (1962)
Combination decanter and ashtray..$14–19

Fish—Green and Gold Glass Figural (1960)
Green, silver, and gold, clear glass base..$30–40

Fish—Ruby Murano Glass Figural (1961)
Ruby-red tone of glass..$30–40

Florentine Majolica (1956)
Round-handled decanter, painted pitcher.....................................$20–30

Gambia (1961)
Black princess, kneeling, holding tray..$8–12

Golden Fakir, Seated Snake Charmer with Flute and Snakes
    1961 gold...$26–37
    1960 black and gray..$26–37

Gondola (1959)
Highly glazed abstract gondola and gondolier in black................$21–27

Gondola (1960)..$14–19

Grapes, Pear Figural...$25–40

Mayan (1960)
Mayan temple godhead mask...$15–25

Mosaic Ashtray (1959), Combination Decanter Ashtray
Black, yellow, green, 11½ in. $15–25
Black, green; miniature, 6 in. $10–14

Nubian
Kneeling black figure...$14–19

Opal Majolica (1957)
Two gold handles, translucent top $14–19

Penguin Murano Glass Figural (1968)
Black-and-white penguin...$25–30

Pheasant Murano Glass Figural (1960)
Red and clear glass on a crystal base $35–45

Pheasant Red and Gold Figural (1960)
Red-and-gold glass bird..$40–60

Primavera Amphora (1958)
Two-handled vase shape $14–19

Puppy Cucciolo Glass Figural (1960)
Amber and green glass..$26–37

Puppy Murano Glass Figural (1960)
Amber glass $26–37

Silver Blue Decanter (1952–1955)
Hand-painted silver flowers and leaves..................................$22–28

Silver Brown Decanter (1952–1955)
Hand-painted silver flowers and leaves..................................$26–37

Sir Lancelot (1962)
Figure of English knight in full armor $14–19

Springbok Amphora (1952)
Leaping African deer $14–19

Squirrel Glass Figural (1968)
Amethyst colored squirrel on crystal base $40–50

Sudan (1960)
African motif in browns, blue, yellow, and gray...........................$14–19

Torre Rosa (1962)
Rose-tinted tower of fruit...$16–24

Torre Tinta (1962)
Multicolor tower of fruit $18–22

Tower of Fruit (1968)
Various fruit in natural colors...$16–24

Tower of Fruit Majolica Torre Bianca (1962)
White-and-gray tower of fruit...$16–24

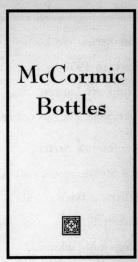

McCormic Bottles

These pieces, like Kentucky Gentlemen and others, are similar in design to the Beam and Brooks bottles but are released in limited numbers.

The McCormic bottles, which originally or still contain McCormick Irish Whiskey, are manufactured in different series, including cars, famous Americans, frontiersmen decanters, and gunfighters. The famous Americans series has been produced most often and represents celebrities from Colonial times to the twentieth century.

Barrel Series

Barrel, with Stand and Shot Glasses 1958..................................$25–30

Barrel, with Stand and Plain Hoops 1968..................................$15–20

Barrel, with Stand and Gold Hoops 1968..................................$20–25

Bird Series

Blue Jay 1971..$20–25

Canada Goose, Miniature..$18–25

Gambel's Quail 1982..$45–55

Ring-neck Pheasant 1982..$45–55

Wood Duck 1980..$30–35

Car Series

Packard 1937 ....$25–35

The Pony Express...$20–25

The Sand Buggy Commemorative Decanter...........................$35–50

Confederate Series

Jeb Stuart...$25–35

Jefferson Davis..$25–30

Robert E. Lee $25–35

Stonewall Jackson...$25–35

Country and Western Series

Hank Williams, Sr., 1980 ....$50–55

Hank Williams, Jr., 1980 ....$70–80

Tom T. Hall 1980..$32–42

Elvis Presley Series

Elvis '55 1979 ....$40–50

Elvis '55 Mini...$25–35

Elvis '55 Mini 1980..$20–30

Elvis '68 1980 ....$40–50

Elvis '68 Mini 1980..$25–35

Elvis '77 1978 ....$65–80

Elvis '77 Mini 1979..$32–40

Elvis Bust 1978...$24–35

Elvis Designer I
Music box plays "Are You Lonesome Tonight?"........................$85–100

Elvis Designer II
Music box plays "It's Now or Never" $140–160

Elvis Gold 1979 ....$180–220

Elvis Karate $100–130

Elvis Sergeant..$190–210

Elvis Silver 1980..$120–135

Famous American Portrait Series

Abe Lincoln with Law Book in Hand...$35–45

Alexander Graham Bell with Apron $10–15

Captain John Smith..$12–20

Charles Lindbergh $24–28

Eleanor Roosevelt $12–20

George Washington Carver $28–40

Henry Ford..$20–25

Lewis Meriwether $16–20

Pocahontas..$30–42

Robert E. Perry $25–35

Thomas Edison $35–45

Ulysses S. Grant with Coffeepot and Cup $15–25

William Clark $15–20

Football Mascots

Alabama Bamas..$26–34

Arizona Sun Devils...$39–48

Arizona Wildcats $21–27

Arkansas Hogs 1972...$42–48

Auburn War Eagles $16–24

Baylor Bears 1972 ....$24–30

California Bears $20–25

Drake Bulldogs, Blue Helmet and Jersey 1974 .... $15–20

Georgia Bulldogs, Black Helmet and Red Jersey $12–19

Georgia Tech Yellowjackets $15–25

Houston Cougars 1972 .... $20–30

Indiana Hoosiers 1974 .... $15–25

Iowa Cyclones 1974 .... $45–55

Iowa Hawkeyes 1974 .... $60–70

Iowa Purple Panthers $32–42

Louisiana State Tigers 1974 .... $15–20

Michigan State Spartans $15–20

Michigan Wolverines 1974 .... $15–25

Minnesota Gophers 1974 .... $8–12

Mississippi Rebels 1974 .... $8–12

Mississippi State Bulldogs, Red Helmet and Jersey 1974 .... $12–18

Nebraska Cornhuskers 1974 .... $12–18

Nebraska Football Player $35–45

Nebraska, Johnny Rogers, No. 1 .... $230–260

New Mexico Lobo $32–40

Oklahoma Sooners Wagon 1974 .... $20–28

Oklahoma Souther Cowboy 1974 .... $14–18

Oregon Beavers 1974 .... $10–18

Oregon Ducks 1974 .... $12–18

Purdue Boilermaker 1974 .... $15–25

Rice Owls 1972 .... $20–30

SMU Mustangs 1972 .... $17–24

TCU Horned Frogs 1972 .... $25–30

Tennessee Volunteers 1974 .... $8–12

Texas A & M Aggies 1972...$22–30

Texas Tech Raiders 1972 ....$20–26

Texas Horns 1972 ....$23–33

Washington Cougars 1974 ....$20–25

Washington Huskies 1974...$15–25

Wisconsin Badgers 1974...$15–25

Frontiersmen Commemorative Decanters 1972

Daniel Boone..$15–22

Davy Crockett $17–25

Jim Bowie $12–15

Kit Carson $14–18

General

A&P Wagon $50–55

Airplane, Spirit of Saint Louis 1969 ....$60–80

American Bald Eagle 1981..$30–40

American Legion Cincinnati 1986 ....$25–35

Buffalo Bill 1979..$70–80

Cable Car $25–30

Car, Packard 1980 ....$30–40

Chair, Queen Anne...$20–30

Ciao Baby 1978 ....$20–25

Clock, Cuckoo 1971..$25–35

De Witt Clinton Engine 1970 ....$40–50

French Telephone 1969 ....$20–28

Globe, Angelica 1971 ....$25–32

Henry Ford 1977 ....$20–24

Hutchinson Kansas Centennial 1972.................................$15–25

Jester 1972 ....$20–28

Jimmy Durante 1981
With music box, plays "Inka Dinka Doo"........................$31–40

Joplin Miner 1972 ....$15–25

J.R. Ewing 1980
With music box, plays theme song from "Dallas".............$22–27

J.R. Ewing, Gold-colored..$50–55

Julia Bulette 1974...$140–160

Lamp, Hurricane $13–18

Largemouth Bass 1982...$20–28

Lobsterman 1979 ....$20–30

Louis Armstrong...$60–70

Mark Twain 1977...$18–22

Mark Twain, Mini...$13–18

McCormick Centennial 1956...$80–120

Mikado 1980 ....$60–80

Missouri Sesquicentennial China 1970 ....$5–7

Missouri Sesquicentennial Glass 1971 ....$3–7

Ozark Ike 1979..$22–27

Paul Bunyan 1979 ....$25–30

Pioneer Theater 1972...$8–12

Pony Express 1972..$20–25

Renault Racer 1969 ....$40–50

Sam Houston 1977 ....$22–28

Stephen F. Austin 1977 ....$14–18

Telephone Operator..$45–55

Thelma Lu 1982 ....$25–35

U.S. Marshal 1979 ....$25–35

Will Rogers 1977 ....$18–22

Yacht Americana 1971 ....$30–38

Gunfighter Series

Bat Masterson $20–30

Billy the Kid...$25–30

Black Bart $26–35

Calamity Jane...$25–30

Doc Holiday $25–35

Jesse James $20–30

Wild Bill Hickok..$21–30

Wyatt Earp $21–30

Jug Series

Bourbon Jug $62–70

Gin Jug $6–10

Old Holiday Bourbon 1956 ....$6–18

Platte Valley 1953 ....$3–6

Platte Valley, half-pint $3–4

Vodka Jug..$6–10

King Arthur Series

King Arthur on Throne...$30–40

Merlin the Wizard with His Wise Old Magical Robe 1979.....$25–35

Queen Guinevere, The Gem of Royal Court $12–18

Sir Lancelot of the Lake in Armor, A Knight of the Round
Table $12–18

The Literary Series

Huck Finn 1980..$20–25

Tom Sawyer 1980..$22–26

Miniatures

Charles Lindbergh Miniature 1978..$10–14

Confederates Miniature Set (4) 1978...$40–50

Henry Ford Miniature 1978 ....$10–14

Mark Twain Miniature 1978 ....$12–18

Miniature Gunfighters (8) 1977..$110–140

Miniature Noble 1978 ....$14–20

Miniature Spirit of '76 1977 ....$15–25

Patriot Miniature Set (8) 1976...$250–350

Pony Express Miniature 1980 ....$15–18

Will Rogers Miniature 1978..$12–16

The Patriots

Benjamin Franklin 1975 ....$13–17

Betsy Ross 1975 ....$20–25

George Washington 1975 ....$20–27

John Paul Jones 1975...$15–20

Patrick Henry 1975 ....$14–18

Patrick Henry, Miniature $12–15

Paul Revere 1975...$20–25

Spirit of '76 1976 ....$50–60

Thomas Jefferson 1975 ....$14–18

Pirate Series

Pirate No. 1 1972..$10–12

Pirate No. 2 1972..$10–12

Pirate No. 3 1972..$8–12

Pirate No. 4 1972..$8–12

Pirate No. 5 1972..$8–12

Pirate No. 6 1972..$8–12

Pirate No. 7 1972..$8–12

Pirate No. 8 1972..$8–12

Pirate No. 9 1972..$8–12

Pirate No. 10 1972..$20–28

Pirate No. 11 1972..$20–28

Pirate No. 12 1972..$20–28

Rural Americana Series

Woman Feeding Chickens 1980 ....$25–35

Woman Washing Clothes 1980 ....$30–40

Shrine Series

Circus..$20–35

Dune Buggy 1976 ....$25–35

Imperial Council..$20–25

Jester (Mirth King) 1972 ....$30–40

The Noble 1976..$25–32

Sports Series

Air Race Propeller 1971..$15–20

Air Race Pylon 1970 ....$10–15

Johnny Rodgers No. 1 1972....................................$160–195

Johnny Rodgers No. 2 1973....................................$70–85

K.C. Chiefs 1969 ....$18–25

K.C. Royals 1971 ....$10–15

Muhammad Ali 1980 ....$20–30

Nebraska Football Player 1972 ....$33–45

Skibob 1971 ....$10–11

Train Series

Jupiter Engine 1969 ....$20–25

Mail Car 1970 ....$25–28

Passenger Car 1970 ....$35–45

Wood Tender 1969 ....$14–18

Miniature Bottles

When a discussion on bottle collecting begins, it's clear that most collectors focus their attention on the physically large bottles such as beer, whiskey, or maybe bitters. But there is a very distinct group of collectors who eschew big finds and set their sights on the small. Their quest for that special find leads them into the world of miniatures. Until I started bottle collecting, the only miniature bottles that I knew of were the ones other passengers bought on airline trips. Today, there is tremendous enthusiasm for miniature bottle collecting. Not only are there specialty clubs and dealers across the United States but throughout the world in the Middle East, Japan, England, Scotland, Australia, and Italy to name just a few. The new collector will soon discover that all miniatures are unique and extremely fascinating in their own way. Because of their low average cost, $1 to $5 per bottle, and the relatively small amount of space required to store them, starting a collection is easy. As is the case with the large bottles, there are some rare and expensive miniatures.

A number of miniatures were manufactured in the 1800s, although the majority date from the late 1920s and the 1950s, with peak production in the 1930s. While miniatures are still produced today, some of the most interesting and sought after are those produced prior to 1950. The state of Nevada legalized the sale of miniatures in 1935, Florida in 1935, and Louisiana in 1934.

If you're looking for a nineteenth-century miniature you might seek out miniature beer bottles. They are a good example of a kind of bottle that was produced for uses other than containing beer. Most of the major breweries produced them as advertisements, novelties, and promotional items. In fact, most of the bottles did not contain beer. A number of these bottles came with perforated caps so that they could be used as salt and pepper shakers. The Pabst Blue Ribbon Beer Company was the first brewery to manufacture a beer bottle miniature commemorating the Milwaukee Convention of Spanish-American War Veterans in 1889. Pabst's last miniature was manufactured around 1942. Most of the miniature beers you'll find today date from before World War II. In 1899 there were as many as 1,507 breweries, of which all produced miniatures.

Beyond the whiskey, beer, and soda pop bottles identified in this chapter, don't overlook earlier chapters that focus on other miniatures, including Luxardo's, Garnier, Lionstone, Drioli, and Barsottini.

Collecting miniature liquor bottles has become a special interest for some. A number of the state liquor stamps from the early 1930s and 1940s have specific series numbers that have a value to stamp collectors.

Beers

Acme Beer, Acme Brewing, Los Angeles $5

American, Embossed "No Deposit, No Return," 1947 .... $10

Arrow Beer, Globe Brewing Co., Baltimore, Md. $7

Apache, Phoenix $2

Ballantine's Ale (Green), P. Ballantine & Sons, Newark, N.J. $3

Berghoff Beer, Berghoff Brewing Corp, est. 1887, Fort Wayne, Ind. $10

Selection of Scotch whiskeys, 1990.

"Having Drunk for Eighty Years
This Poison Cannot Make Me
Fears" (Shafer and Vater), early
1900s.

Blatz Pilsner $3

Burger Bohemian, Brown, 4 in., Burger Brewing Co., Cincinnati,
Ohio $5

Canadian Ace, Chicago $3

Carling's Black Label $3

Coors Beer, Adolf Coors Company, Golden, Colo. $3

Drewry's Old Stock Ale, Drewry's Limited, est. 1877, South
Bend, Ind. $5

Eastside Beer, Zobelein's, Los Angeles Brewing Co., Los Angeles,
Embossed "No Deposit No Return," 1947 .... $12

Edelweiss Beer, Edelweiss Co. $3

Esslingers, 4 in. $9

Falstaff, Super X $3

Falls City Beer, Falls City Brewing Co., Louisville, Ky. $3

Felsenbrau Beer, The Clyffside Brewing Co., Cincinnati, Ohio..... $8

Fort Pitt Beer, Fort Pitt Brewing Co., Pittsburgh (1941–1954),
Formerly Victor Brewing Co., Est. 1907 .... $5

Blue Anchor Navy Rum, 1950s.

Gettelman Rathskeller Beer, A. Gettelman Brewing Co., Est. 1854, Milwaukee, Wisc.. $3

Grain Belt, Minn... $3

Goebel.. $15

Hamm's Preferred Stock... $3

Jax Beer, Jax Brewing Co., New Orleans, La. $4

Kingsbury Pale Beer, Kingsbury Brewing Co., Manitowoc, Wisc. $3

Koehler's Beer, Erie Brewing Co., Erie, Penn. $3

Meister Brau Beer, Peter Hand's Brewing Co., Chicago................ $3

Millers' High Life... $2

Old Shay Beer, Fort Pitt Brewing Co., Jeannette, Penn................. $3

Pabst Blue Ribbon Beer $5

Prager Beer, Atlas Brewing Co., Chicago, Est. 1891...................... $5

Rainier Beer Seattle, U.S.A., embossed, hand blown, Est. 1877 .... $15

Schmidt's Beer, The Schmidt Brewing Co., Detroit $3

Tip Top Bohemian Beer, Sunrise Brewing Co., Cleveland, Ohio ... $3

Walter's Beer, Walter Brewing Co., Pueblo, Colo. $3

Drioli

African Dancer $5

Bull $10

Cat $9

Duck $9

Elephant $5

Fish $7

Jazz Band, set of 6 .... $125

Minstrels, set of 6 .... $45

Owl $7

Rock Group, set of 6 .... $35

Turkey $6

Whiskey

A. J. Cummings, 1930 .... $75

Amber Gold, 1930 .... $75

Belle Isle, 1930 .... $150

Ben Bow, 1934 .... $200

Bottoms Up, 1934 .... $150

Cedar Cliff, 1934 .... $175

Cedaridge, 1934 .... $150

Club Royal, 1930 .... $125

Dr. Dick, 1930 .... $100

50 Grand, 1930 .... $50

Four Bits, 1935 .... $200

Golden Pond, 1932 .... $60

Highland Queen, applied top, Scotland $15

Hilcrest "Special," 1930 .... $50

Kentucky Derby, 1934 .... $75

Kentucky Druggist, 1934 .... $200

L & G, 1931 .... $50

Lucky 7, 1934 .... $175

Monogram, 1934 .... $150

Old Barton Blend, 1930 .... $50

Old Dover, 1933 .... $50

Old Ranger, 1933 .... $175

Phillips Club, 1930 .... $50

Possum Ridge, 1934 .... $150

Quickee's Fernwood, 1933 .... $200

Redville, 1930 .... $50

Schulte's, 1930 .... $50

Southern Pines, 1934 .... $175

Three Musketeers, 1930 .... $80

Tom Horn, 1931 .... $200

Pop-Eye Very Old Demerara Rum, 1950s.

Wilshire's Midget, 1930 .... $150

Wisconsin Club, 1930 .... $50

Soda Pop

Canada Dry $1

Dad's Root Beer $3

Dr. Pepper, Good for Life $2

Fanta $2

Hires Root Beer $2

Hi-Spot $1

Joya, Mexico $3

Life $2

Mission Beverages $2

Nesbitt's of California $2

Orange Crush $3

O-So Grape Soda $1

Royal Crown Cola $2

Pepsi-Cola $2

Sprite, Mexico $1

Squirt, Mexico $1

Whistle (embossed) $3

These bottles, like other figurals, are manufactured to contain Old Blue Ribbon liquor.

The Blue Ribbon bottles are noted for distinct realism of historical themes and depictions of railroad cars from the nineteenth century. In addition, Blue Ribbon is the only manufacturer to produce a hockey series with each bottle commemorating a different hockey team.

Air Race Decanter $18–26

Blue Bird $14–19

Caboose $20–30

Eastern Kentucky University $15–21

Jupiter '60 Mail Car $13–17

Jupiter '60 Passenger Car $16–23

Jupiter '60 Wood Tender $13–17

Jupiter '60 Locomotive $15–22

K.C. Royals $19–26

Pierce Arrow $13–15

Santa Maria, Columbus's Ship $15–20

Titanic Ocean Liner $35–45

Transportation Series

Balloon $9–12

Fifth Avenue Bus $14–21

Prairie Schooner..$10–11

River Queen $10–15

River Queen, Gold..$20–25

Hockey Series

Boston Bruins..$14–18

Chicago Black Hawks...$14–18

Detroit Red Wings..$14–18

Minnesota North Stars $14–18

New York Rangers $14–18

Saint Louis Blues..$14–18

Old Common-wealth Bottles

The Old Commonwealth brand, produced by J. P. Van Winkle and Son, is one of the newer companies (1974) to produce whiskey in collectible decanters. The ceramic decanters themselves are manufactured in the Orient, while the whiskey is made and the bottling is done at the Hoffman Distilling Company in Lawrenceburg, Kentucky.

Today, the majority of the decanters are produced in regular and miniature sizes. The titles of most pieces appear on the bottle's front plaque.

Alabama Crimson Tide 1981
University of Alabama symbol $23–30

Bulldogs 1982
The mascot of the University of Georgia Bulldogs........................$20–30

Chief Illini No. 1 1979
The mascot for the University of Illinois......................................$70–85

Chief Illini No. 2 1981
The mascot for the University of Illinois......................................$55–65

Chief Illini No. 3 1979
The mascot for the University of Illinois......................................$65–75

Coal Miner No. 1 1975
Standard size $80–100
Mini 1980...$20–30

Coal Miner No. 2 1976
Standard size $20–30
Mini 1982 .... $19–23

Coal Miner No. 3 1977
Standard size $28–36
Mini 1981 .... $20–25

Coal Miner—Lunchtime—No. 4 1980
Standard size $33–43
Mini $15–20

Cottontail 1981 .... $25–35

Elusive Leprechaun 1980 .... $24–30

Fisherman, "A Keeper," 1980 .... $20–30

Golden Retriever 1979 .... $30–40

Kentucky Thoroughbreds 1976 .... $30–40

Kentucky Wildcat $32–42

LSU Tiger 1979 .... $45–55

Lumberjack $15–25

Missouri Tiger $35–45

Old Rip Van Winkle No. 1 1974 .... $40–50

Old Rip Van Winkle No. 2 1975 .... $35–45

Old Rip Van Winkle No. 3 1977 .... $30–40

Pointing Setter Decanter 1965 .... $16–23

Quail on the Wing Decanter 1968 .... $7–12

Rebel Yell Rider 1970 .... $23–32

Rip Van Winkle Figurine 1970 .... $32–40

Sons of Ireland 1972 .... $15–20

Sons of Erin 1969 .... $6–9

South Carolina Tricentennial 1970 .... $12–19

Tennessee Walking Horse 1977 .... $24–35

USC Trojans 1980
Standard size $45–55
Mini $11–16

Weller Masterpiece 1963 .... $26–35

Western Boot Decanter 1982
Standard size $20–25
Mini $8–12

Western Logger 1980 .... $25–34

Wildcats 1982 .... $40–46

Wings Across the Continent 1972 .... $16–23

Yankee Doodle $25–32

Modern Firefighters Series

Modern Hero No. 1 1982
Standard size $25–35
Mini $8–12

The Nozzleman No. 2 1982
Standard size $30–40
Mini $17–24

On Call No. 3 1982
Standard size $45–55
Mini $15–24

Fallen Comrade No. 4 1982
Standard size $30–40
Mini $17–25

Waterfowler Series

Waterfowler No. 1 1979 .... $40–50

Here They Come No. 2 1980 .... $32–42

Good Boy No. 3 1981 .... $32–42

Old Fitzgerald Bottles

These bottles are manufactured by the Old Fitzgerald Distilling Company to package its whiskey and bourbon. These bottles are often called Old Cabin Still bottles, for one of the brand names under which they were distributed and sold.

These bottles are issued in both decanter and figural designs in various types and colors portraying different Irish and American subjects. Runs are produced in very limited quantities.

Americas Cup Commemorative 1970 ....$15–22

Blarney Castle 1970 ....$12–19

Browsing Deer Decanter 1967 ....$15–22

California Bicentennial 1970 ....$15–22

Candelite Decanter 1955 ....$9–12

Colonial Decanter 1969 ....$4–7

Crown Decanter $5–9

Gold Coast Decanter 1954 ....$10–15

"Golden Bough" Decanter 1971 ....$4–9

Gold Web Decanter 1953 ....$10–16

Hillbilly 1969, pint $13–18

Hillbilly Bottle 1954, pint $13–18

Hillbilly Bottle 1954, quart $13–18

Hillbilly Bottle 1954, gallon (very rare) $60–85

Jewel Decanter 1951–1952 ....$9–15

Leaping Trout Decanter 1969 ....$11–16

Leprechaun Bottle 1968..$25–32

LSU Alumni Decanter 1970 ....$25–32

Man O' War Decanter 1969 ....$5–9

Memphis Commemorative 1969 ....$8–12

Nebraska 1971 ....$27–32

Nebraska 1972 ....$18–25

Ohio State Centennial 1970 ....$12–18

Old Cabin Still Decanter 1958 ....$16–23

Pilgrim Landing Commemorative 1970...$14–24

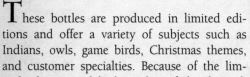

Ski-Country Bottles

These bottles are produced in limited editions and offer a variety of subjects such as Indians, owls, game birds, Christmas themes, and customer specialties. Because of the limited editions and high quality of detailing, these bottles are rated high on the wish lists of most collectors.

Animals

Badger Family
Standard size $35–45
Mini $16–24

Bobcat Family
Standard size $45–60
Mini $16–25

Coyote Family
Standard size $37–48
Mini $17–23

Kangaroo
Standard size $22–32
Mini $18–28

Koala $20–28

Raccoon
Standard size $36–45
Mini $25–30

Skunk Family
Standard size $40–50
Mini $22–26

Snow Leopard
Standard size $36–43
Mini $30–35

Birds

Blackbird
Standard size $34–40
Mini $29–30

Black Swan
Standard size $30–35
Mini $18–24

Blue Jay
Standard size $50–60
Mini $42–49

Cardinal
Standard size $55–70
Mini $35–45

Condor
Standard size $45–55
Mini $25–30

Gamecocks
Standard size $120–130
Mini $40–46

Gila Woodpecker
Standard size $55–65
Mini $26–32

Peace Dove
Standard size $50–60
Mini $20–26

Peacock
Standard size $80–100
Mini $45–60

Penguin Family

Standard size $45–55
Mini $21–27

Wood Duck

Standard size $175–200
Mini $125–150

Christmas

Bob Cratchit

Standard size $40–50
Mini $25–30

Mrs. Cratchit

Standard size $40–50
Mini $25–30

Scrooge

Standard size $40–50
Mini $15–20

Circus

Clown

Standard size $44–52
Mini $27–33

Elephant on Drum

Standard size $35–45
Mini $35–45

Jenny Lind, Blue Dress

Standard size $55–75
Mini $48–60

Lion on Drum

Standard size $31–36
Mini $23–28

Palomino Horse

Standard size $40–48
Mini $30–40

P. T. Barnum
Standard size $32–40
Mini $20–25

Ringmaster
Standard size $20–25
Mini $15–18

Tiger on Ball
Standard size $35–44
Mini $31–37

Tom Thumb
Standard size $20–25
Mini $16–21

Customer Specialties

Ahrens-Fox Engine $140–180

Bonnie and Clyde (pair)
Standard size $60–70
Mini $55–62

Caveman
Standard size $16–23
Mini $18–22

Mill River Country Club..$38–47

Olympic Skier, Gold..$85–110

Olympic Skier, Red
Standard size $22–30
Mini $30–35

Olympic Skier, Blue
Standard size $25–32
Mini $35–40

Political Donkey and Elephant..$50–60

Domestic Animals

Basset Hound
Standard size $45–55
Mini $26–32

Holstein Cow $45–60

Eagles, Falcons, and Hawks

Birth of Freedom
Standard size $85–95
Mini $65–75

Eagle on the Water
Standard size $90–110
Mini $38–45

Easter Seals Eagle
Standard size $48–60
Mini $22–29

Falcon, Gallon..$350–425

Gyrfalcon
Standard size $54–60
Mini $27–34

Happy Eagle
Standard size $85–105
Mini $80–95

Mountain Eagle
Standard size $130–150
Mini $100–120

Osprey Hawk
Standard size $140–160
Mini $100–120

Peregrine Falcon
Standard size $75–85
Mini $18–25

Prairie Falcon
Standard size $65–80
Mini $35–48

Red-Shoulder Hawk
Standard size $60–70
Mini $35–40

Redtail Hawk
Standard size $75–95
Mini $33–40

White Falcon
Standard size $68–75
Mini $30–40

Fish

Muskellunge
Standard size $30–37
Mini $17–21

Rainbow Trout
Standard size $40–50
Mini $24–30

Salmon
Standard size $30–35
Mini $18–22

Trout $27–32

Game Birds

Banded Mallard..$50–60

Chukar Partridge
Standard size $33–40
Mini $16–21

King Eider Duck $50–60

Mallard 1973...$50–60

Pheasant, Mini $52–62

Pheasant, Golden
Standard size $40–45
Mini $24–30

Pheasant in the Corn
Standard size $50–60
Mini $30–39

Pheasants Fighting
Standard size $70–80
Mini $35–45

Pheasants Fighting, half–gallon...............................$145–165

Pintail...$76–85

Prairie Chicken $55–65

Ruffed Grouse
Standard size $40–50
Mini $22–28

Turkey
Standard size $80–100
Mini $100–120

Grand Slam

Desert Sheep
Standard size $75–90
Mini $25–30

Mountain Sheep
Standard size $50–60
Mini $24–30

Stone Sheep
Standard size $50–65
Mini $27–34

Horned and Antlered Animals

Antelope...$45–60

Bighorn Ram
Standard size $65–75
Mini $25–31

Mountain Goat
Standard size $30–45
Mini $38–48

Mountain Goat, gallon $525–600

Whitetail Deer
Standard size $30–95
Mini $34–40

Indians

Ceremonial Antelope Dancer
Standard size $52–62
Mini $36–45

Ceremonial Buffalo Dancer
Standard size $150–185
Mini $32–38

Ceremonial Deer Dancer
Standard size $85–100
Mini $40–48C

Ceremonial Eagle Dancer
Standard size $185–205
Mini $24–34

Ceremonial Falcon Dancer
Standard size $85–100
Mini $34–45

Ceremonial Wolf Dancer
Standard size $50–60
Mini $32–40

Chief No. 1
Standard size $105–125
Mini $14–20

Chief No. 2
Standard size $105–125
Mini $14–20

Cigar Store Indian $32–40

Dancers of the Southwest, Set
Standard size $250–300
Mini $140–175

Owls

Barn Owl
Standard size $48–55
Mini $20–24

Great Gray Owl
Standard size $48–55
Mini $20–25

Horned Owl
Standard size $60–70
Mini $70–80

Horned Owl, gallon $700–800

Saw Whet Owl
Standard size $40–45
Mini $20–25

Screech Owl Family
Standard size $80–90
Mini $68–75

Spectacled Owl
Standard size $70–85
Mini $58–68

Rodeo

Barrel Racer
Standard size $58–68
Mini $20–26

Bull Rider
Standard size $42–49
Mini $22–28

Wyoming Bronco
Standard size $48–66
Mini $25–35

U.S. Trademarks

The words and letters in bold are that company's description and of the trademarks as they appeared on the bottle. Each is followed by the complete name and location of the company and the approximate period of time during which the trademark was used.*

Domestic Trademarks

A—John Agnew & Son, Pittsburgh, PA, 1854–1866.

A IN A CIRCLE—American Glass Works, Richmond, VA, and Paden City, WV, 1909–1936.

A & B TOGETHER (AB)—Adolphus Busch Glass Manufacturing Co, Belleville, IL, and Saint Louis, MO, 1904–1907.

AB Co.—American Bottle Co., Chicago, 1905–1930.

A B G M Co.—Adolphus Busch Glass Manufacturing Co, Belleville, IL and Saint Louis, MO, 1886–1928.

A & Co.—John Agnew and Co., Pittsburgh, PA, Indian Queen, Ear of Corn, and other flasks, 1854–1892.

A C M E—Acme Glass Co., Olean, NY, 1920–1930.

A & D H C—A. & D. H. Chambers, Pittsburgh, PA, Union Flasks, 1842–1886.

*Some foreign companies moved their bottling business to the U.S. in order to be more profitable. So, while they kept their foreign names they actually had bottling operations in this country.

AGEE AND AGEE IN SCRIPT—Hazel Atlas Glass Co., Wheeling, WV, 1921–1925.

A.G.W. Co.—American Glass Works Ltd., 1860–1905.

AGW—American Glass Works, 1880.

ANCHOR FIGURE WITH H IN CENTER—Anchor Hocking Glass Corp., Lancaster, OH, 1955.

A. R. S.—A. R. Samuels Glass Co., Philadelphia, PA, 1855–1872.

A S F W W VA.—A. S. Frank Glass Co., Wellsburg, WV, 1859.

ATLAS—Atlas Glass Co., Washington, PA, and later Hazel Atlas Glass Co., 1896–1965.

AVH—A. Van Hoboken & Co., Rotterdam, the Netherlands, 1800–1898.

BALL AND BALL IN SCRIPT—Ball Bros. Glass Manufacturing Co., Muncie, IN, and later Ball Corp., 1887–1973.

BERNARDIN IN SCRIPT—W. J. Latchford Glass Co., Los Angeles, CA, 1932–1938.

THE BEST—Gillender & Sons, Philadelphia, PA, 1867–1870.

B F B Co.—Bell Fruit Bottle Co., Fairmount, IN 1910.

B. G. Co.—Belleville Glass Co., IL, 1882.

BISHOP'S—Bishop & Co., San Diego and Los Angeles, CA, 1890–1920.

BK—Benedict Kimber, Bridgeport and Brownsville, PA, 1822–1840.

BOYDS IN SCRIPT—Illinois Glass Co., Alton, IL, 1900–1930.

BRELLE (IN SCRIPT) JAR—Brelle Fruit Jar Manufacturing Co., San Jose, CA, 1912–1916.

BRILLIANTE—Jefferis Glass Co., Fairton, NJ, and Rochester, PA, 1900–1905.

C IN A CIRCLE—Chattanooga Bottle & Glass Co., and later Chattanooga Glass Co., 1927–present.

C IN A SQUARE—Crystal Glass Co., Los Angeles, CA, 1921–1929.

C IN A STAR—Star City Glass Co., Star City, WV, 1949–present.

CANTON DOMESTIC FRUIT JAR—Canton Glass Co., Canton, OH, 1890–1904.

C & Co. OR C Co—Cunninghams & Co., Pittsburgh, PA, 1880–1907.

CCCo—C. Conrad & Co. (Beer), 1878–1883.

C.V.Co. No. 1 & No 2—Milwaukee, WI, 1880–1881.

C C Co.—Carl Conrad & Co., Saint Louis, MO. 1876–1883.

C C G Co.—Cream City Glass Co., Milwaukee, WI, 1888–1893

C.F.C.A.—California Fruit Canners Association, Sacramento, CA, 1899–1916.

C G M Co.—Campbell Glass Manufacturing Co., West Berkeley, CA, 1885.

C G W—Campbell Glass Works, West Berkeley, CA, 1884–1885.

C & H—Coffin & Hay, Winslow, NJ, 1838–1842.

C L G Co.—Carr-Lowrey Glass Co., Baltimore, MD, 1889–1920.

CLYDE, N. Y.—Clyde Glass Works, Clyde, N.Y., 1870–1882.

THE CLYDE IN SCRIPT—Clyde Glass Works, Clyde, N.Y., 1895.

C MILW—Chase Valley Glass Co., Milwaukee, WI, 1880.

COHANSEY—Cohansey Glass Manufacturing Co., Philadelphia, PA, 1870–1900.

CS & Co—Cannington, Shaw & Co., St. Helens, England, 1872–1916.

DB—Du Bois Brewing Co., Pittsburgh, PA, 1918.

DEXTER—Franklin Flint Glass Works, Philadelphia, PA, 1861–1880.

DIAMOND (plain)—Diamond Glass Co., 1924–present.

THE DICTATOR—William McCully & Co., Pittsburgh, PA, 1855–1869.

DICTATOR—William McCully & Co., Pittsburgh, PA, 1869–1885.

D & O—Cumberland Glass Mfg. Co., Bridgeton, NJ, 1890–1900.

D O C—D. O. Cunningham Glass Co., Pittsburgh, PA, 1883–1937.

D S G Co.—De Steiger Glass Co., LaSalle, IL, 1867–1896.

Duffield—Duffield, Parke & Co., Detroit, MI, 1866–1875.

Dyottsville—Dyottsville Glass Works, Philadelphia, PA, 1833–1923.

Economy (in script) TRADE MARK—Kerr Glass Manufacturing Co., Portland, OR, 1903–1912.

Electric Trade Mark in script—Gayner Glass Works, Salem, N.J., 1900–1910.

Electric Trade Mark—Gayner Glass Works, Salem, NJ, 1900–1910.

Erd & Co., E R Durkee—E. R. Durkee & Co., New York, Post–1874.

E R Durkee & Co—E. R. Durkee & Co., New York, N.Y., 1850–1860.

Eureka 17—Eurkee Jar Co., Dunbar, W.V., 1864.

Eureka in script—Eurkee Jar Co., Dunbar, WV, 1900–1910.

Everlasting (in script) JAR—Illinois Pacific Glass Co., San Francisco, CA, 1904.

Excelsior—Excelsior Glass Co., Saint John, Quebec, Canada, 1878–1883.

F Inside a jar outline—C. L. Flaccus Glass Co., Pittsburgh, PA, 1900–1928.

F & A—Fahnstock & Albree, Pittsburgh, PA, 1860–1862.

FL or FL & Co.—Frederick Lorenz & Co., Pittsburgh, PA, 1819–1841.

G E M—Hero Glass Works, Philadelphia, PA, 1884–1909.

G & H—Gray & Hemingray, Cincinnati, OH, 1848–1864.

Gilberds—Gilberds Butter Tub Co., Jamestown, NY, 1883–1890.

Greenfield—Greenfield Fruit Jar & Bottle Co., Greenfield, IN, 1888–1912.

H (with varying numerals)—Holt Glass Works, West Berkeley, CA, 1893–1906.

Hamilton—Hamilton Glass Works, Hamilton, Ontario, Canada, 1865–1872.

Hazel—Hazel Glass Co., Wellsburg, WV, 1886–1902.

Helme—Geo. W. Helme Co., Jersey City, NJ, 1870–1895.

Hemingray—Hemingray Brothers & Co., and later Hemingray Glass Co., Covington, KY, 1864–1933.

H. J. Heinz—H. J. Heinz Co., Pittsburgh, PA, 1860–1869.

Heinz & Noble—H. J. Heinz Co., Pittsburgh, PA, 1869–1872.

F. J. Heinz—H. J. Heinz Co., Pittsburgh, PA, 1876–1888.

H. J. Heinz Co.—H. J. Heinz Co., Pittsburgh, PA, 1888–present.

HS in a circle—Twitchell & Schoolcraft, Keene, NH, 1815–1816.

Hunyadi Janos—Andreas Saxlehner, Buda-Pesth, Austria-Hungary, 1863–1900.

I G Co.—Ihmsen Glass Co., Pittsburgh, PA, 1870–1898.

I. G. Co—Ihmsen Glass Co., 1895.

I. G. Co. (Monogram)—Ill., Glass Co. on fruit jar, 1914.

I. P. G. in diamond—Ill., Pacific Glass Corp., 1925–1930.

IG—Illinois Glass, F inside of a jar outline, C. L. Flaccus ½ glass ½ co., Pittsburgh, PA, 1900–1928.

Ill. Glass Co.—1916–1929.

I G—Illinois Glass Co., Alton, IL, before 1890.

I G Co. in a diamond—Illinois Glass Co., Alton, IL, 1900–1916.

Improved G E M—Hero Glass Works, Philadelphia, PA, 1868.

I P G—Illinois Pacific Glass Co., San Francisco, 1902–1932.

JAF & Co., Pioneer and Folger—J. A. Folger & Co., San Francisco, 1850–present.

J D 26 S—Jon Ducan & Sons, New York, 1880–1900.

J R—Stourbridge Flint Glass Works, Pittsburgh, PA, 1823–1828.

JBS monogram—Joseph Schlitz Brewing Co., Milwaukee, WI, 1900.

JT—Mantua Glass Works and later Mantua Glass Co., Mantua, OH, 1824.

JT & Co—Brownsville Glass Works, Brownsville, PA, 1824–1828.

KENSINGTON GLASS WORKS—Kensington Glass Works, Philadelphia, PA, 1822–1932.

KERR IN SCRIPT—Kerr Glass Manufacturing Co., and later Alexander H. Kerr Glass Co., Portland, OR; Sand Spring, OK; Chicago; Los Angeles, 1912–present.

K H & G—Kearns, Herdman & Gorsuch, Zanesville, OH, 1876–1884.

K & M—Knoz & McKee, Wheeling, WV, 1824–1829.

K Y G W AND KYGW Co.—Kentucky Glass Works Co., Louisville, KY, 1849–1855.

LAMB—Lamb Glass Co., Mount Vernon, OH, 1855–1964.

L & W—Lorenz & Wightman, PA, 1862–1871.

L G Co—Louisville Glass Works, Louisville, KY, 1880.

LIGHTNING—Henry W. Putnam, Bennington, VT, 1875–1890.

L I P—Lea & Perrins, London, England, 1880–1900.

L K Y G W—Louisville Kentucky Glass Works, Louisville, KY, 1873–1890.

"MASCOT," "MASON" AND M F G Co.—Mason Fruit Jar Co., Philadelphia, PA, 1885–1890.

MASTADON—Thomas A. Evans, Mastadon Works, and later Wm. McCully & Co., Pittsburgh, PA, 1855–1887.

MG (slant letters)—Maywood Glass, Maywood, CA, 1930–1950.

M.G. CO.—Missouri Glass Co., 1900.

MG. Co.—Modes Glass Co., ID., 1895–1904.

M. G. W.—Middletown Glass Co., New York, 1889.

MOORE BROS.—Moore Bros., Clayton, NJ, 1864–1880.

N B B G Co—North Baltimore Bottle Glass Co., North Baltimore, OH, 1885–1930.

O—Owen Bottle Co.

O-D-1-O & DIAMOND & I—Owens Ill. Pacific Coast Co., CA, 1932–1943. Mark of Owen-Ill. Glass Co. merger in 1930.

P F W—Pacific Glass Works, San Francisco, CA, 1862–1876.

PREMIUM—Premium Glass Co., Coffeyville, KS, 1908–1914.

PUTNAM GLASS WORKS IN A CIRCLE—Putnam Flint Glass Works, Putnam, OH, 1852–1871.

P & W—Perry & Wood and later Perry & Wheeler, Keene, NH, 1822–1830.

QUEEN (IN SCRIPT) TRADE MARK ALL IN A SHIELD—Smalley, Kivian & Onthank, Boston, 1906–1919.

R—Louit Freres & Co., France, 1870–1890.

RAU'S—Fairmount Glass Works, Fairmount, IN, 1898–1908.

R & C Co—Roth & Co., San Francisco, CA, 1879–1888.

RED WITH A KEY THROUGH IT—Safe Glass Co., Upland, IN, 1892–1898.

R G Co.—Renton Glass Co., Renton, WA, 1911.

ROOT—Root Glass Co., Terre Haute, IN, 1901–1932.

S (in a side of a start)—Southern Glass Co., Los Angeles, 1920–1929.

S.B. & G. Co.—Stretor Bottle & Glass Co., IL, 1881–1905.

S.F. & P.G.W.—John Wieland's extra-pale Cac.cal. Bottling Works, San Francisco.

S & C—Stebbins & Chamberlain or Coventry Glass Works, Coventry, Conn., 1825–1830.

S F G W—San Francisco Glass Works, San Francisco, 1869–1876.

S & M—Sykes & Macvey, Castleford, England, 1860–1888.

SQUIBB—E.R. Squibb, M.D., Brooklyn, NY, 1858–1895.

STANDARD (IN SCRIPT, MASON)—Standard Coop. Glass Co., and later Standard Glass Co., Marion, IN, 1894–1932.

STAR GLASS CO—Star Glass Co., New Albany, IN, 1867–1900.

SWAYZEE—Swayzee Glass Co., Swayzee, IN, 1894–1906.

T C W—T. C. Wheaton Co., Millville, NJ, 1888–present.

T S—Coventry Glass Works, Coventry, CT, 1820–1824.

W & CO—Thomas Wightman & Co., Pottsburg, PA, 1880–1889.

W C G Co—West Coast Glass Co., Los Angeles, 1908–1930.

WF & S MILW—William Franzen & Son, Milwaukee, WI 1900–1929.

W G W—Woodbury Glass Works, Woodbury, NJ, 1882–1900.

W T & Co—Whitall-Tatum & Co., Millville, NJ, 1857–1935.

Foreign Trademarks

A IN A CIRCLE—Alembic Glass, Industries Bangalore, India.

BIG A IN CENTER OF IT GM—Australian Glass Mfg. Co., Kilkenny, So. Australia.

A.B.C.—Albion Bottle Co. Ltd., Oldbury, Nr. Birmingham, England.

A.G.W.—Alloa Glass Limited, Alloa, Scotland.

A G B Co.—Albion Glass Bottle Co., England, trademark is found under Lea & Perrins, 1880–1900.

B & C Co. L—Bagley & Co. Ltd., est. 1832, still operating, England.

AVH.A.—Van Hoboken & Co., Rotterdam, the Netherlands, 1800–1898.

BEAVER—Beaver Flint Glass Co., Toronto, Ontario, Canada, 1897–1920.

BOTTLE IN FRAME—Veb Glasvoerk Drebkau, Drebkau, N. L., Germany.

CROWN WITH 3 DOTS—Crown Glass, Waterloo, N.S., Wales.

CS & Co.—Cannington, Shaw & Co., St. Helens, England, 1872–1916.

CROWN WITH FIGURE OF A CROWN—Excelsior Glass Co., Saint Johns, Quebec, and later Diamond Glass Co., Montreal, Quebec, Canada, 1879–1913.

D IN CENTER OF A DIAMOND—Cominion Glass Co., Montreal, Quebec.

D.B. IN A BOOK FRAME—Dale Brown & Co., Ltd., Mesborough, York, England.

FISH—Veb Glasvoerk Stralau, Berlin.

Excelsior—Excelsior Glass Co., Saint John, Quebec, Canada, 1878–1883.

HH—Werk Hermannshutte, Czechoslovakia.

Hamilton—Hamilton Glass Works, Hamilton, Ontario, Canada, 1865–1872.

Hat—Brougba, Bulgaria.

Hunyadi Janos—Andreas Saxlehner, Buda-Pesth, Austria-Hungary, 1863–1900.

IYGE, all in a circle—The Irish Glass Bottle, Ltd., Dublin.

KH—Kastrupog Holmeqaads, Copenhagen.

L on a bell—Lanbert S.A., Belgium.

LIP—Lea & Perrins, London, England, 1880–1900.

LS in a circle—Lax & Shaw, Ltd., Leeds, York, England.

M in a circle—Cristales Mexicanos, Monterey, Mexico.

N in a diamond—Tippon Glass Co., Ltd., Tokyo, Japan.

NAGC—North American Glass Co., Montreal, Quebec, Canada, 1883–1890.

PG—Verreries De Puy De Dome, S. A., Paris.

R—Louit Freres & Co., France, 1870–1890.

S in a circle—Vetreria Savonese. A. Voglienzone, S.A., Milano, Italy.

S.A.V.A., all in a circle—Asmara, Eritrea.

S & M—Sykes & Macvey, Castleford, England, 1860–1888.

T in a circle—Tokyo Seibin., LTD., Tokyo, Japan.

vFo—Vidreria Ind. Figuerras Oliveiras, Brazil.

VT—Ve.Tri S.p.a., Vetrerie Trivemta, Vicenza, Italy.

VX—Usine de Vauxrot, France.

WECK in a frame—Weck Glaswek G. mb.H, ofigen, in Bonn, Germany.

Y in a circle—Etaria Lipasmaton, Athens, Greece.

Bottle Clubs

Bottle Clubs are one of the best sources for beginners, and offer a great opportunity to meet veteran bottle collectors, learn from them, and in general have a good time. The bottle clubs listed here reflect the latest information available at the time of publication and are subject to change. The list represents an excellent cross section of the United States, Europe, and Asia-Pacific. Any active bottle club or organization that requires a change of information or wishes to be included in the next edition of *Bottles: Identification and Price Guide,* should send the required information to Michael F. Polak, P.O. Box 30328, Long Beach, CA 90853.

Listed alphabetically by state, country, and club name.

Domestic Clubs

ALABAMA

Alabama Bottle Collectors Society
2768 Hanover Circle
Birmingham, AL 35205
205–933–7902

Azalea City Beamers Bottle and
Specialty Club
100 Bienville Avenue
Mobile, AL 36606
205–473–4251

Bama Beamers Bottle and Specialty Club
Rt. 1, P.O. Box 72
Sheffield, AL 35660
205–383–6884

Choctaw Jim Beam Bottle and Specialty
Club
218 S. Hamburg Street
Butler, AL 36904
205–459–3140

Heart of Dixie Beam Bottle and
Specialty Club
2136 Rexford Road
Montgomery, AL 36116

Mobile Bottle Collectors Club
8844 Lee Circle
Irvington, AL 36544
205–957–6725

Mobile Bottle Collectors Club
Rt. 4, P.O. Box 28
Theodore, AL 36582

Montgomery, Alabama, Bottle Club
1940A Norman Bridge Court
Montgomery, AL 36104

Montgomery Bottle and Insulator Club
2021 Merrily Drive
Montgomery, AL 36111
205–288–7937

North Alabama Bottle and Glass Club
P.O. Box 109
Decatur, AL 35602–0109

Tuscaloosa Antique Bottle Club
1617 11th Street
Tuscaloosa, AL 35401

Southern Beamers Bottle and Specialty
Club
1400 Greenbrier Road, Apt. G-3
Anniston, AL 36201
205–831–5151

Vulcan Beamers Bottle and Specialty
Club
5817 Avenue Q
Birmingham, AL 35228
205–831–5151

ALASKA
Alaska Bottle Club
8510 E. 10th
Anchorage, AK 99504

ARIZONA
Avon Collectors Club
P.O. Box 1406
Mesa, AZ 86201

Fort Smith Area Bottle Collectors
Association
4618 S. "Q"
Fort Smith, AZ 72901

Kachina Ezra Brooks Bottle Club
3818 W. Cactus Wren Drive
Phoenix, AZ 85021

Phoenix A.B.C. Club
1939 W. Waltann Lane
Phoenix, AZ 85023
602–993–9757

Pick and Shovel A.B.C. of Arizona, Inc.
P.O. Box 7020
Phoenix, AZ 85011

Southern Arizona Historical Collector's
Association, Ltd.
6211 Piedra Seca
Tuscon, AZ 85718

Tri-City Jim Beam Bottle Club
2701 E. Utopia Road,
Sp. #91
Phoenix, AZ 85024
602–867–1375

Valley of the Sun Bottle and Specialty
Club
212 E. Minton
Tempe, AZ 85281

White Mountain Antique Bottle
Collectors Association
P.O. Box 503
Eager, AZ 85925

Wildcat Country Beam Bottle and
Specialty Club
2601 S. Blackmoon Drive
Tucson, AZ 85730
602–298–5943

ARKANSAS
Fort Smith Area Bottle Collectors Assn.
2201 S. 73rd Street
Fort Smith, AR 72903

Hempsted County Bottle Club
710 S. Hervey
Hope, AR 71801

Indian Country A.B. and Relic Society
3818 Hilltop Drive
Jonesboro, AR 72401

Little Rock Antique Bottle Collectors
Club
16201 Highway 300
Roland, AR 72135

Madison County Bottle Collectors Club
Rt. 2, Box 304
Huntsville, AR 72740

Razorback Jim Beam Bottle and
Specialty Club
2609 S. Taylor
Little Rock, AR 72204
501–664–1335

Southwest Arkansas Bottle Club
Star Route
Delight, AR 71940

CALIFORNIA

Amethyst Bottle Club
3245 Military Avenue
Los Angeles, CA 90034

Antique Bottle Club Association of
Fresno
P.O. Box 1932
Fresno, CA 93718

Antique Bottle Collectors of Orange
County
223 E. Pomona
Santa Ana, CA 92707

A, OK Beamers
7650 Balboa Boulevard
Van Nuys, CA 91406
213–787–2674

Argonaut Jim Beam Bottle Club
8253 Citadel Way
Sacramento, CA 95826
916–383–0206

Avon Bottle and Specialties Collectors
Southern California Division
9233 Mills Avenue
Montclair, CA 91763

Bakersfield Bottle and Insulator
Collectors
1023 Baldwin Road
Bakersfield, CA 93304

Bay Area Vagabonds Jim Beam Club
224 Castleton Way
San Bruno, CA 94066
415–355–4356

Bidwell Bottle Club
Box 546
Chico, CA 95926

Bishop Belles and Beaux Bottle Club
P.O. Box 1475
Bishop, CA 93514

Blossom Valley Jim Beam Bottle and
Specialty Club
431 Grey Ghost Avenue
San Jose, CA 95111
408–227–2759

Bodfish Beamers Jim Beam Bottle Club
19 Dow Drive
P.O. Box 864–A
Bodfish, CA 93205
714–379–3280

Bytown Bottle Seekers
P.O. Box 375
Ontario, CA 91761
613–838–5802

California Miniature Bottle Club
1911 Willow Street
Alameda, CA 94501

California Ski Country Bottle Club
212 South El Molino Street
Alhambra, CA 91801

Camellia City Jim Beam Bottle Club
3734 Lynhurst Way
North Highlands, CA 95660

Central Calif. Avon Bottle and
Collectible Club
P.O. Box 232
Amador City, CA 95601

Cherry Valley Beam Bottle and Specialty
Club
6851 Hood Drive
Westminster, CA 92683

Chief Solano Bottle Club
4–D Boynton Avenue
Sulsun, CA 94585

Curiosity Bottle Association
Box 103
Napa, CA 94558

Fiesta City Beamers
329 Mountain Drive
Santa Barbara, CA 93103

First Double Springs Collectors Club
13311 Illinois Street
Westminster, CA 92683

Five Cities Beamers
756 Mesa View Drive, Sp. 57
Arroyo Grande, CA 93420

Fresno Antique Bottle and Collectors
Club
281 West Magill Avenue
Clovis, CA 93612

Glass Belles of San Gabriel
518 W. Neuby Avenue
San Gabriel, CA 91776

Glasshopper Figural Bottle Association
P.O. Box 6642
Torrance, CA 90504

Golden Bear Ezra Brooks Bottle Club
8808 Capricorn Way
San Diego, CA 92126

Golden Bear Jim Beam Bottle and
Specialty Club
8808 Capricorn Way
San Diego, CA 92126

Golden Gate Beam Club
35113 Clover Street
Union City, CA 94587
415–487–4479

Golden Gate Historical Bottle Society
P.O. Box 5331
Richmond, CA 94805

Greater Calif. Antique Bottle Collectors
P.O. Box 55
Sacramento, CA 95801

High Desert Bottle Hunters
P.O. Box 581
Ridgecrest, CA 93558

Highland Toasters Beam Bottle and
Specialty Club
1570 E. Marshall
San Bernardino, CA 92404
714–883–2000

Hoffman's Mr. Lucky Bottle Club
2104 Rhoda Street
Simi Valley, CA 93065

Hollywood Stars–Ezra Brooks Bottle
Club
2200 N. Beachwood Drive
Hollywood, CA 90028

Humboldt Antique Bottle Club
P.O. Box 6012
Eureka, CA 95501

International Perfume Bottle Association
3519 Wycliffe Drive
Modesto, CA 95355

Jewels of Avon
2297 Maple Avenue
Oroville, CA 95965

Jim Beam Bottle Club
139 Arlington
Berkley, CA 94707

*Jim Beam Bottle Club of Southern
California*
1114 Coronado Terrace
Los Angeles, CA 90066

Juniper Hills Bottle Club
Rt. 1, Box 18
Valyerma, CA 93563

Kern County Antique Bottle Club
P.O. Box 6724
Bakersfield, CA 93306

Lilliputian Bottle Club
5626 Corning Avenue
Los Angeles, CA 90056
213–294–3231

Lionstone Bottle Collectors of America
P.O. Box 75924
Los Angeles, CA 90075

Livermore Avon Club
6385 Claremont Avenue
Richmond, CA 94805

Lodi Jim Beam Bottle Club
429 E. Lodi Avenue
Lodi, CA 95240

Los Angeles Historical Bottle Club
P.O. Box 60762
Terminal Annex
Los Angeles, CA 90060
213–332–6751

*Miniature Bottle Club of Southern
California*
836 Carob
Brea, CA 92621

Mission Bells (Beams)
1114 Coronada Terrace
Los Angeles, CA 90026

*Mission Tesore Jim Beam Bottle and
Specialty Club*
7701 E. Zayante Road
Felton, CA 95018
408–335–4317

*Mission Trails Ezra Brooks Bottles and
Specialties Club, Inc.*
4923 Bel Canto Drive
San Jose, CA 95124

Mission Trail Historical Bottle Club
1475 Teton Avenue
Salinas, CA 93906

Modesto Beamers
1429 Glenwood Drive
Modesto, CA 95350
209–523–3440

Modesto Old Bottle Club (MOBC)
P.O. Box 1791
Modesto, CA 95354

*Monterey Bay Beam Bottle and Specialty
Club*
P.O. Box 258
Freedom, CA 95019

Motherlode Antique Bottle Club
P.O. Box 165
Downieville, CA 95936

M. T. Bottle Club
P.O. Box 608
Solana Beach, CA 92075

Mount Bottle Club
422 Orpheus
Encinitas, CA 92024

Mount Diablo Bottle Club
4166 Sandra Circle
Pittsburg, CA 94565

Mount Diablo Bottle Society
1699 Laguna #110
Concord, CA 94520

Mount Whitney Bottle Club
P.O. Box 688
Lone Pine, CA 93545

Napa-Solano Bottle Club
1409 Delwood
Vallejo, CA 94590

National Jim Beam Bottle and Specialty
Club
5005 Cochrane Avenue
Oakland, CA 94618
415-655-5005

Northern California Jim Beam Bottle
and Specialty Club
P.O. Box 186
Montgomerey Creek, CA 96065

Northwestern Bottle Collectors
Association
P.O. Box 1121
Santa Rosa, CA 95402

Northwestern Bottle Collectors
Association
1 Keeler Street
Petaluma, CA 94952

Ocean Breeze Beamers
4841 Tacayme Drive
Oceanside, CA 92054
714-757-9081

Orange County Jim Beam Bottle and
Specialties Club
546 W. Ash Avenue
Fullerton, CA 92632-2702
714-875-8241

Original Sippin Cousins Ezra Brooks
Specialties Club
12206 Malone Street
Los Angeles, CA 90066

Palomar Jim Beam Club
246 S. Las Posas
P.O. Box 125
San Marcos, CA 92069
714-744-2924

Pebble Beach Jim Beam Bottle Club
419 Alvarado Street
Monterey, CA 93940
408-373-5320

Pepsi-Cola Collectors Club
P.O. Box 817
Claremont, CA 91711

Painted Soda Bottle Collectors
Association
9418 Hilmer Drive
La Mesa, CA 91942
619-461-4354

Peninsula Bottle Club
P.O. Box 886
Belmont, CA 94002

Petaluma Bottle and Antique Club
P.O. Box 1035
Petaluma, CA 94952

Quail Country Jim Beam Bottle and
Specialty Club
625 Pleasant
Coalinga, CA 93210

Queen Mary Beam and Specialty Club
P.O. Box 2054
Anaheim, CA 92804

Relic Accumulators
P.O. Box 3513
Eureka, CA 95501

Santa Barbara Beam Bottle Club
5307 University Drive
Santa Barbara, CA 93111

Santa Barbara Bottle Club
P.O. Box 30171
Santa Barbara, CA 93105

*San Bernardino County Historical Bottle
and Collectible Club*
P.O. Box 6759
San Bernardino, CA 92412
619–244–5863

San Diego Antique Bottle Club
P.O. Box 5137
San Diego, CA 92165
619–274–5519

San Diego Jim Beam Bottle Club
2620 Mission Village Drive
San Diego, CA 92112

San Francisco Bay Area Bottle Club
160 Lower Via Casitas #8
Kentfield, CA 94904

*San Joaquin Valley Jim Beam Bottle and
Specialties Club*
4085 N. Wilson Avenue
Fresno, CA 93704

*San Jose Historical Bottle Club
Association*
P.O. Box 5432
San Jose, CA 95150
408–259–7564

San Luis Obispo Antique Bottle Club
124–21 Street
Paso Robles, CA 93446
805–238–1848

Santa Maria Beam and Specialty Club
528 E. Harding
San Maria, CA 93454
805–922–1238

Sequoia Antique Bottle Society
1900 4th Avenue
Kingsburg, CA 93631

*Sequoia Antique Bottle and Collectors
Society*
P.O. Box 3695
Visalia, CA 93278
209–686–1873

*Shasta Antique Bottle Collectors
Association*
Route 1, Box 3147–A
Anderson, CA 96007

Sierra Gold Ski Country Bottle Club
5081 Rio Vista Avenue
San Jose, CA 95129

*Ski-Country Bottle Club of Southern
California*
3148 N. Walnut Grove
Rosemead, CA 91770

Solar Country Beamers
940 Kelly Drive
Barstow, CA 92311
714–256–1485

South Bay Antique Bottle Club
2589½ Valley Drive
Manhattan Beach, CA 90266

Southern Wyoming Avon Bottle Club
301 Canyon Highlands Drive
Oroville, CA 95965

Stockton Historical Bottle Society, Inc.
P.O. Box 8584
Stockton, CA 95204

*Sunnyvale Antique Bottle Collectors
Association*
613 Torrington
Sunnyvale, CA 94087

Superior California Bottle Club
3220 Stratford Avenue
Redding, CA 96001

Taft Antique Bottle Club
P.O. Box 334
Taft, CA 93268

Teen Bottle Club
Route 1, Box 60–TE
Eureka, CA 95501

Tehama County Antique Bottle Club
Route 1, Box 775
Red Bluff, CA 96080
916–527–1680

The California Miniature Club
1911 Willow Street
Alameda, CA 94501

Tinseltown Beam Club
4117 E. Gage Avenue
Bell, CA 90201
213–699–8787

Western World Collectors Association
P.O. Box 409
Ontario, CA 91761
714–984–0614

Wildwind Jim Beam Bottle and Specialty
Club
905 Eaton Way
Sunnyvale, CA 94087
408–739–1558

World Wide Avon Collectors Club
44021 Seventh Street
E. Lancaster, CA 93534
805–948–8849

'49er Historical Bottle Association
P.O. Box 561
Penryn, CA 95663
916–663–3681

COLORADO
Alamosa Bottle Collectors
Route 2, Box 170
Alamosa, CO 81101

American Breweriana Association, Inc.
P.O. Box 11157
Pueblo, CO 81001

Antique Bottle Club of Colorado
P.O. Box 245
Littleton, CO 80160

Avon Club of Colorado Springs,
Colorado
707 N. Farragut
Colorado Springs, CO 80909

Colorado Mile-High Ezra Brooks Bottle
Club
7401 Decatur Street
Westminster, CO 80030

Four Corners Bottle and Glass Club
P.O. Box 45
Cortez, CO 81321

Horsetooth Antique Bottle Collectors, Inc.
P.O. Box 944
Fort Collins, CO 80521

Lionstone Western Figural Club
P.O. Box 2275
Colorado Springs, CO 80901

Mile-Hi Jim Beam Bottle and Specialty
Club
13196 W. Green Mountain Drive
Lakewood, CO 80228
303–986–6828

National Ski Country Bottle Club
1224 Washington Avenue
Golden, CO 80401
303–279–3373

Northeastern Colorado Antique Bottle
Club
P.O. Box 634
Fort Morgan, CO 80701

Northern Colorado Antique Bottle Club
227 W. Beaver Avenue
Fort Morgan, CO 80701

Northern Colorado Beam Bottle and
Specialty Club
3272 Gunnison Drive
Fort Collins, CO 80526
303–226–2301

Ole Foxie Jim Beam Club
7530 Wilson Court
Westminster, CO 80030
303–429–1823
Attn: Shirley Engel, President

Peaks and Plains Antique Bottle Club
P.O. Box 814
Colorado Springs, CO 80901

Pikes Peak Antique Bottle and Collectors
Club
308 Maplewood Drive
Colorado Springs, CO 80907–4326

Rocky Mountain Jim Beam Bottle and
Specialty Club
Alcott Station, P.O. Box 12162
Denver, CO 80212

Southern Colorado Antique Bottle Club
843 Ussie Avenue
Canon City, CO 81212
719–275–3719

Telluride Antique Bottle Collectors
P.O. Box 344
Telluride, CO 8143

Western Figural and Jim Beam Specialty
Club
P.O. Box 4431
Colorado Springs, CO 80930

Western Slope Bottle Club
P.O. Box 354
Palisade, CO 81526
303–464–7727

CONNECTICUT
Connecticut Specialty Bottle Club, Inc.
P.O. Box 624
Stratford, CT 06497

The National Association of Milk Bottle
Collectors
4 Ox Bow Road
Westport, CT 06880–2602
203–227–5244

Somers Antique Bottle Club
27 Plank Lane
Glastonbury, CT 06033–2523

Southern Connecticut Antique Bottle
Collectors Association
34 Dartmouth Drive
Huntington, CT 06484
203–929–5197

Western Connecticut Jim Beam Bottle
and Specialty Club
Route 1, Box 442
Old Hawleyville Road
Bethel, CT 06081
203–744–6118

DELAWARE
Blue Hen Jim Beam Bottle and Specialty
Club
303 Potomac Drive
Wilmington, DE 19803
302–652–6378

Delmarva Antique Bottle Collectors
57 Lakewood Drive
Lewes, DE 19958

Mason-Dixon Bottle Collectors
Association
P.O. Box 505
Lewes, DE 19958

*Tri-State Bottle Collectors and Diggers
Club*
2510 Cratchett Road
Wilmington, DE 19808

FLORIDA

Antique Bottle Collectors of Florida, Inc.
2512 Davie Boulevard
Fort Lauderdale, FL 33312

*Antique Bottle Collectors of North
Florida*
P.O. Box 14796
Jacksonville, FL 32238
904–284–1499

*Association of Florida Antique Bottle
Collectors*
P.O. Box 3105
Sarasota, FL 34230
813–923–6550

Bay Area Historical Bottle Collector
P.O. Box 3454
Apollo Beach, FL 32210

Central Florida Insulator Collectors Club
707 N.E. 113th Street
Miami, FL 33161–7239
305–895–0843

Central Florida Jim Beam Bottle Club
1060 W. French Avenue
Orange City, FL 32763
904–775–7392

Crossarms Collectors Club
1756 N.W. 58th Avenue
Lauderhill, FL 33313

*Deep South Jim Beam Bottle and
Specialty Club*
16100 S.W. 278th Street
Homestead, FL 33031
305–248–7301

Everglades Antique Bottle Club
6981 S.W. 19th Street
Pompano, FL 33068

*Everglades Antique Bottle and Collectors
Club*
400 S. 57 Terrace
Hollywood, FL 33023
305–962–3434

*Florida Panhandle Jim Beam Bottle and
Specialty Club*
706 James Court
Fort Walton Beach, FL 32548
904–862–3469

*Gateway of the Palms Beam Bottle and
Specialty Club*
6621 Katherine Road
West Palm Beach, FL 33406
305–683–3900

Gold Coast Collectors Club
Joseph I. Frakes
P.O. Box 10183
Wilton Manors, FL 33305

Halifax Historical Society
224½ S. Beach Street
Daytona Beach, FL 32018

Harbor City Bottle Collectors Club
1232 Causeway
Eau, FL 32935

Longwood Bottle Club
P.O. Box 437
Longwood, FL 32750

Mid-State Antique Bottle Collectors
88 Sweetbriar Branch
Longwood, FL 32750
407–834–8914

Mid-State Antique Bottle Collectors
3400 E. Grant Avenue
Orlando, FL 32806
407–896–8915

M.T. Bottle Collectors Association, Inc.
P.O. Box 1581
Deland, FL 32720

Northwest Florida Regional Bottle Club
P.O. Box 282
Port Saint Joe, FL 32456

Original Florida Keys Collectors Club
P.O. Box 212
Islamorada, FL 33036

Pensacola Bottle and Relic Collectors
Association
1004 Freemont Avenue
Pensacola, FL 32505

Ridge Area Antique Bottle Collectors
1219 Carlton
Lake Wales, FL 33853

Sanford Antique Bottle Collectors
2656 Grandview Avenue
Sanford, FL 33853
305–322–7181

Sarasota-Manatee Antique Bottle
Collectors Association
Route 1, Box 74–136
Sarasota, FL 33583

South Florida Jim Beam Bottle and
Specialty Club
7741 N.W. 35th Street
West Hollywood, FL 33024

Suncoast Antique Bottle Club
P.O. Box 12712
Saint Petersburg, FL 33733

Suncoast Antique Bottle Club
Association, Inc.
5305 8th Avenue South
Gulfport, FL 33707
813–866–0263

Suncoast Antique Bottle and Specialty
Club
P.O. Box 5067
Sarasota, FL 33579

Tampa Antique Bottle Collectors
P.O. Box 4232
Tampa, FL 33607

Treasure Coast Bottle Collectors
6301 Lilyan Parkway
Fort Pierce, FL 34591

West Coast Florida Ezra Brooks Bottle
Club
1360 Harbor Drive
Sarasota, FL 33579

GEORGIA

Bulldog Double Springs Bottle Collector
Club of Augusta, Georgia
1916 Melrose Drive
Augusta, GA 30906

Coastal Empire Bottle Club
P.O. Box 3714, Station B
Savannah, GA 31404

Coca-Cola Collectors Club International
P.O. Box 49166
Atlanta, GA 30359–1166

The Desoto Trail Bottle Collectors Club
406 Randolph Street
Cuthbert, GA 31740

The Dixie Jewels Insulator Club
6220 Carriage Court
Cummings, GA 30130
707–781–5021

Flint Antique Bottle & Coin Club
c/o Cordele-Crisp Co., Recreation
Department
204 Second Street N.
Cordele, GA 31015

Flint River Jim Beam Bottle Club
Route 3, P.O. Box 6
Camilla, GA 31730
912–336–7034

Georgia Bottle Club
2996 Pangborn Road
Decatur, GA 30033

Georgia-Carolina Empty Bottle Club
P.O. Box 1184
Augusta, GA 30903

Macon Antique Bottle Club
P.O. Box 5395
Macon, GA 31208

Macon Antique Bottle Club
c/o 5532 Jane Run Circle
Macon, GA 31206

The Middle Georgia Antique Bottle Club
2746 Alden Street
Macon, GA 31206

Peachstate Bottle and Specialty Bottle
Club
5040 Vallo Vista Court
Atlanta, GA 30342

Peachtree Jim Beam Bottlers Club
Lakeshore Drive
Daluth, GA 30136
404–448–9013

Peanut State Jim Beam Bottle and
Specialty Club
767 Timberland Street
Smyra, GA 30080
404–432–8482

Southeastern Antique Bottle Club
P.O. Box 657
Decatur, GA 30033

Southeastern Antique Bottle Club
1546 Summerford Court
Dunwoody, GA 30338
707–394–6664

HAWAII

Hauoli Beam Bottle Collectors Club of
Hawaii
45–027 Ka-Hanahou Place
Kaneohe, HI 96744

Hawaii Historic Bottle Collectors Club
P.O. Box 90456
Honolulu, HI 96835
808–955–2130

Hilo Bottle Club
287 Kanoelani Street
Hilo, HI 96720

IDAHO

Buhl Antique Bottle Club
500 12th, N.
Buhl, ID 83316

Eagle Rock Beam and Specialty Club
3665 Upland Avenue
Idaho Falls, ID 83401
208–522–7819

Em Tee Bottle Club
P.O. Box 62
Jerome, ID 83338

Fabulous Valley Antique Bottle Club
P.O. Box 8051
Boise, ID 83707

Idaho Beam and Specialty Club
2312 Burrell Avenue
Lewiston, ID 83501
208–743–5997

Inland Empire Jim Beam Bottle and
Collectors' Club
1117 10th Street
Lewiston, ID 83501

Rock and Bottle Club
Route 1
Fruitland, ID 83619

Treasure Valley Beam Bottle and
Specialty Club
2324 Norcrest Drive
Boise, ID 83705
208–343–6207

ILLINOIS

Antique Bottle Club of Northern Illinois
436 Center
Woodstock, IL 60098

Alton Area Bottle Club
2448 Alby Street
Alton, IL
618–462–4285

Blackhawk Jim Beam Bottle and
Specialty Club
2003 Kishwaukee Street
Rockford, IL 61101

Central Illinois Jim Beam Bottle and
Specialty Club
3725 S. Sand Creek Road
Decatur, IL 62521

Central and Midwestern States Beam
and Specialty Club
44 S. Westmore
Lombard, IL 60148

Chicago Ezra Brooks Bottle and
Specialty Club
3635 W. 82nd Street
Chicago, IL 60652

Chicago Jim Beam Bottle and Specialty
Club
1305 W. Marion Street
Joliet, IL 60436

Dreamers Beamers
5721 Vial Parkway
LaGrange, IL 60525
312–246–4838

Eagle Jim Beam Bottle and Specialty
Club
1015 Hollycrest
P.O. Box 2084 CFS
Champaign, IL 61820
217–352–4035

First Chicago Antique Bottle Club
P.O. Box-A3382
Chicago, IL 60690
708–541–5788

Heart of Illinois Antique Bottle Club
2010 Bloomington Road
East Peoria, IL 61611

Illinois Jim Beam Bottle and Specialty
Club
P.O. Box 13
Champaign, IL 61820

Illinois Bottle Club
P.O. Box 181
Rushville, IL 62681

International Association of Jim Beam
4338 Saratoga Avenue
Downers Grove, IL 60515

Kelly Club
147 North Brainard Avenue
LaGrange, IL 60525

Land of Lincoln Bottle Club
2515 Illinois Circle
Decatur, IL 62526

Lewis and Clark Jim Beam Bottle and
Specialty Club
P.O. Box 451
Wood River, IL 62095

Lionstone Bottle Collectors of America
P.O. Box 2418
Chicago, IL 60690

Louis Joliet Bottle Club
12 Kenmore
Joilet, IL 60433

Metro East Bottle and Jar Association
309 Bellevue Drive
Delleville, IL 62223
618–233–8841

Metro East Bottle and Jar Association
1702 North Keesler
Collinsville, IL 62234

Metro East Bottle and Jar Association
P.O. Box 185
Mascoutah, IL 62234

National Ezra Brooks Club
645 N. Michigan Avenue
Chicago, IL 69611

North Shore Jim Beam Bottle and
Specialty Club
542 Glendale Road
Glenview, IL 60025

Pekin Bottle Collectors Association
P.O. Box 372
Pekin, IL 61555
309–691–5704

Rock River Valley Jim Beam Bottle and
Speciality Club
1107 Avenue A
Rock Falls, IL 61071
815–625–7075

Starved Rock Jim Beam Bottle and
Specialty Club
P.O. Box 177
Ottawa, IL 61350
815–433–3269

Sweet Corn Capital Bottle Club
1015 W. Orange
Hoopeston, IL 60942

The Greater Chicago Insulator Club
34273 Homestead Road
Gurnee, IL 60031
708–855–9136

Tri-County Jim Beam Bottle Club
3702 W. Lancer Road
Peoria, IL 61615
309–691–8784

INDIANA

American Collectors of Infant Feeders
5161 W. 59th Street
Indianapolis, IN 46254
317–291–5850

City of Bridges Jim Beam Bottle and
Specialty Club
1017 N. Sixth Street
Logansnport, IN 46947
219–722–3197

Crossroads of America Jim Beam Bottle
Club
114 S. Green Street
Brownsburg, IN 46112
317–852–5168

Fort Wayne Historical Bottle Club
P.O. Box 475
Huntertown, IN 446748

Hoosier Jim Beam Bottle and Specialty
Club
P.O. Box 24234
Indianapolis, IN 46224

Indiana Ezra Brooks Bottle Club
P.O. Box 24344
Indianapolis, IN 46224

Jelly Jammers
6986 West Boggstown Road
Boggstown, IN 46110

Lafayette Antique Bottle Club
3664 Redondo Drive
Lafayette, IN 47905

Michiana Jim Beam Bottle and Specialty Club
58955 Locust Road
South Bend, IN 46614

Mid-West Antique Fruit Jar and Bottle Club
P.O. Box 38
Flat Rock, IN 47234
812–587–5560

The Ohio Valley Antique Bottle and Jar Club
214 John Street
Aurora, IN 47001

Steel City Ezra Brooks Bottle Club
Route 2, Box 32A
Valparaiso, IN 46383

Three Rivers Jim Beam Bottle and Specialty Club
Route 4
Winchester Road
Fort Wayne, IN 46819
219–639–3041

We Found 'Em Bottle and Insulator Club
P.O. Box 578
Bunker Hill, IN 46914

Iowa

Five Seasons Beam and Specialty Club of Iowa
609 32nd Street, N.E.
Cedar Rapids, IA 52402
319–365–6089

Gold Dome Jim Beam Bottle and Specialty Club
2616 Hull
Des Moines, IA 50317
515–262–8728

Hawkeye Jim Beam Bottle Club
658 Kern Street
Waterloo, IA 60703
319–233–9168

Iowa Antique Bottleers
Route 1, Box 145
Milton, IA 52570
515–675–3740

Iowa Great Lakes Jim Beam Bottle and Specialty Club
Green Acres Mobile Park, Lot 88
Estherville, IA 51334
712–362–2759

Larkin Bottle Club
107 W. Grimes
Red Oak, IA 51566

Midlands Jim Beam Bottle and Specialty Club
Route 4
Harlan, IA 51537
712–744–3686

Quad Cities Jim Beam Bottle and Specialty Club
2425 W. 46th Street
Davenport, IA 52806
319–391–4319

Shot Tower Beam Club
284 N. Booth Street
Dubuque, IA 52001
319–583–6343

Kansas

Air Capital City Jim Beam Bottle and Specialty Club
3256 Euclid
Wichita, KS 67217
316–942–3162

Bud Hastin's National Avon Collector's
Club
P.O. Box 12088
Overland Park, KS 66212

Cherokee Strip Ezra Brooks Bottle and
Specialty Club
P.O. Box 631
Arkansas City, KS 67005

Flint Hills Beam and Specialty Club
201 W. Pine
El Dorado, KS 67402

Jayhawk Bottle Club
7919 Grant
Overland Park, KS 66212

Kansas City Antique Bottle Collectors
5528 Aberdeen
Shawnee Mission, KS 66205
816–433–1398

North Central Kansas Antique Bottle
and Collectors Club
336 E. Wisconsin
Russell, KS 67665
913–483–4380

Southeast Kansas Bottle and Relic Club
Route 2, Box 107
Humboldt, KS 66748

Walnut Valley Jim Beam Bottle and
Specialty Club
P.O. Box 631
Arkansas City, KS 67005
316–442–0509

Wichita Ezra Brooks Bottle and
Specialty Club
8045 Peachtree Street
Wichita, KS 67207

KENTUCKY
Derby City Jim Beam Bottle Club
4105 Spring Hill Road
Louisville, KY 40207

Gold City Jim Beam Bottle Club
286 Metts Court, Apt. 4
Elizabethtown, KY 42701
502–737–9297

Kentuckiana Antique Bottle and
Outhouse Society
4017 Shady Villa Drive
Louisville, KY 40219

Kentucky Bluegrass Ezra Brooks Bottle
Club
6202 Tabor Drive
Louisville, KY 40218

Kentucky Cardinal Beam Bottle Club
428 Templin
Bardstown, KY 41104

Land by the Lakes Beam Club
Route 6, Box 320
Cadiz, KY 42211
502–522–8445

Louisville Bottle Collectors
11819 Garrs Avenue
Anchorage, KY 40223

Pegasus Jim Beam Bottle and Specialty
Club
9405 Cornflower Road
Valley Station, KY 40272
502–937–4376

LOUISIANA
Ark-La-Tex Jim Beam Bottle and
Specialty Club
1902 Carol Street
Bossier City, LA 71112
318–742–3550

Bayou Bottle Bugs
216 Dahlia
New Iberia, LA 70560

*"Cajun Country Cousins" Ezra Brooks
Bottle and Specialty Club*
1000 Chevis Street
Abbeville, LA 70510

Cenia Bottle Club
c/o Pam Tullos
Route 1, Box 463
Dry Prong, LA 71423

*Crescent City Jim Beam Bottle and
Specialty Club*
733 Wright Avenue
Gretna, LA 70053
504–367–2182

Dixie Diggers Bottle Club
P.O. Box 626
Empire, LA 70050

*Historical Bottle Association of Baton
Rouge*
1843 Tudor Drive
Baton Rouge, LA 70815

Ken Tally Jim Beam Bottle Club
110 Ken Tally Estates
Hammond, LA 70401
504–345–6186

New Albany Glass Works Bottle Club
732 N. Clark Boulevard
Parksville, LA 47130

*North East Louisiana Antique Bottle
Club*
P.O. Box 4192
Monroe, LA 71291
318–322–8359

Red Stick Jim Beam Bottle Club
2127 Beaumont, Suite 4
Baton Rouge, LA 70806

Sanford's Night Owl Beamers
Route 2, Box 102
Greenwell Springs, LA 70739
504–261–3658

Shreveport Antique Bottle Club
1157 Arncliffe Drive
Shreveport, LA 71107
504–221–0089

MAINE

Dirigo Bottle Collectors Club
R.F.D. 3
Dexter, ME 04930
207–924–3443

Dover Foxcroft Bottle Club
50 Church Street
Dover Foxcroft, ME 04426

The Glass Bubble Bottle Club
P.O. Box 91
Cape Neddick, ME 03902

Jim Beam Collectors Club
10 Lunt Road
Falmouth, ME 04105

New England Antique Bottle Club
R.F.D. 1, Box 408
North Berwick, ME 03906

New England Bottle Club
45 Bolt Hill Road
Eliot, ME 03903

Paul Bunyan Bottle Club
237 14th Street
Bangor, ME 04401

Pine Tree Antique Bottle Club
Buxton Road
Saco, ME 04072

Pine Tree State Beamers
15 Woodside Avenue
Saco, ME 04072
207–284–8756

Tri-County Bottle Collectors Association
R.F.D. 3
Dexter, ME 04930

Waldo County Bottlenecks Club
Head-of-the-Tide
Belfast, ME 04915

MARYLAND
Baltimore Antique Bottle Collectors, Inc.
P.O. Box 36061
Towson, MD 21286

Blue and Gray Ezra Brooks Bottle Club
2106 Sunnybrook Drive
Frederick, MD 21201

Catoctin Jim Beam Bottle Club
c/o Ron Danner
1 North Chatham Road
Ellicott City, MD 21063
301–465–5773

International Chinese Snuff Bottle Society
2601 North Charles Street
Baltimore, MD 21218

Mason Dixon Bottle Collectors Association
601 Market Street
Denton, MD 21629

Mid-Atlantic Miniature Whiskey Bottle Club
208 Gloucester Drive
Glen Burnie, MD 21061
301–766–8421

MASSACHUSETTS
Baystate Beamers Bottle and Specialty Club
27 Brookhaven Drive
Ludlow, MA 01056
413–589–0446

Berkshire Antique Bottle Association
Box 415
Monterey, MA 01245

Merrimack Valley Antique Bottle Club
c/o M. E. Tarleton
Hillside Road
Boxford, MA 02675

Scituate Bottle Club
54 Cedarwood Road
Scituate, MA 02066

Yankee Pole Cat Insulator Club
c/o Jill Meier
103 Cantebury Court
Carlisle, MA 01741–1860
508–369–0208

MICHIGAN
Central Michigan Krazy Korkers Bottle Club
Mid-Michigan Community College
Clare Avenue
Harrison, MI 48625

Chief Pontiac Antique Bottle Club
c/o Larry Blascyk
13880 Neal Road
Davisburg, MI 48019
313–634–8469

Dickinson County Bottle Club
717 Henford Avenue
Iron Mountain, MI 49801

Flint Antique Bottle Collectors Association
450 Leta Avenue
Flint, MI 48507

Flint Antique Bottles and Collectors Club
6349 Silver Lake Road
Linden, MI 48451

Flint Eagles Ezra Brooks Club
1117 W. Remington Avenue
Flint, MI 48507

Grand Rapids Antique Bottle Club
1368 Kinney N.W.
Walker, MI 49504

Grand Valley Bottle Club
31 Dickinson S.W.
Grand Rapids, MI 49507

Great Lakes Jim Beam Bottle Club of
Michigan
1010 South Harvey
Plymouth, MI 48170
313–453–0579

Great Lakes Miniature Bottle Club
P.O. Box 230460
Fairhaven, MI 48023

Huron Valley Bottle Club
12475 Saline-Milan Road
Milan, MI 48160

Huron Valley Bottle and Insulator Club
2475 West Walton
Waterford, MI 48329–4435

Kalamazoo Antique Bottle Club
1121 Maywood
Kalamazoo, MI 49001

Lionstone Collectors Bottle and Specialty
Club of Michigan
3089 Grand Blanc Road
Swartz Creek, MI 48473

Manistee Coin and Bottle Club
207 E. Piney Road
Mamistee, MI 49660

Metro and East Bottle and Jar
Association
309 Bellevue Park Drive
Fairview Heights, MI 49660

Metro Detroit Antique Bottle Club
410 Lothrop Road
Grosse Point Farms, MI 48236

Michigan Bottle Collectors Association
144 W. Clark Street
Jackson MI 49203

Michigan's Vehicle City Beam Bottles
and Specialty Club
907 Root Street
Flint, MI 48503

Mid-Michee Pine Beam Club
609 Webb Drive
Bay City, MI 48706

Northern Michigan Bottle Club
P.O. Box 421
Petroskey, MI 49770

Old Corkers Bottle Club
Route 1
Iron River, MI 49935

Red Run Jim Beam Bottle and Specialty
Club
172 Jones Street
Mount Clemens, MI 48043
313–465–4883

Traverse Area Bottle and Insulator Club
P.O. Box 205
Acme, MI 49610

West Michigan Avon Collectors
331 Bellevue S.W.
Wyoming, MI 49508

W.M.R.A.C.C.
331 Bellevue S.W.
Grand Rapids, MI 49508

Wolverine Beam Bottle and Specialty
Club of Michigan
36009 Larchwood
Mount Clemens, MI 48043

World Wide Avon Bottle Collectors Club
22708 Wick Road
Taylor, MI 48180

Ye Old Corkers
c/o Janet Gallup
Box 7
Gastor, MI 49927

MINNESOTA

Arnfalt Collectors Beam Club
New Richard, MN 56072

Golpher State Jim Beam Bottle and
Specialty Club
1216 Sheridan Avenue N.
Minneapolis, MN 55411
612–521–4150

Heartland Jim Beam Bottle and
Specialty Club
Box 633
245 Elm Drive
Foley, MN 56329
612–968–6767

Hey! Rube Jim Beam Bottle Club
1506 Sixth Avenue N.E.
Austin, MN 55912
507–433–6939

Lake Superior Antique Bottle Club
P.O. Box 67
Knife River, MN 55609

Minnesota First Antique Bottle Club
5001 Queen Avenue, N.
Minneapolis, MN 55430
612–521–9874

North-Star Historical Bottle Association,
Inc.
3308–32 Avenue So.
Minneapolis, MN 55406
612–721–4165

Paul Bunyan Jim Beam Bottle and
Specialty Club
Route 8, Box 656
Bemidji, MN 56601
218–751–6635

Truman, Minnesota Jim Beam Bottle
and Specialty Club
Truman, MN 56088
507–776–3487

Viking Jim Beam Bottle and Specialty
Club
8224 Oxborough Avenue S.
Bloomington, MN 55437
612–831–2303

MISSISSIPPI

Chimneyville Beam Bottle and Specialty
Club
2918 Larchmont
Jackson, MS 39209–6129
601–352–6069

Gum Tree Beam Bottle Club
104 Ford Circle
Tupelo, MS 38801

Magnolia Beam Bottle and Specialty
Club
1079 Maria Drive
Jackson, MS 39204–5518
601–372–4464

Middle Mississiippi Antique Bottle Club
P.O. Box 233
Jackson, MS 39205

Oxford Antique Bottlers
128 Vivian Street
Oxford, MS 38633

South Mississippi Antique Bottle Club
203 S. Fourth Avenue
Laurel, MS 39440

MISSOURI

Antique Bottle Club of Central Missouri
726 W. Monroe
Mexico, MO 65265
314–581–1391

Antique Bottle and Relic Club of Central
Missouri
c/o Ann Downing,
Route 10
Columbia, MO 65210

Arnold, Missouri Jim Beam Bottle and
Specialty Club
1861 Jean Drive
Arnold, MO 63010
314–296–0813

Barnhart, Missouri Jim Beam Bottle and
Specialty Club
2150 Cathlin Court
Barnhart, MO 63012

Chesterfield Jim Beam Bottle and
Specialty Club
2066 Honey Ridge
Chesterfield, MO 63017

"Down in the Valley" Jim Beam Bottle
Club
528 Saint Louis Avenue
Valley Park, MO 63088

The Federation of Historical Bottle Clubs
10118 Schuessler
Saint Louis, MO 63128
314–843–7573

Festus, Missouri Jim Beam Bottle and
Specialty Club
Route 3, Box 117H
Frederick Road
Festus, MO 63028

Florissant Valley Jim Beam Bottles and
Specialty Club
25 Cortez
Florissant, MO 63031

Greater Kansas City Jim Beam Bottle
and Specialty Club
P.O. Box 6703
Kansas City, MO 64123

Kansas City Antique Bottle Collectors
Association
1131 E. 77 Street
Kansas City, MO 64131

Maryland Heights Jim Beam Bottle and
Specialty Club
2365 Wesford
Maryland Heights, MO 63043

Mineral Area Bottle Club
Knob Lick, MO 63651

Missouri Arch Jim Beam Bottle and
Specialty Club
2900 N. Lindbergh
Saint Ann, Mo 63074
314–739–0803

Mound City Jim Beam Decanter
Collectors
42 Webster Acres
Webster Groves, MO 63119

North-East County Jim Beam Bottle and
Specialty Club
10150 Baron Drive
Saint Louis, MO 63136

Rock Hill Jim Beam Bottle and Specialty
Club
9731 Graystone Terrace
Saint Louis, MO 63119
314–962–8125

Sho Me Jim Beam Bottle and Specialty
Club
Route 7, Box 314-D
Springfield, MO 65802
417–831–8093

Saint Charles, Missouri Jim Beam Bottle
and Specialty Club
122 S. Cardinal
Saint Charles, MO 63301

Saint Louis Antique Bottle Collectors
Association
71 Outlook Drive
Hillsboro, MO 63050

Saint Louis Jim Beam Bottle and
Specialty Club
2900 Lindbergh
Saint Ann, MO 63074
314–291–3256

Troy, Missouri, Jim Beam Bottle and
Specialty Club
121 E. Pershing
Troy, MO 63379
314–528–6287

Valley Bank Park Jim Beam Bottle and
Specialty Club
614 Benton Street
Valley Park, MO 63088

Vera Young, Avon Times
P.O. Box 9868
Kansas City, MO 64134
816–537–8223

Walnut Park Jim Beam Bottle and
Specialty Club
5458 N. Euclid
Saint Louis, MO 63114

West County Jim Beam Bottle and
Specialty Club
11707 Momarte Lane
Saint Louis, MO 63141

NEBRASKA
Cornhusker Jim Beam Bottle and
Specialty Club
5204 S. 81st Street
Ralston, NE 68127
402–331–4646

Mini-Seekers
"A" Acres, Route 8
Lincoln, NE 68506

Nebraska Antique Bottle and Collectors
Club
14835 Drexel Street
Omaha, NE 68137

Nebraska Big Red Bottle and Specialty
Club
N Street Drive-in
200 S. 18th Street
Lincoln, NE 68508

NEVADA
Las Vegas Antique Bottle and
Collectibles Club
3901 E. Stewart #16
Las Vegas, NV 89110
702–452–1263

Las Vegas Bottle Club
2632 E. Harman
Las Vegas, NV 89121
702–731–5004

Lincoln County Antique Bottle Club
P.O. Box 191
Calente, NV 89008
702–726–3655

Reno/Sparks Antique Bottle Club
P.O. Box 1061
Verdi, NV 89439

Virginia and Truckee Jim Beam Bottle
and Specialty Club
P.O. Box 1596
Carson City, NV 89701

NEW HAMPSHIRE
Bottlers of New Hampshire
125A Central Street
Farmington, NH 03835

Central New Hampshire Antique Bottle
Club
RFD 2, Box 1A
Winter Street
Tilton, NH 03276

Granite State Bottle Club
R.F.D. 1
Belmont, NH 03220

Merrimack Valley Antique Bottle Club
776 Harvey Road
Manchester, NH 03103
503-623-4101

New England Antique Bottle Club
4 Francove Drive
Somersworth, NH 03878

Yankee Bottle Club
382 Court Street
Keene, NH 03431-2534

NEW JERSEY

Antique Bottle Collectors Club of
Burlington County
18 Willow Road
Bordentown, NJ 08505

Artifact Hunters Association, Inc.
29 Lake Road
Wayne, NJ 07470

Central Jersey Bottle Club
93 North Main Street
New Egypt, NJ 08533

The Jersey Devil Bottle Diggers Club
14 Church Street
Mount Holly, NJ 08060

Jersey Jackpot Jim Beam Bottle and
Specialty Club
197 Farley Avenue
Fanwood, NJ 07023
201-322-7287

Jersey Shore Bottle Club
P.O. Box 995
Toms River, NJ 08754
908-240-5247

Lionstone Collectors Club of Delaware
Valley
R.D. 3, Box 93
Sewell, NJ 08080

Meadowland Beamers
413 24th Street
Union City, NJ 07087
201-865-3684

New Jersey Ezra Brooks Bottle Club
S. Main Street
Cedarville, NJ 08311

North Jersey Antique Bottle Club
Association
36 Williams Street
Lincoln Park, NJ 07035

South Jersey Heritage Bottle and Glass
Club, Inc.
P.O. Box 122
Glassboro, NJ 08028
609-423-5038

Sussex County Antique Bottle Collectors
Division of Sussex County Historical
Society
82 Main Street
Newton, NJ 07860

Trenton Jim Beam Bottle Club, Inc.
17 Easy Street
Freehold, NJ 07728

Twin Bridges Beam Bottle and Specialty
Club
P.O. Box 347
Pennsville, NJ 08070

West Essex Bottle Club
76 Beaufort Avenue
Livingston, NJ 07039

NEW MEXICO

Cave City Antique Bottle Club
Route 1, Box 155
Carlsbad, NM 88220

Roadrunner Bottle Club of New Mexico
2341 Gay Road S.W.
Albuquerque, NM 87105

NEW YORK

Auburn Bottle Club
297 S. Street Road
Auburn, NY 13021

Ball Metal Container Group
One Adams Road
Saratoga Springs, NY 12866–9036

Big Apple Beamers Bottle and Specialty Club
2901 Long Branch Road
Oceanside, NY 11572
516–678–3414

Capital District Insulator Club
41 Crestwood Drive
Schenectady, NY 12306

Catskill Mountains Jim Beam Bottle Club
6 Gardner Avenue
Middletown, NY 10940

Chautauqua County Bottle Collectors Club
Morse Motel
Main Street
Sherman, NY 14781

Eastern Monroe County Bottle Club
c/o Bethelem Lutheran Church
1767 Plank Road
Webster, NY 14580

Empire State Bottle Collectors Association
P.O. Box 3421
Syracuse, NY 13220
315–689–6460

Empire State Jim Beam Bottle Club
P.O. Box 561
Main Street
Farmingdale, NY 11735

Finger Lakes Bottle Collectors Association
3250 Dubois Road
Ithaca, NY 14850

Genessee Valley Bottle Collectors Association
P.O. Box 15528
Rochester, NY 14615
716–872–4952

Greater Catskill Antique Bottle Club
P.O. Box 411
Liberty, NY 14850

Hudson River Jim Beam Bottle and Specialty Club
48 College Road
Monsey, NY 10952

Hudson Valley Bottle Club
6 Columbus Avenue
Cornwall-on-Husdon, NY 12520

Lions Club of Ballston Spa
37 Grove Street
Ballston Spa, NY 12020

Long Island Antique Bottle Association
46 Evergreen Avenue
Patchogue, NY 11772

Mohawk Valley Antique Bottle Club
1735 State Route 173
Cheektowaga, NY 13037

National Bottle Museum
76 Milton Anenue
Ballston Spa, NY 12020
518–885–7589

National Insulator Association
41 Crestwood Drive
Schenectady, NY 12306

Niagara Frontier Beam Bottle and
Specialty Club
17 Ravensbrook Court
Getsville, NY 14066
716–688–6624

North County Bottle Collectors
Association
Route 1
Canton, NY 13617

Rensselaer County Antique Bottle Club
P.O. Box 792
Troy, NY 12180

Saratoga Type Bottle Collectors Society
531 Route 42
Sparrow Bush, NY 12780
914–856–1766

Southern Tier Bottle and Insulator
Collectors Association
47 Dickinson Avenue
Port Dickinson, NY 13901

Tryon Bottle Badgers
P.O. Box 146
Tribes Hill, NY 12177

Twin Counties Old Bottle Club
c/o Don McBride
Star Route, Box 242
Palenville, NY 12463
518–943–5399

Warwick Valley Bottle Club
P.O. Box 393
Warwick, NY 10990

Western New York Bottle Club
Association
62 Adams Street
Jamestown, NY 14701
716–487–9645
Attn: Tom Karapantso

Western New York Bottle Collectors
87 S. Bristol Avenue
Lockport, NY 14094

Western New York Miniature Liquor
Club
P.O. Box 182
Cheektowaga, NY 14225

West Valley Bottleique Club
P.O. Box 204
Killbuck, NY 14748
716–945–5769

NORTH CAROLINA

Blue Ridge Bottle and Jar Club
Dogwood Lane
Black Mountain, NC 28711

Carolina Bottle Club
c/o Industrial Piping Co.
Anonwood
Charlotte, NC 28210

Carolina Jim Beam Bottle Club
1014 N. Main Street
Burlington, NC 27215

Catawba Valley Jim Beam Bottle and
Specialty Club
265 Fifth Avenue, N.E.
Hickory, NC 28601
704–322–5268

Goldsboro Bottle Club
2406 E. Ash Street
Goldsboro, NC 27530

Greater Greensboro Moose Ezra Brooks
Bottle Club
217 S. Elm Street
Greensboro, NC 27401

Kinston Collectors Club, Inc.
1905 Greenbriar Road
Kinston, NC 28501–2129
919–523–3049

Pelican Sand Dunners Jim Beam Bottle
and Specialty Club
Paradise Bay Mobile Home Park
Lot 17–J, P.O. Box 344
Salter Path, NC 28575
919–247–3290

Tar Heel Jim Beam Bottle and Specialty
Club
6615 Wake Forest Road
Fayetteville, NC 20301
919–488–4849

The Johnnyhouse Inspector's Bottle Club
1972 East U.S. 74 Highway
Hamlet, NC 28345

Western North Carolina Antique Bottle
Club
P.O. Box 18481
Asheville, NC 28814

Wilmington Bottle and Artifact Club
183 Arlington Drive
Wilmington, NC 28401
919–763–3701

Wilson Antique Bottle and Artifact Club
Route 5, P.O. Box 414
Wilson, NC 27893

Yadkin Valley Bottle Club
General Delivery
Gold Hill, NC 28071

OHIO

Beam on the Lake Bottle and Specialty
Club
9151 Mentor Avenue, F 15
Mentor, OH 44060
215–255–0320

Buckeye Bottle Club
229 Oakwood Street
Elyria, OH 44035

Buckeye Bottle Diggers
Route 2, P.O. Box 77
Thornville, OH 44035

Buckeye Jim Beam Bottle Club
1211 Ashland Avenue
Columbus, OH 43212

Carnation City Jim Beam Bottle Club,
c/o Vernon E. Brunt
135 W. Virginia
Sebring, OH 44672
216–938–6817

Central Ohio Bottle Club
931 Minerva Avenue
Columbus, OH 43229

Diamond Pin Winners Avon Club
5281 Fredonia Avenue
Dayton, OH 45431

The Federation of Historical Bottle Clubs
c/o Gary Beatty, Treasurer
9326 Court Road 3C
Galion, OH 44833

Findlay Antique Bottle Club
c/o Shirlee MacDonald
407 Cimarron Court
Findlay, OH 45840
419–422–3183

First Capitol Bottle Club
c/o Maxie Harper
Route 1, Box 94
Laureville, OH 43135

Gem City Beam Bottle Club
1463 E. Stroop Road
Dayton, OH 45429

Greater Cleveland Jim Beam Club
5398 W. 147th Street
Brook Park, OH 44142
216–267–7665

Heart of Ohio Bottle Club
P.O. Box 353
New Washington, OH 44854
419–492–2829

Jeep City Beamers
531A Durango
Toledo, OH 43609
419–382–2515

Lakeshore Beamers
2681 Douglas Road
Ashtbula, OH 44004
216–964–3457

Maple Leaf Beamers
8200 Yorkshire Road
Mentor, OH 44060
216–255–9118

Midwest Minature Bottle Club
5537 Cleander Drive
Cincinnatti, OH 45238

Northern Ohio Jim Beam Bottle Club
43152 Hastings Road
Oberlin, OH 44074
216–775–2177

North Eastern Ohio Bottle Club
P.O. Box 57
Madison, OH 44057
614–282–8918

Northwest Ohio Bottle Club
104 W. Main
Norwalk, OH 44857

Ohio Bottle Club
P.O. Box 585
Barberton, OH 44203
216–753–2115

Ohio Ezra Brooks Bottle Club
8741 Kirtland Chardon Road
Kirtland Hills, OH 44094

Pioneer Beamers
38912 Butternut Ridge
Elyria, OH 44035
216–458–6621

Rubber Capitol Jim Beam Club
151 Stephens Road
Akron, OH 44312

Sara Lee Bottle Club
27621 Chagrin Boulevard
Cleveland, OH 44122

Southwestern Ohio Antique Bottle and
Jar Club
273 Hilltop Drive
Dayton, OH 45415
513–836–3353

St. Bernard Swigin Beamers
4327 Greenlee Avenue
Cincinnati, OH 45217
513–641–3362

Superior Bottle Club
22000 Shaker Boulevard
Shaker Heights, OH 44122

OKLAHOMA
Bar-Dew Antique Bottle Club
817 E. Seventh Street
Dewey, OK 74029

Frontier Jim Beam Bottle and Specialty
Club
P.O. Box 52
Meadowbrook Trailer Village, Lot 101
Ponca City, OK 74601
405–765–2174

Green County Jim Beam Bottle and
Specialty Club
Route 2, P.O. Box 233
Chouteau, OK 74337
918–266–3512

McDonnel Douglas Antique Club
5752 E. 25th Place
Tulsa, OK 74114

Midwest Miniature Bottle Collector
3108 Meadowood Drive
Midwest City, OK 73110–1407

Oklahoma Territory Bottle and Relic
Club
1300 S. Blue Haven Drive
Mustang, OK 73064
405–376–1045

Ponca City Old Bottle Club
2408 Juanito
Ponca City, OK 74601

Sooner Jim Beam Bottle and Specialty
Club
5913 S.E. Tenth
Midwest City, OK 73110
405–737–5786

Southwest Oklahoma Antique Bottle
Club
35 S. 49th Street
Lawson, OK 73501

Tri-State Historical Bottle Club
817 E. 7th Street
Dewey, OK 74029

Tulsa Antique and Bottle Club
P.O. Box 4278
Tulsa, OK 74159–0278
918–446–6774

OREGON

Central Oregon Bottle and Relic Club
671 N.E. Seward
Bend, OR 97701

Central Oregon Bottle and Relic Club
1545 Kalama Avenue
Redmond, OR 97756

Central South Oregon Antique Bottle
Club
708 San Francisco Street
Lakeview, OR 97630

Emerald Empire Bottle Club
P.O. Box 292
Eugene, OR 97401

Empire City Old Bottle Society
1991 Sherman Avenue
Suite #206
North Bend, OR 97459

Frontier Collectors
504 N.W. Bailey
Pendleton, OR 97801

Gold Diggers Antique Bottle Club
1958 S. Stage Road
Medford, OR 97501

Lewis & Clark Historical Bottle and
Collectors Society
8018 S.E. Hawthorne Boulevard
Portland, OR 97501

Lewis and Clark Historical Bottle Society
4828 N.E. 33rd
Portland, OR 97501

Molalla Bottle Club
Route 1, P.O. Box 205
Mulino, OR 97042

Northwest Mini Bottle Club
P.O. Box 6551
Portland, OR 97228

Oregon Antique Bottle Club
Route 3, P.O. Box 23
Molalla, OR 97038

Oregon Beamers Beam Bottle and
Specialty
P.O. Box 7
Sheridan, OR 97378

Oregon Bottle Collectors Association
3565 Dee Highway
Hood River, OR 97031

Pioneer Fruit Collectors Association
P.O. Box 175
Grand Ronde, OR 97347

Siskiyou Antique Bottle Collectors
Association
2715 East McAndrews
Medford, OR 97504

PENNSYLVANIA
American Collectors of Infant Feeders
1849 Ebony Drive
York, PA 17402-4706

Anthracite Jim Beam Bottle Club
406 Country Club Apartments
Dallas, PA 18612

Beaver Valley Jim Beam Club
1335 Indiana Avenue
Monaca, PA 15061

Bedford County Bottle Club
P.O. Box 116
Loysburg, PA 16659
814-766-3215

Camoset Bottle Club
P.O. Box 252
Johnstown, PA 15901

Christmas Valley Beamers
150 Second Street
Richlandtown, PA 18955
215-536-4636

Classic Glass Bottle Collectors
2 Cogan Station, PA 17728

Cumberland Valley Jim Beam Club
P.O. Box 132
Middletown, PA 17057
717-944-5376

Delaware Valley Bottle Club
12 Belmar Road
Halboro, PA 19040

Del-Val Bottle Club
Route 152 and Hilltown Pike
Hilltown, PA 19040

Del Val Miniature Bottle Club
57-104 Delaire Landing Road
Philadelphia, PA 19114

East Coast Double Springs Specialty
Bottle Club
P.O. Box 419
Carisle, PA 17013

East Coast Ezra Brooks Bottle Club
2815 Fiddler Green
Lancaster, PA 17601

Endless Mountain Antique Bottle Club
P.O. Box 75
Granville Summit, PA 16926

Eric Bottle Club
P.O. Box 373
Erie, PA 16512

Flood City Jim Beam Bottle Club
231 Market Street
Johnston, PA 15901

Forks of the Delaware Bottle Club
Association
164 Farmview Road
Nazareth, PA 18064–2500

Friendly Jim's Beam Club
508 Benjamin Franklin H.W. East
Douglasville, PA 19518

Indiana Bottle Club
240 Oak Street
Indiana, PA 15701

Jefferson County Antique Bottle Club
6 Valley View Drive
Washington, PA 15301

Keystone Flyers Jim Beam Bottle Club
288 Hogan Boulevard
Box 42
Lock Haven, PA 17745
717–748–6741

Kiski Mini Beam and Specialty Club
c/o John D. Ferchak Jr.
816 Cranberry Drive
Monroeville, PA 15146
412–372–0387

Laurel Valley Bottle Club
P.O. Box 131
Ligonier, PA 15658
412–238–0946

Ligonier Historic Bottle Club
P.O. Box 188
Ligonier, PA 15658
412–238–4590

Middleton Area Bottle Collectors
Association
P.O. Box 1
Middletown, PA 17057
717–939–0288

Pagoda City Beamers
735 Florida Avenue
Riverview Park
Reading, PA 19605
215–929–8924

Penn Beamers' 14th
15 Gregory Place
Richboro, PA 18954

Pennsylvania Bottle Collectors
251 Eastland Avenue
York, PA 17402
717–854–4965

Pennsylvania Dutch Jim Beam Bottle
Club
812 Pointview Avenue
Ephrate, PA 17522

Philadelphia Bottle Club
8203 Elberon Avenue
Philadelphia, PA 19111

Pittsburgh Antique Bottle Club
235 Main Entrance Drive
Pittsburgh, PA 15228

Pittsburgh Bottle Club
P.O. Box 401
Ingomar, PA 15127

Pittsburgh Bottle Club
1528 Railroad Street
Sewickley, PA 15143

Seaview Jim Beam Bottle and Specialty
Club
362 Lakepoint Drive
Harrisburg, PA 17111
717–561–2517

Susquehanna Valley Jim Beam Bottle
and Specialty Club
64 E. Park Street
Elizabethtown, PA 17022
717–367–4256

Tri-County Antique Bottle and Treasure
Club
R.D. 2, P.O. Box 30
Reynoldsville, PA 15851

Valley Forge Jim Beam Bottle Club
1219 Ridgeview Drive
Phoenixville, PA 19460
215–933–5789

Washington County Antique Bottle Club
R.D. 2, Box 342
Carmichael, PA 15320
412–966–7996

RHODE ISLAND
Little Rhody Bottle Club
210 South Pier Road
Narragansett, RI 02882

SOUTH CAROLINA
Greer Bottle Collectors Club
P.O. Box 142
Greer, SC 29651

Lexington County Antique Bottle Club
201 Roberts Street
Lexington, SC 29072

Palmetto State Beamers
908 Alton Circle
Florence, SC 29501
803–669–6515

Piedmont Bottle Collectors
c/o R. W. Leizear
Route 3
Woodruff, SC 29388

South Carolina Bottle Club
1119 Greenbridge Lane
Columbia, SC 29210

Union Bottle Club
107 Pineneedle Road
Union, SC 29379

Upper Piedmont Bottle and Advertising
Collectors Club
c/o R. W. Leizear
Route 3
Woodruff, SC 29379

TENNESSEE
Cotton Carnival Beam Club
P.O. Box 17951
Memphis, TN 38117

East Tennessee Bottle Society
220 Carter School Road
Strawberry Plains, TN 37871

Memphis Bottle Collectors Club
3706 Deerfield Cove
Bartlett, TN 38135

Middle Tennessee Bottle Collectors Club
1221 Nichol Lane
Nashville, TN 37205

Music City Beam Bottle Club
2008 June Drive
Nashville, TN 37214
615–883–1893

TEXAS
Alamo City Jim Beam Bottle and
Specialty Club
5785 FM 1346, P.O. Box 20442
San Antonio, TX 78220

Austin Bottle and Insulator Collectors
Club
1300 Sunrise, #269
Round Rock, TX 78664

Cowtown Jim Beam Bottle Club
2608 Roseland
Fort Worth, TX 76103
817–536–4335

Dr. Pepper Collectors Club
P.O. Box 153221
Irving, TX 75015

El Paso Insulator Club
c/o Martha Stevens, Chairman
4556 Bobolink
El Paso, TX 79922

The Exploration Society
603 Ninth Street NAS
Corpus Christie, TX 78419
214–922–2902

Foard C. Hobby Club
P.O. Box 625
Crowell, TX 79227

Fort Concho Bottle Club
1703 W. Avenue N.
San Angelo, TX 76901

Foursome (Jim Beam)
1208 Azalea Drive
Longview, TX 75601

Golden Spread Jim Beam Bottle and
Specialty Club
1104 S. Maddox
Dumas, TX 79029
806–935–3690

Gulf Coast Beam Club
128 W. Bayshore Drive
Baytown, TX 77520

Gulf Coast Bottle and Jar Club
P.O. Box 1754
Pasadena, TX 77501
713–592–3078

North Texas Longhorn Bottle Club
4205 Donnington Drive
Plano, TX 75072

Oil Patch Beamers
1300 Fairmont
Longview, TX 75604
214–758–1905

Republic of Texas Jim Beam Bottle and
Specialty Club
616 Donley Drive
Euless, TX 76039

UTAH

Utah Antique Bottle and Relic Club
517 South Hayes
Midvale, UT 84047
801–561–0438

Utah Antique Bottle Club
P.O. Box 15
Ogden, UT 84402

VIRGINIA

Apple Valley Bottle Collectors Club
P.O. Box 2201
Winchester, VA 22604

Bottle Club of the Virginia Peninsula
P.O. Box 5456
Newport News, VA 23605

Buffalo Beam Bottle Club
P.O. Box 434
Buffalo Junction, VA 24529
804–374–2041

Chesapeake Bay Beam Bottle and
Specialty Club
515 Briar Hill Road
Norfolk, VA 23502
804–461–3763

Country Cousins Beam Bottle and
Specialty Club
Route 2, Box 18C
Dinwiddle, VA 23841
804–469–7414

Dixie Beam Bottle Club
Route 4, Box 94–4
Glen Allen, VA 23060

Historical Bottle Diggers of Virginia
242 East Grattar Street
Harrisonburg, VA 22801

Merrimac Beam Bottle and Specialty Club
433 Tory Road
Virginia Beach, VA 23462
804–497–0969

Metropolitan Antique Bottle Club
109 Howard Street
Domfries, VA 22026
804–221–8055

National Privy Diggers Association
614 Park Drive
Mechanicsville, VA 23111
804–746–9854

Old Dominion Beam Bottle and Specialty Club
624 Brandy Creek Drive
Mechanicsville, VA 23111
804–746–7144

Potomac Bottle Collectors
8411 Porter Lane
Alexandria, VA 22308
703–360–8181

Richmond Area Bottle Club Association
7024 Pointer Ridge Road
Midlothian, VA 23112

Shenandoah Valley Beam Bottle and Specialty Club
11 Bradford Drive
Front Royal, VA 22630
703–743–6316

Tidewater Beam Bottle and Specialty Club
P.O. Box 14012
Norfolk, VA 23518

Ye Old Bottle Club
General Delivery
Clarksville, VA 23927

WASHINGTON

Antique Bottle and Glass Collectors
P.O. Box 163
Snohomish, WA 98290

Apple Capital Beam Bottle and Specialty Club
300 Rock Island Road
E. Wenatchee, WA 98801
509–884–6895

Blue Mountain Jim Beam Bottle and Specialty Club
P.O. Box 147, Russet Road
Walla Walla, WA 99362
509–525–1208

Cascade Treasure Club
254 N.E. 45th
Seattle, WA 98105

Chinook Ezra Brooks Bottle Club
233 Kelso Drive
Kelso, WA 98626

Evergreen State Beam Bottle and Specialty Club
P.O. Box 99244
Seattle, WA 98199

Inland Empire Bottle and Collectors Club
7703 E. Trent Avenue
Spokane, WA 99206

Klickital Bottle Club Association
Goldendale, WA 98620

Mt. Rainier Ezra Brooks Bottle Club
P.O. Box 1201
Lynwood, WA 98178

Northwest Jim Beam Bottle Collectors
Association
P.O. Box 7401
Spokane, WA 99207

Northwest Treasure Hunter's Club
E. 107 Astor Drive
Spokane, WA 99208

Pacific Northwest Avon Bottle Club
25425 68th S.
Kent, WA 98031

Seattle Jim Beam Bottle Collectors Club
8015 15th Avenue, N.W.
Seattle, WA 98107

Skagit Bottle and Glass Collectors
1314 Virginia
Mount Vernon, WA 98273

Violin Bottle Collectors Association of
America
21815 106th Street E.
Buckley, WA 98321

Washington Bottle Collectors Association
5492 Hannegan Road
Bellingham, WA 98226

WEST VIRGINIA
Blennerhassett Jim Beam Club
Route 1
26 Popular Street
Davisville, WV 26142
304-428-3184

Wild Wonderful W. Virginia Jim Beam
Bottle and Specialty Club
3922 Hanlin Way
Weirton, WV 26062
304-748-2675

WISCONSIN
Antique Bottle Club of Northern Illinois
P.O. Box 571
Geneva, WI 53147

Badger Jim Beam Club of Madison
P.O. Box 5612
Madison, WI 53705

Belle City Jim Beam Bottle Club
8008 104th Avenue
Kenosha, WI 53140
414-694-3341

Bucken Beamers Bottle Club of
Milwaukee Wisconsin
16548 Richmond Drive
Menomonee Falls, WI 53051
414-251-772

Cameron Bottle Diggers
P.O. Box 276
Camereon, WI 54822

Central Wisconsin Bottle Collectors
1608 Main Street
Stevens Point, WI 54481

Cream Separator Collectors Association
W20772 State Road 95
Arcadia, WI 54612

Heart of the North Beam Bottle and
Bottle Club
1323 Eagle Street
Rhinelander, WI 54501
715-362-6045

Hooten Beamers
2511 Needles Lane
Wisconsin Rapids, WI 54494
715-423-7116

Indianhead Jim Beam Club
5112 Berry Street
Menomonee, WI 54751
715-235-5627

Lumberjack Beamers
414 N. Fifth Avenue
Wausau, WI 54401
715-842-3793

Milwaukee Antique Bottle Club
N. 88 W. 15211 Cleveland Avenue
Menomonee Falls, WI 53051

Milwaukee Antique Bottle and
Advertising Club, Inc.
2343 Met-To-Wee Lane
Wauwatosa, WI 53226
414–257–0158

Milwaukee Jim Beam Bottle and
Specialty Club, Ltd.
N. 95th Street
W. 16548 Richmond Drive
Menomonee Falls, WI 53051

Packerland Beam Bottle and Specialty
Club
1366 Avondale Drive
Green Bay, WI 54303
414–494–4631

Shot Tower Jim Beam Club
818 Pleasant Street
Mineral Point, WI 53565

South Central Wisconsin Bottle Club
c/o Dr. T.M. Schwartz
Route 1
Arlington, WI 53911

Sportsman's Jim Beam Bottle Club
6821 Sunset Strip
Wisconsin Rapids, WI 54494
715–325–5285

Sugar River Beamers
Route 1, Box 424
Brodhead, WI 53520
608–897–2681

WYOMING
Cheyenne Antique Bottle Club
4417 E. 8th Street
Cheyenne, WY 82001

Insubott Bottle Club
P.O. Box 34
Lander, WY 82520

Foreign Clubs

AUSTRALIA
Miniature Bottle Collectors of Australia
P.O. Box 59
Ashburton, Victoria 3147 Australia

CANADA
Bytown Bottle Seekers' Club
7 Queenston Drive
Richmond, Ontario, Canada KOA 2Z0

Four Seasons Bottle Collectors Club
8 Stillbrook Court
West Hill
Ontario, Canada M1E3N7

CHINA
Hong Kong Miniature Liquor Club LTD
180 Nathan Road
Bowa House
Tsim Sha Tsui
Kowloon, Hong Kong
852–721–3200

ENGLAND
The Mini Bottle Club
47 Burradon Road
Burradon, Cramlington
Northumberland, NE 237NF England

GERMANY
Miniatur Flaschensammler Duetschlands
E.V.
Keltenstrasse 1a
5477 Nickenich, Germany

ITALY
Club Delle Mignonnettes
Via Asiago 16
60124 Ancona, AN, Italy

JAPAN

Osaka Miniature Bottle Club
11–2 Hakucho 1-Chome
Habikinoshi, Osaka 583, Japan

Miniature Bottle Club of Kobe
3–5–41, Morigocho
Nada-ku, Kobe, 657 Japan

NEW ZEALAND

Port Nicholson Miniature Bottle Club
86 Rawhiti Road
Pukerua Bay
Wellington, New Zealand

Bottle Dealers

Domestic Dealers

Bert and Margaret Simard
Route 1, Box 49D
Ariton, AL 36311
334–762–2663
Ink bottles and ink wells

Steve Holland
1740 Serene Drive
Birmingham, AL 35215
205–853–7929

Walkers Antique Bottles
2768 Hanover Circle
Birmingham, AL 35205
205–933–7902
Medicines and Crown sodas

Terry and Katie Gillis
115 Mountain Drive
Fort Payne, AL 35967
205–845–4541

C.B. and Barbara Meares
Route 3, Box 161
Fort Payne, AL 35967
205–638–6225

Frank and Nancy Harrison
815 Troy Street
Gadsden, AL 35901
205–546–9112
Glassware and stoneware

Ken Roberts
218 Cumberland Drive
Huntsville, AL 35803
205–880–1460
Glass insulators

Loretta & Mack Wimmer
3012 Cedar Crescent Drive
Mobile, AL 36605

Old Time Bottle House and Museum
306 Parker Hills Drive
Ozark, AL 36360
Stone jugs and fruit jars

Elroy Webb
203 Spanish Main
Spanish Fort, AL 36527
334–626–1067
Bottles, appraisals

Ed's Lapidary Shop
7927 Historic Mobile Parkway
U.S. Highway 90
Theodore, AL 36582
205–653–0713

ARIZONA

Antiques Etc.
5753 W. Glendale Avenue
Glendale, AZ 85301
602–939–2732

Now, Then, and Always, Inc.
7021 N. 57th Drive
Glendale, AZ 85301
602–931–1116

Bruce Young
Lake Havasu City, AZ 86406
520–855–3396
Insulators

Antiques, Interiors and Memories
3026 N. 16th Street
Phoenix, AZ 85016
602–277–0433

The Antique Center
3601 E. Indian School Road
Phoenix, AZ 85018
602–957–3600

The Brewery
1605 N. Seventh Avenue
Phoenix, AZ 85007
602–252–1415
Brewery items

Bryan Grapentine
1939 W. Waltann Lane
Phoenix, AZ 85023
602–993–9757
Bottles and advertising

Ray and Dyla Lawton
Box 374
Pinetop, AZ 85935
602–366–4449

The Antique Center
1290 N. Scottsdale Road
Tempe, AZ
602–966–3350

Keith Curtis
6871 E. Lurlene Drive
Tucson, AZ 85703
602–790–4336

ARKANSAS

Buddy's Bottles
30 N. Taylor
Ashdown, AR 71822
501–898–3790
Hutchinson sodas and medicines

Charles and Mary Garner
620 Carpenter Drive
Jacksonville, AR 72076
501–982–8381

Don and Jackie Leonard
1118 Green Mount Drive
Little Rock, AR 72211
501–224–5432
Bottles

Terry Fields
Route 1, Box 167–7
McCrory, AR 72101
501–697–3132
Bottles and Indian artifacts

Rufus Buie
P.O. Box 226
Rison, AR 71665
501–325–6816

Edwin R. Tardy
16201 Highway 300
Roland, AR 72135
501–868–9548
Coca-Cola bottles

CALIFORNIA

Al Halpern
P.O. Box 2081
Anaheim, CA 92814
714–776–1371
Miniature bottles

D & E Collectibles and Antiques
14925 Apple Valley Road
Apple Valley, CA 92307
619–946–1767
Bottles

Diane Pingree
345 Commercial Street
Auburn, CA 95603
916–885–5537

Tom Chapman
2433 Apache Drive
Bishop, CA 93514
619–872–2427
California and Nevada bottles

Leigh R. Giarde
P.O. Box 366
Bryn Mawr, CA 92318
909–792–8681
Dairy nostalgia

Walter Yeargain
6222 San Lorenzo Drive
Buena Park, CA 90620
714–826–5264
Bottles

Fred Hawley
1311 Montero Avenue
Burlingame, CA 94010
415–342–7085
Miniature bottles

Wayne Hortman
P.O. Box 183
Butler, CA 31006
912–862–3699

Bruce D. Kendall
Erma's Country Store
P.O. Box 1761
Carmel, CA 93921
408–394–3257

Eloise Haltman
P.O. Box 399
Cathedral City, CA 92234
619–328–5321
Glass insulators

Don Ayers
P.O. Box 1515
Chico, CA 95927
916–895–0813
Coca-Cola bottles

Barbara Edmundson
701 E. Lassen #308
Chico, CA 95973
916–343–8460
Shot glasses

Randy Taylor
566 E. 12th Street
Chico, CA 31006
916–342–4928

Tom Bloomenrader
6200 Desimore Lane, #38A
Citrus Heights, CA 95621
916—729–5744

Duke Jones
P.O. Box 642
Citrus Heights, CA 95610
916–725–1989
California embossed beers

John Walker
281 W. Magill Avenue
Clovis, CA 93612
209–297–4613
Bottles

Stoney and Myrt Stone
1925 Natoma Drive
Concord, CA 94519
415–685–6326

Russell Brown
P.O. Box 441
Corona, CA 91720
714–737–7164

Gary and Harriet Miller
5034 Oxford Drive
Cypress, CA 90630
714–828–4778

Jim and Monica Baird
P.O. Box 106
Descanso, CA 91916
619–445–4771
Western Americana

Jay Turner
5513 Riggs Road
El Cajon, CA 92019
619–445–3039
Bottles

Tim Blair
418 W. Palm Avenue
El Segundo, CA 90245
310–640–2089
Los Angeles bottles/whiskeys

Ken Salter
P.O. Box 1549
El Cerrito, CA 94530
510–527–5779
French and U.S. mustards

Floyd Brown
532 South E Street
Exeter, CA 93221
209–592–2525
Marbles, games, and related items

Mike and Joyce Amey
625 Clay Street
Fillmore, CA 93015
805–524–3364

James Musser
P.O. Box T
Forest Knolls, CA 94933
415–488–9491
Heroin, cocaine, and opium bottles

Vincent Madruga
P.O. Box 1261
Gilroy, CA 95021
408–847–0639
Bitters, whiskeys, historicals

Gary and Sheran Johnston
22853 De Berry
Grand Terrace, CA 92313
909–783–4101
Fruit jars

Scott Grandstaff
Box 154
Happy Camp, CA 96039
916–493–2032
Mason's SGCO (monogram) Pat.
1858s

Kitty Roach
Box 409
Happy Camp, CA 96039
916–493–2032
Whittemore bottles

Mike and Deanna Delaplain
P.O. Box 787
Hemet, CA 92343
714–766–9725

Gene and Phyllis Kemble
14733 Poplar Street
Hesperia, CA 92345
714–244–5863

Larry Caddell
15881 Malm Circle
Huntington Beach, CA 92647
714–897–8133

Jim and Sandy Lindholm
2001 Sierra
Kingsburg, CA 93631
209–897–4083
Western bottles, machine and hand-made marbles, free appraisals

Joss Grandeau
P.O. Box 1508
Laguna Beach, CA 92652
714–588–6091
Milk bottles

Fred Padgett
P.O. Box 1122
Livermore, CA 94551–1122
510–443–8841
Glass insulators and bottles

Ted Haigh
1852 Miceltorena
Los Angeles, CA 90026
213–666–4408
Miniature bottles

Chiisasi Bin Imports
P.O. Box 90245
Los Angeles, CA 90009
310–370–8993
Miniature bottles

Louis and Cindy Pellegrini
1231 Thurston
Los Alton, CA 94022
415–965–9060

John and Estelle Hewitt
366 Church Street
Marietta, CA 30060
404–422–5525

Steve Viola
827 Wake Forest Road
Mountain View, CA 94043
415–968–0849
Glass insulators

John Hiscox
10475 Newtown Road
P.O. Box 704
Nevada City, CA 95959
Bottles

Alex Kerr
4709 Forman Avenue
North Hollywood, CA 91602
818–762–6320
Target balls, fruit jars

Chuck Erickson
155 N. Singingwood #58
Orange, CA 92669
714–771–2286
Los Angeles bottles, whiskeys

Gary Frederick
1030 Mission Street
Pasadena, CA 91030
818–799–1917
Soda pop bottles, owls, medicines

Pat and Shirley Patocka
P.O. Box 326
Penryn, CA 95663
916–663–3681
Insulators

Bob's Bottle Shop
c/o Robert Glover
2500 Highway 128
Philco, CA 95466
707–895–3259
Bottles and fruit jars

Mel and Barbara De Mello
P.O. Box 186
Pollock Pines, CA 95726
916–644–6133
Antique advertising

Robert Jones
1866 N. Orange Grove #202
Pomona, CA 91767
909–920–0840
Rexall Drug bottles and related items

J. Bart Parker
P.O. Box 356
Randsburg, CA 93554
619–374–2217
Louis Taussig whiskey items, tokens

Emma's Trunk
c/oBill and Sue Morse
1701 Orange Tree Lane
Redlands, CA 92374
909–798–7865

Byrl and Grace Rittenhouse
3055 Birch Way
Redding, CA 96002
916–243–0320

Ralph Hollibaugh
8266 Cascade Boulevard
Redding, CA 96008
916–243–4672

Doug Hansen
865 Commerce
Redding, CA 96002
916–547–3152

Tom Aldama
15245 Fawndale Road #2
Redding, CA 96003
916–275–1048
Painted label sodas

Shawn McAlister
333 Calle Miramar #C
Redondo Beach, CA 90277
310–791–0440
Whiskeys, bitters, colored sodas

Jeff Hargrove
2002 Midway Road
Ridgecrest, CA 93555
619–446–8986
Glass insulators

Harold and Virginia Lyle
11259 Gramercy Place
Riverside, CA 92505
714–689–3662
Bottles

James Fennelly
520 54th Street
Sacramento, CA 95819
916–457–3695
Ezra Brooks, Jim Beams, ski country

Bill Grolz
22 Mad River Court
Sacramento, CA 95831
916–424–7283
Violin bottles

Frank Feher
1624 Maryland Avenue
West Sacramento, CA 95691
916–371–7731
Glass insulators

George and Rose Reidenbach
2816 P Street
Sacramento, CA 95816
916–451–0063

Grant Salzman
427 Safflower Place
West Sacramento, CA 95691
916–372–7272
Glass insulators

Peck and Audie Markota
4627 Oakhallow Drive
Sacto, CA 95842
916–334–3260

Dwayne and Ofelia Anthony
1066 Scenic Drive
San Bernardino, CA 92408
909–888–6417
Insulators, fruit jars, poison bottles

Clarice Gordon
3269 N. Mountain View Drive
San Diego, CA 92116
619–282–5101
Glass insulators

Norm and Doris James
San Diego, CA 92115
619–466–0652
Insulators

Al Sparacino
743 La Huerta Way
San Diego, CA 92154
619–690–3632
Miniature bottles

Thierry Stanich
946 Terra Bella Avenue
San Jose, CA 95125
408–267–7703
Miniature bottles (cognacs)

Jim Gibson
8573 Atlas View Drive
Santee, CA 92071
Bottles

Bill Groves
2620 Sutter Street
San Francisco, CA 94115
415–922–6248

Randolph M. Haumann
415 Amherst Street
San Francisco, CA 94134
415–239–5807
Colored figural bitters

Terry and Peggy Wright
6249 Lean Avenue
San Jose, CA 95123
408–578–5580

Ed and Diane Kuskie
1030 W. MacArthur #154
Santa Ana, CA 92707
714–435–1054
Bottles

Valvern and Mary Kille Mcluff
214 S. Ranch Road
Santa Maria, CA 93454
805–925–7014

Derek Abrams
129 E. El Camino
Santa Maria, CA 93454
805–922–4208
Whiskeys, Western bottles

Fireside Cellars
1421 Montana Avenue
Santa Monica, CA 90403
310–393–2888
Miniature bottles

Lewis Lambert
Santa Rosa, CA
707–823–8845
Early Western bottles

James Doty
2026 Finch Court
Simi Valley, CA 93063
Insulators

T. R. Schweighart
1123 Santa Luisa Drive
Solana Beach, CA 92075

Flask Liquor, Inc.
12194 Ventura Boulevard
Studio City, CA 91604
818–761–5373
Miniature bottles

Frank and Judy Brockman
104 W. Park
Stockton, CA 95202
209–948–0746

The Glass Bottle
22 Main Street Highway 49
Sutter Creek, CA
209–267–0122
Figurals, perfumes, whiskey, milks

John R. Swearingen
3227 N. Wildhorse Court
Thousand Oaks, CA 91360
805–492–5036
Fruit jars

Rich Burnham
P.O. Box 4056
Torrance, CA 90503
310–320–2552
Civil War relics

David Spaid
2916 Briarwood Drive
Torrance, CA 90505
310–534–4943
Miniature bottles

Steve and Cris Curtiss
34641 S. Bernard Drive
Tracy, CA 95376
209–836–0903
Northern and central California hutch
and sodas

Nancy Clayton
P.O. Box 3566
Tustin, CA 92681–3566
909–395–2727
Miniature bottles

Dennis Rogers
2459 Euclid Crescent East
Upland, CA 91784
909–982–3416
Cathedral pickle bottles

Don and Linda Yount
P.O. Box 4459
Ventura, CA 93004
805–656–2707
Bottles

Tom Eccles
747 Magnolia
West Covina, CA 91791
818–339–9107
Sarsaparilla bottles

Les and Pat Whitman
219 Fir Street
P.O. Drawer KK
Westwood, CA 96137
916–256–3437
Sodas

David Hall
1217 McDonald Avenue
Wilmington, CA 90744
310–834–6368
Glass insulators

Betty and Ernest Zumwalt
5519 Kay Drive
Windsor, CA 95492
707–545–8670

Mitri Manneh
11415 Whittier Boulevard
Whittier, CA 90601
310–692–2928
Miniature bottles

Sleep's Siskiyou Specialties
217 W. Miner
P.O. Box 689
Yreka, CA 96097

COLORADO
Ken Schneider
7156 Jay Street
Arvada, CO 80003
Colorado bottles

Mike and Jodee Holzwarth
2224 Laporte Avenue
Fort Collins, CO 80521
970–224–4464
Colorado bottles

Fort Collins Bottles
Bill Thomas
2000 Rangeview Drive
Fort Collins, CO 80524
303-493-8177
Miniature bottles

Remember When
Ron Jones
2204 W. Colorado Avenue
Colorado Springs, CO 80904
Collectibles

Jim Keilman
3101 F Road
Grand Junction, CO 81501
303-434-3275
Bottles, Bimal miniatures

Marc Sagrillo
555 Aspen Ridge Drive
Lafayette, CO 80026
303-661-9800
Colorado bottles

Marietta LeBlanc
5592 W. Geddes Place
Littleton, CO 80123
303-979-4943
Miniature bottles

Jim Bishop
Box 5554
Snowmass Village, CO 81615
303-923-2348
Miniature liquors

CONNECTICUT

Woodland Antiques
P.O. Box 277
Mansfield Center
Ashford, CT 06250
203-429-2983
Flasks, bitters, inks

Stephen Link
953 Post Road
Fairfield, CT 06430

B'Thea's Cellar
31 Kensington Street
Hartford, CT 06112
203-249-4686

Mary's Old Bottles
White Hollow Road
Lakeville, CT 06039
203-435-2961

Bob's Old Bottles
656 Noank Road
Route 215
Mystic, CT 06355
203-536-8542

Gerald "J" Jaffee and Lori Waldeck
P.O. Box 1741
New Haven, CT 06507
203-787-4232
Poisons and insulators

Time in a Bottle
Gail Quick
Route 25
Hawleyville, CT 06440
203-426-0031

Albert Corey
153 W. Main Street
Niantic, CT 06357
203-739-7493

Bill Stankard
61 Old Post Road
Saybrook, CT 06475
203-388-2435

George E. Johnson
2339 Litchfield Road
Watertown, CT 06795
203-274-1785

Norman and Elizabeth Heckler
Woodstock, CT 06282
203–974–1634

Al and Ginny Way
68 Cooper Drive
Waterbury, CT 06704
203–575–9964
Insulators

FLORIDA

E.S. and Romie Mackenzie
Box 57
Brooksville, FL 33512
904–796–3400

Bud Hastings
P.O. Box 11530
Fort Lauderdale, FL 33339
305–566–0691

M & S Bottles and Antiques
421 Wilson Street
Fort Meade, FL 33841
941–285–9421

Gore's Shoe Repair
410 Orange Avenue
Fort Pierce, FL 33450
Florida bottles and black glass

This-n-That Shop
Albert B. Coleman
P.O. Box 185
Hollister, FL 32047
904–328–3658

Hickory Stick Antiques
400 So. 57 Territory
Hollywood, FL 33023
904–962–3434
Canning jars, black glass, household
bottles

The Browns
6512 Mitford Road
Jacksonville, FL 32210
904–771–2091
Sodas, mineral waters, milk, black
glass

Dwight Pettit
33 Sea Side Drive
Key Largo, FL 33037
305–852–8338

Carl Sturm
88 Sweetbriar Branch
Longwood, FL 32750
407–332–7689
Cure bottles

Gerae & Lynn McLarty
6705 Dogwood Court
New Port Richey, FL 33552
813–849–7166

Mike Kollar
50 Sylvania Place
Ormond, FL 32074

Jon Vander Schouw
P.O. Box 1151
Palmetto, FL 33561
813–722–1375

Hidden Bottle Shop
2656 Grandview
Sandford, FL 32771
813–322–7181

Harry O. Thomas
2721 Parson's Rest
Tallahassee, FL 32308
904–893–3834

L. L. Linscott
3557 Nickllaus Drive
Titusville, FL 32780
305–267–9170
Fruit jars and porcelain insulators

GEORGIA

Wayne's Bottles
Box 183
Bultler, GA 31006
912–862–3699
Odd colors and shapes

Carlo and Dot Sellari
Box 888553
Dunwoody, GA 30338
404–451–2483

James T. Hicks
Route 4, Box 265
Eatonton, GA 31024
404–485–9280

Dave and Tia Janousek
2293 Mulligan Circle
Laurenceville, GA 30245

Schmitt House Bottle Diggers
5532 Jane Rue Circle
Macon, GA 31206
912–781–6130

Bob and Barbara Simmons
152 Greenville Street
Newnan, GA 30263
404–251–2471

HAWAII

The Hawaiian Antique Bottle Shop
Kahuku Sugar Mill
P.O. Box 495
Honolulu, HI 96731
808–293–5581
Hawaiian sodas, whiskeys, medicines,
and milks

The Hawaii Bottle Museum
1044 Kalapaki Street
P.O. Box 25153
Honolulu, HI 96825
808–395–4671
Hawaiian bottles, Oriental bottles, and
pottery

IDAHO

John Cothern
Route 1
Buhl, ID 83316
208–543–6713

Jim and Barb Sinsley
1048 N. 14th Street
Coeur d'Alene, ID 83814
208–667–2211
Bitters bottles

Rudy Burns
1238 Eagle Hills Way
Eagle, ID 83616

Idaho Hotel
Jordan Street, Box 75
Silver City, ID 86350
208–495–2520

ILLINOIS

Ronald Selcke
4N236 Eighth Avenue
Addison, IL 60101
312–543–4848

Sean Mullikin
5014 Alicia Drive
Alton, IL 62002
312–466–7506

Mike Spiiroff
1229 Alton Street
Alton, IL 62002
618–462–2283

Wayne and Jacquline Brammer
309 Bellevue Drive
Belleville, IL 62223
618–213–8841

Marvin and Carol Ridgeway
450 W. Cart
Cerro Gordo, IL 61818
217–763–3271

Casad's Antique
610 South State Street
Champaign, IL 61820
217–356–8455
Milk bottles

Tom and Gladys Bartels
5315 W. Warwick
Chicago, IL 60641
312–725–2433

Ernest Brooks
9023 S. East End
Chicago, IL 60617
312–375–9233

First Chicago Bottle Club
P.O. Box A3382
Chicago, IL 60690

Jerry McCann
5003 West Berwyn
Chicago, IL 60630
312–777–0443
Fruit jars

Joe Healy
3421 W. 76th Street
Chicago, IL 60652

William Kiggans
7747 South Kedzle
Chicago, IL 60652
312–925–6148

Carl Malik
8655 S. Keeler
Chicago, IL 60652
312–767–8568

Louis Metzinger
4140 N. Mozart
Chicago, IL 60618
312–478–9034

L. D. and Barbara Robinson
1933 So. Homan
Chicago, IL 60623
312–762–6096

Paul R. Welko
5727 S. Natoma Avenue
Chicago, IL 60638
312–582–3564
Blob tops and Hutchinson sodas

Al and Sue Verley
486 Longwood Court
Chicago, IL 60411
312–754–4132

Jim Hall
445 Patridge Lane
Deerfield, IL 60014
312–541–5788

John and Claudia Panek
816 Holmes
Deerfield, IL 60015
312–945–5493

Ray's and Betty Antiques
Box 5
Dieterich, IL 62424
217–925–5449
Bitters

Keith and Ellen Leeders
1728 N. 76th Avenue
Elmwood, IL 60635
708–453–2085

Jeff Cress
3403 Morkel Drive
Godfrey, IL 62035
618–466–3513

Jim and Jodi Hall
5185 Conifer Lane
Gurnee, IL 60031
708–541–5788
Bottles—all types

Doug and Eileen Wagner
9225 S. 88th Avenue
Hickory Hills, IL 60457
312–598–4570

Jim and Perry Lang
628 Mechanic
Hillsboro, IL 62049
217–532–2915

Art and Pat Besinger
611 Oakwood
Ingelside, IL 60041
312–546–2367

John Murray
301 Hillgrove
LaGrange, IL 60525
312–352–2199

Lloyd Bindscheattle
P.O. Box 11
Lake Villa, IL 60046

Russ and Lynn Sineni
1372 Hillcrest Road
Lemont, IL 60439
312–257–2648

Neal and Marianne Vander Zande
18830 Sara Road
Mokena, IL 60448
312–479–5566

Joe Molloy
P.O. Box 225
Newton, IL 62448
618–783–8741
Miniature bottles

Tom and Ann Feltman
425 North Oak Street
O'Fallon, IL 62269
618–632–3327

Vern and Gloria Nitchie
300 Indiana Street
Park Forest, IL 60466
312–748–7198

Ken's Old Bottles
119 East Lahon
Park Ridge, IL 60068
312–823–1267
Milks, inks, sodas, whiskeys

Harry's Bottle Shop
612 Hillyer Street
Pekink, IL 61555
309–346–3476
Pottery, beer, sodas, medicines

Oertel's Bottle House
Box 682
Pekin, IL 61555
309–347–4441
Peoria pottery, embossed picnic beer
bottles, fruit jars

Bob Rhinberger
Route 7
Quincy, IL 62301
217–223–0191

Bob and Barbara Harms
14521 Atlantic
Riverdale, IL 60627
312–841–4068

Ed McDonald
3002 23rd
Sauk Village, IL 60511
312-758-0373

Jon and Char Granada
631 S. Main
Trenton, IL 62293
618-224-7308

Ben Crane
1700 Thompson Drive
Wheaton, IL 60187
312-665-5662

Scott Garrow
2 S. 338 Orchard Road
Wheaton, IL 60187

B. Hall
940 E. Old Willow Road
Wheeling, IL 60090
312-541-5788
Sodas, inks, medicines

Steve Miller
623 Ivy Court
Wheeling, IL 60090
312-398-1445

Michael Divis
1652 Tappan
Woodstock, IL 66098
815-338-5147

Mike Henrich
402 McHenry Avenue
Woodstock, IL 66098
815-338-5008

INDIANA

Ed and Margaret Shaw
Route 1, Box 23
Boggstown, IN 46110
317-835-7121

Connie Hackman
11757 Whisper Bay Court
Carmel, IN 46033
317-846-3629
Miniature bottles

Tony and Dick Stringfellow
714 Vine
Clinton, IN 47842
317-832-2355

Bob and Morris Wise
409 E. Main
Flora, IN 46929
219-967-3713

Annett's Antiques
6910 Lincoln Highway E.
Fort Wayne, IN 46803
219-749-2745

Gene Rice
61935 CR37, Route 1
Goshen, IN 46526

Wayne Wagner
23558 Creek Park Drive
Goshen, IN 46526

George and Nancy Reilly
Route 10, Box 67
Greenfield, IN 46140
317-462-2441

John and Dianna Atkins
3168 Beeler Avenue
Indianapolis, IN 46224
317-299-2720

Herrell's Collectibles
265 E. Canal Street
Peru, IN 46970
317-473-7770

Fort Harrod Glass Works
160 N. Gardner Road
Scottsburg, IN 47170
812-752-5170

Harry and Dorothy Frey
5210 Clinton Road
Terre Haute, IN 47805
812–466–4642

Doug Moore
9 Northbrook Circle
Westfield, IN 46074
317–896–3015

IOWA
The Bottle Shop
206 Chestnut
Elkader, IA 52043
319–245–2359
Sarsaparilla and bitters

John Wyss
1941 Grant Wood Drive
Iowa City, IA 52240
319–337–9965
Miniature bottles

Ralph and Helen Welch
804 Colonial Circle
Storm Lake, IA 50588
712–732–4124

KANSAS
Mikey Stafford
507 On the Mall
Atchison, KS 66002
913–367–0056
Antiques and books

Donald Haury
208 Main
Halstead, KS 67056
316–283–5876
316–835–2356

Mike Elwell
Route 2, Box 30
Lawrence, KS 66044
913–842–2102

Stewart and Sons Old Bottle Shop
610 E. Kaskaskia
Paola, KS 66071
913–294–3434
Drugstore bottles, blob-top beers

Joe and Alyce Smith
4706 West Hills Drive
Topeka, KS 66606
913–272–1892

KENTUCKY
Michael and Kathy Kolb
6 S. Jefferson
Alexandria, KY 41001
606–635–7121

Paul Van Vactor
100004 Cardigan Drive
Jeffersontown, KY 40299

Roy and Cordie Willis
Heartland of Kentucky
Lebanon Junction, KY 40150
502–833–2827
Jim Beam, ski country bottles

Gene Blasi
5801 River Knolls Drive
Louisville, KY 40222
502–425–6995

Jerry Phelps
8012 Deronia Avenue
Louisville, KY 40222
502–425–2561

Paul and Paulette Van Vavtor
300 Stilz Avenue
Louisville, KY 40299
502–895–3655

Earl and Ruth Cron
808 N. 25th Street
Paducah, KY 42001
502–443–5005

Sheldon Baugh
252 West Valley Drive
Russellville, KY 42276
502–726–2712
Shaker bottles

LOUISIANA

Sidney and Eulalle Genius
1843 Tudor Drive
Baton Rouge, LA 70815
504–925–5774

Bobby and Ellen Kirkpatrick
7313 Meadowbrook Avenue
Baton Rouge, LA 70808

Sheldon L. Ray Jr.
P.O. Box 17238
LSU
Baton Rouge, LA 70893
504–388–3814

Hilly Trading Company
Bob Willett
3171 Highway 167
Dubach, LA 71235
318–255–6112
318–777–3424

Cajun Pop Factory
P.O. Box 1113
Jennings, LA 70546
318–824–7078
Hutchinson, blob-tops, pontil sodas

Everett L. Smith
100 Everett Drive
Monroe, LA 71202
318–325–3534
Embossed whiskeys

Ralph and Cheryl Green
515 Elizabeth Street
Natchitoches, LA 71457

Bep's Antiques
3923 Magazine Street
New Orleans, LA 70115
504–891–3468
Import bottles

Dr. Charles and Jane Aprill
484 Chestnut
New Orleans, LA 70118
504–899–7441

The Dirty Digger
1804 Church Street
Ruston, LA 71270
318–255–6112

MAINE

F. Barrie Freeman Antiques
Paradise Hill Road
Bethel, ME 04217
207–824–3300

John and Althea Hathaway
Bryant Pond, ME 04219

Don McKeen Bottles
McKeen Way, P.O. Box 5A
E. East Wilton, ME 04234

Spruce's Antiques
Main Street, P.O. Box 295
Milford, ME 04461
207–827–4756

Morse and Applebee Antiques
U.S. Route 1, Box 164
Searsport, ME 04974
207–548–6314
Early American glass

Wink's Bottle Shop
Route 235
Waldoboro, ME 04572
207–832–4603

Daniel R. Winchenbaugh
RFD 4, Box 21
Waldoboro, ME 04572
207–832–7702

MARYLAND

Pete's Diggins
Route 40 West, RR 3, Box 301
North East, MD 21901
301–287–9245

Fran and Bill Lafferty
Box 142
Sudlersville, MD 21668

MASSACHUSETTS

Gloria Swanson Antiques
611 Main Street
Dennis, MA 02675
508–385–4166

Joe and Kathy Wood
49 Surplus Street
Duxbury, MA 02332
617–934–2221

Metamorphosis
46 Teewaddle, RFD 3
Leverett, MA 01002
Hair tonics and medicines

Shop in My Home
211 East Street
Mansfield, MA 02048
617–339–6086
Historic flasks

The Applied Lip Place
26 Linden Street
North Easton, MA 02356
617–238–1432
Medicines, whiskeys

Carlyn Ring
59 Livermore Road
Wellesley, MA 02181
617–235–5675

Leo A. Bedard
62 Craig Drive, Apt. 7A
West Springfield, MA 01089
Bitters, whiskeys, medicines

MICHIGAN

John Wolfe
1622 E. Stadium Boulevard
Ann Arbor, MI 48104
313–665–6106

Pat Keefe
2290 Hiller Road W.
Bloomfield, MI 48324
313–363–2068
Miniature bottles

Jim and Robin Meehan
25 Valley Way
Bloomfield Hills, MI 48013
313–642–0176

Old Chicago
316 Ross Drive
Buchanan, MI 49107
616–695–5896
Hutchinson sodas, blob-top beers

Fred and Shirley Weck
8274 S. Jackson
Clarklake, MI 49234
517–529–9631

Chief Pontiac Antique Bottle Shop
13880 Neal Road
Davisburg, MI 48019
313–634–8469

Michael and Christina Garrett
19400 Stout
Detroit, MI 48219
313–534–6067

Ray and Hillaine Hoste
366 Main Street
Dundee, MI 48131
313-529-2193

E & E Antiques
9441 Grand Blanc Road
Gaines, MI 48436
517–271–9063
Fruit jars, beer bottles, milks

Dewey and Marilyn Heetderks
21 Michigan N.E.
Grand Rapids, MI 49503
616–774–9333

Sarge's
111 E. Hemlock
Iron River, MI 49935
906–265–4223
Old mining town bottles, Hutchinsons'

Mark and Marty McNee
1009 Vassar Drive
Kalamazoo, MI 49001
616–343–9393

Lew and Leon Wisser
2837 Parchmount
Kalamazoo, MI 49004
616–343–7479

The Jar Emporium
Ralph Finch
19420 Saratoga
Lathrup, MI 48076
313–569–6749
Fruit jars

Chris and Becky Batdorff
516 Maple Street
Manistee, MI 49660
616–723–7917

Don and Glennie Burkett
3942 West Dunbar Road
Monroe, MI 48161
313–241–6740

Copper Corner Rock and Bottle Shop
4th and Lincoln
Stambaugh, MI 49964
906–265–3510
Beers, Hutchinsons, medicines

Anvil Antiques
3439 Hollywood Road
Saint Joseph, MI 49085
616–429–5132
Insulators

John and Kay Petruska
21960 Marathon Road
Stugis, MI 49091
616–651–6400

James Clengenpeel
316 Ross Drive
Wuchanan, MI 49107
616–695–5896

MINNESOTA

Jim Conley
P.O. Box 351
Excelsior, MN 55331
612–935–0964

Steve Ketcham
P.O. Box 24114
Minneapolis, MN 55424
612–920–4205

Neal and Pat Sorensen
132 Peninsula Road
Minneapolis, MN 55441
612–545–2698

Doug Shilson
3308–32 Avenue So.
Minneapolis, MN 55406
612–721–4165
Bitters, beers, and sodas

Ron and Vernie Feldhaus
5117 W. 92nd Street
Bloomington, MN 55437
612–835–3504

MISSISSIPPI
Vieux Beloxie Pottery Factory
Restaurant
U.S. 90 E.
Biloxi, MS 39530
601–374–0688
Mississippi bottles

Robert A. Knight
516 Dale Street
Columbia, MS 39429
601–736–4249
Mississippi bottles and jugs

Robert Smith
623 Pearl River Avenue
McComb, MS 39648
601–684–1843

Jerry Drott
710 Persimmon Drive
P.O. Box 714
Starkville, MS 39759
601–323–8796
Liniments, drug store bottles

Ted and Linda Kost
107 Columbia
Vicksburg, MS 39180
601–638–8780

MISSOURI
Dave Hausgen
Route 1
Elsberry, MO 63343
314–898–2500

Sam and Eloise Taylor
3002 Woodlands Terrace
Glencoe, MO 63038
314–273–6244

Bob and Debbi Overfield
2318 Chestnut Street
Hannibal, MO 63401
314–248–9521

Mike and Carol Robinson
1405 N. River
Independence, MO 64050
816–836–2337

Donald Kimrey
1023 W. 17th Street
Kansas City, MO 64108
816–741–2745

Robert Stevens
1131 E. 77th
Kansas City, MO 64131
816–333–1398

The Bottle House
Route 1, Box 111
Linn Creek, MO 65052
314–346–5890

Gene and Alberta Kelley
1960 Cherokee
Saint Louis, MO 63126
314–664–7203

Jerry Mueller
4520 Langtree
Saint Louis, MO 63128
314–843–8357

Terry and Luann Phillips
1014 Camelot Gardens
Saint Louis, MO 63125
314–892–6864

Hal and Vern Wagner
10118 Schuessler
Saint Louis, MO 63128
314–843–7573
Historical flasks, colognes, early glass

Barkely Museum
U.S. 61
Taylor, MO
314–393–2408

Joseph and Jean Reed
237 E. Morgan
Tipton, MO 65081
816–433–5937

Randy and Jan Haviland
American Systems Antiques
Westphalia, MO 65085
314–455–2525

MONTANA
Lavaur Scow
Box 959
Boulder, MT 59632
406–225–3290
Montana embossed bottles

NEBRASKA
Born Again Antiques
1402 Williams Street
Omaha, NE 68108
402–341–5177

Karl Person
10210 W Street
Omaha, NE 68127
402–331–2666

Fred Williams
5712 N. 33rd Street
Omaha, NE 68111
402–453–4317

NEVADA
Lost River Trading Company
Larry Gray
401 W. Main
Beatty, NV 89003
702–553–2233

Doug Southerland
Box 1345
Carson City, NV 89702

Loren D. Love
P.O. Box 412
Dayton, NV 89403
702–246–0142
Beer cans, bottles

Ed Hoffman
P.O. Box 6039
Elko, NV 89802
702–753–2435
Coins and paper

Don and Opal Wellman
P.O. Box 521
Fallon, NV 89406
702–423–3490

Coleen Garland
Mithell's Mercantile
Gold Point, NV 89440
Soda pop and beer bottles

Anita's Antiques and Collectibles
2030 E. Charleston
Las Vegas, NV 89104
702–388–1969

Bottle Collector's Liquor Shop
1328 Las Vegas Boulevard, S.
Las Vegas, NV 89104
702–382–6645
Miniature bottles

James Campiglia
4371 Lucas
Las Vegas, NV 89120
702–456–6855
Casino collectibles, postcards, bottles

Frank Gafford
5716 West Balzar
Las Vegas, NV 89108

William V. Wright
220 S. Bruce Street
Las Vegas, NV 89101
Nevada collectibles, bottles

Allen Wilson
P.O. Box 29
Montello, NV 89830
702–776–2511
Bottles

Ronald J. Freeman
450 Douglas Fira
Reno, NV 89511
702–849–9543
Miniature whiskey bottles

Marty Hall
15430 Sylvester Road
Reno, NV 89511
702–852–6045
Western whiskeys and Nevada bottles

Fred Holabird
14040 Perlite Drive
Reno, NV 89511
702–851–0836
Nevada bottles and paper items

Richard Moritz
5025 S. McCarran Boulevard
Box 186
Reno, NV 89502
702–329–4358
Nevada bottles

Larry and Jann Shoemaker
P.O. Box 50546
Reno, NV 89513
702–747–6095
Bottles

Willy Young
80 Promontory Pointe
Reno, NV 89509
702–746–0922
Fire grenades

Don and Bonnnie McLane
1846 F Street
Sparks, NV 89431
702–359–2171

Walt Walker
P.O. Box 21
Verde, NV 89439
702–345–0171
Bottles

Mark Twain's Museum of Memories
Joe Curtis
P.O. Box 449
Virginia City, NV 89440
Bottles

Ann Hunt-Laird Antiques
119 North Main Street
Yerington, NV 89447
702–463–5641

New Hampshire

Dave and Carol Waris
Boston Post Road
Amherst, NH 03031
603–882–4409

Bob and Betty Morin
R.D. 3, Box 280
Dover, NH 03820

Lucille Stanley
9 Oak Street
Exeter, NH 03833
603–772–2296

Murray's Lakeside Bottle Shop
Benson Shores
P.O. Box 57
Hampstead, NH 03841
603–329–6969

Jim and Joyce Rogers
Harvey Road, Route 10
Manchester, NH 03103
603–623–4101

House of Glass
25 High Street
Troy, NH 03465
603-242-7947

NEW JERSEY
Richard and Lesley Harris
Box 400
Branchville, NJ 07826
201-948-3935

Phil and Flo Alvarez
P.O. Box 107
Califon, NJ 07830
201-832-7438

Ed and Carole Clemens
81 Chester Place, Apt. D-2
Englewood, NJ 07631
201-569-4429

John Orashen
R.D. 6, Box 345-A
Flemington, NJ 08822
201-782-3391

Tom and Marion McCandless
62 Lafayette Street
Hopewell, NJ 08525
609-466-0619

Howell Township
Bruce and Pat Egeland
3 Rustic Drive
Howell, NJ 07731
201-363-0556

Sam Fuss
Harmony Road
Mickleton, NJ 08056
609-423-5038

Old Bottle Museum
4 Friendship Drive
Salem, NJ 08079
609-935-5631

NEW MEXICO
George Petroff
1401 Pennsylvania NE #3143
Albuquerque, NM
505-875-0312
Miniature bottles

Irv and Ruth Swalwell
8826 Fairbanks
Albuquerque, NM 87112
505-299-2977

Krol's Rock City and Mobile Park
Star Route 2, Box 15A
Deming, NM 88030
Hutchinson sodas, inks, Avons

Zang Wood
P.O. Box 890/#21 Road 3461
Flora Vista, NM 87415
505-334-8966
Seltzers, Hutchinsons

Tino Romero
2917 Canada del Humo
Santa Fe, NM 87505
505-474-6353
Poisons, inks, Dr. Kilmer, and New
Mexico

NEW YORK
Brewster Bottle Shop
297 South Street
Auburn, NY 13021
315-252-3246
Milk bottles

Tom and Alice Moulton
88 Blue Spruce Lane, R.D. 5
Ballston Lake, NY 12019

Jim Chamberlain
R.D. 8, 607 Nowland Road
Binghamton, NY 13904
607-772-1135

Jo Ann's Old Bottles
R.D. 2, Box 638
Port Crane, NY 13833
607-648-4605

Edward Petter
P.O. Box 1
Blodgett Mills, NY 13738
607-756-7891
Inks

Old Bottle Shop
Horton Road
P.O. Box 105
Blooming Grove, NY 10914
914–496–6841

Al Manuel
1225 McDonald Avenue
Brooklyn, NY 11230
718–253–8308
Miniature bottles

J.J.'s Pontil Place
1001 Dunderberg Road
Central Valley, NY
914–928–9144

John Kovacik
11 Juniper Drive
Clifton Park, NY 12065
518–371–4118

Richard Strunk
R.D. 4, Grooms Road
Clifton Park, NY 12065
Flasks, bitters, Saratogas

The Bottle Shop Antiques
P.O. Box 503
Cranberry Lake, NY 12927
315–848–2648

Leonard and Joyce Blake
1220 Stolle Road
Elma, NY 14059
716–652–7752

Tony Natelli
153–31 79th Street
Howard Beach, NY 11414
718–738–3344
Miniature bottles

Kenneth Cornell
78 Main
Leroy, NY 14482
716–768–8919

The Bottle Shop
P.O. Box 24
Loch Sheldrake, NY 12759
914–434–4757

Manor House Collectibles
R.D. 1, Box 67
Monticello, NY 12701
914–794–3967
Whiskeys, beers, sodas

Chris Davis
522 Woodhill
Newark, NY 14513
315–331–4078
Bottles and glass

David Byrd
43 E. Kenwood Drive
New Windsor, NY 12550
914–561–7257

Chuck Moore
3 East 57th Street
New York, NY 10022

Bottles Unlimited
245 East 78th Street
New York, NY 10021
212–628–8769
Eighteenth- and nineteenth-century
bottles

Schumer's Wine and Liquors
59 East 54th Street
New York, NY 10022
Miniature bottles

Bob and Dawn Jackson
107 Pine Street
Powhatan Point, NY 43942
614–795–5565

Burton Spiller
169 Greystone Lane, Apt. 13
Rochester, NY 14618
716–244–2229

Robert Zorn
23 Knickerbocker Avenue
Rochester, NY 14615
716–254–7470

Dick and Evelyn Bowman
1253 LaBaron Circle
Webster, NY 14580
716–872–4015
Insulators

NORTH CAROLINA

Vieve and Luke Yarbrough
P.O. Box 1023
Blowing Rock, NC 28605
704–963–4961

Bob Morgan
P.O. Box 3163
Charlotte, NC 28203
704–527–4841

Clement's Bottles
5234 Willowhaven Drive
Durham, NC 27712
919–383–2493
Commemorative soft drink bottles

Howard Crowe
P.O. Box 133
Gold Hill, NC 28071
704–279–3736

Vernon Capps
Route 5, Box 529
Goldsboro, NC 27530
919–734–8964

Rex D. McMillan
4101 Glen Laurel Drive
Raleigh, NC 27612
919–787–0007
North Carolina blobs, saloon bottles,
colored drug store bottles

NORTH DAKOTA

Robert Barr
102 N. Ninth Avenue
Mandan, ND 58554

OHIO

Don and Barb Dzuro
5113 W. Bath Road
Akron, OH 44313
216–666–8170

Jim Salzwimmer
3391 Tisen Road
Akron, OH 44312
216–699–3990

Allan Hodges
25125 Shaker Boulevard
Beachwood, OH 44122
216–464–8381

Schroll's Country Shop
3 miles east of county line on County
Road 33
Bluffton, OH
419–358–6121

Albert and Sylvia Campbell
R.D. 1, Box 194
Byesville, OH 43723
614–439–1105

Kenneth and Dudie Roat
7775 Kennedy Lane
Cincinnati, OH 45242
513–791–1168

Joe and Mary Miller
2590 N. Moreland Boulevard
Cleveland, OH 44120
216–721–9919

Don and Paula Spangler
2554 Loris Drive
Dayton, OH 45449
513–435–7155

Roy and Barbara Brown
8649 Dunsinane Drive
Dublin, OH 43017
614–889–0818

Roger Durflinger
P.O. Box 2006
Frankfort, OH 45628
614–998–4849

Gilbert Nething
P.O. Box 96
Hannibal, OH 43931
Hutchinson sodas

R. J. and Freda Brown
125 S. High Street
Lancaster, OH 43130
614–687–2899

Sonny Mallory
P.O. Box 134
Lewistown, OH 43333
513–686–2185

Harold A. Waxman
1928 Camberly Drive
Lydnhurst, OH 44124
216–449–4765
Miniature bottles, whiskey, rye, scotch

John and Margie Bartley
160 S. Main
North Hampton, OH 45319
513–964–1080

Bob and Phyllis Christ
1218 Creekside Place
Reynoldsburg, OH 43068
614–866-2156

Ballentine's Bottles
710 W. First Street
Springfield, OH 45504
513–399–8359

Larry R. Henschen
3222 Delrey Road
Springfield, OH 45504
513–399–1891

Tom and Deena Caniff
1223 Oak Grove Avenue
Steubenville, OH 43952
614–282–8918
Fruit jars

Bob and Mary Ann Willamagna
711 Kendall Avenue
Steubenville, OH 43952
614–282–9029

Doug and Joann Bedore
1483 Ritchie Road
Stowk, OH 44224
216–688–4934

Bob Villamagna
1518 Madison Avenue
P.O. Box 56
Toronto, OH 43964
614–537–4503
Tri-State area bottles, stoneware

Paul Stookey
3015 W. Tate Route 571
Troy, OH 45373
513–698–3392
Miniature bottles

Bill Orr
1680 Glenwood Drive
Twinsburg, OH 44087
216–425–2365
Miniature bottles

Michael Cetina
3272 Northwest Boulevard N.W.
Warren, OH 44485
216–898–1845

Al and Beth Bignon
480 High Street
Washingtonville, OH 44490
216–427–6848

The Bottleworks
70 N. Main Street
P.O. Box 446
Waynesville, OH 45068
513–897–3861

Elvin and Cherie Moody
Trails End
Wellington, OH 44090
216–647–4917

Bill and Wanda Dudley
393 Franklin Avenue
Xenia, OH 45385
513–372–8567

OKLAHOMA
Ronald and Carol Ashby
831 E. Pine
Enid, OK 73701
Rare and scarce fruit jars

Johnnie W. Fletcher
1300 S. Blue Haven Drive
Mustang, OK 73064
405–376–1045
Kansas and Oklahoma bottles

Joe and Hazel Nagy
3540 N.W. 23
Oklahoma City, OK 73107
405–942–0882

Larry and Linda Shope
310 W. 44th
Sandsprings, OK 74063
918–363–8481

OREGON
Juanita Rubio
4326 Old Stage Road
Central Point, OR 97502
Miniature bottles

Tom and Bonnie Kasner
380 E. Jersey Street
Gladstone, OR 97027
503–655–9127
Insulators, marbles, bottles, jars

Robert and Marguerite Ornduff
Route 4, Box 236–A
Hillsboro, OK 97123
503–538–2359

R.E. Barnett
P.O. Box 109
Lakeview, OR 97630
503–947–2415
Western whiskey bottles

Gerald M. Burton
611 Taylor Street
Myrtle Creek, OR
503–863–6670

Alan Amerman
2311 S.E. 147th
Portland, OR 97233
503–761–1661
Fruit jars

The Glass House
4620 S.E. 104th
Portland, OR 97266
503–760–3346
Fruit jars

PENNSYLVANIA
R. S. Riovo
686 Franklin Street
Alburtis, PA 18011–9578
610–966–2536
Milk bottles, dairy go-withs

Ernest Hurd
5 High Street
Bradford, PA 16701
814–362–9915

Dick and Patti Mansour
458 Lambert Drive
Bradford, PA 16701
814–368-8820

Claude and Ethel Lee
643 Bolivar Drive
Bradford, PA 16701
814–362–3663
Jars, bottles, pocket knives

John and Mary Schultz
R.D. 1, Box 118
Canonsburg, PA 15317
412–745–6632

The Old Bottle Corner
508 South Main Street
Coudersport, PA 16915
814–274–7017
Fruit jars, blob tops

James A. Hagenback
102 Jefferson Street
East Greenville, PA 18041
215–679–5849

Jere and Betty Hambleton
5940 Main Street
East Petersburg, PA 17520
717–569–0130

Al and Maggie Duffield
12 Belmar Road
Hatboro, PA 19040
215–675–5175
Hutchinsons, inks

Barry and Mary Hogan
3 Lark Lane
Lancaster, OH 17603

Ed Lasky
43 Nightingale
Levittown, PA 19054
215–945–1555

Harold Bauer Antique Bottles
136 Cherry Street
Marienville, PA 16239

Chuck Henigin
3024 Pitch Fork Lane
McKees Rocks, PA 15136
412–331–6159

Harold Hill
161 E. Water Street
Muncy, PA 17756
717–546–3388

Allen Holtz
R.D. 1
Pipersville, PA 18947
215–847–5728

Carl and Gail Onufer
210 Newport Road
Pittsburg, PA 15221
412–371–7725
Milk bottles

R. A. and Ester Heimer
P.O. Box 153
Roulette, PA 16746
814–544–7713

Butch and Gloria Kim
R.D. 2, Box 35
Strongstown, PA 15957

RHODE ISLAND
Wes and Diane Seemann
Box 49
Kenyon, RI 02836
203–599–1626

Normand Provencal
84 Rowe Avenue
Warwick, RI 02889
401–739–4148
Miniature bottles

SOUTH CAROLINA
Bob Durham
704 W. Main Street
Eashey, SC 29640

Tony and Marie Shank
P.O. Box 778
Marion, SC 29571
803-423-5803

TENNESSEE
Charlie Barnette
100 N. Coffey Street
Bristol, TN 37620
615-968-1437
Whiskeys, druggists' patent medicines

Ronnie Adams
7005 Charlotte Drive
Knoxville, TN 37914
615-524-8958

Terry Pennington
415 N. Spring Street
McMinnvillek, TN 37110
Jack Daniels, amber Coca-Cola

Bluff City Bottlers
4630 Crystal Springs Drive
Memphis, TN 38123
901-353-0541
Common American bottles

Larry and Nancy McCage
3772 Hanna Drive
Memphis, TN 38128
901-388-9329

Tom Phillips
2088 Fox Run Cove
Memphis, TN 38138
901-754-0097

TEXAS
Robert Snyder
4235 W. 13th
Amarillo, TX 79106

Mack and Alliene Landers
P.O. Box 5
Euless, TX 76039
817-267-2710

Bennie and Harper Leiper
2800 W. Dallas
Houston, TX 77019
713-526-2101

Gerald Welch
4809 Gardenia Trail
Pasadena, TX 77505
713-487-3057

Jimmy and Peggy Galloway
P.O. Drawer A
Port Isabel, TX 78578
512-943-2437

Chuck and Reta Bukin
1325 Cypress Drive
Richardson, TX 75080
214-235-4889

Sam Greer
707 Nix Professional Building
San Antonio, TX 78205
512-227-0253

Ken Malone
3110 Garfield
Wichita Falls, TX 76308
817-691-6397
New Mexico bottles

UTAH
Betty's Antiques and Collectibles
1181 South Main
Cedar City, UT 84720
801-586-7221
Depression glass and pottery

Bruce Duggar
1617 W. 4800 South
Salt Lake City, UT 84123

Dave Emett
1736 North Star Drive
Salt Lake City, UT 84116
801-596-2103
Utah crocks and jugs

Shady Lane Antiques
Marie and Mont Bradford
276 W. Saint George Boulevard
Saint George, UT 84770
801–628–7716

Dark Canyon Trading Company
Janice and Gary Parker
212 W. 200N (24–4)
Blanding, UT 84511
Bottles, pottery, art

VERMONT

Kit Barry
88 High Street
Brattleboro, VT 05301
802–254–2195

VIRGINIA

A. E. Steidel
6167 Cobbs Road
Alexandria, VA 22310

Dick and Margie Stockton
2331 N. Tuckahoe Street
Arlington, VA 22205
703–534–5619

Tom Morgan
3501 Slate Court
Chesterfield, VA 23832

White's Trading Post
Boutchyards Olde Stable
Fredericksburg, VA 22401
703–371–6252
Fruit jars

Vic and Betty Landis
Route 1, Box 8A
Hinton, VA 22801
703–867–5959

Early American Workshop
Star Route
Huntly, VA 22640
703–635–8252
Milk bottles

John Tutton
Route 1, Box 261
Marshall, VA 22115
703–347–0148

Lloyd and Carrie Hamish
2936 Woodworth Road
Richmond, VA 23234
804–275–7106

Jim and Connie Mitchell
5106 Glen Alden Drive
Richmond, VA 23234

WASHINGTON

Kent Beach
1001 Harding Road
Aberdeen, WA 98520
206–532–8556
Owl bottles and related items

Ron Flannery
1821 Jackson Drive N.W.
Bremerton, WA 98312
360–373–7514
Bottles

Pete Hendricks
3005 S. 302nd Place
Federal Way, WA 98023
206–874–6345
Owl bottles

Ed and Tami Barber
45659 S.E. 129th
North Bend, WA 98045
206–888–1179
Early American bottles

John W. Cooper
4975 120th Avenue S.E
Bellevue, WA 98006
206–644–2669
Bottles

WISCONSIN

Mike and Carol Schwartz
Route 1
Arlington, WI 53911
608–846–5229

Jeff Burkhardt
12637 N. River Forest Circle
Mequon, WI 53092
414-243-5643

Bor Markiewicz
11715 W. Bonniwell Road
Mequon, WI 53092
414-242-3968

George Aldrich
3211 West Michigan Street
Milwaukee, WI 53208
414-933-1643
Miniature bottles

Richard Schwab
65-5 Lareen Road
Oskosh, WI 54901
414-235-9962

Bill and Kathy Mitchell
703 Linwood Avenue
Stevens Point, WI 55431
715-341-1471

George and Ruth Hansen
Route 2, Box 26
Wautoma, WI 54962
414-787-4893

Foreign Dealers

AUSTRALIA
John Lynch
P.O. Box 78
Charters Towers QLD 4820, Australia

Stephen Trill
5 Acacia Avenue
Warwick, Australia 4370

CANADA
Ed Gulka
5901 44th Street
Lloydminister, Alberta T9V 1 V6
403-875-6677

Peter Austin
Off Road Bottles and Collectibles
P.O. Box 171
Pontypool, Ontario, L0A 1K0
705-277-3704
Canadian Codd bottles

Ron Nykolyshyn
8820 138th Avenue
Edmonton, Alberta T5E 2A8 Canada
Miniature vodka bottles

ENGLAND
Rob Goodacre
44 Arundel Close, BH 25 SUH
New Milton Hants
01425 620794
Overseas direct dial:
011-44-1425-620794
Bitters, whiskeys, pictorials

Robin A. Gollan
6 Broom Mead
Bexleyheath, Kent
DA6 7NY England
011-441-1322-524246
Miniature cognac bottles

NETHERLANDS
Willy Van den Bossche
Kniplaan 3 NL
2251 AK Voorschoten, Nederland

CHINA
Hong Kong Miniature Liquor
Collection Shop 107
Astor Plaza
380 Nathan Road
Kowloon, Hong Kong
Fax: 852-314-8022
Miniature bottles

Man's Chan
Dragon Empire Trading Co.
Bowa House
180 Nathan Road
Tsimshatsui, Kowloon, Hong Kong
852-721-3200
Fax: 852-314-8022

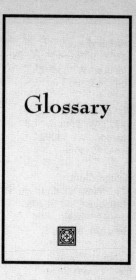

Glossary

Amethyst-Colored Glass A clear glass that when exposed to the sun or bright light for a long period of time will turn various shades of purple. Only glass that contains manganese is subject to this process.

Amber-Colored Glass Nickel was added in the glass production to obtain this common bottle color. It was believed that the resulting dark color would prevent the sun from damaging the contents of the bottle.

Annealing The gradual cooling of hot glass in a cooling chamber or annealing oven.

Applied Lip On bottles manufactured before 1880 the lip was applied after removal from the blowpipe. This may be only a ring of glass trailed around the bottle neck.

Automatic Bottle Machine Invented in 1903, this machine revolutionized the bottle industry.

Aqua-Colored glass The natural color of glass. The particular shade produced was dependent on the iron oxide used in the glass production. It was commonly produced until the 1930s.

Barber Bottle In the 1880s these colorful bottles decorated the shelves of barbershops and usually were filled with bay rum.

Batch A mixture of the ingredients necessary for the manufacture of glass.

Battledore A wooden paddle used by a glassblower to flatten the bottom or sides of a bottle.

Bitters An herbal, purportedly medicinal, mixture and flavoring, which contained a great quantity of alcohol, usually corn whiskey.

Black Glass This type of glass, produced between 1700 and 1875, is actually a dark olive green color created by the carbon used in the glass production.

Blob Seal A way of identifying an unembossed bottle. Manufacturers applied a molten coin-shaped blob of glass to the shoulder of this bottle, into which a seal with the logo, name of the distiller, date, or product name was impressed.

Blob Top A large thick blob of glass that was placed around the lip of soda or mineral water bottles. A wire held the stopper, which was seated below the blob and anchored the wire when the stopper was closed, to prevent the carbonation from escaping.

Blown-in Mold Process by which the gather of glass is blown into a mold to take the shape of the mold. The lips on these types of bottles were added later and the bases often have open pontil scars.

Blowpipe A hollow iron tube wider and thicker at the gathering end than at the blowing end. Glassblowers used them to pick up the molten glass, which was then blown in a mold or free-blown outside the mold. Pipes vary from 2½ to 6 feet in length.

Cobalt-Colored Glass This color was used with patented medicines and poisons to distinguish them from other bottles. Excessive amounts resulted in the familiar "cobalt blue" color.

Crown Cap A metal cap formed from a circular tin plate crimped on its edge to fit tightly over the rolled lip of a bottle. The inside of the cap was filled with a cork disk, which created an airtight seal.

Cullet Cleansed and broken glass added to the batch to bring about rapid fusion.

Date Line The mold seam or mold line on a bottle. The length of this line provides collectors with a clue to the bottle's approximate age.

Decolorizer A compound that is added to natural aquamarine bottle glass to render the glass clear.

Dip Mold A one-piece mold open at the top.

Embossed Lettering Raised print denoting the name of the product or manufacturer on the bottle.

Fire Polishing The reheating of glass to eliminate unwanted blemishes.

Flared Lip Bottles produced prior to 1900 have lips that have been worked out or flared out to reinforce the strength of the opening.

Flint Glass Glass composed of a silicate of potash and lead.

Free-Blown Glass Items of this nature are produced with a blowpipe and do not utilize a mold.

Gaffer The word for the master blower in the early glass houses.

Gather The gob of molten glass adhering to the blowpipe in the first stage of the free-blown process.

Glory Hole The small furnace used for the frequent reheatings necessary during the making of a bottle. The glory hole was also used in fire polishing.

Green Glass Refers to a composition of glass and not a color. The green color was caused by the iron impurities in the sand, which could not be controlled by the glassmakers.

Ground Pontil Refers to the smooth circle that remains when a rough pontil scar has been ground off.

Imperfections Include bubbles or tears of all sizes and shapes, bent shapes and necks, imperfect seams, and errors in spelling and embossing.

Improved Pontil Bottles having an improved pontil appear as reddish or blackish on the base.

Kick-up The deep indentation in the bottom of many bottles. This is formed by placing a projected piece of wood or metal in the base of the mold while the glass is still hot. Wine bottles are usually indented.

Laid-on Ring A bead of glass that has been trailed around the neck opening to reinforce the opening.

Lady's Leg Bottles that are shaped like long curving necks.

Manganese Utilized as a decolorizer between 1850 and 1910. Will also cause glass to turn purple under extreme heat.

Melting Pot This was a clay pot used to melt silicate in the glass-making process.

Metal The molten glass.

Milk Glass Tin is added in glass production to obtain this colored glass, which was primarily used for cosmetic bottles.

Mold, Full-Height, Three-Piece The entire bottle was formed in the mold, and two seams run the height of the bottle to the lip on both sides.

Mold, Three-Piece Dip In this mold the bottom part of the bottle mold was one piece and the top, from the shoulder up, was two separate pieces. Mold seams appear circling the bottle at the shoulder and on each side of the neck.

Opalescence This is seen on the frosty bottle or variated-color bottle that has been buried in mud or silt; the minerals in these substances have interacted with the glass to create these effects.

Paste Mold These were made of two or more pieces of iron and were coated with a paste to prevent scratches on the glass. The seams were eliminated as the glass was turned in the mold.

Pontil, Puntee, or Punty Rod The iron rod attached to the base of a bottle by a gob of glass to hold the bottle during the finishing.

Pontil Marks To remove the bottle from the blowpipe, an iron rod with a small amount of molten glass was applied to the bottom of the bottle for handling while the neck and lip were finished. A sharp tap removed the bottle from the pontil, leaving a jagged glass scar.

Pressed Glass Glass that has been pressed into a mold to take the shape of the mold or the pattern within the mold.

Pucellas Called "the tool" by glassmakers. This tool is essential in shaping both the body and opening in blown bottles.

Pumpkinseed A small round flat flask, often found in Western areas. Generally made of clear glass, the shape resembled the seed of the grown pumpkin. These bottles are also known as "Mickies," "Saddle Flasks," and "Two-Bit Ponies."

Round Bottom A soda bottle made of heavy glass designed in the shape of a torpedo. This enabled the bottle to lie on its side, keeping the liquid in contact with the cork, and preventing the cork from drying and popping out of the bottle.

Sheared Lip After the bottle was blown, a pair of scissorlike shears clipped the hot glass from the blow-pipe. No top was applied and sometimes a slight flange was created.

Sick Glass Glass bearing a superficial decay or deterioration that takes on a grayish tinge caused by erratic firing.

Slug Plate A metal plate about two by four inches with a firm's name on it, which was inserted into a mold and customized bottles for a glasshouse's clients. By simply exchanging plates the glasshouse could use the same mold for many companies.

Snap Case Also called a "snap tool." This tool replaced the pontil rod and enabled the worker to hold the bottle with a tool that had vertical arms curving out from a central stem. The snap case gripped the bottle and held it firmly during finishing of the neck and lip. The use of the snap case eliminated the pontil scars or marks; however, it did at times produce grip marks on the sides of the finished bottle.

Whittle Marks Bottles formed in carved-wood molds have these distinctive marks. A similar effect was produced when forming hot glass on cold molds early in the morning. "Goose pimples" resulted on the surface of these bottles. As the day progressed and the mold warmed, later bottles were smooth.

Bibliography

Books

Agee, Bill. *Collecting All Cures.* East Greenville, Pa.: Antique Bottle & Glass Collector, 1973.

Ayers, James. *Pepsi-Cola Bottles Collectors Guide.* Mount Airy, N.C.: R. J. Menter Enterprises, 1995.

Barnett, R. E. *Western Whiskey Bottles.* Bend, Ore.: Maverick Publishing, 1992.

Beck, Doreen. *The Book of Bottle Collecting.* Gig Harbor, Wash.: Hamlin Publishing Group, Ltd., 1973.

Bound, Smyth. *19th Century Food in Glass.* Sandpoint, Idaho: Midwest Publishers, 1994.

Cleveland, Hugh. *Bottle Pricing Guide, 3rd Edition.* Paducah, Ky.: Collector Books, 1993.

Creswick, Alice M. *Redbook Number 6: The Collectors Guide to Old Fruit Jars.* Grand Rapids, Mich.: Privately published 1992.

Dale, Van P. *American Breweries II.* North Wales, Pa.: Eastern Coast Brewiana Association, 1995.

DeGrafft, John. *American Sarsaparilla Bottles.* East Greenville, Pa.: Antique Bottle & Glass Collector, 1980.

Diamond, Freda. *Story of Glass.* New York: Harcourt, Brace, 1953.

Dumbrell, Roger. *Understanding Antique Wine Bottles*. Ithaca, N.Y.: Antique Collectors Club, 1983.

Edmundson, Barbara. *Historical Shot Glasses*. Chico, Calif.: Self-published, 1995.

Eilelberner, George, and Serge Agadjanian. *The Compleat American Glass Candy Containers Handbook*. New York: Adele Bowden, 1986.

Ferraro, Pat and Bob. *A Bottle Collector's Book*. Sparks, Nev.: Western Printing & Publishing, 1970.

Field, Anne E. *On the Trail of Stoddard Glass*. Dublin, N.H.: William L. Bauhan, 1975.

Fletcher, W. Johnnie. *Kansas Bottle Book*. Mustang, Okla.: Self-published, 1994.

———. *Oklahoma Bottle Book*. Mustang, Okla.: Self-published, 1994.

Gardner, Paul Vickens. *Glass*. New York: Smithsonian Illustrated Library of Antiques, Crown Publishers, 1975.

Graci, David. *American Stoneware Bottles, A History and Study*. South Hadley, Mass.: Self-published, 1995.

Hastin, Bud. *26th Anniversary Avon Products & California Perfume Co. Collector's Encyclopedia*. Kansas City, Mo.: Bud Hastin's Publications, 1995.

Holabird, Fred, and Jack Haddock. *The Nevada Bottle Book*. Reno, Nev.: R. F. Smith, 1981.

Holiner, Richard. *Collecting Barber Bottles*. Paducah, Ky.: Collector Books, 1986.

Hudgeons, Thomas E., III. *Official Price Guide to Bottles Old & New*. Orlando, Fla.: House of Collectibles, 1983.

Hudson, Paul. "Seventeenth-Century Glass Wine Bottles and Seals Excavated at Jamestown," *Journal of Glass Studies*, vol. 3. Corning, N.Y.: The Corning Museum of Glass, 1961.

Hunter, Frederick William. *Stiegel Glass*. New York: Dover Publications, 1950.

Innes, Lowell. *Pittsburg Glass 1797–1891*. Boston: Houghton Mifflin, 1976.

Jackson, Barbara and Sonny. *American Pot Lids*. East Greenville, Pa.: Antique Bottle & Glass Collector, 1992.

Jarves, Deming. *Reminiscences of Glass Making.* New York: Hurd and Houghton, 1865.

Kendrick, Grace. *The Antique Bottle Collector.* Ann Arbor, Mich.: Edwards Brothers, 1971.

Ketchum, William C., Jr. *A Treasury of American Bottles.* Los Angeles: Rutledge Publishing, 1975.

Klesse, Brigitt, and Hans Mayr. *European Glass from 1500–1800, The Ernesto Wolf Collection.* Germany: Kremayr and Scheriau, 1987.

Knittle, Rhea Mansfield. *Early American Glass.* New York: Garden City Publishing Company, 1948.

Kovel, Terry and Ralph. *The Kovels' Bottle Price List.* New York: Crown Publishers, 1992.

Kovill, William E., Jr. *Ink Bottles and Ink Wells.* Taunton, Mass.: William L. Sullwold, 1971.

Lee, Ruth Webb. *Antique Fakes and Reproductions.* Northborough, Mass.: Privately published, 1971.

Leybourne, Doug. *Red Book #7, Fruit Jar Price Guide.* North Muskegon, Mich.: Privately published, 1995.

Maust, Don. *Bottle and Glass Handbook.* Uniontown, Pa.: E. G. Warman Publishing, 1956.

Markowski, Carol. *Tomart's Price Guide to Character & Promotional Glasses.* Dayton, Ohio: Tomart Publishing, 1993.

McCann, Jerry. *1996 Fruit Jar Annual.* Chicago: J. McCann Publisher, 1996.

McDougald, John and Carol. *1995 Price Guide for Insulators.* St. Charles, IL.: Self-published, 1995.

McKearin, Helen, and George S. *American Glass.* New York: Crown Publishers, 1956.

———. *Two Hundred Years of American Blown Glass.* New York: Crown Publishers, 1950.

McKearin, Helen, and Kenneth M. Wilson. *American Bottles and Flasks and Their Ancestry.* New York: Crown Publishers, 1978.

Megura, Jim. *Official Price Guide Bottles.* New York: House of Collectibles, 1991.

Meinz, David. *So Da Licious, Collecting Applied Color Label Soda Bottles.* Norfolk, Va.: Self-published, 1994.

Milroy, Wallace. *The Malt Whiskey Almanac.* Glasgow, Scotland: Neil Wilson Publishing, 1989.

Munsey, Cecil. *The Illustrated Guide to Collecting Bottles.* New York: Hawthorn Books, 1970.

Namiat, Robert. *Barber Bottles with Prices.* Randor, Pa.: Wallace Homestead Book Company, 1977.

Nielsen, Frederick. *Great American Pontiled Medicines.* Cherry Hill, N.J.: The Cortech Corporation, 1978.

Northend, Mary Harrod. *American Glass.* New York: Tudor Publishing, 1940.

Odell, John. *Digger Odell's Official Antique Bottle & Glass Price Guide.* Morrow, Ohio: Odell Publishing, 1995.

Ostrander, Diane. *A Guide to American Nursing Bottles.* York, Pa.: ACIF Publications, 1992.

Pepper, Adeline. *The Glass Gaffers of New Jersey.* New York: Charles Scribner's Sons, 1971.

Petretti, Alan. *Petretti's Coca-Cola Price Guide,* 9th ed. New York: Homestead Book Company, 1994.

Putnam, H. E. *Bottle Identification.* New York: Putnam Publishers, 1965.

Ring, Carlyn. *For Bitters Only.* Concord, Mass.: The Nimrod Press, 1980.

Russell, Mike. *Collectors Guide to Civil War Period Bottles and Jars.* Greenville, Pa.: Antique Bottle & Glass Collector, 1995.

Schwartz, Marvin D. "American Glass," *Antiques* 1 (1974) *Blown and Molded,* Princeton, N.J.: Pyne Press.

Seeliger, Michael. *H. H. Warner: His Company & His Bottles.* East Greenville, Pa.: Antique Bottle & Glass Collector, 1974.

Sloan, Gene. *Perfume and Scent Bottle Collecting.* Randor, Pa.: Wallace Homestead Book Company, 1986.

Snyder, Bob. *Bottles in Miniature.* Amarillo, Tex.: Snyder Publications, 1969.

———. *Bottles in Miniature II.* Amarillo, Tex.: Snyder Publications, 1970.

———. *Bottles in Miniature III.* Amarillo, Tex.: Snyder Publications, 1972.

Spaid, M. David, and Harry A. Ford. *101 Rare Whiskey Flasks (Miniature).* Palos Verdes, Calif.: Brisco Publications, 1989.

Spillman, Jane Shadel. *Glass Bottles, Lamps, and Other Objects.* New York: Alfred A. Knopf, 1983.

Sweeney, Rick. *Collecting Applied Color Label Soda Bottles.* La Mesa, Calif.: Painted Soda Bottles Collectors Association, 1995.

Thompson, J. H. *Bitters Bottles.* Watkins Glen, N.Y.: Century House, 1947.

Toulouse, Julian Harrison. *Bottle Makers and Their Marks.* Camden, N.J.: Thomas Nelson, 1971.

Townsend, Brian. *Scotch Missed (The Lost Distilleries of Scotland).* Glasgow, Scotland: Neil Wilson Publishing, 1994.

Tyson, Scott. *Glass Houses of the 1800s.* East Greenville, Pa.: Antique Bottle & Glass Collector, 1971.

Tucker, Donald. *Collectors Guide to the Saratoga Type Mineral Water Bottles.* East Greenville, Pa.: Antique Bottle & Glass Collector, 1986.

Tutton, John. *Udderly Delightful.* Stephens City, Va.: Commercial Press, 1989.

Umberger, Joe and Arthur. *Collectible Character Bottles.* Tyler, Tex.: Corker Book Company, 1969.

Van Rensselaer, Stephen. *Early American Bottles and Flasks.* Stratford, Conn.: J. Edmund Edwards Publisher, 1969.

Von Spiegel, Walter, *Glas.* Munich, Germany: Battenberg Verlag, 1979.

Watkins, Laura Woodside. *American Glass and Glassmaking.* New York: Chanticleer Press, 1950.

Watson, Richard. *Bitters Bottles.* New York: Thomas Nelson & Sons, 1965.

———. *Supplement to Bitters Bottles.* New York: Thomas Nelson & Sons, 1968.

Wilson, Kenneth M. *New England Glass and Glass Making.* New York: Thomas Y. Crowell Company, 1972.

Zumwalt, Betty. *Ketchup, Pickles, Sauces.* Sandpoint, Idaho: Mark West Publishers, 1980.

Periodicals

Bottles & Bygones. 30 Brabant Road, Cheadle Hulme, Cheadlek, Cheshire, SKA 7AU England.

Bottles & Extra Magazine. 88 Sweetbriar Branch, Longwood, FL 32750–2783.

British Bottle Review. 5 Ironworks Row, Elsecar Project, Wath Road, Elsecar, Barnsley, S. York, S74, 8HJ England.

Canadian Bottle & Stoneware Collector. Bowmanville, Ontario, Canada.

Fruit Jar Newsletter. FJN Publishers, 364 Gregory Avenue, West Orange, NH 07052–3743.

Antique Bottle & Glass Collector. Jim Hagenbuch, 102 Jefferson Street, P.O. Box 187, East Greenville, PA 18041.

Crown Jewels of the Wire. Carol McDougald, P.O. Box 1003, Saint Charles, IL 60174–1003.

The Miniature Bottle Collector. Brisco Publications, P.O. Box 2161, Palos Verdes Peninsula, CA 92074.

Treasure Hunter's Gazette. George Streeter, Publisher and Editor, 14 Vernon Street, Keene, NH 03431.

Auction Companies

ABIC Absentee Auctions
P.O. Box 310
Bowmanville, Ontario, Canada L1C 3L1
Peter Austin
705–277–3704

Armans of Newport
207 High Point Avenue
Portsmouth, RI 02871

BBR Auctions
5 Ironworks Row, Wath Road
Elsecar, Barnsley
S. Yorkshire, S74 844, England
0226–745156

CB & SC Auctions
179D Woodridge Cres
Nepean, Ontario K2B 712, Canada
Rhonda Bennett
613–828–8266

Garth's Auctions
2690 Stratford Road
Box 369
Delaware, OH 43015
614–362–4771

Glass Works Auctions
Box 187
East Greenville, PA 18041
215–679–5849

Gore Enterprises
P.O. Box 158
Huntington, VT 05462
William D. Emberley
802–453–3311

Harmer Rooke Galleries
32 East 57 Street
New York, NY 10022
212–751–1900

Howard B. Parzow
P.O. Box 3464
Gaithersburg, MD 20885–3464
301–977–6741

Norman C. Heckler & Co.
79 Bradford Corner Road
Woodstock Valley, CT 06282
203–974–1634

Pacific Glass Auctions
1507 21st Street, Suite #203
Sacramento, CA 95814
800–806–7722

R Newton-Smith Antiques
88 Cedar Street
Cambridge, Ontario
Canada N1S IV8
519–623–6302

Shot Glass Exchange
Box 219 BE.
Western Springs, IL 60558
708–246–1559

Skinner
375 Main Street
Bolton, MA 01740
508–779–6241

Stuckey Auction Co.
315 West Broad Street
Richmond, VA 23225
804–780–0850

The Pop Shoppe
Jim Millar
2180 Ellery Avenue
Clovis, CA 93611–0652
209–298–7531

T.B.R. Bottle Consignments
P.O. Box 1253
Bunnell, FL 32110
904–437–2807

Victorian Images
Box 284
Marlton, NJ 08053
609–985–7711

WM Morford
R.D. #2
Cazehovia, NY 13035
315–662–7625